A

C000157620

B O O K

The Philip E. Lilienthal imprint
honors special books
in commemoration of a man whose work
at University of California Press from 1954 to 1979
was marked by dedication to young authors
and to high standards in the field of Asian Studies.
Friends, family, authors, and foundations have together
endowed the Lilienthal Fund, which enables UC Press
to publish under this imprint selected books
in a way that reflects the taste and judgment
of a great and beloved editor.

KOREA **KF**
FOUNDATION

한국국제교류재단

The Korea Foundation has provided financial assistance for
the undertaking of this publication project.

The publisher gratefully acknowledges the generous support
of the Philip E. Lilienthal Asian Studies Endowment Fund of
the University of California Press Foundation, which was
established by a major gift from Sally Lilienthal.

# Assimilating Seoul

ASIA PACIFIC MODERN

Takashi Fujitani, Series Editor

# Assimilating Seoul

*Japanese Rule and the Politics of Public
Space in Colonial Korea, 1910–1945*

Todd A. Henry

UNIVERSITY OF CALIFORNIA PRESS
*Berkeley · Los Angeles · London*

University of California Press, one of the most
distinguished university presses in the United States,
enriches lives around the world by advancing scholarship
in the humanities, social sciences, and natural sciences.
Its activities are supported by the UC Press Foundation
and by philanthropic contributions from individuals and
institutions. For more information, visit www.ucpress
.edu.

University of California Press
Berkeley and Los Angeles, California

University of California Press, Ltd.
London, England

First Paperback printing 2016

Library of Congress Cataloging-in-Publication Data

Henry, Todd A., 1972–.
    Assimilating Seoul : Japanese rule and the politics
of public space in colonial Korea, 1910–1945 / Todd A.
Henry.
        pages   cm. (Asia Pacific modern ; 12)
    Includes bibliographical references and index.
    ISBN 978-0-520-27655-0 (cloth : alk. paper)
    ISBN 978-0-520-29315-1 (pbk.: alk. paper)
    ISBN 978-0-520-95841-8 (ebook)
    1. Seoul (Korea)—History—20th century.   2. Seoul
(Korea)—Ethnic relations—History—20th century.   3.
Public spaces—Social aspects—Korea—Seoul—History—
20th century.   4. Koreans—Cultural assimilation—
Korea—Seoul—History—20th century.   5. Japanese—
Korea—Seoul—History—20th century.   6. Korea—
History—Japanese occupation, 1910–1945.   I. Title.
    DS925.S457H46   2014
    951.95—dc23                          2013038505

23   22   21   20   19   18   17   16
10   9   8   7   6   5   4   3   2   1

# Contents

# Illustrations

# Note on Place Names

If one accepts my argument that the public spaces of the Korean peninsula have been the object of considerable attention and a source of perennial contestation, then it should come as little surprise that the
nomenclature of these spaces has witnessed a similarly turbulent history. The city that is the focus of this book, for example, boasts several
names depending on the regime that controlled it. These include
Namgyŏng (Koryŏ dynasty, 918–1392), Hanyang (Chosŏn dynasy,
1392–1910), Hwangsŏng (Great Han Empire, 1897–1910), Keijō
(Kyŏngsŏng; colonial period, 1910–45), and Seoul (1945–present).
Although some of these names for the capital were used interchangea-
bly as categories of practice, *Assimilating Seoul* deploys them as categories of analysis in order to capture the historicity of this city. As a matter
of principle, I have made an effort to honor Korean names for places
that predated the colonial period, while using Japanese terms for those
that colonial authorities came to control in the first half of the twentieth
century. However, where Koreans tended to dominate—in the "northern village" of Chongno (J: shōro; 鍾路), for example—I have taken the
liberty of using indigenous terms. As this example shows, one can
deploy at least three versions of the same name for one single place. The
following chart, organized alphabetically according to the Korean term
and providing English names when they are referenced in the text, is
intended to guide the reader through the complex and contested topography of Seoul that follows.

## KEY SITES

| KOREAN | JAPANESE | CHINESE | ENGLISH |
|---|---|---|---|
| An'guk-dong | Ankoku-dō | 安國洞 | |
| Ch'angdŏkkung | Shōtokukyū | 昌德宮 | Ch'angdŏk Palace |
| Ch'anggyŏnggung/wŏn | Shōkeikyū/en | 昌慶宮/苑 | Ch'anggyŏng Palace/Garden |
| Ch'ilp'ae | Shichihai | 七牌 | |
| Ch'ongdokbu ch'ŏngsa | Sōtokufu chōsha | 総督府廳舍 | Government-General Building |
| Ch'ŏnggyech'ŏn | Seikeisen | 清溪川 | Ch'ŏnggye Stream |
| Chongmyo | Sōbyō | 宗廟 | Royal Family's Ancestral Shrine |
| Chongno | Shōro | 鍾路 | |
| Ch'ŏngnyangni | Seiryōri | 清凉里 | |
| Chŏngsŏn-bang | Teizen-bō | 貞善坊 | |
| Chosŏn sin'gung | Chōsen jingū | 朝鮮神宮 | Korea Shrine |
| Chujak taero | Suzaku tairo | 朱雀大路 | |
| Chung'angch'ŏng | Chūōchō | 中央廳 | Capitol Hall |
| Ch'ungmuro | Chūburo | 忠武路 | Formerly Honmachi Street |
| Han'gang | Kankō | 漢江 | Han River |
| Hanwŏn'gung | Kan'inkyū | 閑院宮 | Hanwŏn Palace |
| Hanyang | Kan'yō | 漢陽 | Chosŏn Period Seoul |
| Honghwamun | Kōkamon | 弘化門 | Honghwa Gate |
| Hongnŭng | Kōryō | 弘陵 | |
| Hŭngnyemun | Kōreimon | 興禮門 | Hŭngnye Gate |
| Hwa-dong | Ka-dō | 花洞 | |
| Hwanggŭm-jŏng | Kōgane-machi | 黃金町 | |
| Hwangsŏng | Kōjō | 皇城 | Great Han Empire Period Seoul |
| Hwan/wŏn'gudan | Enkyūden | 圜/圓丘壇 | Ring Hall Altar |
| Hyejŏm-dong | Keiten-dō | 鞋店洞 | |
| Hyoja-dong | Kōshi-dō | 孝子洞 | |
| Ihyŏn | Riken | 梨峴 | |

| | | | |
|---|---|---|---|
| Insa-dong | Jinji-dō | 仁寺洞 | |
| Inwangsan | Niōsan | 仁王山 | Mount Inwang |
| Kaegyŏng/Kaesŏng | Kaikyō/Kaijō | 開京/開城 | |
| Koyang | Kōyō | 高陽 | |
| Kŭnjŏngjŏn | Kinseiden | 勤政殿 | Central Hall |
| Kŭnjŏngmun | Kinseimon | 勤政門 | Kŭnjŏng Gate |
| Kwanghŭimun | Kōkimon | 光熙門 | Kwanghŭi Gate |
| Kwanghwamun | Kōkamon | 光化門 | Kwanghwa Gate |
| Kyŏngbokgung | Keifukukyū | 景福宮 | Kyŏngbok Palace |
| Kyŏnghoeru | Keikairō | 慶會樓 | Kyŏnghoe Pavilion |
| Kyŏnghŭigung | Keikikyū | 慶熙宮 | Kyŏnghŭi Palace |
| Kyŏngsŏng | Keijō | 京城 | Colonial Period Seoul |
| Kyŏngsŏng cheguk taehak pyŏngwŏn | Keijō teikoku daigaku byōin | 京城帝国大学病院 | Keijō Imperial University Hospital |
| Kyŏngsŏng hoguk sinsa | Keijō gokoku jinja | 京城護國神社 | Seoul Nation-Protecting Shrine |
| Kyŏngsŏng sinsa | Keijō jinja | 京城神社 | Seoul Shrine |
| Kyŏngsŏng-yŏk | Keijō-eki | 京城驛 | Seoul (Central) Train Station |
| Kyŏng'un-dong | Keiun-dō | 慶雲洞 | |
| Kyŏng'ungung | Keiunkyū | 慶運宮 | Kyŏng'un Palace |
| Map'o | Maho | 麻浦 | |
| Myŏngch'i-jŏng | Meiji-machi | 明治町 | |
| Naeja-dong | Naishi-dō | 内資洞 | |
| Nambyŏlgung | Nanbetsukyū | 南別宮 | Nambyŏl Palace |
| Namch'on | Nanson | 南村 | Southern Village |
| Namdaemun | Nandaimon | 南大門 | South Gate |
| Namsan | Nanzan | 南山 | South Mountain |
| Piwŏn | Hien | 祕苑 | Secret Garden |
| Pon-jŏng | Hon-machi | 本町 | |
| Posingak | Fushinkaku | 普信閣 | Belfry |
| Pukch'on | Hokuson | 北村 | Northern Village |
| Pukhansan | Hokkansan | 北漢山 | Mount Pukhan |

| | | | |
|---|---|---|---|
| Sajikdan | Shashokudan | 社稷壇 | Altar to State Deities |
| Samp'ant'ong | Misaka dōri | 三坂通 | Misaka Avenue |
| Sejongno | Seisōro | 世宗路 | Sejong Boulevard |
| Sich'ŏng | Shichō | 市廳 | City Hall |
| Simsegwan | Shinseikan | 審勢館 | Hall to Assess Conditions |
| Sin-jŏng | Shin-machi | 新町 | |
| Sŏdaemun | Saidaimon | 西大門 | West Gate |
| Sunhwawŏn | Junkain | 順化院 | Junkain Hospital |
| Taean-dong | Daian-dō | 大安洞 | |
| Taehanmun | Daikanmon | 大漢門 | Taehan (Great Han) Gate |
| T'aep'yŏngno | Taiheiro | 太平路 | Taihei Boulevard |
| T'apdong kongwŏn | Pagoda kōen | 塔洞公園 | Pagoda Park |
| T'oegyero | Taikeiro | 退溪路 | Formerly Yamato-machi Avenue |
| Tŏksugung | Tokujukyū | 德壽宮 | Tŏksu Palace |
| Tongdaemun | Tōdaimon | 東大門 | East Gate |
| T'onggwanbu ch'ŏngsa | Tōkanfu chōsha | 統監府廳舍 | Residency-General Building |
| Tongnimmun | Dokuritsumon | 獨立門 | Independence Gate |
| Tonhwamun | Tonkamon | 敦化門 | Tonhwa Gate |
| Uk-jŏng | Asahi-chō | 旭町 | |
| Ŭljiro | Isshiro | 乙支路 | Formerly Kōgane-machi Avenue |
| Umigwan | Yūbikan | 優美館 | |
| Wangsimni | Ōjūri | 往十里 | |
| Wŏn'gaksa | Enkakuji | 圓覺寺 | Wŏn'gak Temple |
| Yŏngdŭngp'o | Eitōho | 永登浦 | |
| Yongsan | Ryūzan | 龍 山 | |
| Yŏng'ŭnmun | Geionmon | 迎恩門 | Yŏng'ŭn Gate |
| Yugŭijŏn | Rokuiten | 六矣廛 | Six Licensed Stores |

# Preface and Acknowledgments

In the process of writing this book, I have realized anew that some, if not all, history is autobiographical. This preface is thus a way for me both to acknowledge that truism and to thank the many individuals whom I have met along the arduous but rewarding path of producing a scholarly monograph. I am often asked in South Korea and Japan as well as in the United States and elsewhere why a white American-born scholar—more specifically, of Jewish ancestry—would decide to write a book about the Japanese rule of colonial Korea and its capital city. My usual answer to that ethnocentric question is to say, "Well, of course! Now, let me tell you my story." As are all serendipitous experiences, the path leading to this study began in unexpected ways. Looking back on that journey with the perspective of hindsight, I can now say that it started by befriending several Japanese exchange students living in Corrientes, Argentina (where I was an exchange student), and in Milwaukee, Wisconsin (where I attended high school). Hoping to better interact with these friends and their compatriots, I chose to minor in Japanese language and literature at The George Washington University, a decision that subsequently took me to Osaka as an exchange student between 1993 and 1995. A childhood neighbor (the Florsheims) with business connections to an Osaka merchant (the Yasudas) led me to pursue a homestay in the southern part of the city, a meeting ground for the country's disenfranchised ethnic and class minorities, including *burakumin* outcastes, resident Koreans, paupers, and gangsters, to identify just a few. That experience—of being surrounded by nearly invisible minorities, but ones clearly known and implicitly despised by at least some of my Japanese friends due to their "unfortunate" residence (i.e., my own neighborhood of Hanazono-chō)—forced me to think seriously about the spatial dimensions of power relations, including my own positionality as an upwardly mobile queer "Jewbu" (Jewish-Buddhist) and, of course, much more. It also led me to master the Korean language and to become a specialist of the peninsula's recent past, especially that of one of its most important contact zones. *Assimilating Seoul* is one attempt to understand the social and cultural relations of Japanese rule through the city's lived spaces. I also hope that this book can be read for what it says about wider themes animating the critical humanities, ones that ultimately pertain to my life and those of others both like and unlike me.

As this brief description of the project's serendipitous genesis suggests, the many people and institutions who have made it possible are numerous and far-flung. Words alone cannot do justice to the immense debt of gratitude I feel for those who have guided, taught, supported, and loved me along this wonderful journey of discovery. I first want to thank Sonja Ivanovich, my high school social studies teacher, and my college Japanese instructors, Kimura Takeo and Fukui Nanako, for opening my horizons well beyond the boundaries of the US nation-state. All of them remain role models for my pedagogical and scholarly work. Iwasaki (formerly, Katō) Wakako, Tateiwa Tarō, Shimada Yōhei, Kuwahira Eiji, and their respective families have been loyal friends and generous hosts for more than twenty years. At Sophia University in Tokyo where I was a Japanese government–supported master's student from 1996 until 1999, I had the good fortune of working with Miwa Kimitada, Takahashi Hisashi, and Kate Nakai Wildman, all of whom taught me much about modern Japan, especially in relation to its East Asian neighbors. At UCLA, where I completed my PhD in 2006, my advisors were and continue to be unfailing sources of wisdom, support, and friendship. The early loss of the brilliant and inspiring Miriam Silverberg, the person who opened the door for me to become a professional historian, has been an especially painful burden to bear, but she would be happy to know that her feisty spirit lives on in me and so many of her students. John Duncan and Namhee Lee expanded my horizons of Korean history, pulling me backward and forward into the pre- and postcolonial periods. I thank both of them for their generosity and support over the years, and I am proud to claim myself as part of the "Westwood faction" of Koreanists. Edward Soja turned me on to questions of space and place, and his work continues to provide great inspiration. I also want to thank past and present UCLA professors Fred Notehelfer, Herman Ooms, Michael Bourdaghs, Seiji Lippit, Tim Tangherlini, Mariko Tamanoi, Gi-Wook Shin, Rodgers Brubaker, and Michael Salman for their warm-hearted encouragement and intellectual camaraderie over the years. My graduate student friends, many of whom are some of the leading scholars in their respective fields, have made the transition to young professor all the more satisfying. They include Serk-bae Suh, Aimee (Nayoung) Kwon, Youngju Ryu, Chris Hanscom, Mickey Hong, Ellie Choi, Sonja Kim, the late Sophia Kim, Charles Kim, Min Suh Son, Hijoo Son, Seung-ah Lee, Kim Jŏng-il, Kim Hyŏng-uk, Howard Kahm, Paul Cha, Paul Nam, Paul Chang, Jennifer Jung Kim, Jane Kim, Kelly Jeong, Stella Xu, Makiko Mōri, Emily Anderson, Kristine Dennehy, Elyssa Faison, Michiko Takeuchi, Ann Marie Davis, John Swain, Haeng-ja Chung, Hiromi Mizuno, Eiichiro Azuma, David Eason, Hye Seung Chung, David Scott Diffrient, Eng-beng Lim, and Sung (Eun) Choi. Along the way, I have been fortunate to befriend other supportive colleagues, including Greg Pflugfelder, John Treat, Micah Auerback, Jordan Stein, Robert Chang, Michael Robinson, Jun Yoo, Eunjung Kim, Lisa Kim Davis, Jennifer Yum, Kim T'ae-ho, Yumi Moon, Dafna Zur, Eugene Park, Jenny Wang Medina, Jina Kim, Suk-Young Kim, Michael Berry, Rosalie Fanshel, Rachael Miyung Joo, Janice Kim, John DiMoia, Watanabe Naoki, Jordan Sand, Sarah Thal, Sharon Hayashi, Stephen Miller, Pak Yun-jae, Stephen Epstein, Hwansoo Ilmee Kim, Helen Lee, Mark Driscoll, Leo Ching, Matty Wagehaupt, Jinhee Lee, Vladimir Tikhonov, Kyong-mi Kwon Kwon, Joy Kim, Hyung Il Pai, Sunyoung Park, Kyung Moon Hwang, Nicole Cohen, Charles Armstrong, Koen De Ceuster, Chŏng Ta-ham, Se Woong (Ken) Koo, Roald Maliangkay, Kim Ŭn-sil, Yim Ji-hyŏn, Kim Sang-hyŏn, Kyung Hyun Kim, Su Yun Kim, Hyung Gu Lynn, Ted Hughes, Steven Chung, Yŏn-mi Kim, Raja Adal, Mark Caprio, Ken Ruoff, and Pak Tae-gyun.

Two years of dissertation research with grants from the Korea Foundation and the Fulbright Commission allowed me to interact with a tremendous coterie of Japanese and South Korean scholars. At Seoul National University, individuals who were especially supportive of my work include my teachers of Korean history, Kwŏn T'ae-ŏk, Yi T'ae-jin, and Chŏng Kŭn-sik, and their talented students, Ch'oe Pyŏng-t'aek, Chŏng Sang-u, Yŏm Pok-kyu, Pak Chun-hyŏng, Kim Tae-ho, Kim

Paek-yŏng, Chu Yun-jŏng, Kim Su-jin, Park Se-hun, Ko Tong-hwan, and Chŏn U-yŏng. I also want to thank An Ch'ang-mo, a fellow student of Seoul who, through his well-guided tours, has taught me much about the city's geography, history, and culture. At Kyoto University's Institute for Research in Humanities, my deepest gratitude goes to Mizuno Naoki who continues to be one of the most knowledgeable and generous supporters of my work, including with his last-minute help gathering many of the images that appear in this book. Takagi Hiroshi, Komagome Takeshi, and Yi Sŭng-yŏp also assisted me in developing ideas about Japanese rule and colonial Korea, while Yamamoto Tatsuya became a bosom buddy. Other Japan-based scholars who have aided me at various points include Matsuda Toshihiko, Itagaki Ryūta, Hashiya Hiroshi, Kawase Takuya, Hiura Satoko, Suga Kōji, Aoi Akihito, Narita Ryūichi, Yamaguchi Kōichi, and Matsutani Motokazu. I also want to acknowledge my heartfelt gratitude to the many librarians, archivists, and other individuals who helped me find documents and images across Japan, South Korea, and the United States. I am especially indebted to Ellie Bae, for her many visits to Japan's National Diet Library, and to the staffs of UCLA, UCSD, UC Berkeley, Colorado State University, Harvard University, Seoul National University, Yonsei University, the University of Seoul, the Seoul Museum of History, the National Library of Korea, Kyoto University, Tokyo University, Hokkaidō University, the International Research Center for Japanese Studies, and the Saitō Makoto Memorial Library. I thank Benjamin Pease for the maps that adorn this book and for making their production a rewarding process.

As a junior scholar, I have been supported by a number of important institutions and individuals. Although largely from afar, Andre Schmid and Tak Fujitani, now colleagues at the University of Toronto, have been close confidantes and indefatigable supporters at every juncture of my career. Michael Kim of Yonsei University also generously offered his time, knowledge, and laughter. At Colorado State University, my first academic job, I benefited greatly from the support and friendship of numerous colleagues, especially Ruth Alexander, Mark Fiege, May Fu, Elizabeth Jones, Anne Little, Thaddeus Sunseri, and Gamze Yasar. A year respite from teaching, a leave supported by the Korea Foundation, allowed me to rework a long and clumsy dissertation into a more tightly argued and temporally expanded book. I thank the staff of Harvard University's Korea Institute, Susan Lawrence, Myung-suk Chandra, and Catherine Glover, and their counterparts at the Reischauer Institute for

Japanese Studies for their support. The intellectual team of David McCann, Carter Eckert, and Sun Joo Kim on the Korea side and Andrew Gordon, Ian Miller, and Ted Bestor on the Japan side made my stay at Harvard especially productive, as did Carol Gluck's visit to Cambridge for my manuscript workshop. That year also allowed me to form new relationships with a fantastic group of postdoctoral fellows, including Se-mi Oh, Jonathan and Jessamyn Abel, Chelsea Foxwell, Ayu Majima, Trent Maxey, and Jun Uchida. My new academic home at UCSD has been an excellent place to finish this first project and begin new ones. I am especially thankful to Seth Lerer, John Marino, Pamela Radcliff, Nayan Shah, Joe Esherick, Cathy Gere, Mark Hendrickson, Nancy Kwak, Weijing Lu, Natalia Molina, Patrick Patterson, Paul Pickowicz, Rebecca Plant, Jeremy Presholdt, Sarah Schneewind, Joe Hankins, Lisa Yoneyama, Lisa Lowe, Ari Larissa Heinrich, Ping-hui Liao, Jin-Kyung Lee, Eun-Young Jung, Stephen Haggard, Jong-sung You, Jeyseon Lee, Patrick Anderson, and David Serlin. In the final stages of revisions, Susan Whitlock came to my editorial rescue, encouraging me to revisit what seemed like completely ossified prose but what soon became an enjoyable process of (re)writing. I also want to thank two reviewers of my initial manuscript for their very useful feedback and encouragement as well as the editorial staff of UC Press, especially Reed Malcolm, Stacy Eisenstark, Chalon Emmons, and Robert Demke, for guiding me through the uncharted waters of book publication. Subvention support from the Association for Asian Studies, the Korea Foundation, and UCSD's Office of Research Affairs helped offset production costs.

Parts of this book appeared, in earlier versions, as articles or book chapters and are being reprinted here with permission. Chapters 1, 4, and 5 are based, in part, on the following publications, respectively: "Respatializing Chosŏn's Royal Capital: The Politics of Japanese Urban Reforms in Early Colonial Seoul, 1905–19," in *Sitings: Critical Approaches to Korean Geography,* edited by Timothy Tangherlini and Sallie Yea (Honolulu: University of Hawai'i Press, 2007): 15–38; "Sanitizing Empire: Japanese Articulations of Korean Otherness and the Construction of Early Colonial Seoul, 1905–19," *Journal of Asian Studies* 64, no. 3 (Aug. 2005): 639–75; and "Cheguk ŭl kinyŏm hago, chŏnjaeng ŭl tongnyŏ hagi: Singminji malgi (1940 nyŏn) Chosŏn esŏ ŭi pangnamhoe," *Asea yŏn'gu* 51, no. 4 (Winter 2008): 72–112.

Last but certainly not least, I reserve the most heartfelt thanks to the members of my immediate family for the love and support they have shown me over the years. I cannot imagine my life without them.

Although no longer with me on this earth, my grandparents, Henrietta, Mack, Muriel, Harry, and Charlie, always remind me from where I came and where I am going. My uncle Tom and aunt Jane, both formidable intellectuals in their own right, have been wonderful companions and listeners to my ideas. My brothers Greg and Doug have always accepted me for what I do and who I am. I could not ask for more from my siblings, and I hope that they feel the deep love I have for them and their families. Through thick and thin, my parents, Lyle and Nancy, have formed the emotional pillar of my life. Their labor of love for me is without conditions and knows no limits. Their commitment to all aspects of my life is the thing that I strive to achieve in my own relationships, and it is thus to them that I lovingly dedicate this book.

*Seoul*
*May 2013*

# Assimilation and Space

*Toward an Ethnography of Japanese Rule*

In the fall of 1925, after nearly fifteen years of planning and over five years of construction, the Government-General, the colonial state that had ruled over Korea since its annexation by Japan in 1910, unveiled an imposing Shintō shrine atop Namsan (literally, South Mountain). Although the mountain had marked the southern edge of Hanyang, the former capital of the Chosŏn dynasty (1392–1910), Namsan was quickly becoming the geographic center of a growing metropolis known in Japanese as Keijō (Kyŏngsŏng; present-day Seoul), the empire's showcase city on the peninsula.[1] Until its destruction in 1945, Korea Shrine—whose deities (Amaterasu, the mythical ancestress of the Japanese polity, and Emperor Meiji, Japan's first modern monarch [r. 1868–1912]) symbolized the ideology of an unbroken imperial line—was one of the most powerful public sites in colonial Korea and one to which millions of residents, from both Keijō and throughout the peninsula, paid their respects. These visits of worship, compulsory for all able-bodied residents of Keijō during the Asia-Pacific War (1937–45), formed part of an ambitious project to turn the colonized population into dutiful, and ultimately loyal, subjects of the emperor. However, Koreans remained economically and politically disadvantaged in comparison to most of their privileged Japanese counterparts, exemplified by their relatively low class position and underrepresentation in the higher ranks of administration. Fearing the negative outcomes of such blatant discrimination, Ogasawara Shōzō, a Japanese proponent of Shintō, had tried unsuccessfully to install native deities at Korea Shrine in order to more effectively "assimilate" *(tonghwa; J: dōka)* the colonized masses. However, his experience visiting the shrine's unveiling ceremony on October 15, 1925, demonstrated that assimilation might prove difficult, if not impossible. As he recalled:

> At approximately eight o'clock in the evening, I left my inn wearing a light, unlined garment and a half-length, Japanese-style coat. Using the front approach, I paid my respects to the gods [J: *sampai shita*]. Both Japanese and Koreans continually climbed the stone stairs. However, when they arrived in front of the offertory hall, the former removed their hats and bowed, whereas the latter turned around and went home. I stood in front of the offertory hall for more than an hour. But, not one Korean paid his or her respect to the gods. According to our common sense, paying one's respects to the gods means making a ceremonial bow and offering a prayer. Koreans do not pay their respects before the gods; I could [thus] confirm that they [merely] look around [J: *sankan*].
> What is the cause for this [behavior]? Will Korea Shrine end up being a shrine only for the Japanese?[2]

The creation of a government shrine atop Namsan aimed at directing the thoughts and actions of the colonized population captures the central premise of this book, namely, that Keijō's public spaces are an important, if overlooked, crucible for examining the development of Japanese rule. In this particular case, Shintō practices of emperor worship functioned as the outward signs by which critical observers like Ogasawara attempted to judge the loyalty of Koreans. Accused of simply "looking around" Namsan, colonized visitors purportedly lacked the reverence attributed to their Japanese counterparts, who, like Ogasawara, respectfully prayed before the newly installed deities of Korea Shrine. This failure of assimilation—a central, albeit vaguely defined, policy of Japanese rule—suggested the need for the colonial state and its proxies to repeatedly examine and train Koreans according to what Michel Foucault once called a "regime of truth."[3] As extant records and subsequent memories of shrine visits demonstrate, many members of the colonized population resented being subjected to intrusive forms of surveillance that grew out of racialized claims that they were inferior. However, with the exception of some Christian protestors for whom emperor worship equated idolatry, most Koreans came to perform the rituals expected of them at this powerful public site, especially after wartime mobilization began in 1937.[4]

Despite these outward gestures of compliance, Ogasawara's apprehension also reveals that, at least as of 1925, most of the colonized population did not act, let alone think, according to official expectations of reverence. Indeed, forging the critical link between the venerated ancestors of the Japanese imperial house and those of individual Korean clans remained a significant, if not insurmountable, obstacle to assimilation. Although positioned more as intractable objects of Japanese rule rather than as self-governing subjects of colonial power, the nonchalant Koreans captured in Ogasawara's anxious remarks point to a contentious politics of place that a critical history of public space must also take into consideration. The government monument atop Namsan did, after all, command a spectacular view of the city below and, as a popular site of tourism, Korea Shrine often drew colonized residents for leisure visits, some to experience its natural surroundings and others perhaps simply to impress a romantic date.[5] As such, the site's attractions, like the other public spaces discussed in this book, did not always advance the assimilatory ideology of Japanese rule—in this case, the site created unrealistic expectations that Korean subjects would worship the imperial deities of a nation that, just fifteen years earlier, had forcefully occupied the peninsula and colonized its inhabitants.

## JAPANESE ASSIMILATION AS CONTESTED EXPERIMENTS OF COLONIAL GOVERNMENTALITY

Following the complex nuances of such colonial encounters, *Assimilating Seoul* attends to both the structures of Japanese rule and, to the extent possible, the multivocal agency of the subjects who filled its cracks. Building on efforts launched by Kim Paek-yŏng, Jun Uchida, and others, my work seeks to disaggregate colonial authority by examining how various forms of assimilation—spiritual as well as material and civic—operated on the grounds of colonial society and in its public spaces.[6] In particular, I view official efforts to redirect the divine affiliations (spiritual), productive energies (material), and collective ethics (civic) of colonial subjects—the criteria deemed necessary for them to "become Japanese"—as contested experiments of colonial governmentality. This analytical framework was first developed to study liberal societies in the modern West, but it was subsequently adapted to examine those of its imperial territories. Typically, studies of liberal governmentality have focused on the late-eighteenth-century shift from sovereignty—that is, a centralized, coercive, and unlimited form of power aimed at protecting the security of the monarch's territory—to a more diffuse, persuasive, and limited form of power known as governmentality.[7] In this new paradigm, lassiez faire concerns over political economy and its population led modern states to act indirectly as managers of individual freedom and encouraged citizens to become increasingly self-governing, a feature of liberal rule now famously described as "the conduct of conduct."

In a comparative study of the American and Japanese empires, Takashi Fujitani has argued persuasively that the Government-General did not always act as if most colonized Koreans could become reliable subjects of self-government, at least not until wartime mobilization necessitated that they be more fully included in the biopolitical concerns of the late colonial state.[8] When viewed from this macroscopic level, the Government-General failed to extend its subjectivizing efforts beyond the confines of most Japanese settlers and some bourgeois Koreans, and it only tentatively adopted the inclusionary strategies of nation-building simultaneously deployed in the metropole. However, a microscopic analysis of the city's infrastructure, Namsan's Shintō shrines, the expositions of Kyŏngbok Palace, and local hygiene campaigns demonstrates how public spaces became targeted points of intervention aimed at transforming nonelite inhabitants from disobedient objects of rule into self-regulating, if not self-governing, subjects of power. For their part, subaltern actors, although virtually excluded from political institutions, used these same sites according to their own attitudes and interests, many of which did not converge with those of the state. In this sense, the city's public spaces became a dynamic meeting ground between, on the one hand, the ideas and policies that set the parameters of Japanese rule and, on the other hand, the practices of individuals who occupied, visited, and inhabited those lived spaces.

To approach the colonial politics of place-making, my analysis of Keijō's public spaces builds, in part, on previous studies of Japanese assimilation, but reframes them in two important ways. The first involves a considerable widening of what this term meant in colonial practice. To date, most studies have understood assimilation in the narrow context of things one might label distinctly Japanese, limiting their discussion to the realm of what I am calling the spiritual.[9] To be sure, mandatory visits to Shintō shrines and classroom education aimed at inculcating imperial ethics and the "national language" (Japanese) constituted some of the most important manifestations of assimilation.[10] However, practices aimed at reorienting subjects' spiritual affiliations toward the emperor constituted only one part of what colonial officials regularly referred to as *dōka (tonghwa)*, or "assimilation," as well as *tōgō (tonghap)* and *yūgo (yunghap),* or "integration" and "incorporation." Indeed, both explicit invocations of assimilation and implicit references to its combinatory logic can be found in a wide range of modern discourses and practices that included, in addition to spiritual matters, the colonial economy, politics, and, of course, culture. Heeding Komagome Takeshi's incisive reminder that scholars should specify the inherently nebulous contours and shifting meanings of assimilation, my analysis includes practices of rule—the promotion of industriousness at spectacular expositions and the development of hygienic ethics in neighborhood campaigns, for example—that might otherwise be captured under the more universal rubric of modernization.[11] To varying degrees, authorities in all modern empires sought to manage the highly uneven process of development for the benefit of their own ethnic and class interests. In Keijō, such forms of capitalist exploitation not only forced Koreans to imbibe the modern gospel of productivity and cleanliness as subordinated and nonthreatening members of the labor force but also encouraged them to become loyal subjects of the Japanese emperor.[12]

In addition to expanding the conceptual boundaries of assimilation, my study recasts these transformative projects by analyzing their ideological underpinnings. To date, most studies have tended to adopt top-down approaches, using elite debates or state policies as the main criterion by which to assess this amorphous but powerful strategy of rule. In the field of education, for example, scholars of state policy have assessed the role that common schools played in teaching the national language and inculcating reverence for the imperial house. Focusing on the colonial nature of these institutions, they exposed the difficulty of acquiring the necessary skills for upward mobility, an area of discrimination that nationalist critics worked to eliminate.[13] Similarly, scholars of intellectual debates have highlighted the attitudes of Japanese theorists whose ideas undergirded these discriminatory policies. Although equally top-down, these studies demonstrated how elite writers sought to justify foreign domination in the eyes of colonized subjects and in relationship to Euro-American powers.[14] Although successful in explaining the intellectual roots and institutional forms of assimilation, they have not fully explored how these ruling tactics aimed to reorient the everyday practices of colonized Koreans and, to a lesser extent, Japanese settlers. By bowing before Shintō shrines and engaging in other performative rituals, imperial subjects did, to varying degrees, seek empowerment by "becoming Japanese," only to discover that the promises of inclusion in the imperial nation-state went largely unfulfilled. As a result, they often found themselves in a frustrating predicament, which Dipesh Chakrabarty has, in another colonial context, elegantly described as the "waiting room" of history.[15] That officials left most Koreans (as well as women, leftists, the lower classes, and other peripheral members of Japan's empire) uncomfortably suspended between the duties of subordinated subjects and the rights of enfranchised citizens lies at the very crux of assimilation—a ruling strategy that offered them the lure of modernity's rewards alongside their bewildering deferment.[16] *Assimilating Seoul,* a title meant to capture the nearly impossible process of "becoming Japanese," focuses on this contradictory and experimental project of rule—one that was neither fully implemented by government officials nor wholeheartedly embraced by colonized subjects.

By elucidating the limitations of top-down analyses, I do not mean to suggest that scholars ignore the ideas behind and policies for assimilation, since both remain important for understanding the governing rationalities of Japanese imperialism. However, in order to move beyond the highly ideological rhetoric of government officials and elite theorists, it is necessary to denaturalize the authority of the colonial state. All too often, Korean-language scholarship has uncritically assumed the Government-General's omnipotence, framed under the simple, yet misleading rubric of *ilche* (literally, imperial Japan). By contrast, the chapters that follow will subject efforts at *differentially incorporating* Koreans into the larger imperial community to an ethnographic analysis of specific projects that, in their various spiritual, material, and civic guises, projected the vague and contested parameters for how this multiethnic polity should develop.

Drawing on anthropological approaches to (post)colonial state formations, I begin with the unorthodox presumption that the Government-General's ability to integrate and to exclude the colonized population, although perhaps stable when viewed from within, was, in practice, highly variable and partial as it moved outward from its seat of authority. This disjuncture between internal coherence and external fragility gave rise to voluble discourses about assimilation that suggested ongoing reservations about the practical difficulties of incorporating most Koreans, subjects whose allegedly low "level of civilization" *(mindo)* placed them on the outer edges of the imperial community. For this reason, Japanese notions of assimilation were often supplanted by French theories of association, especially during the 1920s and 1930s, when a countervailing force of "cultural rule" allowed Koreans a certain amount of living space within a settler-dominated society.[17] Even then, officials were often forced to call on their disciplinary proxies—especially the police but also local elites—to engage in social control in order to shore up the appearance of governmental authority.[18]

This reformulation of Japanese rule shifts the analytical focus away from the a priori dominance of the colonial state to a closer examination of its contested relationships with various state and nonstate actors—relationships that, through mundane and ritual forms, helped constitute the Government-General's presence in the lives of Keijō's residents. That officials could project their authority in some, but certainly not all, of the city's spaces requires that students of Japanese colonialism heed Thomas Blom Hansen and Finn Stepputat's call to "move beyond the state's own prose, categories, and perspective and study how the state appears in everyday and localized forms."[19] Thus, rather than approach assimilation from the exclusive halls of the Government-General or from the desks of elite writers, I start from grounded histories of how individuals and groups operated in public places and then work my way upward to a broader understanding of the various forms of power informing those lived spaces.[20]

Some scholars, accepting Foucault's model of epistemological break and its Eurocentric pretensions to universality, have argued that such a model of governmentality cannot possibly capture the racializing workings of imperial domination—a radical departure from liberalism that Partha Chatterjee once called "the rule of colonial difference" to describe the British Raj.[21] In response to these postcolonial critiques, other scholars such as David Scott have sought to reframe the question by further problematizing, rather than further reifying, liberal forms of rule, while closely examining "the formation of historically heterogeneous rationalities through which the political sovereignties of colonial rule were constructed and operated."[22] Similarly, governmentality studies have exposed the surprising prevalence of illiberal forms of rule aimed at subpopulations deemed temporarily, if not permanently, incapable of self-government—a pattern especially characteristic of colonial situations, but one also intrinsic to metropolitan societies. Modern Japan—an imperial nation-state that, like its Euro-American counterparts, only extended the right to vote to less than half of its population before 1945, to say nothing of the disenfranchised masses living in its colonies—fits with Barry Hindess's incisive observation that "the majority of individuals governed by states committed to individual liberty in fact belonged to the subject peoples of Western imperial possessions."[23]

Building on these approaches, my analysis of Keijō's public spaces considers various modalities of rule along a shifting continuum that included both sovereign power and governmentality, but that often favored the former at the expense of the latter. It treats the political rationalities of the Government-General—a sovereign entity that, at best, extended only the spirit of the Meiji Constitution to colonial Korea—as comparable to, albeit less successful in its subjectifying reach than, similarly uneven processes of nation-building occurring in imperial Japan.[24] In locating my study between metropole and colony, modernity and coloniality, and inclusion and exclusion, I aim to specify how the operation of Japanese rule produced a spectrum of gradated positions that exposed the contradictions inherent in these dichotomies. Much like Gary Wilder's study of the French imperial nation-state, my analysis refuses to fetishize one privileged vantage point, elucidating instead the intrinsic tension between emancipatory and oppressive forces.[25]

To capture the disjointed relationship between these antinomies, *Assimilating Seoul* explores one of the most notable products of colonialism—namely, its glaring excesses and neglects.[26] It treats these contradictions as both structural and contested features of Japanese rule, rather than using them to prove the Korean case as an aberrant or warped version of a unitary, Western modernity—a tendency found in much nationalist history writing.[27] The seat of Japanese authority on the peninsula, Keijō offers a particularly instructive vantage point from which to observe how the creative reinscription of sovereign power in new projects of governmentality often veered in illiberal and authoritarian directions. An excessive reliance on the police, a coercive force whose numbers and efficacy increased during the period of Japanese rule, is perhaps the best example of how the Government-General disciplined the colonized masses despite pretensions to less heavy-handed forms of subjectification.[28] Throughout, colonial officials tended to ignore the well-being of poor Koreans, who, like unreliable paupers at home, were seen as requiring a protracted period of cultural education before qualifying as self-governing subjects. Although Korean nationalists vociferously criticized this negligent strategy of deferral, they simultaneously embraced the liberating prospects of colonial governmentality, an understudied feature of Japanese rule that Pak Se-hun has called "guided voluntarism."[29] Chapter 4, for example, shows how they demanded the state eliminate police-led sanitation inspections, suggesting steps by which a similar class of local leaders could certify the hygienic practices of subaltern neighbors. Even as colonized elites accelerated the contested process of becoming subjects of their own self-government, they operated as disciplinary proxies of the Government-General, staging similarly excessive spectacles aimed at controlling the allegedly unhygienic habits of their poorer counterparts. Such practices demonstrate how sovereign logics continued to inform increasingly diffuse modes of power, although ones that still failed to deeply permeate the city's microspaces.

Using the uneven development of Keijō's infrastructure as its example, chapter 1 reveals another "awkward amalgam"[30] of governmentality, sovereignty, and discipline in colonial Korea. This chapter recounts how the Government-General poured tremendous effort and financial resources into designing Taihei Boulevard, the city's main north-south axis. Similarly excessive displays of state authority characterized the political and spiritual termini of this spectacular thoroughfare—the Government-General building, the former home of Kyŏngbok Palace and the stage for two major colonial expositions (chapter 3), and Korea Shrine, the site of the opening episode and subsequent visits of worship (chapter 2). Although such forms of excess marked Keijō's arterial infrastructure, its capillary network of narrow and meandering roads remained largely outside the disciplinary gaze and biopolitical concerns of the colonial state. Even during the late 1920s, when government officials finally began to address the unsanitary conditions of Korean neighborhoods, efforts to radically respatialize the "northern village" (pukch'on) suffered from a lack of financial commitment by the Government-General. As a result, officials were forced to rely on impoverished residents and ambivalent elites to fund these fanciful projects. When provided the opportunity to voice their opinions, nationalist critics bemoaned inequalities in urban welfare, highlighting the immoral underside of Japanese rule while demanding a more equitable share of public resources. The uneven nature of Keijō's development thus became a source of considerable controversy for colonized elites, demonstrating how the contradictory structures of Korean modernity opened up possibilities for contestation and negotiation among a diverse group of inhabitants. In this way, public spaces, "contact zones" as the following section describes them, functioned as sites of popular encounters with assimilation, experienced both through the periodic hosting of spectacular events and as an ongoing process of everyday engagement with the harsh realities of Japanese rule.

## AN ETHNOGRAPHY OF KEIJŌ'S PUBLIC
## SPACES AS "CONTACT ZONES"

Through an ethnography of colonial projects, this book demonstrates how the wide-ranging invocations of assimilation worked in a tense relationship with the city's social spaces. By affixing the adjective "social" to the analytical term "space," I seek to foreground how the sites addressed in the following chapters manifested a living and stubborn dynamism often exceeding the neatly conceived visions of colonial governmentality that gave birth to them. This understanding of space as a place of struggle derives, in part, from ideas offered by Henri Lefebvre, who, in the creation of his own analytical framework of capitalism, categorized previous studies of human spatiality in two ways. According to his schema, one group of scholars analyzed the material productions and reproductions of space as physically manifest in, for instance, the built environment of cities. By contrast, other analysts sought to decode space according to its ideational representations, as exemplified in, say, an urban planner's design for a public park. In an effort to combine and transcend these limiting approaches, Lefebvre suggested a form of analysis that comprehends space "as directly *lived* through its associated images and symbols, and hence the space of 'inhabitants' and 'users.'" "This," he continues, "is the dominated—and hence passively experienced—space which the imagination seeks to change and appropriate. It overlays physical space, making symbolic uses of its objects."[31] Adopting this approach, *Assimilating Seoul* highlights the constant mutability of space and the ability of at least some human agents to manipulate its material forms and thereby reconstruct its ideational representations.

The urban spaces of specific concern to this book can be characterized by their close and inseparable connection to the forms of colonial subjectification outlined above. To varying degrees, these places invited inhabitants and users of space to develop intimate relationships with the projects of rule promoted by the Government-General but ones that functioned in localized and site-specific contexts. Out of convenience, I will use the term "public" as a *category of analysis* to describe these sites. However, lest this term be confused with notions of openness, freedom, and access often associated with liberal societies, I historicize their function as a *category of practice* located within colonial society.[32] In other words, my attention will be focused on how human agents engaged with these sites and thereby gave them meanings, including ones that did not coincide with the political rationalities of the Government-General. It is perhaps best to think of these sites with the unwieldy but more nuanced term "the officially sanctioned, social." This historicized gloss for the Japanese *kōkyō (konggong),* usually rendered as "public," more accurately captures the interconnected nature of these places as embodying particular governing logics while allowing members of colonial society to actively negotiate their way through them.

I will analyze these negotiations in terms of what Mary Louise Pratt has called contact zones, a phrase she uses "to invoke the spatial and temporal copresence of subjects previously separated by geographic and historical disjunctures, whose trajectories now intersect."[33] In Keijō, major thoroughfares, Shintō shrines, palace grounds, and other public sites functioned as contact zones insofar as government officials and local elites used them to promote a variety of assimilation projects. These projects occurred at different frequencies across time, ranging from daily house cleanings (chapter 4) to annual shrine celebrations (chapters 2 and 5) and periodic colonial expositions (chapter 3).[34] On both extraordinary and quotidian levels, assimilation projects interpolated individuals with a series of ideological messages about what it meant to "become Japanese." The center of colonial authority and home to the largest population of Japanese settlers, Keijō was surely a unique site—one that exposed residents to the contradictory logics of colonial rule in ways more intense than could be achieved in most other urban locales, to say nothing of their rural counterparts.[35] Indeed, nowhere else in colonial Korea could one feel the power of a public space like Namsan, home to several Shintō monuments, including Korea Shrine, the highest-ranking institution of its kind on the peninsula. Although it would be mistaken to assume that such excessive displays of authority represented the reality of Japanese rule writ large, seemingly exceptional sites like Namsan and Kyŏngbok Palace not only mobilized Keijō's residents, but also drew visitors from other parts of the Korean peninsula, the Japanese metropole, and throughout the empire—a strategy of rule that only accelerated during the Asia-Pacific War. Understood in this way, the city's contact zones, themselves often framed as models for other locations, extended far beyond the city's geographic bounds, if only in the same uneven ways as in the capital itself.

Keijō's assimilation projects engaged a cross section of colonial society that, in addition to ethnicity, became increasingly divided along class, gender, and generational lines. With these divisions in mind, I highlight the innovative ways in which different groups of actors used public spaces to appropriate, deflect, or challenge the contradictory logics of Japanese rule. To capture the nuances of these engagements, the pages that follow pursue an analysis of cultural events through what one interpreter of the postlinguistic turn has called "social semantics." This approach not only focuses on the semiotic structures used to stage colonial celebrations, but also analyzes how the actions of participants produced variable understandings of these events according to the different positions they occupied within society. As Gabriel Spiegel has written, "By reappropriating meanings (by *resignifying*) as a way of responding to or making sense of events as they happen, historical actors construe their culture from the point of view of their self-preservation and self-promotion, and creatively bend it to the conditions of daily life."[36]

Although largely excluded from institutionalized forms of politics and often positioned as obdurate objects of control by both colonialists and nationalists, even some of the poorest Koreans managed to turn assimilation projects to their own needs. For example, in the early 1930s, a time of economic depression, impoverished newcomers to Keijō formed their own relationship to the city's yearly Shintō festivals, celebrations designed to promote sentiments of loyalty for the imperial house. Rather than cheering the passing procession like Japanese settlers and their wealthy Korean counterparts, some members of the "lumpen proletariat," as the local press anxiously called them, used this public gathering to steal money from the pockets of onlookers. Such defiant uses of this mobile shrine space undermined a colonial governmentality aiming to produce a uniform set of imperial loyalties among residents and instead revealed the class and ethnic biases of spiritual assimilation. Police officers, neighborhood representatives, and other state proxies kept unsanctioned practices under careful, if ineffective, forms of surveillance, and, when necessary, they also used the threat of punishment to enforce compliance with public norms. The group of pickpockets, part of a local gang of wayward youths, was, for example, swiftly apprehended. With battles raging in China starting in 1937 and the onset of hostilities with the United States in 1941, noncompliance with cultural practices embodying loyalty for the Japanese empire took on increasingly perilous consequences. But even before the wartime period, pursuing personal interests in ways that contravened normative standards of conduct carried negative consequences including monetary fines, physical punishment, and social ostracism.

Capturing the nuances of subjects actively engaged with assimilation projects requires a form of analysis often pursued by anthropologists who study "the field," which cultural historians of colonialism have also begun to adopt as a way of writing about the past with greater ethnographic sensibilities.[37] However, unlike fieldwork, which enables anthropologists to produce their own cultural data, my ethnographic history is, by its very nature, limited by the forms and norms of the archive from which I draw my examples. That censorship could and did silence Korean voices, especially during the 1910s and again in the early 1940s, means that my analysis of Keijō's spatiality must rely, at least in part, on Japanese-language reports published in newspapers, journals, and other sources.[38] For example, the social columns of the *Keijō nippō* (Seoul daily), a newspaper with close associations to the Government-General, offer some of the most illuminating accounts of Shintō celebrations and shrine visits, in part because this semiofficial publication was invested in promoting a public image of a multiethnic community moving in the direction of assimilation. Thus it formed part of the colonial archive, which functioned, as Ann Stoler has innovatively suggested, "as both transparencies on which power relations were inscribed and intricate technologies of rule in themselves."[39] However, even officially sanctioned sources like the *Keijō nippō,* often neglected in studies of the colonial period, can expose the contradictions and tensions of colonial governmentality. For example, these same sources reveal the unequal and uneven ways in which a limited number of Koreans came to participate in public events, such as shrine festivals. That the colonized population remained largely absent in festival-related reports published in the pages of the *Maeil sinbo* (Daily news), the Korean-language counterpart to the *Keijō nippō,* also shows how pervasive forms of exclusion, often advanced by Japanese settlers against the inclusionary rhetoric of the Government-General, filtered into officially sanctioned representations of the city's public spaces.

I take the same approach of reading both *along* and *against* the archival grain when examining vernacular publications, all too often valorized in South Korean historiography as the authentic voice of the colonized.[40] To be sure, the Korean-language media, which flourished during the 1920s and 1930s, presented a far more critical assessment of colonial rule, using the lens of ethnic discrimination to question the universalist pretensions so often touted in government sources. For example, editorialists writing in the *Tonga ilbo* (Eastern daily) and *Chosŏn ilbo* (Korean daily) excoriated Japanese authorities for neglecting the sanitary conditions of Chongno and other Korean-populated neighborhoods. However, in critiquing the Government-General for instituting a highly discriminatory program of public health, these nationalist pundits, who shared the same class background and cultural assumptions as their colonialist counterparts, could not help but actively endorse the very regime of hygienic modernity promoted by officialdom.[41] In this sense, Korean-language newspapers also formed part of a repository of colonial knowledge and, therefore, they need to be analyzed as such.

When read critically, these sources also provide a way to resuscitate, if only partially and imperfectly, what Michel Foucault once called "subjugated knowledges."[42] Although subaltern voices regularly appear in Korean accounts as politicized inscriptions of nationalist knowledge, my critical ethnography attempts to link the everyday practices of nonelite residents to the larger structures of power that invariably informed them. So, for example, nationalist writings in the vernacular press that harshly criticized poor Koreans for concealing diseases (or the symptoms thereof) during deadly outbreaks closely mirrored the critiques of colonialist accounts. Yet below these overlapping agendas for hygienic modernity lay the subjugated knowledges that animated these individuals to hide their ailments as a strategy to parry the intrusive presence of the hygiene police and the ostracizing gaze of sanitation cooperatives. Moreover, biomedical treatments for contagious diseases were far more costly than herbal remedies and, at a time when ailments like cholera remained largely incurable, impoverished Koreans did not necessarily consider the former more effective than the latter. Finally, reporting a loved one to the local police station or the neighborhood sanitation cooperative often led to hospital quarantine. Such measures made it impossible for a patient's own family members to care for the sick, a long-standing Korean tradition.[43] Even these basic observations on bodily health cannot possibly capture the complex subjectivities informing agents' engagements with Japanese rule, and their subjugated knowledges thus remain an inherent, if not marked, limitation of *Assimilating Seoul*.

## THE BOOK'S TEMPORAL AND SPATIAL COORDINATES

Although the narrative structure of this book reflects an explicitly spatial approach to the contradictory dynamics of assimilation, each chapter also proceeds temporally across the thirty-five years of Japanese rule. By attending to change over time, I show how a variety of human

agents, both government officials and nonstate actors, attributed different meanings to the city's public sites, meanings largely determined by
their shifting subject positions within colonial society. However, these
dynamics of space- and place-making follow a slightly different trajectory than most Korean histories, a revision that requires some explica-
tion. To move beyond the Government-General's own language and its
strategies of rule, my narrative suspends methods of periodization conventionally used to describe the colonial era. Instead, I offer a less totalizing model whose turning points more accurately reflect the changing
nature of Keijō's lived spaces.

In most accounts, the colonial period is described as beginning with a
decade of "military rule" (1910–19), epitomized by the repression carried out by police officers against resistant Koreans. *Assimilating Seoul,*
although not minimizing these acts of state violence, aims to better
understand their historical causes, often cited as self-evident proof of
Japanese inhumanity. Instead, I suggest the need to critically examine
these acts as important signs exposing the inherent limitations of early
colonial rule, even in the capital of Keijō. This ironic predicament—the
coexistence of brutal violence and administrative impotence—affected
not only the newly colonized population of ethnic Koreans but also a
significant number of Japanese settlers who had already taken residence
in the city by the time of annexation. Only around 1915, after nearly five
years of coercively pacifying and consolidating both ethnic communities,
did the Government-General begin to more effectively control the future
direction of life in Keijō and, by extension, the various regions under its
bureaucratic purview. It was at this historical juncture that the colonial
state held its first exposition—a major media event aimed at persuading
Koreans that the exploitative nature of colonial modernization might
somehow benefit them. Although typically associated with the ruling
strategies of the ensuing decade, important spectacles like the Industrial
Exhibition in 1915 began at an earlier date, only to be modified and
expanded during the 1920s. These strategies of persuasion produced an
inherently makeshift and limited form of early colonial governmentality,
one that continued to rely on violent tactics of social control.

Another common characteristic of accounts of the colonial period is
a focus on the role played by the March First Movement of 1919—an
anticolonial and nationalist uprising spurred on by promises of self-
determination in the post–World War I era. Typically, this movement
stands as a crucial connection between the first decade of military rule
and the second decade of "cultural rule," both terms created by the

Government-General in response to the unprecedented challenge to its authority in 1919.[44] Although not completely inaccurate, this narrative obscures two interrelated points upon which my study of Keijō is premised. First, even before 1919, government officials, realizing the futility of draconian forms of social control, had begun to experiment with more persuasive strategies associated with cultural rule. A similarly uncritical approach to cultural rule after 1919 fails to account for the continued use of coercion. Second, although the ideas and policies of cultural rule did begin to appear shortly after 1919, it was not until the mid-1920s that this revised form of colonial governmentality gained traction in the assimilation projects that the Government-General had supported only tentatively during the 1910s.[45] So, for example, in terms of public infrastructure, Keijō's basic network of roads and the architectural monuments highlighting them finally took shape around 1925, following more than ten years of urban reforms.

In suggesting 1915 and 1925 as important turning points, my narrative also underscores the important role that Japanese settlers played in the direction and pace of assimilation. In many ways, this group of expatriates, themselves fractured by internal differences, functioned as key intermediaries, or "brokers" as Jun Uchida calls them, between the authority of the Government-General and the lives of colonized Koreans.[46] As mentioned above, the early colonial state not only sought to establish administrative control over newly colonized Koreans, but also struggled to rein in the semiautonomous institutions of expatriate Japanese, whose numbers increased from nearly forty thousand in 1910 to more than 150,000 by 1940.[47] Even after the Government-General abolished the settlement's legal authority in 1914, settlers continued to play an important role in inflecting governing rationalities as they filtered down into public life, reshaping them according to their own interests rather than those of the colonial state. My examinations of city planning (chapter 1) and Shintō shrines (chapter 2), for example, show how expatriate leaders labored to protect the commercial interests and cultural dominance of their community against official attempts at social integration and cultural assimilation, even if that meant excluding, subordinating, or racializing Koreans as detestable "others."[48] In fact, only in the mid-1920s did their interests begin to converge with those of the colonial government, leading Japanese settlers to reposition themselves as more aggressive proponents of assimilation.

The third and final shift in my narrative occurred in the late 1930s with the onset of the Asia-Pacific War. However, like the earlier turning points in 1915 and 1925, 1937 stands less as a break than as a threshold around which earlier experiments of colonial governmentality were transmuted into new forms. Chapter 5 thus addresses the wartime project of imperial subjectification (J: *kōminka; hwangminhwa*) as both an extension of and a departure from earlier modes of assimilation. This approach borrows, in part, from Leo Ching's definition of imperial subjectification as "a colonial ideology that, by concealing and erasing the internal contradiction of *dōka,* radically transformed and circumscribed the manner in which colonial subjectivity and identity were allowed to be articulated and repressed."[49] However, the epistemic break posited by Ching for identity formations in late colonial Taiwan overstates the case for the relationship between colonial power and space during the same period in Korea. The mutually constitutive relationship between assimilationist rationalities and individual practices continued, in large part, to shape the direction of wartime rule. To be sure, the late colonial state did launch unprecedented efforts at what I will call "emotional engineering," seeking to weaken ethnic-based identifications in the production of a more unified community of loyal subjects. However, even these novel attempts at imperial subjectification inherited a fragmented social fabric characterized by differences based on ethnicity as well as class, gender, generation, and region. The wartime regime had no choice but to recuperate these important differences into a multiethnic rhetoric of inclusion and coprosperity.

These three periods (1910–25, 1925–37, and 1937–45) form the temporal coordinates of my explorations of Keijō's public spaces. To set the stage, chapter 1 traces how the Government-General sought to transform the royal/imperial city of Hanyang/Hwangsŏng into a Japanese colonial capital. This chapter shows that early colonial planners, downplaying recent changes promoted by the leaders of the Great Han Empire (1897–1910), pursued their own respatializing program of urban reforms drawn from Meiji Japan (1868–1912). However, their attempts to impose a grid and rotary system of roads to facilitate the circulation of goods and people succeeded in reshaping only a small portion of the city's existing arterial structure. Although framed as promoting what officials liked to call the "public good," even these street improvements required heavy-handed policies of land confiscation, undercutting efforts to create a community of civic-minded residents. The second half of chapter 1 demonstrates how the city planning movement of the mid-1920s to early 1930s widened the scope of urban reforms, while introducing a series of updated methods (land readjustment and a betterment levy) and new objects of attention (Korean neighborhoods). However, financial limitations and ongoing resistance meant that Keijō continued to develop in highly uneven ways, as the modern logics of circulation and sanitation penetrated only the city's thoroughfares. As in other colonial cities, these roads came to embody the excessive (sovereign) power of the Government-General, particularly in the architectural monuments along Taihei Boulevard.

Chapters 2, 3, and 4 address how three different projects of rule operated in and through the city's public spaces. Chapter 2 focuses on spiritual assimilation, examining how Shintō shrines and their cultural activities were used to instill a sense of loyalty toward the Japanese imperial house. To date, scholars of colonial shrines have tended to assume that the imposition of forced shrine worship in 1937 also characterized earlier periods.[50] By contrast, I argue that this wartime phenomenon derives from an earlier history of struggle and competition by a wide range of social actors and cultural agents who exploited the internal contradictions of colonial Shintō. In particular, I show how spiritual assimilation began as a tentative arrangement in which the local Japanese custodians of Seoul Shrine, the only Shintō complex in Keijō before the unveiling of Korea Shrine in 1925, tended to exclude the colonized population from festival celebrations rather than follow the assimilationist rhetoric of the Government-General. As Ogasawara Shōzō's comments at the beginning of this chapter indicate, only after 1925 did colonized residents begin to make visits of worship to Korea Shrine, a solemn and uninviting complex that many continued to treat as a tourist site rather than as a place of reverence. The second half of chapter 2 demonstrates how these unconventional shrine practices reflected the increasingly competitive atmosphere of Shintō politics. I explain this marked shift by describing the Government-General's placement of the mammoth Korea Shrine in a position higher atop Namsan than the smaller Seoul Shrine. In response to this unprecedented challenge to their authority, the Japanese leaders of Seoul Shrine began to use the selective and subordinated incorporation of Koreans into festival celebrations more frequently as one of several new strategies aimed at maintaining and expanding their power vis-à-vis the colonial state.

Chapter 3 uses the former Kyŏngbok Palace grounds—the site of the new Government-General building and two major expositions held during the colonial period—to examine what I am calling material assimilation. With this term, I mean to suggest the process by which colonial officials promoted the uneven development of the Korean economy within the Japanese empire. The periodic staging of expositions played a central role in both displaying modern "progress" and inculcating in their Korean visitors (and Japanese tourists) the attendant ethics of diligence, efficiency, and frugality. At the exhibition of 1915, for example, designers promoted an image of industriousness through the universal idiom of Western architecture and machinery, powerful symbols of development that they carefully juxtaposed with the open grounds of an "anachronistic" palace. Although some educated Koreans successfully decoded and cautiously embraced this modernizing vision, nonelites tended to relate to the exhibition more as a captivating world of recreation and commerce. Later, during the Great Depression of 1929, the Korea Exposition, originally planned to commemorate fifteen years of Japanese rule in 1925, also aimed to impress audiences with displays of colonial progress. At the same time, its organizers sought to more fully place the peninsula's development within the imperial economy, a pattern that assumed increasingly autarkic forms as a Pan-Asian bloc was formed during the 1930s.[51] Designed in part as a strategy to lure Japanese tourists from the metropole, the exposition of 1929 highlighted what its architects liked to call the "pure Korean style" of display halls lining the main corridor. These palace-like structures also created a new east-west axis, which shifted the palace's spatiality away from its original north-south orientation. The brazen respatialization of Kyŏngbok Palace and the re-creation of an ersatz aesthetics came under harsh criticism by nationalists writers who decried these tactics of cultural rule as colonial violence. According to their incisive critiques, the nod to a Korean style also masked a discriminatory logic of wealth distribution orchestrated by the Government-General in conjunction with Japanese entrepreneurs. The Korea Exposition only exacerbated the impoverishing effects of colonialism by persuading and even coercing poor Koreans from the countryside to attend this costly commemoration.

If Shintō shrines gradually directed colonized subjects to embody an idealized form of Japanese spirituality and industrial expositions encouraged them to accept the exploitative logic of colonial progress, then what I call civic assimilation in chapter 4 conditioned Koreans to adopt the hygienic ethics of an equally discriminatory system of public health. Focusing on neighborhood life, this chapter examines how seasonal cleanups and other local campaigns aimed to link the health of individual bodies to that of a larger collective. In particular, I argue that police enforcement of sanitary regulations and popular resistance to the high cost and unwelcome consequences of biomedical treatments produced considerable obstacles to institutionalizing a viable system of public health in early Keijō (1910–15). Although Japanese pundits once denigrated it as Korea's "shit capital," Keijō assumed its infamous reputation as the empire's "diseased city" during the late 1920s and early 1930s. As an outpouring of concerned medical reports now showed, Japanese expatriates warded off contagious diseases far less successfully than allegedly less hygienic Koreans, even as the latter succumbed to death at a comparatively higher rate than the former. Chapter 4 also reveals how competing agendas of hygienic modernity advanced by Japanese colonialists and Korean nationalists converged over politically charged questions of urban sanitation and hygienic welfare. Although neither campaign managed to cure the diseased city, their combined efforts cast an increasingly wide net of power across Keijō's neighborhoods, an expansive web that even the subaltern population could never fully escape.

Chapter 5 argues that, with the onset of the Asia-Pacific War, the disparate projects and sites of assimilation merged, giving rise to an unprecedented moment in the city's spatiality. In particular, new pressures to prove one's loyalty toward the imperial house led to significant changes in the use of public space and the creation of new sites capable of advancing the wartime goal of "uniting Japan(ese) and Korea(ns) as one body" (J: *naisen ittai; naesŏn ilch'e*). For example, the increasingly militarized and solemn precincts of Namsan's Shintō shrines began to penetrate Korean homes through the installation of household altars and the distribution of Ise talismans. Although never fully successful, these measures were intended to force Koreans to more strongly identify with emperor-led battles. Further, the celebrations of 1940, staged to commemorate the twenty-six-hundredth anniversary of the Japanese nation, inspired Koreans to become active participants in the Asia-Pacific War, even if most remained on the home front. To this end, events like the sacred torch relay and the Great Korea Exposition aimed to create an imagined community of Pan-Asian subjects. Held at sites across the peninsula, these celebrations generated a compressed topography of the wartime empire—one that encouraged the colonized population to expand their vision as imperial subjects, while subordinating their local and familial affiliations. Although some Koreans with close ties to the military began think of themselves in this way, the late colonial state never managed to fully erase the ethnic, class, and other differences that had also helped shape previous projects of assimilation. Now strategically reincorporated into the multiethnic rhetoric of late colonial ideology, these differences continued to determine how imperial subjectification functioned during the final years of an increasingly deadly war.

As the epilogue suggests, recent memories of this war, the violent culmination of thirty-five years of Japanese rule, explain how Koreans began to refashion Keijō's most symbolic spaces after 1945—in part, by forcing Japanese officials to destroy Namsan's Shintō shrines and replacing them with anticolonial monuments of the nation. In 1995, exactly fifty years later after liberation, the postcolonial state finally succeeded in razing the former Government-General building, another powerful reminder of the colonial period, which, until that national celebration, had served as Capitol Hall (1948–86) and the National Museum (1986–95). In its place today stands a semirestored version of Kyŏngbok Palace, a costly project of decolonization that will not be completed until at least 2030, if not later. Much like Namsan's memorial to An Chung-gŭn, the Korean patriot who killed the first Resident-General (Itō Hirobumi) in 1909, the nationalized palace grounds, used in part to claim legitimacy over a peninsula still divided into two rival regimes, aim to remind domestic and international visitors of the imagined glory of the Chosŏn dynasty (1392–1910). By returning to this romanticized past, the South Korean planners of contemporary Seoul, much as their colonial predecessors sought to minimize the peninsula's precolonial history, continue to bypass the period when Japanese officials violently remade the royal/imperial capital into a showcase for Japanese modernity.

# CHAPTER I

# Constructing Keijō

*The Uneven Spaces of a Colonial Capital*

This chapter traces the Government-General's attempts to transform the symbolic and material landscape of Hanyang, royal city of the Chosŏn dynasty, into the colonial capital of Keijō (Kyŏngsŏng). Through an initial period of urban reforms and a later phase of city planning, the colonial state remade the skeletal and aesthetic frames of Keijō even as it neglected considerable parts of the city, especially in the Korean-populated northern village. To borrow a metaphor used by Gyan Prakash in his study of colonial India, the smooth and sanitary circulation envisioned by officials only reached the city's main arteries, rather than penetrating to the capillary level of everyday life.[1] The result was a multilayered built environment, characterized by unlikely juxtapositions of old and new, neglect and excess, and chaos and order. Like other modern cities in the metropole to which planners frequently compared it, Keijō developed in highly uneven ways, a phenomenon further exacerbated by ethnic, class, and other divisions produced through Japanese rule. By its very definition, then, "constructing Keijō" remained a contentious project, one that led concerned officials to invest tremendous financial and ideological resources in transforming this historic capital into the peninsula's showcase city. Although certainly less grandiose in their designs, a diverse group of residents also made assertive claims on the city's spaces, where those who were well placed could seize enriching possibilities, but where many more of the less fortunate residents remained vulnerable to its disrepairs.

## FROM ROYAL HANYANG TO IMPERIAL HWANGSŎNG, 1394–1910

When Japanese officials annexed the Korean peninsula in 1910, they inherited a city with more than five hundred years of history. Shortly after establishing the Chosŏn dynasty in 1392, the first king, Yi Sŏng-gye (T'aejo), constructed a new royal city at Hanyang to distance himself from Kaegyŏng (present-day Kaesŏng), the main center of power during the Koryŏ dynasty (918–1392).[2] Chosen for its geomantic propitiousness, Hanyang developed according to an adaptation of Chinese planning principles, incorporating elements that would legitimate and protect the new dynasty. As figure 1 illustrates, the city followed many continental precedents.[3] For example, Chosŏn planners placed the royal family's ancestral shrine (Chongmyo) to the east of the king's main palace (Kyŏngbokgung) and an altar to the state deities (Sajikdan) to the west. Following the Confucian belief in the five elements and their virtues as described in the *Book of Changes*, the city's five central points, the (1) East, (2) West, (3) South, and (4) North Gates and (5) the Belfry—which corresponded to (1) wood for benevolence, (2) gold for righteousness, (3) fire for propriety, (4) water for wisdom, and (5) earth for trust—were laid out around Kyŏngbok Palace. The main north-south axis (Chujak Taero) emanated from the palace, while the city's other main arteries included Chongno, which extended from the West Gate (Sŏdaemun) to the East Gate (Tongdaemun), and another road extending from the Belfry (Posingak) to the South Gate (Namdaemun). Officials had also ensured that the city met the geomantic prescription that it be surrounded by four auspicious mountains, through which the proper amount of energy *(ki)* could pass. From these nearby mountains flowed a major source of the city's water supply, the Ch'ŏnggye Stream.[4] Although departing from Chinese cities with square or rectangular enclosures, Chosŏn officials constructed an oval wall to defend an urban basin naturally surrounded by four major mountain ranges.

During the mid- to late Chosŏn period, the capital city experienced significant changes. In particular, while continuing to function as a political center, Hanyang also grew into a commercial hub. According to Ko Tong-hwan, both the national circulation of metallic currency and the implementation of the Uniform Land Tax Law during the latter half of the seventeenth century spurred the development of an urban economy based on commercial currency. Poor harvests and epidemics during this period drew desperate peasants to the expanding suburban

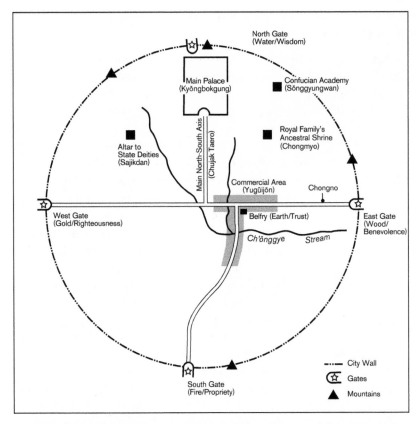

FIGURE I. Late-fourteenth-century design of Hanyang. Map adapted from Im Tŏk-sun, "Chosŏn ch'ogi Hanyang chŏngdo wa sudo ŭi sangjinghwa," in *Sŏul ŭi kyŏnggwan pyŏnhwa*, ed. An Tu-sun (Seoul: Sŏulhak yŏn'guso, 1994), 47.

areas just outside the city's walls. These developments led to a metropolitan population that grew from just over eighty thousand in 1657 to nearly two hundred thousand in 1669, a level it retained until the end of the Chosŏn dynasty.[5] Within the city's walls, the commoner markets of Ihyŏn and Ch'ilp'ae came to complement the Six Licensed Stores (Yugŭijŏn), a commercial area located along Chongno that provided goods for the royal palaces. As a result, the majority of Hanyang's population was engaged in some form of commercial enterprise by the eighteenth century. Meanwhile, new, nonelite forms of culture and entertainment developed around the middle classes of the so-called *chung'in,* bureaucratic specialists in foreign languages, law, and medicine.[6]

With the onset of imperialist aggression during the late nineteenth century, protecting the economic and political autonomy of the dynasty became a growing concern for Chosŏn's leaders, some of whom sought to refashion the royal city of Hanyang into the imperial capital of Hwangsŏng. After the Sino-Japanese rivalry over the peninsula (1894–95), the assassination of Queen Min by the Japanese military (1895), and King Kojong's flight to the Russian Legation (1896), concerned officials of the newly established Great Han Empire—a novel political, economic, and cultural system aimed at promoting national independence by reasserting the power of the throne—launched the Kwangmu Reforms (1897–1904) under the slogan of "old foundation, new participation" *(kubon sinch'am)*.[7] An effort to use Western technology to buttress monarchical authority and develop a modern infrastructure, these reforms aimed to make the city capable of representing and defending the fledgling Korean nation-state at a dangerous time of imperialist intrusions. According to Yi T'ae-jin, the campaign included several important changes, including (1) the destruction of temporary commercial stalls jutting from the city's two main commercial thoroughfares, thus restoring these boulevards to their original width and facilitating smoother conveyance; (2) the creation of roads centered on Emperor Kojong's new court/residence at Kyŏng'un (later Tŏksu) Palace, thereby establishing a radial system of streets linking the new imperial capital to its suburbs; and (3) the erection of buildings and other structures asserting national autonomy under the Korean monarch, such as the Independence Gate, Pagoda Park (built on Wŏn'gak Temple grounds in Chongno where Chosŏn kings accepted petitions from their subjects), and a memorial monument commemorating the fortieth anniversary of Kojong's coronation in 1863 (also a popular site of gatherings). (See figure 2.)

Most Korean historians have understood these changes as part of a program of "internal development" *(naejaejŏk paljŏn)* and gradual modernization. Yi T'ae-jin, for example, has argued that the Kwangmu Reforms, advanced in large part by Korean diplomats with experience living in Washington, DC, likely adopted the American capital as a conceptual model, an exemplary embodiment of the empire's commitment to "old foundation, new participation."[8] In truth, the leaders of the Great Han Empire were engaged in a globalized process of nation-state building, the native and nonnative elements of which cannot be easily disaggregated because of the city's (and the nation's) position in an overlapping network of semicolonial structures. On the one hand,

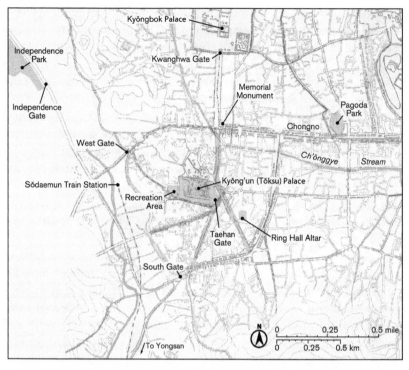

FIGURE 2. Late-nineteenth-century plan for Hwangsŏng. Map adapted from *Jissoku shōmitsu saishin Keijō zenzu* (Keijō: Nikkan shobō, 1907).

some elites sought to establish greater political autonomy by down-playing China's historical influence and thereby promoting Korea's cultural primacy. The symbolic valence of this project was concretely manifested in the construction of the Western-style Independence Gate, overwriting the ritual site where Qing envoys had been regularly received by the Chosŏn court (Yŏng'ŭn Gate). However, as Andre Schmid has shown, other purifying tactics of official nationalism ironi-cally relied on the hoary symbols of the Middle Kingdom, undercutting efforts to displace the Sino-centric world of Chosŏn's recent past. Such difficulties took concrete shape in the Ring Hall Altar (Hwan'gudan or Wŏn'gudan), a new national structure built for Kojong's elevation in 1897 from king to emperor on the very site of Qing envoys' former residence (Nambyŏl Palace), but which uncannily resembled Beijing's Altar of Heaven.[9]

On the other hand, these projects to create an imperial capital that exuded self-confidence in official nationalism vis-à-vis a declining China were carried out with and against imperial powers after the Sino-Japanese War, particularly Russia and Japan, but also the United States. Indeed, the very spaces of Hwangsŏng came to reflect the precarious geopolitical position in which the Great Han Empire found itself during this period. It was not by coincidence, then, that the center of the new imperial capital, Kyŏng'un Palace, was constructed in close proximity to the city's foreign legations. In his pioneering work on the Great Han Empire's urban planning projects, Kim Kwang-u uncovered that a secret passageway and bridge were built to link the Russian Legation (where Kojong briefly resided after the Sino-Japanese War) to the new imperial palace complex.[10] Other modernizing projects were similarly tied to the semicolonial politics of concessions during this period.[11] For example, the Great Han Empire employed two American entrepreneurs, Henry Collbran and H. R. Bostwick, to introduce new technology and to finance the construction of a streetcar system, power lines, street lamps, water pipes, and telephone lines.[12] Among the streetcar lines, one was laid symbolically from Kyŏng'un Palace, across the main thoroughfare of Chongno, to Hongnŭng, the site of Queen Min's tomb on the city's eastern fringe. Meanwhile, these monarch-centered projects led to a series of popular riots among local Korean residents, who viewed this foreign technology, managed by American engineers and operated by Japanese conductors, as both a geomantic intrusion onto their communal living space and a public threat to property-holding patterns.[13]

As these riots suggest, Hwangsŏng's perilous position within the transnational politics of East Asian imperialism necessitated internal political changes that were also reflected in city spaces. In spite of Confucian rhetoric calling for a popularly oriented nation, the kind of Korean people envisioned by the elite architects of the Great Han Empire was closer to dutiful subjects rather than citizens endowed with individual rights. Therefore, where once virtually the entire city consisted of royal spaces, government officials now created stronger connections between the symbolic center of the monarchy and groups of socially stratified Koreans. The new streetcar line linking the imperial palace complex with the commercial district along Chongno was one particularly symbolic manifestation of this important transformation. Indeed, the new imperial city witnessed a noticeable increase in the number of contact zones between the sovereign and his subjects, including the area in front of the Taehan Gate (the entrance to Kyŏng'un Palace), where Hwangsŏng's residents gathered for new national events, such as Kojong's elevation in 1897 from king to emperor.[14] That these changes reflected new strictures on personal freedoms is supported by the fate of the short-lived Independence Club (1896–98), a group closely associated with the urban reforms of this period.[15] In fact, when some members pushed for a more participatory constitutional system, the Korean court quickly disbanded the club and centralized state authority under the newly elevated emperor, Kojong.

With Japan's victory against Russia in 1905 and the subsequent establishment of a semicolonial protectorate government, the monarch-centered project to transform Hwangsŏng into a national center became nearly impossible, especially after Kojong's forced abdication in 1907. When Japan annexed the peninsula in 1910, early colonial officials hijacked these reforms and began to institute their own improvements, remaking the city's spaces into a showcase of Japanese modernity. However, the modern project of physically and symbolically transforming the capital initiated by the leaders of the Great Han Empire continued after 1910. The major change was, of course, that thereafter a colonial state now attempted to use spatial reorganization to incorporate Koreans as subjects of the Japanese emperor.

## THE LIMITS OF "URBAN REFORMS," 1910–1925

With the promulgation of the Annexation Treaty on August 29, 1910, Japanese authorities moved to gain full control over the symbolic topography not just of Seoul, but of the entire peninsula. To this end, they changed the name of the colony back to Chōsen (Chosŏn) from its previous designation, the Great Han Empire, a name associated with a nationalizing state under Emperor Kojong. In addition to "Great Han," the name "Hwangsŏng" as a designation for the capital of this former empire was prohibited.[16] Instead, officials symbolically "renamed" the city Keijō, invoking the Chinese character for capital. As the political center of Japan's empire on the peninsula, this symbolic change mirrored the recent history of Edo, the seat of shogunal authority during the Tokugawa period (1600–1868), which had been renamed Tokyo (literally, eastern capital) in 1868, replacing the ancient city of Kyoto (literally, capital city from 794 until 1868) as the new imperial capital.[17] In the case of Japan, Tokyo did not emerge as the nation's symbolic center until 1889 due to the historical weight of Kyoto and the emperor's peregrinations outside of the new capital—practices recently reenacted by protectorate officials who had dispatched Sunjong (the last Korean emperor; r. 1907–10) on nationwide processions to promote

Japan's control over the peninsula.[18] Although the Korean capital was itself never relocated like Kyoto/Tokyo, the transformation of Han-yang/Hwangsŏng into Keijō was neither immediate nor uncontested, and it required spatial interventions that spanned the first fifteen years of Japanese rule (1910–25).[19]

This project of respatialization was, like the annexation itself, launched on the path of subordinating and then desacralizing the Korean royal house. It thus began in symbolic fashion with the strategic reconstruction of the city's palaces, whose private grounds Japanese officials converted into civic parks and other public monuments. Made accessible for the first time, these once sacred sites were used to interpolate the Korean masses as subordinated members of the new imperial community. Before annexation, Japanese commentators—drawing on recent experiences of converting domanial complexes from the Tokugawa period into parks, schools, and other public spaces—commonly referred to Kyŏng'un Palace, Kojong's residence, as the "kingdom's castle" (J: ōjō; wangsŏng) or the "imperial castle" (J: kōjō; hwangsŏng). Already by 1907, protectorate officials had begun to downplay the symbolic importance of Kyŏng'un Palace, when they forced Kojong to abdicate in favor of his young son, Sunjong, Korea's last (puppet) emperor, whose residence was then relocated to Ch'angdŏk Palace. Between 1908 and 1911, Japanese officials, following the Meiji model of "modernizing" Ueno Park under imperial auspices, transformed the adjacent Ch'anggyŏng Palace into another public site, outfitted with a royal museum, zoo, and garden.[20] Meanwhile, authorities quickly moved to destroy or sell buildings related to Kyŏnghŭi Palace, which had functioned as part of the ruling palace complex during the Great Han Empire.[21] Parts of Kyŏng'un Palace, symbolically renamed Tŏksu Palace after Kojong's 1907 abdication, remained, although it was stripped of its modernizing emperor and the powerful symbols he wielded. In 1910, officials built a Western-style art museum on the grounds of this palace and, in 1914, replaced the Ring Hall Altar with another modern facility, the railway-operated Chōsen Hotel.[22] A similar fate awaited Kyŏngbok Palace, the "old castle" (J: kyū-ōjō; ku-wangsŏng), the king's main residence until its destruction by Hideyoshi's invasions of the 1590s. Although partially rebuilt during the reign of Kojong's regent father, the Hŭngsŏn Taewŏn'gun (1863–73), this "old castle" had remained in disuse until its symbolic opening to public viewing in 1908.[23] During the colonial period, this desacralized site became home to the new Government-General building (est. 1926) and the stage for several spectacular expositions. In this this way, Kyŏngbok Palace grounds aimed to display Japan's authority over the peninsula's ineluctable "progress" and Koreans' subordinated participation in colonial modernization.

In addition to the symbolic deconstruction and reconstruction of Hanyang/Hwangsŏng's palace grounds, Japanese officials also sought to rearrange roads and neighborhoods in order to advance both colonial authority and capitalist accumulation. First carried out in late-nineteenth-century Tokyo, these "urban reforms" (J: *shiku kaisei; sigu kaejŏng;* literally, "re-forming city districts") included widening and straightening extant roads, expanding waterways for sewage and, as mentioned above, refashioning domanial and religious spaces into civic parks and plazas.[24] Together, they aimed at a partial upgrade of the existing city rather than the systematic transformation of space that would characterize the planning movement of the 1920s and 1930s. In early Keijō, planners, borrowing the German term for urban regulations *(Regulierung der Städte),* focused their efforts on sanitizing, widening, and straightening the city's main arteries and constructing new ones in order to establish a more rationalized system of roads.[25] Over these roads, officials hoped to lay a series of radials connected to three symbolic rotaries in the creation of what bureaucrats liked to call a "civilized city," a term downplaying similar modernizing techniques recently used by the Great Han Empire.

This ambitious plan, modeled on the one first implemented in colonial Taipei, had failed in Tokyo, where entrenched landowners prevented its implementation.[26] To be sure, the protectorate and early colonial governments, backed by a coercive military force, had far greater leverage to impose urban reforms in Korea than officials in the metropole. However, even in Keijō, these efforts did not go uncontested, particularly by Japanese settlers who, as residents of the peninsula since the early 1880s, sought to influence the city according to their own interests. The Residency-General and its successor, the Government-General, were themselves far from monolithic or coherent, either in their motives or in the exercise of their authority. Even the most ambitious planners soon realized that the city's existing structure and perennial finance problems would severely limit what they could accomplish. As a result, (semi)colonial officials, drawing on modernizing tactics developed in Meiji Japan and its fledgling empire, succeeded in implementing only a limited program of urban reforms.

For their part, Japanese settlers played an important, if distracting, role in the development of early Keijō. During the protectorate period, for example, expatriate leaders petitioned the Residency-General to make road improvements around Hon-machi, the historic center of their community. In 1907, settler elites submitted a proposal to widen this narrow but important street.[27] Concerned primarily with their own living space, local leaders envisioned a city that would promote their commercial interests at the expense of the northern village. Later, in 1911, an 824,000-yen plan submitted to the Government-General included an expansion of Honmachi Street in the direction of the South Gate and the Kwanghŭi Gate. To fortify their presence in the southern village, settler leaders also hoped to upgrade an auxiliary road south of Honmachi Street to divert heavy traffic, a proposal that bore fruit only in the late 1920s.[28] Mirroring a project recently advanced by the Great Han Empire, the final component of this expatriate initiative aimed to connect the nearby boomtown of Yongsan—the new home to the Japanese military, railroad facilities, and a growing settler population—to the burgeoning commercial area of Map'o along the Han River.[29]

Although Japanese settlers sought considerable government support to finance this Hon-machi–centered plan, it did not coincide with the state's own vision of transforming a wider portion of the city into a showcase for Japanese modernity. That plan began to take shape in May 1912, when officials announced that a new Government-General building, to be erected on the grounds of Kyŏngbok Palace, would replace the smaller former Residency-General building, which sat in the heart of the settler community. In addition to creating a new political center in the northern village, officials also decided to build a major Shintō complex, eventually located in close proximity to the settler-managed Seoul Shrine. At a joint cost of three hundred thousand yen, the new Government-General building and Korea Shrine would form the political and sacerdotal termini of the city's main thoroughfare, Taihei Boulevard, linking the train station in the south to Kyŏngbok Palace in the north.[30]

Having heard rumors as early as 1911 that the Government-General building would eventually move away from Hon-machi, some members of the Japanese settler association reacted to this plan with disbelief. Fearing that the heart of the city would ultimately shift northward to the Korean neighborhoods of Chongno, some insular expatriates even called for excluding the colonized population from a new system of urban administration, which, in 1914, put the two ethnic communities together.[31] Seeking to retain a voice in Keijō's development, Fuchigami Tadasuke, director of the settler community's road widening committee, reiterated the interests of Japanese expatriates by demanding that the Government-General expand Honmachi Street.[32] At a cost four times more than repairs planned for Taihei Boulevard, colonial officials rejected this grandiose plea. Even some settlers considered the project a fiscal fantasy, while others lambasted it as hidebound for only including a corner of the southern half of the city rather than embracing the entire city.[33]

In June 1912, Mochiji Rokusaburō (1867–1923), a veteran bureaucrat who had served in early colonial Taiwan and was now appointed to head the Civil Engineering Bureau, identified both the practical and symbolic import of Keijō, placing the city within the global contexts of modern imperialism and urban planning.[34] As he wrote, "A great colonial city in the [Japanese] empire and in the grand logic of the world, [Keijō] has come to stand in a position deserving notable attention as Korea's railway connection to Asia." In addition to being a transportation hub, the new colonial capital also served as a gauge for what Mochiji called the "country's level of civilization" and its "barometer of culture." Judging Keijō by these universal standards, he concluded that Korea was the most undeveloped country. To transform the capital into the most advanced and civilized city, Mochiji recommended that officials straighten and widen Keijō's irregular and winding streets. In particular, he recommended the new city-style of London recently adopted in Dairen (C: Dalian), a reference to the system of rotaries designed by Russian city planners before Japan gained control over this Manchurian port city in 1905.[35]

The globally circulating ideas of city planning invoked by Mochiji are clearly seen in the first urban reform plan for Keijō (1913–17), which was issued in June 1912 and which was to have an astounding cost of three million yen (see figure 3).[36] Building on reforms made during the Great Han Empire, this ambitious plan aimed to superimpose a radial and grid system of roads onto the city's existing street formation. While north-south and east-west roads would create the grid, the diagonal roads would form three rotaries, each converging on an important power center in the early colonial city. Officials located one such plaza in front of Kyŏngbok Palace where Taihei Boulevard met Chongno, the main east-west axis during the Chosŏn dynasty. This plaza aimed to displace Tŏksu (formerly Kyŏng'un) Palace, the center of power during the Great Han Empire. As figure 3 shows, constructing a plaza in front of Kyŏngbok Palace (the planned site of the Government-General building) would require three new radial roads emanating in northwesterly, northeasterly, and southeasterly directions.

Urban reformers planned a second plaza in Kōgane-machi where Kōganemachi Avenue (present-day Ŭljiro), an east-west thoroughfare,

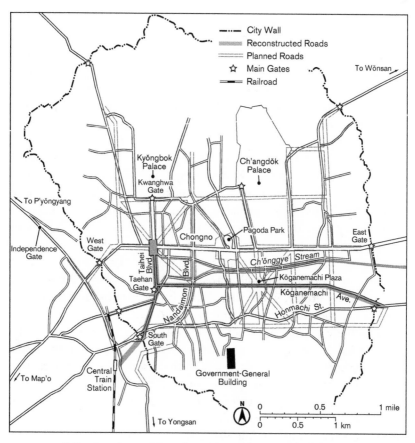

FIGURE 3. Keijō plan of 1913. Map adapted from *Chōsen sōtokufu kanpō* 81 (Nov. 6, 1912): 34.

bisected the southern half of the city.[37] This proposal aimed to placate the commercial interests of the expatriate community, which repeatedly petitioned the Government-General to include Honmachi Street in its urban reforms.[38] Although these efforts fell upon deaf ears, officials did plan to make most street improvements in the southern village, including repairs actually completed on Kōganemachi Avenue, one of four major arteries that converged on the plaza. Another radial emanating northwesterly from Kōgane-machi would have connected this Japanese-dominated area to a third plaza in the heart of the northern village. The Taean-dong Plaza would have also linked Kyŏngbok Palace and Pagoda Park, the only civic space of its kind in the northern village.

The significance of these urban reforms becomes clear in the context of the colonial state's desire to promote "assimilation," a term officials often used to describe the city's respatialization.[39] From the start, these efforts focused on amalgamating the city's Korean and Japanese populations through a unified administrative system. To this end, officials promulgated a law in 1914 that disbanded the legal authority of the Japanese community and other foreign settlements still retaining extraterritorial privileges. Two years later, the Government-General passed another ordinance that placed both Koreans and Japanese under the official supervision of neighborhood representatives. The north-south road projects completed during the first phase of urban reforms embodied attempts to connect the Korean neighborhoods of the northern village to the settler community of the southern village.[40] The most important of these north-south roads continued to be Taihei Boulevard, a central axis officials hoped to extend (along with train and telephone connections) southward to connect the central city to the boomtown of Yongsan.[41] In the fall of 1917, 150,000 residents gathered to celebrate the unveiling of a bridge built across the Han River just south of Yongsan. The new bridge, which linked the historic core in the northern village to the booming parts of southern Keijō, symbolized one important shift in the city's development.[42] Featuring both Japanese *geisha* and Korean *kisaeng* in another popular symbol of assimilation, the festive unveiling ceremony marked the end of the first phase of urban reforms and inaugurated the second phase (1919–24).

As figure 4 shows, the Government-General's second urban reform plan not only included the southward extension of Taihei Boulevard in the direction of Yongsan, but also highlighted the northern terminus of this thoroughfare. While the new plan was significantly scaled back from its predecessor from 1913 and made almost no reference to the ambitious project of superimposing radial and grid roads onto the precolonial configuration of streets, it still showcased the growing authority of the Government-General at the expense of the disenfranchised settler community. In particular, the plan jettisoned the aforementioned proposal for an interlocking system of centers, including the Kōganemachi Plaza, leaving the future site of the Government-General building as the only plaza.[43] Officials had already used this site to stage the Industrial Exhibition of 1915, the first major spectacle of its kind in colonial Korea. Now urban reformers continued to highlight the former grounds of Kyŏngbok Palace by relocating the one remaining plaza from the plan of 1913 to the area in front of the palace's main gate, Kwanghwamun. During the second phase of urban reforms, this plaza, enlarged more than two times the width of the broadest city thoroughfare, worked to spotlight

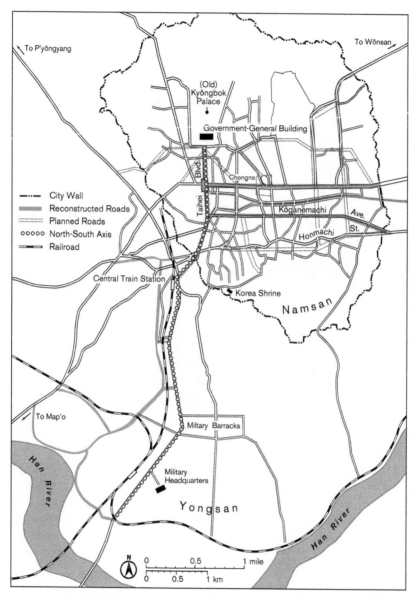

To P'yŏngyang

To Wŏnsan

(Old)
Kyŏngbok
Palace

Government-General Building

Taihei Blvd.

Chongno

Kōganemachi Ave.

Honmachi St.

- · - Link City Wall
▬▬▬ Reconstructed Roads
═══ Planned Roads
ooooo North-South Axis
═══ Railroad

Central Train Station

Korea Shrine

Namsan

To Map'o

Miltary Barracks

Military
Headquarters

Yongsan

Han River

Han River

N

| 0 | | 0.5 | | 1 mile |
| 0 | 0.5 | 1 km | | |

FIGURE 4. Keijō plan of 1919. Map adapted from: *Chōsen sōtokufu kanpō* 2062
(June 25, 1919): 310–11.

the new Government-General building at the expense of the expatriate community.

Even as colonial officials subordinated the insular initiatives of settler elites, their plan from 1919 continued to favor the southern village, although ultimately producing only a rudimentary system of gridded roads. Largely a result of financial limitations, planners completed only fifteen of forty-two roads (35.7 percent) designated for reconstruction during the first decade of colonial rule.[44] Of the street improvements successfully completed, many also underwent considerable revisions in their final implementation. Such modifications not only tempered the respatialization of early Keijō but also privileged the living spaces of Japanese settlers. A good example of such ethnic discrimination is evidenced by a north-south avenue planned to connect eastern Hon-machi and Pagoda Park. As Gotō Yasushi has shown, officials completed only half of this artery. Faced with fiduciary restrictions, they abandoned their original plan to pave a new street, straightening and widening a nearby road instead.[45] More important, this upgraded road extended only from Hon-machi to Kōganemachi Avenue, an area primarily inhabited by Japanese settlers. By contrast, officials neglected the area north of Kōgane-machi. Bisected by the Ch'ŏnggye Stream, this overpopulated and unsanitary part of Keijō was inhabited primarily by indigent Koreans.[46] Neglect of slums like those along the Ch'ŏnggye Stream resulted in considerable continuities, rather than radical departures, from the precolonial system of roads.

This spatial holdover, in turn, ensured that the existing contours of administrative districts tended to override more intrusive plans to rationalize and even "assimilate" neighborhood formations. Following the pre-Meiji tradition of constructing commoner areas in a grid pattern of rectangular blocks (J: chō), urban reformers aimed to create uniform administrative units. According to this plan, a straight road would bisect approximately three subblocs (J: chōme), thus creating one rectangular unit. Such respatializations depended on the successful implementation of gridded roads, only partially completed before 1925. As a result, the existing principle of "natural" neighborhoods tended to prevail, especially in areas where colonized Koreans resided. "Natural" neighborhoods refer to communal living spaces consisting of a number of plots (p'ilji) and divided by a few cul de sacs or by one minor (but not necessarily straight) road. Comparing land register maps produced by the Great Han Empire and the early colonial state, Sŏ Hyŏn-ju has demonstrated that the Government-General reconstructed only eight (14.5

percent) of fifty-five "natural" Korean neighborhoods by bisecting two or more of these neighborhoods with a new road.[47] In other words, 85.5 percent of the city's Korean neighborhoods retained their precolonial administrative boundaries, despite the construction of a modest grid network of thoroughfares around them. The stark contrast between excessive attention to the city's arterial contours and woeful neglect of much of its capillary organization reveals, in spatial terms, the highly uneven and disjointed state of early Keijō.

Strategic disregard for the city's colonized neighborhoods was also reflected in the names associated with administrative districts and in the ways local residents likely identified with their immediate surroundings. In the southern village, officials modified the names of most districts, often by changing their administrative suffixes from the Korean *dong* to the Japanese *machi*. They took similar measures to "Japanize" several districts in the northern village, adding or subtracting a Chinese character where necessary. Yet in spite of these changes, few districts with distinctly Japanese names—of famous people, places related to the empire, or sites referring to the expatriate settlement—coincided with areas where Koreans tended to reside. In fact, almost every district in the northern village retained names that had existed since the Chosŏn dynasty, thus leaving them markedly unassimilated.[48] The notable continuity of neighborhood names in these Korean-populated areas is another important indication that urban reforms did not deeply penetrate the city's existing spatiality.[49] The unevenness of these reforms, in turn, helped produce the administrative appearance, if not the sociocultural reality, of two distinct ethnic enclaves, a binary configuration that Korean nationalists only further strengthened by demanding a more egalitarian redistribution of public resources for "their" numerically underrepresented neighborhoods. At the same time, considerable instances of interethnic mixing in terms of residential patterns and working conditions undercut highly politicized divisions between the northern and southern villages, demonstrating that the boundary between them was, at least to some degree, porous and artificial.[50]

Although early colonial power failed to reach the capillary level, street improvements did produce remarkably strong effects on individuals living and working along Keijō's arterial infrastructure. In order to transform them into showcase thoroughfares, officials required inhabitants to relinquish land and property. To this end, the Government-General passed the Land Confiscation Law of 1911 and a series of other ordinances, such as the Regulations Controlling Urban Construction and the Regulations Controlling Roads of 1913. Extended from the metropole but significantly widened in terms of their coverage and enforcement, these laws imposed heavy fines on individuals who failed to surrender holdings in exchange for monetary compensation. Meanwhile, the colonial state also sought to imbue Keijō with a notion of social criminality, one that would allow it to move away from the vengeful hand of sovereign power toward gentler punishments aimed at defending the urban collective. Through a combination of punishments and rewards, authorities thus intensified the stakes in promoting what official newspapers championed as "civic morality" *(kongdŏksim;* J: *kōtokushin)*. Criticizing stalwart landowners who refused to contribute to the public good, the Government-General encouraged residents to reform their attitudes according to street improvements. In this way, authorities hoped to transform human mores in support of state goals and to bring back into the fold of civic normalcy individuals who had temporarily transgressed top-down reorderings of urban space. The discourse of civic morality thus points to experiments with new forms of subjectification aimed at producing illegalities commensurate with modern capitalism and property rights. However, police coercion in these processes frequently undercut pretentions to governmentality, reinstituting the sovereignty of an external force that struggled to widely disseminate its political and economic rationalities.

Government reports published in the *Maeil sinbo,* the Korean-language version of the *Keijō nippō,* reveal considerable resistance to urban reforms and, in response to this situation, the repeated use of racializing discourses on civic morality. Exhortative articles repeatedly chastised colonized residents for refusing to cooperate with the land survey, a project central to establishing a modern system of property ownership and closely tied to constructing a rationalized system of roads. Published in the same year as the first urban reform plan, one article put the matter in these ideologically dichotomous terms: "Civilized people wholeheartedly welcome and approve this [project], but those lacking knowledge rely on barbarian traditions. . . . Thus, misunderstandings regarding the land and building surveys are many, as are wild rumors that taxes will increase or that dim-witted people's homes and land will be confiscated without warning."[51] Deploying an assimilationist rhetoric of imperial benevolence, officials took pains to explain that expropriated land would be properly compensated.[52] Despite financial inducements, the *Maeil sinbo* continued to carry admonitory accounts of "stubborn" Koreans, a countervailing reference to racialized conceptions of ethnic difference. In stark contrast to their "civilized" Japanese counterparts who surrendered themselves to the public good, these colonized stalwarts were accused of overstating their property out of extreme self-interest—a "selfish" behavior that, according to colonialist stereotypes, came to define Koreans as essentially clannish.[53] Such clan-induced selfishness, Japanese pundits claimed, "forced" officials to implement the Land Confiscation Law. Urban reformers also complained about frequent and unpredictable land transfers, including cases of falsified property sales and even "unfilial" instances wherein they accused Korean sons of selling their fathers' land as their own property.[54] The intersection of spatial and racial domination thus deprived the colonized population of their venerated traditions of Confucianism, customs that nationalists would soon redeploy to condemn the immorality of Japanese rule.

Meanwhile, the official accounts that "civilized" Japanese settlers also failed to relinquish their property strained the racist dichotomies that supposed only Koreans lacked a sense of civic morality. In an article published in 1911, the *Maeil sinbo* reported that two Koreans and one Japanese living along Nandaimon Boulevard, a major thoroughfare slated for widening, refused to surrender their property. In the end, Pak Sŏn-ho and Yun Ch'ang-sŏk grudgingly acquiesced, but Hamaoka Ryōsuke refused to comply, forcing officials to apply legal sanctions. The article then complained that Japanese settlers like Hamaoka, despite considerable knowledge and wealth, could conduct themselves without common sense, relegating them to the position of "uncivilized" Koreans.[55] Throughout the 1910s, compromising accounts of other uncooperative Japanese settlers continued to fill the pages of the *Maeil sinbo*. An editorial from 1913, for example, reported that few Koreans refused to sell their land or sold only at exorbitantly high prices, whereas settlers continued to commit such "selfish" acts. How, the author anxiously wondered, could Japanese as "forerunners of civilization" hold such "perverse ideas"?[56] Although some settlers may have wielded enough power to resist government impositions, doing so disrupted both official discourses aimed at "enlightening" Koreans and the implementation of urban reforms. As a result, police officers often deployed another set of regulations criminalizing "minor offenses" (J: *keihanzai; kyŏngbŏmjoe*), the colonial version of which provided them even greater latitude in enforcing measures necessary to ensure public safety, commercial transactions, and a sanitary environment along the city's main thoroughfares.[57]

Even as the practices of some expatriates undermined colonialist dichotomies, officials continued to exhort Koreans to actively promote what officials liked to call a "unity of interests." Although still poorly operationalized due to frequent police interventions, this governing rationality aimed to create greater subjective connections between government-led street improvements and the potentially enriching benefits of capitalist development. As one *Maeil sinbo* editorialist explained in 1912, "Generally speaking, roads have a direct connection with civilized transportation; . . . if transit is convenient, import and export frequent, and the coming and going of people trouble-free, there will naturally be unlimited profits."[58] However, official neglect of thoroughfares in the northern village made it difficult, if not impossible, for most residents to buy into the "enlightened" use of public roads. The same editorialist, although writing to excoriate Koreans for their lack of industry, conceded that Keijō's narrow and uneven streets overlapped like snakes, making it difficult for people to pass. Even Chongno, the main commercial thoroughfare of the precolonial city, remained congested due to the unregulated erection of commercial stalls, preventing the "civilized" circulation of goods and people.[59] Deploying both a capitalist logic of accumulation and a colonialist rhetoric of assimilation, officials hoped that destroying these structures would help create an urban infrastructure wherein Koreans themselves would carry out their duties as diligent subjects while simultaneously making a profit.

This assimilationist ideology of profit-making was similarly deployed to persuade residents to embrace a related idea of urban reform that caught the attention of the early colonial state. With the advent of electricity, which had first been used on the peninsula in 1886 to illuminate Kyŏngbok Palace, Japanese pundits called for the expansion of this new technology beyond elite, private locales, establishing night markets to strengthen the link between profit-making roads and their enriching use by local residents. These writers often related the "enlightened" use of public spaces to the efficient use of time, which would "contribute to the prosperity of states and to the development of humanity," to quote one early colonial proponent of night markets.[60] Reiterating Orientalist views of native "backwardness" used to excoriate uncooperative landlords, this particular pundit argued that Korean merchants had squandered opportunities to make profits by closing their doors after dusk, which he criticized as the country's most uncivilized and anachronistic practice. Having recently rescinded the ban on Korean women using streets during the day when the city's gates and markets were open, the next logical step, he argued, was to install streetlights and other electrical devices necessary for nocturnal business. Soon the Government-General's official newspaper exhorted the colonized population: "After you lose a day's profit, a month's profit, and a year's profit, what would be the point of lamenting the downfall of your business? I hope you all do business, not only during the daytime, but also at night. If you work diligently, you will make some profit."[61] Thus personal profit served as the rhetorical enticement to use public roads in this "enlightened" way. Not coincidentally, establishing night markets along the city's thoroughfares also allowed officials to reincorporate into the urban economy those itinerant hawkers recently displaced by the destruction of their temporary stalls.

Still other writers promoted social education facilities such as parks, theaters, music halls, clubs, libraries, art museums, and zoological gardens as a means of assimilating Korean residents through officially sanctioned uses of public space. Matsui Shigeru (1866–1945), a protectorate-period police bureaucrat, had considered these institutions the most effective way to advance civic morality among the colonized population.[62] Adopting an assimilationist model of Confucian paternalism, Matsui had proposed the need to fully "enlighten" expatriates who, as elder brothers, could then direct their younger Korean siblings toward civilization.[63] After annexation, similar pundits called for a highbrow theater, a proper club, and a major Shintō shrine as a way of improving the city's "taste."[64] However, in practice, the sensibilities of the Japanese middle class did not necessarily reflect the everyday reality of the early colonial city, where lower-class Japanese peddlers roamed the streets for profit and many metropolitan women found themselves in the booming entertainment districts.[65] As a result, the colonial police had to enforce "proper" standards of civic morality among *both* unruly Japanese and noncompliant Koreans, thereby undermining the experiment of instituting a self-governing form of colonial rule.

Meanwhile, the Government-General continued to try to hide the coercive hand of its police proxies in public sites reconstructed to serve recreational and educational purposes. Such was the case with Pagoda Park, which officials of the Great Han Empire had created on the grounds of Wŏn'gak Temple to establish stronger links between the Korean monarch and his subjects. When completed in 1900, the park was open to the public on Sundays, while the Korean Imperial Household used it during the rest of the week.[66] Citing this "private" domination of public space as proof of Hwangsŏng's backwardness, colonial officials decided to open the park to the public on a daily basis in late July 1913. To further establish their regime's modernity, they also upgraded the park with benches, flowers, walking paths, electrical lighting, and trees.[67] But newspaper reports repeatedly criticized Koreans for uprooting trees, damaging foliage, and otherwise mistreating this public site. Ignoring the material privation underlying these acts, colonial officials instead assailed such behavior as selfish and uncivilized, seeking to control it by championing the public good. As one *Maeil sinbo* article explained: "Regardless of the conditions of their construction, parks are not the private property of an individual; rather, they belong to the public. Hence, they should be carefully treated with civic spirit. If . . . this spirit of tender care is weak or damaged, it is fair to say this person is without civic morality."[68] By bringing detractors of this project back into the collective fold through discursive, legal, and other punishments, the Government-General gradually began to saturate parks, roads, and other public sites with the ideology of civic morality. Rather than simply punish deviant individuals through sovereign power, officials urged residents to reform "wayward" practices that continued to undercut their efforts to defend society, an ideology necessary to mask the forceful expropriation of land for urban reforms.

## CITY PLANNING AS "CULTURAL RULE," 1925–1934

Although only implemented in piecemeal fashion, street improvements continued to dominate urban reforms during the early 1920s. By the mid-1920s, officials began to respond to the structural limitations of early colonial rule by seeking to further entrench the powers of city planning, a transnational movement circulating both within Japan's empire and across the modern world. Pursued with considerable contestation among the Government-General, the municipal government, and semigovernmental organizations, the project to create what planners now grandiosely called "Great Keijō" (Tae Kyŏngsŏng) widened the scope of earlier urban reforms and offered a series of updated methods. Rather than operating primarily in a negative register by forbidding certain practices, this intensified form of power created an increasingly positive economy aimed at integrating the productive capacities of the city and its multiethnic inhabitants. However, utopian invocations of the city as an organically united social body concealed even more invasive projects such as land readjustment, a planning technique that aimed to superimpose the city's rudimentary system of gridded roads onto the microspaces of dilapidated neighborhoods. In a similar way, land readjustment called on taxpaying landowners to relinquish a portion of their land in exchange for anticipated increases in property values and commercial profits. Thus while its success in transforming Keijō remained limited, city planning converged with the Government-General's harmonizing tactics of "cultural rule," which also aimed to co-opt bourgeois Koreans (and Japanese) as active supporters of Keijō's markedly uneven modernization.[69]

As discussed in the introduction, most histories of Korea continue to use the nationalist uprising of 1919 as the central event explaining colonial politics during the 1920s. To be sure, this epochal event helps account for the rapid increase in divide-and-rule strategies typically associated with cultural rule, including the introduction of a civilian police force, relaxation on Korean-language media, and support for moderate political organizations. However, other transnational developments linked the metropole and colony to wider, global phenomena such as city planning. In fact, in the very year that the colonial military squelched the March First Uprising, the imperial Diet in Tokyo passed the City Planning Law and the Urban Buildings Law. Together, these metropolitan laws replaced the urban reforms implemented hitherto, setting in motion what André Sorensen has described as "a comprehensive planning system that would regulate whole city areas and allow planned urban growth." Drawing on German and French precedents, the new system included zoning regulations as well as financial measures, such as a tax on increases in land values, a betterment levy for landowners benefiting from planning projects, and land expropriation procedures.[70] While the Government-General did not pass similar laws until 1934, a belated development often criticized as proof of the colony's "warped modernization" (oegok toen kŭndaehwa), Keijō officials did actively borrow new planning techniques from the laws of 1919, especially land readjustment and the betterment levy.[71] They also drew on transnational networks of personnel and organizations to localize city planning, making its global idioms and practices fit both the challenging conditions and contentious politics of colonial urbanism.[72]

Like its Euro-American counterparts, Japanese planning stressed scientific accuracy and rational forecasting.[73] In other words, planners believed that the careful, empirical study of roads, parks, traffic, and sanitation would produce the information necessary to efficiently reorder city spaces. To this end, Gotō Shimpei (1857–1929)—a German-trained doctor and veteran statesman who became Home Minister in

1916—established the Tokyo-based Urban Research Association (URA) in 1917.[74] Staffed by other prominent Home Ministry bureaucrats, including Ikeda Hiroshi (1881–1939), university professors, Diet members, and newspaper journalists, URA served as an extragovernmental organ. This organization published its latest research in a monthly journal entitled *Urban Digest (Toshi kōron)*, an important forum for debates on city planning. Before going on to become Foreign Minister in 1918, Gotō created a formal city planning section within the Home Ministry. He also founded the Urban Planning Research Association, a semigovernmental advisory board that became an institutional model for the Keijō City Planning Research Association (KCPRA; est. 1921).

Gotō's successor as Home Minister, Mizuno Rentarō (1868–1949), functioned as another important link between metropolitan and colonial planners. During his tenure, Mizuno passed the aforementioned planning laws of 1919, before becoming Director-General of Political Affairs under Governor-General Saitō Makoto (r. 1919–27). He also served as chairman of KCPRA, a post he retained even after his return to the Home Ministry in 1922. Many of Mizuno's subordinates who helped formulate the language of the laws of 1919 visited Keijō, offering lectures to colonial planners. These individuals include the Tokyo Imperial University architecture professors Sano Toshikata (1880–1956) and Uchida Yoshikazu (1885–1972) and their protégé, the Home Ministry's Kasahara Toshirō (1882–1969). Sano later became an honorary member of KCPRA, as did the prolific architect Kataoka Yasushi (1876–1946). In addition to the visits officials from the metropole made to the colony, members of KCPRA made frequent research trips to the metropole and to Manchuria to meet with local planning leaders. For example, Hizuka Shōta, a member of KCPRA and a city councilman, visited the Tokyo-based Urban Planning Research Association in late March 1922, consulting with Gotō, Uchida, and Mizuno.[75] The frequency and depth of such interactions between metropole and colony suggest the need to treat planning movements within the Japanese empire as one unit of analysis, while specifying their local inflections.[76]

Like debates published in *Urban Digest*, the colonial planning discussed in *Keijō Digest (Keijō ihō)*, the municipal government's monthly bulletin, focused on the scientific transformation of urban space into an organic system. However, in contrast to their metropolitan counterparts, Keijō officials faced the added burden of overcoming deep social divisions along class and ethnic lines, a difficulty few publicly admitted. Kawano Makoto, for instance, a technician working for the municipal government, simply urged colonial planners to transcend superficial alterations made during the previous decade. As he explained in 1922, "If we look at the city as one organic body, . . . measures such as the repair of roads and the maintenance of cleanliness are one part of efforts to complete the unification of that organic body—namely, the road and sewage plans. . . . In the future, we must therefore move forward with a unified plan, [relating these parts] to one another."[77] The organic metaphors Kawano used to describe Keijō's development assumed a more systematic and ideological form in the writings of Sano Toshikata, who, speaking at KCPRA's inaugural meeting in the fall of 1921, likened the idealized arrangement of domestic space to that of the city. As he wrote: "When house plans are well arranged, living conditions are comfortable. Based on the convenience level of a home's corridors, which are just like the streets of a city, the hard work of the family is done expeditiously or, conversely, in a tiresome way. . . . Only when a myriad of such perfect homes congregate is a splendid city born."[78] Drawing on emperor-centered notions of the family-state (J: *kazoku kokka; kajok kukka*), Sano even proposed reconstructing Keijō as a "family-city" (J: *kazoku toshi; kajok tosi*)—a metaphor commonly used by planners writing in metropolitan journals.[79] By "family-city," Sano was referring to a unified urban community consisting of male-dominated households, all linked to the paterfamilias through the ideology of "imperial loyalty and filial piety as one" (J: *chūkō itchi; ch'unghyo ilch'i*).

To implement this organic notion of urban society, officials placed an increasingly heavy burden on individual residents, although the government ironically refused to institute a system of self-rule allowing local elites to lead debates on "Great Keijō." As Jun Uchida has argued, continuing exclusion from colonial politics led Japanese elites and their Korean counterparts to engage in informal campaigns aimed at securing a stronger claim to national/imperial citizenship. These efforts included participation in new local assemblies, advisory councils that functioned largely at the behest of the mayor, but which members also used to advance their own interests—collective tools of communication that Yun Hae-dong has innovatively termed "colonial publicness" *(singminji konggongsŏng;* J: *shokuminchi kōkyōsei)*.[80] Despite official expectations that disenfranchised residents would support city planning, even some councilmen voiced serious concerns about the knowledge and commitment of the urban masses. As Tanaka Hanshirō, a Japanese member of the local Chamber of Commerce, warned in the fall of 1920: "Generally speaking, Keijō residents not only lack basic concepts about urban administration, but also do not possess strong convictions about the city. . . . If residents lack a basic self-awareness to participate in the affairs of urban administration, there is absolutely no hope for the advancement and development of municipal affairs." As local elites exposed the negative consequences of disenfranchising colonial society, some planners remained optimistic that a united community could overcome the obstacles of creating a modern metropolis. Thus Sano Toshikata argued that planning officials, although limited financially, could rely on Keijō's families to unite in a spirit of mental largesse.[81] By contrast, more skeptical officials, such as Iwai Chōzaburō of the Government-General's Civil Engineering Bureau, echoed concerns voiced by Japanese leaders like Tanaka, condemning Koreans' lack of understanding, effort, and support for city planning as the primary obstacle of this difficult project.[82]

To elicit popular support for city planning, colonial officials focused their efforts on encouraging residents to consider themselves organic parts of a greater urban whole, filling the front pages of the *Keijō Digest* with hortative terms also used by their metropolitan counterparts, such as "self-awareness," "training," and "social solidarity."[83] In one piece entitled "Urban Residents and Training," planners expressed concerns about the city's growing population, which increased from approximately 246,000 in 1920 to 343,000 by 1925. According to this article, rural residents could alleviate social problems by relying on relatively strong communal bonds. By contrast, Keijō, home to an increasingly large population of newcomers from the countryside, required welfare agencies, job introduction offices, and other social services that could train inhabitants to deal with urban problems. To this end, the authors encouraged denizens to acquire a thorough knowledge of sewers, hygiene, waste disposal, home building, tax payments, parks, and transportation.[84] Another article, entitled "Social Solidarity and Training," focused on strengthening the spiritual foundations of urban life. To remedy the harmful effects of modernity, the authors recommended popular education and edification, strategies of "social solidarity" simultaneously invoked in the metropole.[85] As they wrote, "Without making the mistake of moving away from the dualistic concept of individual and society and harmonizing both material and spiritual dimensions [of modern life], we can cultivate the needs of [our] age: individual probity and personal ability."[86] Given the unprecedented need to rely on the capacities of Keijō's population suggested by these colonial planners, individual cooperation with city planning would greatly determine the ability of officials to transform their ideals into a built reality.

As with earlier urban reforms, settler leaders continued to play an important role in promoting city planning to protect the commercial interests of their own community, not all of which coincided with the political aims of the Government-General. As early as 1912, expatriates had voiced concerns about damage regularly caused by the monsoon flooding of the Han River, especially along the highly vulnerable areas of Yongsan. Chronic floods led settler elites to petition the early colonial state to institute preventive measures, and the Government-General responded by channeling creeks in some areas and building levees around them.[87] However, these makeshift responses did not prevent a series of unprecedented floods that completely inundated Yongsan and neighboring areas in the summer of 1920. It took another deluge in 1922 and repeated petitions from settler organizations to convince the Government-General to embark on a comprehensive scheme for flood control. However, particularly heavy rains during the summer of 1925 demonstrated that even newly built levees did not adequately protect the residents of this area.[88] As Japanese settlers continued to seek flood protection, local leaders used natural disasters to further develop the southern village at the expense of the northern village.

However, as Kim Paek-yŏng has shown, the deluge of 1925 appears to have finally convinced government officials that a design focused narrowly on the flood-prone areas of Yongsan for the city's expansion was inadequate to the task of building a "Great Keijō."[89] Instead, the Government-General continued to pursue its own plans to transform Keijō into a showcase city, using the impending unveiling of its administrative complex on Kyŏngbok Palace to build a nearby residential compound, rather than focus only on the enclave of expatriates. This plan naturally provoked anxiety among settler elites who repeated long-standing fears that the colonial state was privileging the northern village over the southern village. For their part, Korean nationalists writing in the reemergent vernacular press voiced their own concerns, fretting that the government's new residential compound would result in a Japanese invasion of the one area where colonized inhabitants dominated, at least numerically. To accommodate predicted increases in the Korean population, they called for residential expansion into the city's eastern and western suburbs, including Map'o, Ch'ŏngnyangni, and Wangsimni.[90] In the end, resistance by both Korean and Japanese elites forestalled the Government-General's plan for a "northern advance," resulting in a compromise between expatriate leaders and government officials. As a result, planners decided to locate the city's geographical center atop Namsan and made the southern village the locus of future commercial development in the direction of Inch'ŏn.

Amid these contestations over the city's future, government officials and local business leaders established KCPRA in the summer of 1921. Founded to systematically and scientifically survey the colonial capital, KCPRA was divided into twelve departments like its Tokyo model, the Urban Planning Research Association (UPRA). Each department carried out a different aspect of city planning: regional development, communications, sanitation, public safety, economics, education, parks, social facilities, administrative systems, architecture, housing, and finances.[91] Unlike UPRA, KCPRA comprised a comparatively high number of middle-class professionals. This difference derived from limits on the government money available to fund KCPRA, which therefore relied more heavily on prominent businessmen for both financial and administrative support.[92] Reliance on the private sector, in turn, allowed Japanese settlers and a smaller number of Korean elites to use KCPRA as an interest group, which voiced their opinions on how best to transform Keijō into a modern metropolis. It was no coincidence, then, that KCPRA's first organizational meeting took place in the offices of the Keijō Chamber of Commerce, an important organization for promoting the business interests of the settler community. However, Keijō's development was ultimately led by the colonial state, which, over time, relegated KCPRA and other semigovernmental organizations to an advisory role.[93] During the early 1920s, the Government-General centralized responsibility for urban reforms within the general affairs division of the municipal government in an unsuccessful attempt to promulgate colonial planning laws. By early January 1925, however, the division's four-hundred-person staff did complete 80 percent of its surveys, far surpassing those outlined by KCPRA in 1921.[94]

These surveys led to the city's first official planning proposal. Published in April 1926, the plan incorporated some proposals favored by Japanese settlers and, to a lesser extent, those of Korean leaders, while seeking to consolidate the city's capacities into one organic unit. On the one hand, a proposal to connect the commercial city of Keijō to the industrial city of Inch'ŏn along the Han River responded to ideas previously championed by the Japanese business leaders of KCPRA.[95] On the other, the plan from 1926 also recommended expanding the city eastward toward Ch'ŏngnyangni and westward toward Yŏngdŭngp'o. Officials offered this concession to the marginalized Korean participants in city planning who had championed developing this region as a way to deal with the city's growing population. To overcome such competing interests, the plan of 1926, reiterating the harmonizing rhetoric of experts, called for the "systematic operation [of Keijō] as an organic body." With scientific data on population increases, transportation routes, sanitation facilities, and building regulations, officials sought to harness Keijō's resources in the creation of a unified urban system.[96] Road development, the basis for the efficient circulation of an increasing number of goods and people within the city, perhaps best exemplifies this assimilatory rationality. According to the plan of 1926, streets accounted for approximately 7 percent of Keijō's surface, a figure considerable less than the 25 to 30 percent boasted by other modern cities.[97] To meet these universal standards, planners proposed a street network that built on the urban reform plan of 1919, but extended roads into the city's suburban areas.[98] But these infrastructural improvements required 150 million yen, an astronomical sum even when supplemented by a hefty betterment levy. As a result, Korean pundits greeted this proposal with harsh criticisms, calling it illusionary and fanciful. Even some members of the Keijō Municipal Council, an organization dominated by Japanese business elites, predicted that the plan of 1926 would never leave the drawing board and, indeed, such was its doomed fate.[99]

While officials desperately searched for additional sources of funding to implement a comprehensive city plan, they had some success in promoting outward transformations of public space at the larger, arterial level that they hoped would eventually inspire the collective energies of urban residents and Keijō visitors. For instance, they allocated 520,000 yen to transform Taihei Boulevard into what planners liked to call Keijō's Champs-Élysées. Seeking to create a world-class capital on par with Paris, planners widened this symbolic thoroughfare to a remarkable sixty-two meters, consisting of a twenty-meter central roadway, a thirteen-meter passage for vehicular traffic, and a six-meter pedestrian walkway. To add further functionality as a city parkway, they also included a grassy outer fringe lined with trees and benches where residents could take a break from their everyday schedules of hard work.[100] In addition, a series of newly unveiled monuments along Taihei Boulevard aimed to redirect the collective attention of residents and visitors alike in ways conducive to Japanese rule. Sites like the Keijō Train Station (est. 1925) beckoned individuals to enjoy their modern facilities. Upon entering the station—a cutting-edge, three-story, red-and-white brick building with concrete reinforcements that one newspaper article described as "popularly oriented" to capture its mass dimensions—visitors found themselves in a large hall boasting a vaulted dome fitted with brightly colored stained glass. Other modern accoutrements such as elevators, flush toilets, restaurants, and a barbershop awaited thousands of passengers as they made their way to and from the capital city.[101]

A short northward journey around the South Gate brought one to City Hall, another new site along Taihei Boulevard. Located across from the Great Han Empire's former palace complex, this modern structure, designed with stones the same color as Koreans' white clothing, encouraged the colonized population (and Japanese settlers) to focus on the present and their roles in supporting city planning.[102] Often referred to as Keijō's "civic center," City Hall was designed with a large plaza where celebrations and other communal activities frequently took place.[103] For example, on October 30, 1926, more than six thousand students and other well-wishers converged here to participate in the building's unveiling ceremony. Holding small flags emblazoned with the municipal government's insignia, school children sang Keijō's new song and yelled, "Long live the municipal government!" three times. Officials also mobilized the members of seventy local civic groups to participate in a paper lantern procession, whose nighttime march ended at the plaza, where a crowd of over twenty thousand people gathered.[104] In addition to public gatherings, City Hall also came to function as a transportation pivot, with five major roads passing through it.[105] So important did this building figure in the minds of city planners that they designated this area an "urban center," likening it to the heart of the city's organic body.[106]

Finally, the northern terminus of Taihei Boulevard was home to the new Government-General building on the former palace grounds of Kyŏngbok Palace, so long the focal point of city planning. Understandably, most Korean-language studies have discussed this imposing neoclassical structure as a violent symbol of Japanese domination aimed at erasing Chosŏn's laudable history.[107] Even at the time of its unveiling, some concerned Japanese intellectuals, such as the folk craft specialist Yanagi Muneyoshi (1889–1961) and the architect and modernologist Kon Wajirō (1888–1973), harshly criticized the monument, fearing that it would alienate most Koreans rather than assimilate them.[108] Yet it is worth considering how the palace's selective destruction also constituted a significant reconstruction. Like other monuments lining Taihei Boulevard, this site was open to the public, if only in periodic and limited ways. To lure visitors, officials put in a modern garden, hundreds of trees, and a series of gravel pathways. For a small fee, visitors could enter the Government-General Art Museum, a permanent fixture from the exhibition of 1915. Opened in the spring of 1925, a new park constructed on the northwestern quadrant of the grounds also beckoned visitors to enjoy cherry blossoms, a cultural symbol of Japan found at many city parks and Shintō shrines.[109]

Although officials did successfully transform Keijō's main arteries into showcases of Japanese modernity, not all Koreans, of course, experienced these sites according to the rosy dreams of urban planners. For example, Pak T'ae-wŏn's short story "A Day in the Life of Kubo the Novelist," published in 1934, describes Taihei Boulevard, the most symbolic thoroughfare of the colonial state, as a place of intense alienation and even illness, contradicting top-down views of city planning as a movement promoting a collective spirit and public health. Although perhaps "publicly oriented" insofar as Keijō's train station elicited crowds, Pak portrays this building as a site of utter loneliness, packed with impersonal and distrustful visitors as well as travelers suffering from a litany of maladies.[110] As mentioned above, planners often referred to City Hall as Keijō's civic center, which, like the train station, drew residents—in this case, to participate in mass celebrations. However, even after an entire day of wandering the city, Pak never once mentions this landmark. Instead, he dwells on the disreputable fate of the nearby site that City Hall and another Western-style building, an art museum, had displaced, Tŏksu Palace, the Great Han Empire's symbolic center before Japanese annexation. His arresting description of this area suggests the nostalgia and ire likely felt by at least some well-educated Koreans, if not the general populace: "But the shabbiness, the shabbiness of the old palace, this is also something that weighs down on one's heart."[111]

Whereas elite writers like Pak highlighted the disrespect shown to former palace grounds as destructive efforts to promote street improvements, most lower-class inhabitants would likely have pointed to their own downtrodden neighborhoods as the most contemptuous aspect of Japanese rule. Indeed, the far greater challenge for colonial planners was to implement the organic ideals of a functional city beyond the arterial level, especially in the dilapidated areas of the northern village that they themselves had largely neglected. The ultimate test case for penetrating the city's capillaries was land readjustment (LR), a respatializing technique borrowed from the Japanese planning laws of 1919. This technique involved building local networks of gridded roads and other public facilities such as parks, thereby redividing lands into subblocks. Such invasive projects required that residents pool the ownership of land within a project area, a costly imposition many opposed.[112] Given these obstacles, planners frequently resorted to the language of organic harmony, seeking to transform the ailing parts of the urban body into a well-functioning mechanism. Sakai Kenjirō, a Keijō bureaucrat who became the head of the temporary urban planning division in 1926, used such metaphors to describe the integral role that colonized residents would play in facilitating LR. As he wrote:

> In city planning, streets are the skeleton, transportational routes the arteries, and conveyers the blood. With these [elements], a city proceeds to grow, while buildings serve as the city's veritable muscles. Keijō's muscles are, in fact, extremely disordered and emaciated. Their organization does not form a fixed system or unity, but is an assemblage of muscular nodes that are poor and in ruins; with those winding roads and cul de sacs, it is barely living. The skeleton, heart, and blood of Keijō are complete, but no muscle adheres [to that body]. For this to happen, the city's residents must rely on their [own] awakening. What is that awakening? It is one thing: land readjustment.[113]

Under this self-governing logic, planners called on Koreans to make personal sacrifices for the public good by supporting LR and thus helping to remedy the sanitary problems of the northern village. By the mid-1920s, this area had become a serious and contested issue among health experts, if only because Japanese settlers continued to suffer from relatively high rates of contagious diseases. Such concerns appeared prominently in yet another city plan published in 1928, one that fell on deaf ears like its predecessor from 1926. As the authors of the plan of 1928 anxiously wrote about the city's Korean enclave, "There are many cul de sacs and clogged sewer water overflows when it rains, [causing] residential areas to virtually lose their value and putting transportation, security, and sanitary conditions in a truly lamentable situation."[114] Officials invoked LR as a costly but effective way of transforming dilapidated neighborhoods through grid-like reconstructions, just as the city's main thoroughfares had partially reshaped its macrospatiality.

The plan of 1928 provides good examples of this project, especially the aim to reconfigure district five in western Chongno (figure 5). According to detailed calculations, this district comprised 84 percent residential lands, 14 percent lands occupied by roads, and only 2 percent parkland. Planners sought to decrease residential lands by 7 percent, making room to expand district roads by 2 percent

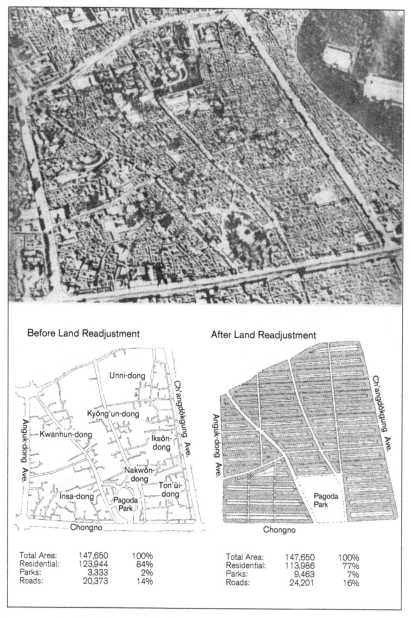

Before Land Readjustment

Unni-dong

Kyŏng'un-dong

Kwanhun-dong

Iksŏn-dong

Anguk-dong Ave.

Ch'angdŏkgung Ave.

Nakwŏn-dong

Ton'ŭi-dong

Insa-dong

Pagoda Park

Chongno

| Total Area: | 147,650 | 100% |
|---|---|---|
| Residential: | 123,944 | 84% |
| Parks: | 3,333 | 2% |
| Roads: | 20,373 | 14% |

After Land Readjustment

Anguk-dong Ave.

Ch'angdŏkgung Ave.

Pagoda Park

Chongno

| Total Area: | 147,650 | 100% |
|---|---|---|
| Residential: | 113,986 | 77% |
| Parks: | 9,463 | 7% |
| Roads: | 24,201 | 16% |

FIGURE 5. Land readjustment plan for western Chongno. Map adapted from *Keijō toshi keikaku chōsasho* (Keijō: Keijōfu, 1928), plates between 270 and 271.

Pagoda Park by 5 percent.[115] Although the proposed increase in lands occupied by local roads in district five contrasted with an average increase of 3.5 percent in the other four districts marked for LR, the qualitative difference in neighborhood space it would create was dramatic. Take, for example, Insa-dong. Located in the southwestern corner of district five, this neighborhood was bound on the south and west by two straight thoroughfares. However, the northern and eastern boundaries of Insa-dong were slightly angled, the former forming a cul de sac. Only one local road passed through the neighborhood, while other alleys produced a number of dead ends. According to the plan of 1928, a series of north-south and east-west streets would connect four existing roads that bounded Insa-dong, thus creating a local grid.

To facilitate such sweeping projects, colonial officials, having yet to pass laws enforcing LR and other planning principles, had to rely on the civic-minded actions of Korean landowners. They could only hope that local elites would come to see the common interests of class and ethnicity and relinquish a portion of their land in return for future increases in land values and improvements in Koreans' standard of living. For example, officials expected Insa-dong residents to cede 6 percent of that neighborhood's land and pay five yen (10 percent) of the costs associated with reconstructing each 3.3-square-meter area of land (fifty yen).[116] To encourage Koreans to make public sacrifices, colonial planners proposed creating landowner cooperatives, joint organizations of proprietors who pooled their individual resources.[117] Having traveled to the metropole in 1927 to study finance methods for city planning, Sakai described how he hoped Korean landowners would participate in these public projects: "Having established landowner cooperatives, they would take plans made for them by the municipal government and reform those cul de sacs, dead ends, and circuitous roads. If landowners contribute a portion of their property, splendid roads and districts can be built. If [this land] is reallocated and replotted, reshaping it into regulated areas, landowners will not only profit in terms of business, public safety, and sanitation, but the city will actually be able to use that land effectively."[118] In addition to providing financial support for government-led projects, these cooperatives would create locally imposed sanctions, compelling all members to participate if at least two-thirds of residents owning at least two-thirds of the land under discussion agreed. Unlike the system of forced land confiscations implemented during the urban reforms of the 1910s, this strategy of cultural rule produced greater local "autonomy" for neighborhood landowners, or at least the illusion thereof.

Although Sakai remained optimistic about landowners' commitments to LR, more sober planners expressed serious concerns about ill-financed attempts to transform the microspaces of Korean neighborhoods. Naoki Rintarō, former head of the Tokyo Reconstruction Bureau, was one such critic. Invited to Korea by KCPRA in late 1928, Naoki questioned the feasibility of carrying out LR in the northern village, whose dense neighborhoods left little room for planners to maneuver.[119] In terms of financial support, he remained pessimistic that Koreans, whom he deplored as wont to engage in lengthy discussions, would support these projects. Even the spirit of generosity and self-sacrifice he contrastingly credited to Tokyoites after the Great Kantō Earthquake of 1923 did not ensure popular support for LR, often forced on reluctant landowners.[120] In the colony, Naoki reminded optimists, cooperation with officials was further complicated by the high percentage of mortgages on Korean properties and the widespread suspicion that fees would accrue on their loans. Since the only other option, forced dislocation, threatened to disaffect the colonized population altogether, Naoki encouraged officials to focus their efforts on the rapidly developing suburbs, where some desperate Korean residents might relocate without officials having to expel these indigents from the dense city center. Given that the redevelopment of the northern village no longer appeared in the Government-General's city plan of 1930, Naoki's realistic conclusion seems to have convinced colonial planners to abandon this difficult project. As late as 1932, officials were, in fact, still complaining that Korean landowners refused to make even a 5 percent contribution of their land, a figure far lower than the 10 to 30 percent customarily offered by their counterparts in the metropole.[121] Only after the passage of the Town Planning Act in 1934 did colonial officials begin to implement LR, limiting these invasive and unpopular projects to developing areas in the suburbs.[122]

Similar difficulties plagued efforts to institute a viable betterment levy (BL)—a metropolitan technique of finance that taxed local residents between 25 and 50 percent of project costs in exchange for speculated increases in property and land values.[123] Even as they hoped to transfer this planning strategy to the colony, officials quickly realized a significant obstacle—namely, ethnic-based inequities of wealth, which increasingly divided the affluent few from the impoverished masses. According to a sobering account published in 1926, Keijō's residents possessed combined financial holdings of 410 million yen. Although seemingly high, this figure equaled that of only small metropolitan cities such as Kumamoto, whose population was less than half that of Keijō. Moreover, many Koreans living in the colonial capital found themselves in dire financial straits, with approximately half of the city's seventy thousand families categorized as poor. What property and land wealthier Koreans could afford was typically held as collateral security. Consequently, many of their holdings were auctioned off, resulting in property transactions in excess of one hundred per month.[124] Cognizant of these socioeconomic disparities, colonial planners concluded that an equal BL might provide future profits to land- and property-owning Japanese, but would likely not produce the same benefits for most Koreans.[125]

Colonized elites writing in the nationalist press came to a similar conclusion, voicing serious concerns that the proposed BL might plunge their already vulnerable working-class neighbors into further destitution. In an article published in the *Tonga ilbo,* the authors estimated that as many as 80 percent of Keijō's Korean families lived in residences held under collateral security, while only 20 percent owned their own homes. With so many families already unable to pay taxes, the imposition of a betterment levy, they feared, would only exacerbate already precarious living conditions. Such measures might even force some Koreans to sell what little they possessed and leave the city, a reality admitted by a few concerned Japanese planners.[126] Another *Tonga ilbo* article captured this widely held fear, criticizing the BL as part of a profligate city plan benefiting affluent expatriates.[127] Korean elites participating in Japanese-dominated advisory committees opposed this planning technique on similar grounds. In March 1927, the Korean members of KCPRA protested the group's decision to implement the BL, questioning a strategy that imposed an unfair tax on planning projects.[128] Finally, poorer Koreans themselves resisted the tax, calling on colonial planners to postpone the betterment levy until transportation and sanitary conditions in the northern village improved. Only then, one editorial concluded, would their opposition gradually subside.[129]

Despite protests from colonized critics, ambitious planners doggedly pushed ahead with plans to implement a BL, made effective in April 1930. The levy remained essential to support a two-phase, ten-year project totaling eleven million yen that aimed to complete the city's rudimentary network of gridded roads. Many Koreans opposed this

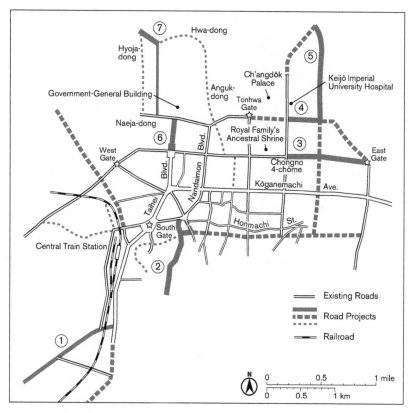

FIGURE 6. First phase road network plan, 1928–33. Map adapted from *Keijō nippō*, March 4, 1929.

project not only due to its unequal financing scheme but also for its callous treatment of Chosŏn dynasty monuments. For funds, the plan relied on the Government-General and the municipal government to pay 40 and 30 percent of costs, respectively, with residents of designated planning areas to shoulder the additional 30 percent.[130] As figure 6 shows, five of the seven roads marked for reconstruction during the first phase (1928–33) fell within the northern village, forcing Koreans to pay a significant portion of costs for road and sewer construction.

In the end, ongoing opposition compelled officials to cancel the BL altogether or tax at a relatively low rate. Because construction had already begun on the east-west axis from the Government-General building to the Keijō Imperial University Hospital, officials exempted residents living along the western segment from Tonhwa Gate to Keijō

Imperial University Hospital (dotted line next to #4 in figure 6).[131] Although the *Keijō nippō* used the availability of government funds to explain this exemption from the BL, the concession also aimed to placate members of the Korean aristocracy who vehemently opposed a thoroughfare that would have bisected the ancestral shrine (Chongmyo) of the former royal family.[132] In 1922, similar complaints, lodged by high-ranking nobles and the last emperor, Sunjong, had forced officials to reroute this intrusive road away from the culturally sensitive monument.[133] Meanwhile, other streets falling in neighborhoods heavily populated by Koreans—segments from Chongno 4-chōme to the East Gate (#3 in figure 6) and from Hwa-dong to Anguk-dong (dotted line), for example—were taxed at the relatively low rates of 5 and 4 percent, respectively.[134]

As officials encountered opposition from colonized residents, tax revenue had become all the more important because of the Great Depression, which put a considerable strain on government finances. In Keijō, the economic downturn resulted in a 68 percent reduction of the 850,000-yen budget for first phase of road projects, causing officials to cancel or postpone many of them.[135] The segment from Naeja-dong to Hyoja-dong (#7 in figure 6) offers an example of how these two factors contributed to obstruct city planners' goals. Located slightly north and west of the Government-General building, this area was populated almost entirely by Koreans, many of the propertied class.[136] As a result, officials set the BL at 17 percent, a rate more than four times that of areas inhabited by poorer Koreans. Although financial problems likely influenced officials' later decision to postpone construction on this segment, newspaper articles suggest that local opposition to the BL posed an equally, if not more, troublesome obstacle. One particularly confrontational editorial published in the fall of 1929 warned that if planning authorities did not win the favor of local residents, the project to construct a road in this area would eventually fail.[137] The *Tonga ilbo* continued to argue that only fully funded projects dedicated to improving roads and sewers in the dilapidated neighborhoods of the northern village would convince non-landholding Koreans that the BL was somehow in their interest. Questioning the universal ideology of colonial development, the nationalistic critics of another article condemned the highly uneven nature of city planning in the form of a deferential yet pointed question: "Isn't there a need," they asked, "to consider anew the degree to which the high-speed construction of Great Keijō directly and indirectly improves *our* lives, and the extent to which the urban development enhances *our* livelihood?"[138]

It is worth noting that even as wealthier Korean authors often used the plight of those less well-off to criticize the inherent inequalities of colonial planning, other members of the emergent Korean bourgeoisie used their privileged class position to take advantage of street improvements. Such was the case with the eastern half of Chongno (#3 in figure 6), upgraded as part of the ten-year plan of 1928. A report published in the *Keijō nippō* contrasted the thatched-roof buildings of this relatively undeveloped area to the "splendid, modern beauty" of two- and three-story brick buildings lining the western half of Chongno.[139] By constructing a widened asphalt road and sidewalks, officials hoped to rejuvenate the area around the East Gate, prompting nearby merchants to compete with their better-established counterparts in western Chongno. Shortly after the upgrade's completion in the spring of 1933, Kim An-bo, the Korean leader of the Eastern Development League, led a campaign to challenge the merchants of western Chongno. Kim and his associates used a number of marketing strategies to attract consumers entering the city from the rapidly developing suburbs of eastern Keijō, including the distribution of coupons for future purchases.[140] These promotional efforts helped create another popular site where consumers could lightheartedly stroll around the East Gate, or what Japanese liked to call *tonbura*.[141] All this pleased city planning officials, to whom Korean business competition signified a more important outcome, the completion of a widened thoroughfare extending the entire length of Chongno.[142] The Eastern Development League is an important reminder that colonial rule, although clearly privileging Japanese settlers, also opened up new opportunities for entrepreneurial Koreans to use the transformation of public space to their own class advantage.

It was not until the passage of the Town Planning Act in 1934 that, after fifteen years of debate, the Government-General instituted mechanisms that could more fully enmesh Koreans in the city's highly uneven public infrastructure.[143] In 1936, a year before the outbreak of the Asia-Pacific War, colonial officials finally applied this act to create a Great Keijō three and a half times larger than its previous size. As a result, the population increased to more than nine hundred thousand by the early 1940s, making the city the seventh largest in the Japanese empire. To merge the disparate spaces of Great Keijō into one organic unit, planners reorganized neighborhoods in the northern village along the lines of the administrative units in the southern village and renamed other land-marks—railroad stations, for example—so that they too formed part of an increasingly unified urban body, at least on a symbolic level.[144] Before Japan's attack on Pearl Harbor in 1941 undercut its financial where-withal, the late colonial state also invested considerable resources in cre-ating thoroughfares that connected the downtown area to newly incor-porated areas, zoned suburbs subjected to a number of government-led LR projects.[145] The various regions of Great Keijō and their diverse com-munities thus became more integrated parts of the wartime city.

Before this historical threshold, however, officials managed only to provide what one Japanese-language report from 1932 referred to as a "reconstructive and surgical treatment of the existing city."[146] To be sure, colonial efforts to displace former Chosŏn royalty, themselves assimilated into the Japanese imperial house as subordinated members, had largely succeeded, although not without considerable criticism and protest by at least some Korean elites.[147] Government measures to disas-sociate the Korean monarchy from an autonomous nation took their most concrete form in the selective destruction of the city's palaces, whose grounds became public spaces showcasing Japanese modernity and colonial authority. However, elaborate plans to transform Han-yang/Hwangsŏng into a capital on par with cities in the metropole and in Euro-American empires continually faltered at the level of the city's capillaries, revealing both the spatial and operational limits of colonial governmentality before 1937. Failure was especially apparent in the Korean-populated neighborhoods of the northern village, which contin-ued to suffer at the expense of the settler-dominated southern village. Even at the arterial level, into which the Government-General funneled considerable resources, financial setbacks and local opposition resulted in the completion of only seventeen of forty-seven (36 percent) streets marked for repairs since the urban reforms of the 1910s and early 1920s.[148]

That perennially frustrated city planners resorted to corporeal meta-phors of disease and organic calls for unity reveals the difficulties they encountered in financing projects of urban renewal. While they sought through rhetoric to more effectively bind the capacities of the city to the governing rationality of increasingly invasive projects, such as LR and a BL, they soon realized the futility of these unpopular and costly projects. As a result, they remained ideas to ponder and schemes to implement in only makeshift and uneven ways. As the following chapters reveal, such limitations also characterized the city's microsites, public spaces that also became the source of considerable attention and manipulation by government officials and their elite proxies as well as an area of intense controversy and contestation among a much larger and diverse group of less fortunate inhabitants.

# CHAPTER 2

# Spiritual Assimilation

*Namsan's Shintō Shrines and
Their Festival Celebrations*

Like the development of Keijō's public infrastructure examined in chapter 1, specific city sites, interconnected parts of the larger urban fabric, played important roles in the contested process of colonial subject formation. This chapter focuses on the spiritual dimensions of that project by examining Namsan, home to the city's Shintō complex. This complex included Seoul Shrine, a community institution founded by Japanese settlers in 1898, and Korea Shrine, a mammoth monument erected by the Government-General in 1925.[1] Even before the Asia-Pacific War (1937–45) mandated that all subjects (both Japanese and especially Koreans) identify with the imperial house, Namsan was at the center of an idealized project of emperor-led assimilation, one that used Shintō rituals to cultivate reverence for an ever-expanding multinational community.

One of the main factors complicating this project of spiritual assimilation, which even the colonial state embraced only halfheartedly before 1925, was the fraught relationship between its obligation of imperial allegiance and an already circumscribed commitment to religious freedom. According to the Government-General, shrine rituals constituted a civic duty of all imperial subjects regardless of their personal faith. Extended from the metropole, this ideology, notably opposed by several Korean Protestants during the 1920s and 1930s, was also regularly undercut by the religious nature of Seoul Shrine, the only public institution capable of exposing Koreans to unfamiliar imperial rituals before the establishment of Korea Shrine.[2] Moreover, as Yamaguchi Kōichi has shown, only in 1925 did the Government-General separate shrine Shintō, those state-administered institutions and practices associated with civic rituals, from sect Shintō and other officially sanctioned religions, such as Buddhism and Christianity, all of which were seen as useful, if potentially disruptive, forces of social mobilization.[3] During the late 1920s and early 1930s, some priests protested against the non-religious status in which the Government-General had placed shrine Shintō, urging teachers to mobilize school children to participate in overtly religious rituals, such as purification ceremonies.[4] In part due to the colonial state's failure to draw more than a porous and contested boundary between civic rites and religious practices, shrine Shintō had a far less unified and monolithic effect on the city's inhabitants than most accounts have suggested. Spiritual assimilation was, in fact, poorly operationalized, and it was done in highly makeshift ways prior to the government's unveiling of Korea Shrine in 1925. That year, an important threshold in the city's spatial transformation, charted in the previous chapter, proved to be an equally significant turning point in the history of colonial Shintō insofar as it established the necessary infrastructure for emperor worship.

Although discussions ensured thereafter that Seoul Shrine might be granted an official ranking in an empire-wide hierarchy of Shintō institutions, the Government-General did not successfully yoke this local institution until the promulgation of new shrine regulations in 1936.[5] Before then, its exceptional status outside of metropolitan conventions allowed the Japanese leaders of Seoul Shrine the room they needed to defend against the colonial state's interference into the daily management of shrine Shintō, one of the few aspects of self-rule that settlers continued to administer after the annexation.[6] Having closely guarded their expatriate shrine and its cultural activities as a bastion of colonial privilege, ethnocentric parish leaders only reluctantly followed state orders to "assimilate" Koreans into their ethnic community before 1925 and continued to do so only in highly subordinated ways. In addition to already popular *kisaeng* entertainment and ancient court music, indigenous deities and Korean costumes were finally incorporated into Seoul Shrine and its grand festival in 1929. Two years later in 1931, colonized parish leaders took charge of leading the annual procession for the first time, a task they carefully negotiated in order to satisfy their more powerful Japanese counterparts and to distinguish themselves from less fortunate Koreans. To be sure, such inclusionary concessions certainly aimed to elicit greater support from colonized spectators. However, these increasingly aggressive measures of spiritual assimilation also targeted the colonial state, which had seriously undermined settler control over colonial Shintō by placing the much larger Korea Shrine higher atop Namsan and by linking this mammoth complex to Seoul Shrine through a back approach that led from the former to the latter. Although competition between the Government-General and expatriate leaders now led to joint efforts aimed at more effectively reaching the colonized population, the masses remained intrigued but uncommitted subjects of this governmentality. Even after the inclusion of Korean deities in the Japanese-dominated pantheon in 1931, the raucous play of Seoul Shrine, rather than solemn worship at Namsan, was the primary experience through which Koreans encountered colonial Shintō. For these reasons, efforts to transform them into loyal subjects of the Japanese empire tended to falter.

## SEOUL SHRINE AND THE MAKESHIFT NATURE OF EARLY COLONIAL SHINTŌ

During its early tenure, the Government-General made clear its intention to follow Meiji (1868–1912) precedents of using Shintō practices to unify a divided polity around common loyalties to the imperial house.[7] It did so by first extending legal authority over Seoul Shrine, the spiritual core of the expatriate community, and using its parish organization and festival celebrations to gradually incorporate Koreans. As part of Keijō's urban reforms, early colonial officials also began the long-term planning and construction of their own government shrine, not completed until 1925. As they slowly laid the infrastructure to spread Shintō, they gained control over the sacerdotal symbols of Korea's royal house, which, during the Great Han Empire, had played an increasingly powerful role in promoting official nationalism.[8] Having recently extinguished the sovereignty of the Korean monarchy, Japanese officials quickly moved to downgrade its national rites. To this end, they forbade members of the royal house from conducting rituals at Sajikdan, an altar that had been used by Chosŏn kings to worship the gods of the earth and harvest since the Silla period (57 BCE–935 AD). The altar itself remained, but colonial authorities discontinued its semiannual rituals in early 1911 on the grounds that they did not conform to the Japanese imperial system.[9] Meanwhile, the Government-General encouraged high-ranking members of the former royal family, now reconstituted into a system of nobility, to regularly visit Seoul Shrine and make Shintō offerings, both of which were to demonstrate their subordination to Japan's monarchy.[10] For example, on October 1, 1913, the yearly commemoration of annexation day, Prince Yi Kang (1877–1955), the fifth son of King/Emperor Kojong (1852–1919), who was later arrested for his nationalistic activities in Manchuria, and Yi U (1912–45), the prince's second son who served as an officer in the Japanese imperial army during the Asia-Pacific War, joined the Governor-General and other officials in paying their respects to Amaterasu, the mythical ancestress of the Japanese nation, offering monetary donations to this imperial deity.[11]

But despite officially voiced hopes that all Koreans living in the early colonial capital would fall under its spiritual sway, Seoul Shrine—a small and unassuming Shintō structure built in close proximity to an expanding population of expatriate parishioners—only gradually came to incorporate the colonized population after annexation. Before 1925, when the Government-General finally unveiled its own Shintō complex atop Namsan, the early colonial state had to rely on the expatriate custodians of Seoul Shrine to transform the loyalty of Koreans into that of their Japanese counterparts. And yet, ironically, the expatriate population the shrine served was itself by no means permanent or stable, militating against the creation of a unified sense of loyalty even among settlers.[12] Comprising individuals from diverse origins throughout the metropole, the expatriate community was, in fact, divided by considerable class, status, and gender differences. Moreover, settlers closely guarded their powerful, if inchoate, "Japaneseness" as a symbol of their ethnic superiority. As a result, both Seoul Shrine's expatriate stewards and other Japanese leaders tended to discriminate against Koreans as "uncivilized," rather than accept the same ancestry theory (tongjoron; J: dōsoron) of the Government-General.[13] They thus responded ambivalently to official directives aimed at extending the cult of the modern emperor to the multiethnic landscape of early Keijō.[14] Tensions between the parochial interests of shrine leaders and the inclusionary rhetoric of the new colonial state thus resulted in a highly makeshift arrangement of spiritual assimilation during the first fifteen years of Japanese rule.

Although frequented by both Korean and Japanese officials, Seoul Shrine remained in the administrative hands of settlers, an institutional arrangement the early colonial state sought to control through new bureaucratic regulations. When the Government-General abolished the legal status of the Japanese settlement in 1914 and erected a unified urban administration system in 1916 (which, as the previous chapter demonstrated, included neighborhoods inhabited by both ethnic groups), it also expanded the constituency of Seoul Shrine beyond the Japanese enclave, requiring that the shrine's leaders include one Korean as a major parish representative in each of the city's four five-person parish districts. In addition, official regulations also stipulated that Koreans would serve as regular parish representatives in the shrine administration.[15] As a result of these regulations, Koreans quickly came to comprise approximately 35 percent of the total number of parish leaders. However, they continued to occupy a subordinated position, which Kim Tae-ho has described as an "honorary membership."[16] Indeed, that only 20 percent of Korean shrine leaders (as opposed to 56 percent of their Japanese counterparts) doubled as popularly elected neighborhood administrators suggests the strong likelihood that the Government-General handpicked these proxies to expand the membership of a Shintō institution that its Japanese leaders still dominated.[17]

Even after the administrative reordering of Keijō and its parish organization, Seoul Shrine's ethnocentric leadership continued to undercut the Government-General's officially stated goal of spiritual assimilation. For one thing, the exclusion of Koreans from the shrine functioned as an expedient tool for disgruntled leaders to wield power over one of the few settler institutions that the new colonial state could not completely control, even after the dismantling of their legal authority. As a result, most Koreans had few direct contacts with Shintō and remained at a considerable distance from its ritual activities. If they encountered Amaterasu at all, it was not in shrine prayers for the imperial house but through the raucous play of festival celebrations.[18] Indeed, these celebrations constituted one of the few contact zones where Shintō could impinge, however lightly, on the consciousness of Koreans.[19] As part of the administrative reorganization mentioned above, parish leaders created a routine schedule for annual shrine celebrations in coordination with the colonial government. Official supervision of this schedule is reflected in the nature of the festivals, most of which were closely linked to the newly created cult of the Japanese emperor.[20] For example, October 17 and 18, the dates for the grand festival, were timed to coincide with celebrations held at Ise Shrine in Mie Prefecture. Dedicated to venerating Amaterasu, the solemn complex of Ise reigned at the spiritual apex of an empire-wide hierarchy of modern Japanese shrines.[21]

The cultural activities performed by the participants of the grand festival consisted of an uneasy coupling of "prayer" and "play."[22] From the perspective of priests, solemn ceremonies conducted on the grounds of Seoul Shrine at the beginning of the celebration were intended to extend to and blend with the sacred procession that followed by transferring the divine spirit to a portable shrine, typically carried by young settler men. In spite of this emphasis on somber ritual, the procession also included elements that contravened carefully constructed signs of order and hierarchy, giving rise to instances of what Sonoda Minoru has called "sacred transgression." As Sonoda writes, "On the one hand are highly defined rites of seclusion and purification, tedious rites in which one's emotions and responses are trained and focused through bodily actions and behavior of the most restrained and solemn kind. But on the other hand, there is also generally an expectation of a thorough liberation of mind and body, a [temporary] destruction of the existing order."[23]

The colonial state would have preferred to represent Japanese settlers as a unified national community of reverent subjects, especially to newly colonized Koreans. However, even reports on early colonial festivals published in the semiofficial newspaper, the *Keijō nippō,* frequently reveal this uneasy mixture of prayer toward Japan's imperial ancestress and a host of Shintō-related forms of play. A good example of this tension can be found in the newspaper images featured in figure 7. In the top half of this illustration, shrine clergy and other important figures show their respect for the city's guardian deity, Amaterasu, by performing a ceremonial bow at the grand festival's opening ceremony. In contrast to the solemnity of the opening ceremony's prayers, the remainder of the festival was marked by play, shown in the bottom half of the illustration: amateur sumo, though presented as an offering to the guardian deity, naturally entertained festival participants. In addition, the grand festival became known for its yearly display of fireworks, children's fencing matches, flower arranging, and Hakata *niwaka,* a form of comedy from Kyūshū, the home island of many settlers. Another highlight of the festival included the parading of the Japanese *geisha* from Shin-machi. Like other forms of festival entertainment, these women not only pleased the guardian deity with their dancing, but also attracted festival audiences, including men who would become nighttime customers after seeing them perform on the streets during the day.

The element of boisterous play frequently took on greater external importance than its counterpart of reverent prayer, dashing the hopes of government officials that Shintō rituals would at least display, if not impart, a "proper" sense of Japanese spirituality to Korean spectators.

FIGURE 7. Prayer and play at Seoul Shrine. Source: *Keijō nippō*, Oct. 17, 1917.

For example, the formal attire worn by the Japanese *geisha* during the festival procession, consisting of a white loose-sleeve jacket and a crimson skirt-like bottom, mimicked the everyday clothes worn by Heian period (794–1185) court nobles, an outfit typically reserved for the predominantly male members of the procession (see figure 8a). That females wore this kind of attire during the festival—described in newspaper

FIGURE 8a. *Geisha* in shrine procession. Source: *Keijō nippō*, Oct. 19, 1918.

FIGURE 8b. *Kisaeng* in shrine procession. Source: *Keijō nippō*, Oct. 19, 1918.

accounts as an "exceptional practice"[24] by women "dressed up like young men"[25]—suggests that a limited form of cross-dressing was allowed for the performers of this special event. Perhaps encouraged by these officially sanctioned parameters for festival play, some enthused onlookers of the Shintō procession also appeared in dress of the opposite sex. Such acts of transgression, also common to festival celebrations in the metropole, became so pronounced in Keijō in 1917 that the colonial police issued entertainment regulations, which included a strict proscription against popular forms of transvestitism.[26] Government officials apparently found that these playful practices were too loosely related to expectations of prayer and thus complicated their ability to reach Koreans with a coherent representation of Japanese reverence for Amaterasu.

Moreover, Koreans' early exposure to this Shintō ritual was limited by the procession route for the annual grand festival, which I read as an embodiment of Keijō's social geography. Surely, the northern and southern villages separated by the Ch'ŏnggye Stream functioned to some extent as disparate ethnic enclaves, although this division may never have been as stark as some nationalist accounts have asserted.[27] Indeed, a wide range of popular celebrations and public campaigns served as cultural bridges, promoting social interactions between Koreans and Japanese.[28] The annual grand festival is an important example of these interethnic (and intraethnic) linkages, in this case, of a Japanese-dominated festival procession penetrating the residential spaces of colonized Koreans and thereby piquing their interest in the spectacle of this Shintō celebration. On the route for the first day (October 17), the shrine procession before 1919 restricted its course to the areas of the southern village where its most important contributors lived and worked, honoring the well-to-do merchants of Hon-machi as well as one of the festival's main attractions, the Japanese *geisha* of the settlement community's pleasure quarter, Shin-machi. However, the parade route on the second day (October 18) gestured toward the undeniable power of the new colonial government by proceeding northward along Taihei Boulevard, the city's main north-south axis, at whose termini would soon sit Keijō's official spiritual and political centers—Korea Shrine and the new Government-General building, both unveiled around 1925. Using this modern thoroughfare to cross the city's ethnic divide at the Ch'ŏnggye Stream, the portable shrine reached the Korean-dominated neighborhoods of Chongno. However, the procession's excursion into a relatively small area of the northern village was brief, ending after thirty minutes when it returned to the more familiar and comfortable confines of the southern village before completing the festival on the grounds of Seoul Shrine. Although this token gesture at spiritual assimilation may have pleased the colonial government, the temporal brevity and limited reach of the procession suggest ongoing reservations among settlers about how to incorporate colonized Koreans into the Japanese shrine community without undercutting their own interests and identities as a privileged minority of colonizers.

Perhaps even more disturbing to government officials was the failure of some members of the early colonial settler community, particularly those of the new middle and lower classes, to participate fully in Seoul Shrine's activities as part of a strongly defined identity as loyal "Japanese."[29] Uneven manifestations of national identity among settlers were, in part, a function of the diverse geographic provenance of the expatriate population, some of whom, the authors of the *Keijō nippō* were quick to point out, refused to make expected contributions to the parish organization.[30] In addition, socioeconomic status and length of residence within the settler community help to explain why some newly arrived officials and businessmen refused to participate in the ritual ceremonies of Seoul Shrine. As members of Japan's new middle class of white-collar professionals and government employees, newcomers to Keijō were outsiders to the city's grand festival, an expatriate practice that had come to define established merchants, traders, and other members of the old middle class.[31] For lower-class Japanese residents, who composed as much as one-third of the early settler population, it would have been even more difficult to make regular shrine donations or to take time away from work during festival celebrations.[32] Lower-class settlers, too, failed to meet the merchant elite's expectations of "proper" spiritual practice, thus becoming an ongoing target of officials' harangues.

Of course, the Korean counterparts to these expatriates were of an even lower socioeconomic class. As suggested above, in addition to some affluent Korean elites who served in the shrine's parish organization, the former Korean royalty and the newly reorganized aristocracy did make regular donations to the shrine in return for preferential treatment from the early colonial state. From the Government-General's standpoint, such symbolic gestures, frequently publicized in the colonial press, suggest that these model Koreans actively supported Seoul Shrine as new imperial subjects. However, the bulk of the city's colonized population, as much as 60 percent of which lived in poverty during the colonial period, struggled to muster the financial resources or the emotional commitments to make regular shrine donations. As a result, parish officials could advocate only that Koreans make small, token contributions to the parish organization.[33]

Even as the colonized masses paid far less than their Japanese counterparts, they still struggled to understand the rationale for these semi-coercive donations. A particularly embarrassing article from 1918—one of several edifying reports on Shintō published in the Korean-language counterpart to the *Keijō nippō*, the *Maeil sinbo*—revealed that most Koreans tended to view shrine contributions as another burdensome and pointless tax, rather than as a practice embodying reverence for Amaterasu.[34] As even Yun Ch'i-ho (1864–1945), an American-educated reformist and nationalist who eventually cooperated with the Japanese after his imprisonment in 1913, wrote with great frustration, "Shinto-ism [sic] is so intensely Japanese that it can have no possible meaning outside of Japan. To force the Koreans to pay for the support of a religion in which they could have no earthly interest can't be said to be the freedom of conscience."[35] Although a strong faith in Christianity clearly colored this critique of Shintō's interference with religious freedom, Yun's comments also underscore the widespread chasm between forced practices of charity and self-generated sentiments of loyalty.

Suffering from a dearth of support by Keijō's colonized residents, parish leaders, under pressure from government officials, attempted to boost popularity for the shrine by mobilizing the city's *kisaeng* to participate in the grand festival procession (see figure 8b).[36] In precolonial times, most female performers of this elite class privately entertained Korean nobles and aristocrats by singing and dancing as well as offering them conversation and company during meals and parties. The appearance of *kisaeng* in public events such as festival processions, industrial expositions, and even hygiene campaigns thus allowed nonelite Koreans to encounter these women for the first time. At the same time, the downfall of the Chosŏn court as a result of Japan's annexation had forced many *kisaeng* into the city's flourishing sex industry, which came to include a new group of Japanese clients who enjoyed ogling them as they marched in the annual festival procession.[37]

To some extent, *kisaeng* were able to take advantage of their inclusion in the procession. Although organizers' motives were clearly aimed at enlarging their audience by subjecting these performers to the male gaze of a broader population of Korean and Japanese men, an increasingly competitive sex market created opportunities for innovative *kisaeng* vying to maintain their reputation as bona fide entertainers. As members of cooperatives that were newly established and regulated by the colonial state, they found in popular events, including the festival procession, an opportunity to promote themselves and their respective guilds. Regardless of how different classes, genders, and generations of Koreans might have responded to the inclusion of these women in the Japanese-dominated procession, the colonial press aggressively played up the notable presence of *kisaeng,* one of the few distinctly Korean groups to appear in festival celebrations before 1925. The *Keijō nippō* even featured them in photographic close-ups (figure 8b and figure 9, top), a highly charged representation, given that Korean festival participants rarely appeared in such a focal way. Not unlike photographs of individual *kisaeng* published in city guides and on tourist postcards, these images surely whetted the appetite of the male reading public, encouraging them to visit houses of Korean entertainers. To make these exoticized women more familiar to a Japanese audience, the *Keijō nippō,* in another gesture of cultural assimilation, reported that a number of *kisaeng* had learned metropolitan forms of entertainment, such as playing the *taiko* drums, which they performed at the festival celebration in 1915.[38] In these ways, *kisaeng* women appeared as an easily recognizable element of Korean society that had been incorporated into the Japanese-dominated procession.

Yet the expatriate leaders of the parish organization remained ambivalent about the Government-General's ideology of spiritual assimilation. Not only did they strictly limit the incorporation of Koreans into Shintō rituals, but even those whom organizers co-opted to participate, such as *kisaeng,* were symbolically subordinated to their Japanese counterparts. Although official media frequently referred to *kisaeng* in the same breath as their Japanese counterparts, *geisha,* the former clearly occupied a lower status within the cultural hierarchy of the festival. As figures 8a and 8b show, festival organizers granted *geisha* the privileges of pulling their own float and appearing in ceremonial dress, while *kisaeng* initially marched without a float to pull and, instead of wearing festival attire, appeared in what one *Keijō nippō* report called "everyday clothing," which consisted of a Korean skirt and blouse.[39]

While *kisaeng* at least seemed to be active participants in the procession, other Koreans appear in festival photographs from colonial newspapers as passive, anonymous onlookers. Such images suggest that some, if not most, of Keijō's colonized population maintained a skeptical, albeit perhaps intrigued, stance toward the Shintō procession. Indeed, newspaper photographs of Korean onlookers typically show

men in attire associated with the former *yangban* class, a garb of fine
white woven hemp and a black cylindrical hat made of horsehair *(kat)*.
In these images, they tend to stand at a distance from the center of festival activities, symbolized by the portable shrine carrying the divine
body of Amaterasu.[40] In figure 9 (bottom), for example, a group of such
men have ventured out onto Taihei Boulevard, the main route linking
the southern and northern villages and thus an important contact zone.
In this photograph, the procession, as is common practice in Shintō
festivals, briefly stopped in front of the *Keijo nippō* offices, where officials performed a short ceremony before the portable shrine, shown in
figure 9 (center) being carried by local boy scouts, and then continued
its journey. This spectacle drew a significant crowd, including a group
of Korean men. On the one hand, their presence on the street suggests a
budding interest in the festival celebration. On the other hand, they
appear to display little interest in its deeper ritual meaning, as is demonstrated by the stance of the man circled in the lower left hand corner of
figure 9 (bottom), who observes the event with his arms nonchalantly
crossed behind his back and his wrists firmly interlocked.

This interpretation of Koreans' bodily comportment as indicating
both their growing attraction to the playful spectacle of the festival and
their ongoing indifference to the proprieties of Shintō reverence is further supported by a number of media reports from the period before
1925. In the fall of 1916, for example, the *Maeil sinbo* warned Koreans
not to poke their heads out of second-story windows to view the festival
below, an irreverent act that might cause the procession to stop and
produce a disturbance.[41] A couple of years later, a Japanese festival
committee member accused the colonized population of committing
just such a blasphemy against Amaterasu. According to his account,
several Koreans had peeked through the curtains of streetcar windows
to glance at the passing procession during the grand festival of 1918. In
doing so, they looked down on the portable shrine carrying the guardian deity, an act of impropriety in Shintō practice. As this parish administrator explained, "Divine worship—which is to say, revering one's
ancestors—has, from ancient times, been the first priority in life for
both Japanese and Koreans, and so we must earnestly strive not to disrespect the god's happiness."[42] On the one hand, this statement did recognize cultural differences between the colony's multiethnic communities. That is to say, looking down in Korea may not have constituted a
sign of ritual disrespect as it did in the Japanese tradition. Whether or
not they were similarly chastised, photographs from the same period

FIGURE 9. *Kisaeng* in shrine procession (top), boys scouts carrying portable shrine (middle), and Korean men observing festival procession (bottom). Source: *Keijō nippō*, Oct. 19, 1918.

reveal that Koreans did, in fact, watch ceremonial events from an elevated position, including at Kojong's elaborately staged funeral procession of 1919.[43] On the other hand, by appealing to a putatively common tradition of ancestor worship, the author echoed arguments for spiritual assimilation often voiced by the Government-General and its intellectual proxies. He thus urged Koreans to associate the existing tradition of paying respect to deceased family members with the new colonial practice of revering Amaterasu, the mythical ancestress of the Japanese imperial nation. His contemptuous words about practices that equated improprieties with Shintō suggest that most colonized Koreans had yet to make that crucial connection, at least as of the late 1910s. Nevertheless, the act of looking (down) at the festival procession from the passing streetcar does indicate that at least some, if not many, Koreans had become attracted to the increasingly recognizable spectacle of the city's annual grand festival.

Whatever commitments the colonized population may have made to Seoul Shrine during the first decade of Japanese rule, the major anticolonial uprising of March First, which began in 1919 and continued into the spring of the following year, severely jeopardized the already beleaguered project of incorporating Koreans into the shrine's spiritual orbit. Although the relative wealth of settlers ensured that Seoul Shrine and its festival celebrations would continue, Koreans' violent mistreatment by the Japanese police and military convinced them of the futility of making further contributions to an institution that continued to oppress them. In the wake of the March First Movement, the city's colonized residents also refused to display Japanese flags on festival occasions, a practice that the *Keijō nippō* harshly condemned as violating one's duty as an imperial subject.[44] These "violations" continued at least until the fall of 1925.[45] Worse still from the perspective of the colonial state was that many already skeptical Korean elites renounced their positions in Seoul Shrine's parish organization, leaving officials with fewer intermediaries through whom to reach the city's colonized population.[46]

Forced to make minor concessions to disgruntled Koreans, shrine leaders, likely at the behest of the colonial government, redoubled their efforts to expand the role of existing festival participants and to co-opt other native cultural groups under the euphemistic slogan of "harmonizing Japanese and Koreans" (J: *naisen yūwa; naesŏn yunghwa*). These efforts began with the further incorporation of the former royal family, the most reliable and subordinated segment of the colonized population. In the fall of 1919, the Government-General persuaded the Yi family to contribute an ancient Korean musical troupe to the festival procession, a form of entertainment hitherto confined to the elite ranks of the court.[47] Consisting of a fourteen-member band praised by the *Keijō nippō* as "classically elegant and dazzlingly ornate" while also displaying a "primitive rhythm," this royal marching troupe was to add another level of solemnity and a distinctive color to the procession.[48] Conspicuously marked as both anachronistic and foreign, the troupe followed behind the lead of the *hōren*, a ceremonial palanquin commonly used by the Japanese emperor. This strategic positioning of the Korean musical troupe reflected the subservient status that the troupe (and Koreans more generally) occupied within the cultural hierarchy of the Japanese-dominated festival. On the other hand, that festival organizers mobilized a cultural symbol directly associated with the royal house in the immediate aftermath of the March First Movement, an uprising that began amid rumors that the Japanese had poisoned the former Korean king/emperor (Kojong), signaled the state's makeshift efforts to more fully persuade the colonized masses of their inclusion in the city's Shintō community.

Festival organizers were aided in this project by the city's *kisaeng* entertainers, who, rather than opt out of this event as a form of protest like Korean parish leaders, sought to redefine the terms of their inclusion, demanding a more equal position vis-à-vis the higher-ranked Japanese *geisha*. As a result of their efforts, the proactive *kisaeng*, whose numbers in the festival procession more than doubled from 120 in 1920 to three hundred in 1921, took charge of their own float for the first time.[49] They also began to march side by side with their *geisha* counterparts, a multiethnic appearance heralded by the *Keijō nippō* as an example of the government's new approach to pacifying disgruntled Koreans, but which these female entertainers actively exploited as an opportunity for commercial profit.[50]

The inclusion of the ancient musical troupe and the increased visibility of the *kisaeng* set the stage for a strategic modification of the festival route, whose daring course into the geographical heart of Korean nationalism also demonstrated a bold effort to "harmonize Japanese and Koreans" through Shintō celebrations.[51] As mentioned above, before 1919, Seoul Shrine's procession centered its peregrinations on the southern village's settler community, making only a brief journey into a limited area of Chongno on the second day. Beginning in the fall of 1919, the portable shrine extended its journey along Chongno during the second day of festivities, covering the entire stretch of this important commercial thoroughfare.[52] In doing so, the Japanese shrine procession strategically passed right in front of Pagoda Park, the very site where the March First Movement had begun less than a year earlier. Thus, although the Government-General now hurried its own plans to complete Korea Shrine as a spiritual counterweight to anticolonial nationalism, state officials continued to rely on increasingly aggressive displays of Seoul Shrine's festival procession in a makeshift attempt to capture the spiritual affinities of the city's colonized population.

Despite measures to involve more Koreans as both participants in and observers of the Japanese-dominated festival, a number of obstacles continued to hamper the Government-General's efforts to impart a unified sense of "Japaneseness" to Koreans. To begin with, a series of economic downturns and natural disasters during the early 1920s forced parish leaders to abridge the festival procession. In 1922, for example, a shortage of funds led them to abbreviate the route during the first day and to cancel the second day of celebrations altogether. Furthermore, reports in the *Keijō nippō* from the early 1920s reveal that some Japanese residents failed to make what commentators considered sufficient monetary contributions to the parish organization.[53] Criticizing such behavior as irreverent, these articles noted that some poorer Japanese settlers complained that shrine "donations" were being forced upon them like a tax. Because working-class Japanese perceptions of parish donations as levies mirrored the attitudes of their colonized counterparts, some particularly concerned pundits, invoking the racialized epithet *yobo* to refer to noncompliant Koreans, even concluded that a significant portion of expatriates had indeed become "Koreanized."[54] Lower-class settlers were also criticized for their unwillingness to make strong emotional attachments to Seoul Shrine, allegedly demonstrated by their failure to take rest from work, prepare ceremonial rice with beans, and enjoy themselves with relatives and friends.[55] Meanwhile, as late as 1925, the colonial media bemoaned the fluid presence of the settler population generally, more than 60 percent of whom still chose to send their remains back to the metropole, rather than have family members memorialize them in the colony.[56]

Evidence suggests that even after Seoul Shrine's festival resumed its standard route (including the entire stretch of Chongno following the abbreviation in 1922) the colonized population never became particularly active participants in the festival or supporters of the parish organization.[57] With the exception of the former royal family and a few neighborhood elites, most Koreans were still unable or unwilling to make substantial shrine donations, which they continued to view as an ethnically skewed levy providing them with few personal benefits. According to one account, Koreans contributed only 17 percent of total parish donations as of 1925, a figure more than 4 percent lower than Yun Ch'iho reported they were forced to donate (fifteen hundred yen) in 1919.[58] Scant contributions by Koreans, the majority of Keijō's population, endangered the financial stability of Seoul Shrine's parish organization, which had to rely on semicompulsory contributions from wealthier Japanese residents. At the same time, the impoverished state of many Korean neighborhoods meant that vast numbers of colonized parishioners in the northern village could not participate in making festival decorations and other offertory objects for Shintō celebrations. These activities aided an increasing number of middle-class settlers who gradually put down roots in the colony, thus establishing a firmer "Japanese" identity.

Occasionally, reports in the *Keijō nippō* did mention Korean-domi-nated districts in the same breath as Japanese-populated ones, employing an assimilationist rhetoric to suggest harmonious, multiethnic participa-tion in Shintō festivals.[59] However, whereas Japanese settlers in Hon-machi, Asahi-chō, Kōgane-machi, and other neighborhoods in the south-ern village were frequently mentioned as contributing festive floats and other shrine offerings, not one specific neighborhood known for a high concentration of Koreans was mentioned even once as participating in such a capacity before 1925. This discursive absence, in the very pages that aimed to promote the Government-General's makeshift attempts at spiritual assimilation, reveals a significant gap between the ideological pretensions of the early colonial state and the reality that most Koreans continued to remain at a psychological distance from the festival celebra-tions of Seoul Shrine, to say nothing of their geographic separation from its sacred grounds.

Even when the post-1919 procession did enter neighborhoods in which the colonized population resided, nationalist authors writing in Korean-language newspapers, such as the *Tonga ilbo* and the *Chosŏn ilbo,* and in other vernacular publications that reemerged after the March First Movement rarely, if ever, made mention of the shrine festivals. Moreover, Korean references to these celebrations usually described them as unfamiliar events carried out "on the side of the Japanese" *(ilbon saram p'yŏn esŏ),* an observation reflecting the city's divided topogra-phy.[60] Such discursive silences and distancings of Japanese rituals suggest the discomfort that many Koreans must have felt toward the slow but mounting imposition of Shintō onto the landscape of their colonized cap-ital. With the completion of Korea Shrine in 1925, new pressures to express reverence for the imperial house through visits of worship would challenge the colonized population in new and unprecedented ways.

## KOREA SHRINE AND THE CONTESTED PRACTICES OF COLONIAL SHINTŌ

The unveiling of Korea Shrine—an imposing Namsan structure that offi-cials strategically built adjacent to and above Seoul Shrine[61]—also affected Japanese parish leaders' relationship to the Government-General and its lukewarm efforts to assimilate Koreans through Shintō rituals. Before 1925, Seoul Shrine's celebrations had sought to unify Keijō's geographically and socioeconomically diverse group of expatriates around the figure of Amaterasu. At the same time, the shrine's custodians had largely excluded Koreans from their spiritual community, a stance they adopted to counter the colonial state's intrusions on their political autonomy and to thereby bolster their community's sense of identity and privilege vis-à-vis subordinated ethnic others. While the uprising of 1919 and the Government-General's violent measures to pacify this unexpected outburst of anticolonial nationalism had begun to convince Japanese shrine leaders that more fully including the city's disgruntled Korean population would better protect their own interests, it was with the establishment of Korea Shrine that these leaders began to more aggressively adopt the Government-General's own tactics of cultural co-optation in order to ensure the survival and growth of their settler institution. As a result, spiritual assimilation became an increasingly competitive field of practice between the custodians of Seoul Shrine and those of Korea Shrine, whose respective agendas complemented each other at times, while at other times contravening one another.

Even before 1925, tensions between the colonial state and settler leaders had emerged over spiritual control of Namsan. As soon as plans for Korea Shrine were announced in 1916, prominent expatriates voiced their disquiet that Seoul Shrine might become a satellite of Korea Shrine or be abolished altogether, a concern that resurfaced periodically in the late 1910s and early 1920s.[62] During the decade after 1925, the leaders of Seoul Shrine struggled more intensely to retain a viable place for their spiritual community in the face of the government's more dominant Korea Shrine. These struggles began in earnest with the impending inauguration of Korea Shrine in the fall of 1925, in contestations over the timing and rituals of festival celebrations and the order of shrine visits. From the start, government officials drew on the incorporative power of Seoul Shrine, using its parish organization to mobilize the colonized population to worship the Japanese deities installed at Korea Shrine (Amaterasu and the Meiji Emperor). To this end, they set the date of Korea Shrine's grand festival to coincide with that of Seoul Shrine, provoking parish leaders to guard their own traditions. For example, they vowed not to relinquish important ritual privileges, such as the carrying of the portable shrine.[63] As a result of their protests, the colonial government agreed to allow the city's residents to celebrate the grand festival of Seoul Shrine (8 AM start time) *before* celebrating the grand festival of Korea Shrine (10 AM start time).[64]

Meanwhile, despite officially voiced expectations that residents would uniformly visit Korea Shrine before making their way down to Seoul Shrine, leaders of the latter also expressed their hope that visitors might continue to give priority to the city shrine by stopping there before proceeding upward to the national Shintō complex.[65] As Kugimoto Tōjirō, the manager for Seoul Shrine, wrote less than a month before the unveiling ceremony in 1925: "In the future, I would like for people [to stop] at Seoul Shrine on their way home from paying their respects at Korea Shrine, [visited] via the front approach, in the same way that visitors to Seoul Shrine from Hon-machi [subsequently] pay their respects to Korea Shrine [via the back approach]." A report published in the *Keijō nippō* revealed that many residents did, in fact, embrace Kugimoto's wishes, at least during the inaugural ceremonies of 1925. Disobeying a sign leading from Seoul Shrine to Korea Shrine that read, "Do not enter from here!," these residents chose to ascend Namsan via the back approach, visiting Seoul Shrine *before* they paid their respects at Korea Shrine.[66]

Another ambiguity Seoul Shrine's leaders actively exploited to contend with the more potent Korea Shrine was the supposed separation of officially sanctioned religions (sect Shintō as well as Christianity and Buddhism) from shrine Shintō. Though this separation was crucial to the colonial state's position that worship of the imperial house at Namsan did not constitute an infringement on religious freedoms, officials struggled to articulate a clear division between these permeable categories. When Korea Shrine was finally completed in 1925, government officials discouraged Shintō priests from conducting wedding rites and other religious ceremonies at this shrine on the grounds that it was to serve as a nonreligious facility promoting civic loyalties for the imperial house.[67] The Japanese custodians of Seoul Shrine seized on the volatile issue of Shintō weddings, using money obtained from these ceremonies to promote their position vis-à-vis Korea Shrine. First conducted by the imperial family during the Meiji period, shrine weddings had increased in popularity among middle-to-upper class families who could afford the high costs of two to four thousand yen.[68] Between 1913 and 1925, the number of Japanese couples tying the knot in front of Seoul Shrine had increased from ten to 127, encouraging the head priest to standardize ceremony rites and even to publish wedding vows.[69]

When priests at Korea Shrine ignored official instructions to perform eight wedding ceremonies during the final months of 1925 and forty-two more in 1926, the leaders of Seoul Shrine complained that the Government-General had reneged on its policy of banning Shintō weddings at Korea Shrine, demanding that these "private" rituals be stopped all together.[70] Their main concern seems to have been financial: parish representatives stressed the vital source of income that shrine weddings provided. Without that income, they argued, Seoul Shrine would be jeopardized financially, especially in light of a new 150,000-yen reconstruction project that included expanded facilities for wedding ceremonies and banquets.[71] Despite these protests, priests continued to perform wedding ceremonies at Korea Shrine (whose numbers increased from sixty-three in 1927 to 327 in 1936), thereby undercutting the Government-General's position on the nonreligious nature of this Shintō complex. Faced with this challenge to their economic autonomy, the parish leaders of Seoul Shrine aggressively competed over income from these religious rites, conducting approximately three hundred wedding ceremonies in 1932 at their newly modeled shrine (as compared to just 151 performed at Korea Shrine during the same year).[72]

While Shintō weddings appealed primarily to Japanese expatriates, Seoul Shrine's leaders proactively installed indigenous deities to attract Koreans to their institution. During the planning of Korea Shrine, Japanese advocates of sect Shintō (and members of the Korean aristocracy) had favored the enshrinement of a native set of so-called development gods as a tactic of spiritual assimilation.[73] If adopted, this practice would have followed a precedent already established at other high-ranking Shintō institutions with close associations to Japanese imperialism, such as Sapporo Shrine (1869) and Taiwan Shrine (1900). Rejecting this precedent, colonial pundits downplayed the popularity of one particularly powerful native deity, Tan'gun, the mythical godfather of the Korean nation. Having just squelched an anticolonial riot that enveloped the peninsula, the Government-General instead decided to staunchly impose the myth of an unbroken line of Japanese rulers embodied in the primordial goddess, Amaterasu, and the modern emperor, Meiji.[74] Launching discussions just months after the completion of Korea Shrine in 1925, the expatriate leaders of Seoul Shrine quickly took advantage of this ethnocentric decision, finally convincing government leaders to incorporate native deities, including Tan'gun, into their own pantheon in 1929.[75] As with Korean cultural attractions previously included in the annual grand festival, such as kisaeng performers and an ancient musical troupe, parish officials carefully subordinated indigenous deities to Amaterasu, writing the former's names in small letters and positioning the latter at the center of a new plaque hung in the offertory hall.[76] In this way, Japanese parish leaders creatively deployed their own tactics of spiritual assimilation, attempting to convince at least some Koreans to offer loyalty to Seoul Shrine.

Tensions between the administrators of these two shrines not only affected their uneasy institutional relationship, but also shaped how the city's colonized population negotiated requirements to pay reverence to the Japanese imperial house during the second half of 1920s and the first half of the 1930s. From the start, the Government-General sought to overcome these tensions by mobilizing popular support for Seoul Shrine in order to promote the position of Korea Shrine, which, as the only officially ranked government shrine on the peninsula, lacked a locally supported parish organization.[77] During Korea Shrine's inaugural festivities, for example, government officials summoned Korean neighborhood administrators to encourage residents to follow their colonizers by displaying Japanese flags, constructing garland arches, and participating in festival processions—activities in which most neighborhoods heavily populated by Koreans had only rarely participated before 1925.[78] These efforts reportedly led to the decoration of Korean neighborhoods with standard Shintō offerings, such as paper lanterns, straw ropes, and a number of ornamental arches. However, this "unprecedented scene of gratefulness toward the shrine," as the *Keijō nippō* heralded it, included offertory practices that diverged considerably from their Japanese counterparts, such as the display of red ribbons instead of Japanese flags.[79] That the colonized apparently failed to fly as many flags as their colonizers wished may have reflected ongoing resentment against Japanese rule, which also haunted the leaders of Seoul Shrine in the aftermath of the anticolonial uprising of 1919. Given the cost of making neighborhood offerings, the use of red ribbons may also have constituted an economical way for relatively poor Koreans to convince Japanese officials of their dutifulness to the new shrine.[80]

Although virtually no Korean-language publications document their subjective experiences, a critical analysis of Japanese testimonies suggests that the colonized masses remained at a psychological distance from the alienating aura of Korea Shrine, with its enshrinement of Japanese deities and increasingly mandatory visits to worship them. As discussed above, before 1925, most Koreans living in the capital city had encountered Shintō through Seoul Shrine's festival celebrations, primarily as passive observers of the passing procession. With the establishment of Korea Shrine, however, officials began to mandate that school children, company employees, and other groups climb the 382 stairs to the top of this lofty complex to perform a series of standardized ritual practices, which included bowing, clapping, and ringing a bell before the gods.[81]

Perhaps due to the novelty and unfamiliarity of the shrine and its ritual practices, Japanese reports on Koreans' visits to Korea Shrine frequently described the colonized as "onlooking" (J: *sankan; ch'amgwan*) rather than "worshiping" (J: *sampai; ch'ambae*).[82] Ogasawara Shōzō's description of the enshrinement ceremony at Korea Shrine, quoted at length at the start of this book, is one of the best examples that deployed these dichotomized tropes to mark the imagined (if not real) gap separating Japanese citizens from Korean subjects and to thereby encourage the latter to model their spiritual practices after the former. Unable to understand the reasons for Koreans' "improprieties," Ogasawara clearly feared that the Government-General might fail to incorporate the colonized population into the city's Shintō community because it had staunchly refused to enshrine deities native to the peninsula. Although contrary in their implications, his concern in 1925 that Korea Shrine would become an exclusive place for Japanese echoed the estrangement that colonized elites like Yun Ch'i-ho had themselves voiced as early as 1919. According to Ogasawara's own account, this sacred place continued to alienate most Koreans. Even official statistics reveal that the number of colonized visitors to Korea Shrine actually decreased from 171,774 in 1926 to 95,230 in 1933, while the number of Japanese visitors grew from 301,498 to 456,882 during this same period.[83] In addition to this quantitative setback, Japanese pundits also worried about insufficient changes in Koreans' attitudes toward the shrine. For his part, Ogasawara wrote later, in 1933, "The rare [Korean] who removes his or her hat watches the scene of solemn and reverent Japanese bowing, somehow trying to merely imitate such an attitude."[84] According to this critique, Koreans' shrine practices, although perhaps approximating those of their idealized Japanese counterparts, were not performed spontaneously, suggesting that the colonized population had yet to internalize sentiments of imperial reverence.

While upbraiding Koreans for similar problems, racist pundits who also criticized shrine "onlooking" questioned the corrigibility of what they viewed as an essential and immutable Korean trait. According to one anecdote from a publication in 1933 that purportedly aimed to eradicate Japanese settlers' discrimination toward Koreans (but ironically may have reinforced it), the Korean leader of an unnamed religious organization in Keijō endured the cold of New Year's Day and ventured up Namsan to pay his respects to the Japanese deities installed at Korea Shrine, an unusual practice given most Koreans' tendency to avoid visiting the shrine at this time of year.[85] However, before he managed to clap his hands and offer a bow, Japanese settlers glowered at him, and one complained, "I wonder if there are Koreans who really have sincerity in practicing shrine worship." "I doubt it," responded a fellow expatriate. "How can Koreans have a sense of faith when [these] *yobo* have [only] come to look around?"[86] On the one hand, these racist comments suggest that the colonized could not—or, perhaps, should not, according to these Japanese settlers—be incorporated into the larger community of the emperor's subjects. On the other hand, they neatly converged with the assimilationist remarks of Ogasawara, who also observed that Koreans continued to visit Shintō sites primarily as if they were recreational arenas rather than sacred grounds promoting imperial reverence. The problem of "sightseeing" became so troublesome during the fall festival of 1929—also the time of the Korea Exposition—that officials had to harshly admonish Korean tourists, some of whom reportedly took *kisaeng* escorts on nighttime pleasure rides to Korea Shrine without paying their proper respects to the deities.[87]

That the colonized masses continued to associate Shintō shrines with recreation may also have resulted from the increasingly enthusiastic efforts of Seoul Shrine's parish leaders. Indeed, their own projects of spiritual assimilation—advanced in concert with the colonial state, but waged against its intrusive power—seem to have kept Koreans focused on the popular spectacle of the city's Shintō celebrations, rather than on the tedium of ritual proprieties atop Namsan. Only a year after Korea Shrine's inaugural festivities, for example, local parish leaders began to discuss how they could more effectively manage the city's joint festival celebration to advance their own interests. As in the past, one way to promote their standing in the eyes of the Government-General involved expanding the geographical scope of the annual procession into the neighborhoods of the city's Korean population. To this end, they directed the festival procession not only to traverse the main thoroughfare of the northern village, Chongno, as it had from 1919 on, but also to enter the district's residential areas.[88] According to a report from the fall of 1926, the procession made its first entry that year into the neighborhoods of An'guk-dong. Predictably, the *Keijō nippō* described the appearance of the portable shrine in the epicenter of the northern village as drawing crowds of enthusiastic Koreans who took to the streets to greet it.[89] However, this same report failed to describe in any detail how the colonized population might have responded to the expansion of shrine Shintō into their living space in ways other than lighthearted "onlooking."

Repeated in years to come, this unprecedented penetration of the festival procession deep into the city's Korean neighborhoods is just one example of parish leaders' active appropriation of the Government-General's strategy of cultural co-optation, which selectively showcased "Koreanness" within a hierarchically structured, multiethnic empire. In order to incorporate the colonized population into their shrine's expanding spiritual orbit, festival organizers also encouraged the ongoing participation of the city's *kisaeng* in the festival procession during the late 1920s and early 1930s. In 1928, for example, the *Keijō nippō*, repeating a media tradition of spotlighting these exoticized performers, published an article about a group of "Japanized" *kisaeng* entertainers. The article celebrated how these women, having previously learned to play the Japanese *taiko* drums, expanded their repertoire by performing a Japanese form of hand dancing typically undertaken by their *geisha* counterparts.[90] (When read against the assimilationist grain of the colonial archive, this article suggests that these dynamic women appropriated cultural forms closely associated with settlers to further promote their professional status within a festival hierarchy that still favored Japanese participants.) Furthermore, parish officials mobilized a number of local residents to join the festival in 1929 in a special Korean procession (figure 10a).[91] Like their *kisaeng* counterparts, these festival participants appeared in a native style of dress, thus continuing to mark them as sartorially unassimilated to the standard style of clothing worn by their ethnic Japanese counterparts. On the other hand, their participation in the festival supported parish leaders' ongoing efforts to more fully integrate the colonized population into its shrine's community, which now included Koreans as a distinct and subordinated group.

The increasingly competitive nature of spiritual assimilation acquired new meanings in the fall of 1931, when Korean administrators, hitherto limited to a supporting role in the Japanese-dominated parish organization, organized the grand festival for the first time. With shrine leaders' decision to allow Korean parish leaders to take charge of the festival in 1931, members of the city's colonized population took it upon themselves to prove their ability to honor Seoul Shrine's guardian deities, a group that now included distinctly Korean ones. According to one celebratory report, Koreans from the Food and Beverage Establishments Co-Operative contributed a gorgeously decorated float that circulated the city with thirty beautiful *kisaeng* aboard.[92] The construction of festival floats and the display of Shintō decorations by local Korean interests were unprecedented for the colonized community, which had been relegated to the sidelines of the procession. Now, they became increasingly active in the festivities of Seoul Shrine, and were thus gradually drawn into its cultural orbit.

In spite of their newfound enthusiasm for Seoul Shrine, the colonized leaders of the grand festival in 1931 also sought to maintain some control over their incorporation into the Japanese-dominated procession. Under the lead of Chŏn Sŏng-uk—a long-standing member of the parish organization and the neighborhood administration system—the Korean members of the festival commission decided to avoid carrying out that year's shrine rites in a purely Japanese style. Although wearing a Shintō-style ceremonial hat and pants, they donned a new form of garb consisting of a white-collared black robe—a contrast that clearly distinguished them from the white clothes of shrine priests and those of Korean commoners.[93] To highlight the native dimension of this special occasion, they also increased the participants in the horse-riding Korean procession from fifty to sixty, all of whom wore the new ceremonial outfit, although their horsehair hats appear native in style (figure 10b).

Emphasizing these participants' Koreanness, however, challenged festival commissioner Chŏn to present his members of the procession as sufficiently loyal to his Shintō counterparts but as not excessively "Japanese" to lower-class Korean spectators. The issue of footwear nicely encapsulates this performative dilemma. Published in the Shintō journal *News of the Imperial Nation (Kōkoku jihō)*, Chŏn's reminiscences suggest that Koreans found unsuitable the combination of digitated socks and hemp-soled sandals (J: *asaura [zōri]*) typically worn by the Japanese participants of Shintō festival processions. Although he did not specify the particular reason, such anxieties likely derived from the fact that the colonized population used the shape of a person's feet that this footwear produced—what they derogatorily called *jjokbari* (literally, cloven feet)—as a racialized epithet against Japanese.[94] In this sense, wearing the digitated socks and the accompanying sandals might have demoted these local elites, perhaps already seen as collaborators in the eyes of lower-class Korean spectators, given their participation in pro-Japanese organizations, to the level of their despised colonizers.[95] Without delving into these intraethnic complications, the head priest of Seoul Shrine ultimately intervened to justify their unconventional appearance,

FIGURE 10a. Korean procession. Source: *Jinja kyōkai zasshi* 30, no. 12 (Dec. 1931): 29.

FIGURE 10b. Hybrid ceremonial outfit. Source: *Jinja kyōkai zasshi* 30, no. 12 (Dec. 1931): 29.

sanctioning the use of socks that were not divided to accommodate a Japanese thong (J: *tabi*) and Korean-style rubber shoes *(komusin)*. Although now worn by elites, these mass produced shoes were frequently worn by commoners during the early twentieth century, yet another measure that would have tempered their "Japanese" appearance in this Shintō festival. In the end, the head priest also found this footwear a good match for the black ceremonial attire chosen by the Korean festival committee. Indeed, he could not help himself from boasting about their outfits as another successful example of the "harmonizing of Japanese and Koreans."

In his official account, Chŏn himself mentions this "harmony" and other colonialist metaphors such as "egalitarian imperial benevolence" (J: *isshi dōjin; ilsi tong'in*) to argue that Seoul Shrine's gods treated both Japanese and Koreans equally. Although such statements seem to reiterate the ideology of spiritual assimilation, his reminiscences also point to the difficulties that colonized elites faced in asserting themselves as dutiful Japanese while also appearing identifiably Korean. Chŏn wrote of the anxiety he felt at the prospect of wearing a special ceremonial outfit, up to then donned only by Japanese festival commissioners. Deferentially referring to himself as an "outsider" (J: *mongaikan*), he even suggested that the most wealthy and prominent Japanese wear the outfit in his place. Chŏn seems to have put aside his anxieties only after Japanese shrine officials convinced him to wear the ceremonial dress.[96] However, the fact that even this most outspoken Korean advocate of spiritual assimilation struggled to demonstrate his dutifulness as a colonial subject suggests the tensions inherent in Koreans' incorporation into the imperial community, a process clearly managed by Japanese shrine leaders, but one also carefully negotiated and rearticulated by native members of the parish organization.

Even as their elite counterparts struggled to position themselves within the cultural hierarchy of the festival, nonelite onlookers of the procession attached their own meanings to this increasingly popular event. Although it is unclear how they responded to the inclusion of native cultural forms in the Korean-organized festival of 1931 (and, later, 1936), earlier reports suggest that colonized crowds met the Japanese procession by creating their own form of cheer, a practice that the *Maeil sinbo* implicitly described as an example of assimilated cultural difference. At the festival in 1928, for example, portable shrine bearers followed the customary practice of repeatedly shouting the Japanese word "Wasshoi!" (Heave-ho!) to animate procession members and the onlooking crowd. However, rather than simply repeat these unfamiliar words, Koreans responded by yelling "ŏlsa tunddung"—a combination of the word "ŏlsa" (hurrah!), an expression customarily used to cheer on native music and theatrical performances, with the onomatopoeia "tungdung," which captured the sound of the festival drums.[97] This kind of engagement with the passing procession points both to the event's increasing resonance among the city's colonized population and to Koreans' ability to significantly reinterpret the meanings of the festival procession in terms other than the prescribed forms of imperial reverence.

At the same time, the poorest members of the colonized population struggled to find the material resources necessary to respond to the procession in any constructive way.[98] Rather than enhancing their loyalties to the deities of Seoul Shrine, the annual festival procession became an opportunity to profit by picking pockets or engaging in other forms of petty theft. For example, two Korean men (ages twenty-eight and thirty-five) allegedly stole six and two yen, respectively, from the pockets of two Japanese women during the festival of 1933.[99] To check various forms of pilfering (and molestation), the local police ordered two plain-clothes units to patrol the streets during the festival of 1934, keeping a careful eye on loafers, lumpen proletariat, and other potential instigators.[100] Although no incidents of pickpocketing appear in the local press from that year, reports from the following year suggest that the problem continued to plague local officials. Even before the celebration of 1935 began, articles appearing in both the *Keijō nippō* and the *Maeil sinbo* detailed seven incidents wherein Koreans, most of whom were born outside of Keijō and relocated to the capital city in search of work, reportedly committed various forms of theft, including a man who admitted to thirty incidents of pilfering.[101] Another report from 1935 mentions a twelve-year-old Korean boy, born in South Kyŏngsang Province but without a local residence, who allegedly stole money from a (Korean?) woman watching the festival procession as it passed along Chongno. A subsequent police investigation discovered that four other teenage subordinates, forming part of a local gang, had also pickpocketed festival-goers at crowded places throughout Keijō.[102]

While similar incidents may have taken place in earlier periods and gone unreported, the increasing attention they received from the early 1930s onward suggests that the economic downturn of this time seriously hampered attempts to effectively implement spiritual assimilation, particularly among the city's growing population of indigent

Koreans. In response, the colonial government erected an array of local institutions in Keijō—welfare committees, spiritual inculcation groups, and a reorganized system of neighborhood associations—aimed at shoring up social solidarity by providing a minimum level of material welfare, served up with a heavy dose of moral demands.[103] And yet, the pickpocketing continued.

The thievery of indigent Koreans is perhaps the most revealing example of the limits of spiritual assimilation, from its remarkably tentative beginnings with the annexation in 1910 to its increasingly aggressive tactics during the early 1930s. Between the incorporative rhetoric of the Government-General and the objects of its stated policy lay a complex and dynamic realm of social actors and cultural practices whose varied interactions militated against the production of a community of subjects unified in their loyalty to the imperial house. Whether between Japanese parish leaders and their Korean counterparts, elite and nonelite members of the colonized community, or female entertainment women and their male spectators, the ethnic-, class-, and gender-specific relationships shaped by everyday life in colonial Korea attest to the varied roles that individuals and groups played in determining what meaning and effect the intrusive presence of shrine Shintō came to have in colonial Korea, especially before the outbreak of the Asia-Pacific War in 1937.

# CHAPTER 3

# Material Assimilation

*Colonial Expositions on the Kyŏngbok
Palace Grounds*

Alongside its efforts at assimilating Koreans spiritually, the Government-General also embarked on using public space to make spectacular displays of modernization that aimed to convince the colonized population that Japanese rule could enrich their lives. With these expositions, rather than asking Koreans to identify with a distant emperor or even a tutelary deity closer by, government officials encouraged them to focus on the more immediate lure of "progress" and to embrace industry as their own personal ethic. Like other colonial governmentalities, material assimilation carried two, interrelated meanings. In one form, "industry" referred to the full range of the colony's economic development, albeit as a hierarchical and exploitative system that privileged Japanese entrepreneurs and a small coterie of Korean capitalists. But it also denoted popular participation in the potentially enriching project of modernization as diligent, if subordinated, subjects. In this way, the Government-General sought to produce a public milieu through which Koreans could identify with the "progressive" fate of an empire that relegated most of them to the lower classes. Those subjective engagements were, as a result, complex and depended on the sex, region, and age of the spectators, many of whom struggled to benefit from the highly uneven development of the colonial economy. Although a small group of male nationalists responded to this predicament by upbraiding designers for promoting blatantly exploitative representations of "Korea" and its desacralized palace grounds, most uneducated exposition visitors preferred to indulge in commercial and recreational attractions, using these spectacular events to pursue personal motives and identities that quietly subverted ideological displays of industry.

## PROTECTORATE PERIOD PRECURSOR: THE KEIJŌ EXHIBITION OF 1907

As discussed in chapter 1, the public spaces of Seoul—the city's palace grounds, in particular—came to function as arenas of competition during the final years of the Chosŏn dynasty, symbolizing what modernizing elites around the world then referred to as one's "level of civilization." As Andre Schmid has reminded us, that many Korean intellectuals and policy makers adopted the universal language of progress as a tactic of official nationalism carried dangerous consequences for a state whose existence was imperiled by imperialist powers deploying those same strategies of modernization.[1] Such power dynamics were perhaps no more evident than in expositions, those great media events promoted by government and business elites in order to create what Robert W. Rydell once called a "symbolic universe" for groups stratified along class, racial, and national lines.[2] Like other modernizers, late Chosŏn leaders actively participated in the competitive politics of these international events, albeit from a position of relative weakness. To this end, they established displays at the Columbian Exhibition in Chicago (1893) and the Universal Exposition in Paris (1900) as well as at similar events held in Osaka (1903) and Tokyo (1907).[3] Officials in the Great Han Empire also took measures to host expositions on the peninsula, but it was not until the protectorate period that such events took place.[4]

Although discussed as a "collaborative" event between Japanese and Korean businessmen, the Keijō Exhibition of 1907, a small-scale precursor to expositions that would be held in 1915 and 1929, was clearly dominated by the former, backed by the increasingly aggressive tactics of the Residency-General.[5] In fact, just months before the exhibition opened its gates on September 1, Japanese officials forced their Korean counterparts to sign a second protectorate treaty, reducing the peninsula to a de facto colony.[6] Such blatant tactics of imperialism, unsuccessfully protested by Emperor Kojong before his dethronement in late 1907, led to opposition by concerned Koreans, including the violent activities of the righteous armies *(ŭibyŏng;* J: *gihei).* Hoping to counter anti-imperial resistance, Japanese organizers envisioned a collaborative exhibition that would not only foster commerce, but also help "soften the thoughts of Koreans."[7] To this end, they chose a site for the exhibition in 1907 that was described in one colonial report as occupying a central position between the city's Japanese and Korean neighborhoods.[8] Although organizers presented Kōganemachi Avenue as an equal meeting point between these two ethnic groups, the Meiji-machi (Tonghyŏn) site was, in fact, located in the heart of the settler community, which was dominated by economically powerful expatriate merchants. This ethnic imbalance was also dramatized in the display halls, which favored goods imported by settlers over those made by Koreans. Unlike later exhibitions, which displayed state-of-the-art gadgets and luxury products, the event in 1907 resembled a market where basic goods were exhibited not only for individuals to inspect, but also for them to purchase. Yet only twenty-three indigenous vendors managed to exhibit goods at ten displays, while Japanese merchants put on over 160 exhibits of metropolitan products.[9] This disparity clearly reflected the peninsula's politically and economically inferior position vis-à-vis Japan, a problem often cited by the Korean press, but that its concerned writers could do little to remedy.[10]

Even as the exhibition in 1907 privileged the interests of Japanese merchants, designers included a number of recreational facilities that enticed exhibition-goers to embrace the logic of progress through light-hearted diversions focused on the sensory details of modernity. For example, the main exhibition hall, a three-story building displaying various objects of art, included rooftop facilities where visitors could enjoy a relaxing beverage at the beer garden or the teahouse while enjoying a panoramic view of the city. Organizers also built a music room with phonographs and a stage where *geisha* and *kisaeng* entertained three times a week and a military band played on Sundays. Outside the event grounds, the festival-like mood permeated the city streets with an array of equally inviting attractions. For example, the Korean Electrical Lighting Company sponsored an illuminated flower-covered streetcar that operated into the night. Meanwhile, the Exhibition Promotion Committee installed five electrified arches outside the South Gate, in front of Daiichi Bank, at the Meiji-machi intersection, in the red-light district of Shin-machi, and along Chongno.[11] In the city's Korean neighborhoods, local leaders spent more than two thousand yen installing newfangled electrical devices as well as flags to draw the people's attention to the excitement of the exhibition.[12]

Like the expositions in 1915 and 1929 that followed, the event in 1907 aimed to convince (semi)colonized visitors to accept foreign domination by allowing them to benefit, however unevenly, from the enriching potential of national "progress." As one Korean-language report optimistically explained about industry, "[it] does not stop at the personal profit of a single individual," but also helps "develop public profit."[13] To disseminate this gospel of progress, organizers encouraged the event's two hundred thousand participants—nearly 75 percent of whom were Korean—to engage in a spirit of competition with fellow visitors and exhibitors.[14] As visitors engaged in bidding wars for basic goods, exhibitors vied to win the attention of a committee that judged and awarded prizes for the best items. The Korean crown prince and future emperor, Sunjong, lent official sanction to this competitive atmosphere when he attended the awards ceremony on November 9, conferring prizes on winners from a systematically categorized list of products.[15] Visitors could also participate in the boisterous mood of commercial competition, using their tickets to enter a lottery. On November 12 and 13, event organizers announced, three thousand display items would be presented as giveaways to winning ticket holders. On the following day, designated as Ladies' Day, five thousand lucky women, including Korean females who broke the taboo of going out during the daytime, won lottery prizes aimed at drawing them onto the grounds.[16]

The competitive spirit of the exhibition in 1907 spilled out onto city streets, a development encouraged by its industry-minded organizers to strengthen the link between displays of development and residents' own practices of industry. One report described Keijō's high-end Japanese eateries (J: *ryōtei*), whose female waitresses served sexual pleasures as well as food and beverages, engaged in extreme competition to outdo one another. Some especially eager entertainers spent more than one thousand yen on attractive decorations, including fancy dresses ordered from the metropole and materials to make flower-decorated carts.[17] Much as the women of Shin-machi participated in Seoul Shrine's festival procession, the female workers of these establishments used decorations to parade around the southern village, stopping to perform dances at various locations. City merchants participated in the atmosphere of commercial competition by establishing stalls along designated thoroughfares, including Misaka Avenue, which extended from Yongsan to the South Gate.[18] Licensed merchants also erected temporary stalls along Meijimachi Street, located near the exhibition site.[19]

Despite the entrepreneurial spirit of some merchants and entertainers, the assimilatory effects of the Keijō Exhibition in 1907 were limited for most participants, a function of both Japan's imperialist tactics and Koreans' unpredictable engagements with this unfamiliar event. The Residency-General's blatant push to make the peninsula a formal Japanese colony clearly undercut officials' naïve goal of using a collaborative event between Japanese and Koreans "to harmonize their thoughts about each other without ever communicating with each other."[20] The decision to disband the Korean military in 1907, the same year as the exhibition, was particularly counterproductive in this regard, causing armed uprisings against the protectorate government. Such opposition, in turn, prevented officials from collecting local products that would attract a large Korean audience.[21] Further, although extant sources give little idea of how Koreans (or Japanese) responded to this ideology of progress, fragmentary evidence suggests that they faced considerable obstacles in identifying, decoding, and internalizing the exhibition's message. Perhaps most obstructive in this regard was the event's carnivalesque atmosphere, a perennial "problem" faced by the designers of future spectacles. Like the organizers of shrine festivals discussed in the previous chapter, exhibition designers expressed concerns about overindulgence in exhibition play. As one Korean exhibitor remarked at the opening ceremony, "The aim of the exhibition is not to be a playground."[22] However, reports reveal that exhibition-goers were most attracted to the festive dimensions of the event, including entertainment by *geisha* and *kisaeng* as well as the flower-decorated train traversing the flag- and lantern-decorated streets.[23] On November 12 and 13, the days of the lottery, for example, many visitors never even entered the display halls, and instead dashed for booths distributing door prizes.[24] In the end, the playful nature of the exhibition contributed to a dilution of the gospel of industry, a political message already compromised by Japan's blatant maneuvers to extinguish the Chosŏn dynasty.

Even before annexation in 1910, protectorate and business officials sought to build on this small-scale event, using the city's beleaguered palace grounds to tout Japan's material prowess and promote the commercial interests of powerful settlers. In the summer of 1908, the director of the exhibition in 1907 met with the Korean Minister of Agriculture, the mayor, the Japanese settlement association, and local business leaders to plan a large-scale event. Calling it the Korean Exhibition for Industrial Promotion, officials allocated a budget of five hundred thousand yen, nearly ten times greater than that of the Keijō Exhibition. In addition, organizers wanted to use a more symbolically potent location than the Meiji-machi site. Initially, they discussed Kyŏngbok Palace,

Hanyang's primary palace until the 1590s, but later decided to survey Kyŏnghŭi Palace, the focal point of modernizing reforms during the Great Han Empire.[25] Hosting a major display of Japan's industrial might at this site would also have highlighted the alleged ineptitude of Kojong, whom the protectorate government had forced to abdicate in favor of his young son, Sunjong. In the end, however, the Korean government, already compromised by the aggressive tactics of the Residency-General, failed to muster the necessary funds, forcing Japanese organizers to postpone it indefinitely.[26]

## THE DISPLAY AND PROMOTION OF COLONIAL INDUSTRY AT THE EXHIBITION OF 1915

Although financial limitations continued to hamper the early colonial state, the annexation removed whatever impediment the protectorate government had faced in collaborating with the Great Han Empire.[27] Thereafter, officials embarked on an even more aggressive plan to use the city's palace grounds as symbolic stages on which to promote Japan's material superiority and thereby convince newly colonized Koreans that modernization could somehow benefit them as agricultural and industrial laborers. In the fall of 1913, for example, government authorities, having already decided to construct the new Government-General building on the grounds of Kyŏngbok Palace, used this sacred site to host a birthday celebration for the recently deceased Meiji Emperor, the monarch who had overseen the capitalist development of the Japanese metropole and the evisceration of the Korean royal house. Seeking to transform the grounds of this private residence into a site of public festivities, officials arranged Japanese flags and martial arts performances on both sides of the main gate, Kwanghwamun. In a symbolic gesture exposing this scared site to the colonial public, they constructed a ceremonial space in front of the central hall, Kŭnjŏngjŏn, once used by Chosŏn monarchs to rule over an independent dynasty. After a ritual conducted by Shintō priests, guests enjoyed a garden party where vendors sold beer, sweet sake, and cigarettes. To further popularize this new public space, *geisha* and *kisaeng* entertained audiences, while Hakata (Fukuoka) performers staged a popular comedy show.[28]

Having already become a ceremonial and recreational stage for public events, Kyŏngbok Palace was transformed even more spectacularly for the Industrial Exhibition of 1915. Held to commemorate the first five years of colonial rule, this event strategically juxtaposed Japan's "modern" accomplishments with the "deplorable" fate of Korea's own (under)development. While the palace site was chosen in part for practical reasons (according to the Government-General's report, other possible sites lacked convenient transportation access and sufficient display space and needed considerable infusions of money for additional construction), it also served two symbolic purposes. First, it coincided with and confirmed a noticeable shift in the city's center of gravity from the Japanese settlement, the location of the Keijō Exhibition of 1907, to the Korean-populated northern village, the traditional urban center. Second, and perhaps more important, officials hoped to induce exhibition-goers to view the place's contents as "historic relics," rather than enlivening symbols of an autonomous Korean nation. "Ruins, long since damaged and decayed, many of which are also dirty and unattractive" were the disparaging terms used by planners to literally "sweep away" 123 palace buildings, including residences, halls, libraries, gates, and other structures.[29] As many as two-thirds of these structures early colonial officials transferred to wealthy Japanese, high-end eateries, and Buddhist temples.[30] They also destroyed a number of important buildings, including (1) the Honghwa Gate, which stood in front of the Kŭnjŏng Gate; (2) the nearby Yuhwa, Yŏngsŏng, and Hyŏpsaeng Gates; (3) the Yangje Bridge, which crossed the Kŭmch'ŏn Stream in front of the Kŭnjŏng Gate; and (4) three stone monuments.[31] By removing structures around the palace's main hall, officials expanded the area in front of Kŭnjŏngjŏn, which became the exhibition's main ceremonial space, and also made room for the postexhibition construction of the new Government-General building.

Officials believed that the goal of the event—namely, showing recent socioeconomic advancements and promoting their future development—should be inscribed into the event grounds, as it would be in the displays themselves. By infusing the exhibition space with this ideological message, they hoped to facilitate visitors' internalization of the spectacle's exploitative rationality of "progress" as self-governing practice. As one Japanese-language newspaper article explained, each element of design should have a specific effect on Koreans' consciousness: "The construction of bridges and the dredging of sewers intend to bring about some awareness of transportation and an understanding of hygiene. The structures around the gardens, which ought to add scenic beauty, should be made to correspond to the design of enticing Koreans to appreciate the natural landscape."[32] Although planners championed functional "simplicity" in reconstructing the palace grounds, they took far greater aesthetic license when it came to the display halls. Aiming to create an awe-inspiring aura of grandeur that would mask the highly uneven logic of colonial modernization, designers eschewed a recognizably "Japanese" style of architecture and, instead, drew from an eclectic variety of Renaissance, Secessionist, and other modern aesthetics of Western derivation.[33] Their choices not only mirrored styles used in metropolitan expositions during the early twentieth century, but also reflected the top-down projection of sovereign power. Such instrumentalism left little room to portray Korea. Indeed, the only place where visitors could encounter indigenous traditions was inside the exhibition halls, which were constructed by exploiting native pine and cedar.

A good example of the grand aesthetics favored by designers is found in the main exhibition hall (Building One), the first structure visitors encountered after passing through the Kwanghwa Gate (see figure 11a). Like other structures flanking the main ceremonial space, this hall exhibited a renaissance air of rationality, a feature best exemplified in the building's geometric design and its set of equidistant pillars. Embellishing various buildings with surface decoration and linear ornamentation, architects used a "Secession style," a reference to the fin-de-siècle Viennese movement promoting artistic innovation and freedom of aesthetic work. One can observe this decorative linearity in the symmetrical vertical openings on the columns and in the equidistant pilasters along the building's façade. Colonial designers' focus was not simply on reproducing or improvising with Western architectural forms, but on the subjectifying effect the exposition structures would produce in viewers. To inspire awe, they gave Building One two central towers measuring 25.5 meters, a height far exceeding that of the city's tallest two-story building.[34] Figure 11a shows how this dominating structure also obscured spectators' view of the palace's main ceremonial space, Kŭnjŏng Hall. Two other exhibition halls—the Machine Building to the north and the Special Forestry Building to the south (see figure 11b)—also blocked a view of Kŭnjŏng Hall by creating an architectural cordon on its eastern side. Even as these awe-inspiring monuments conveyed Japan's shared modernity with the West, they clearly dominated the remaining palace structures, evoking a stance the colonial government considered necessary to the peninsula's material development.

The strategic juxtaposition of Korea's past as premodern, closed, and defunct with Japan's present as modern, open, and progressive also colored visual representations of the event. In the promotional poster

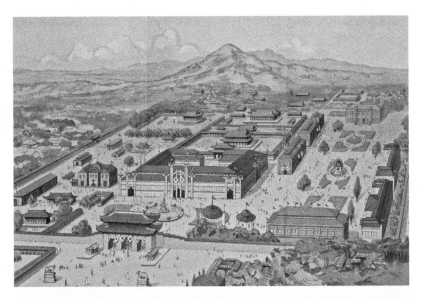

FIGURE 11a. Building One on illustrated exhibition grounds. Source: "Kyōshinkai kaijō keifukukyū no zu." Image courtesy of Seoul Museum of History.

FIGURE 11b. Special Forestry Hall's obstruction of Kŭnjŏng Hall. Source: "Shisei 5 nen kinen Chōsen bussan kyōshinkai, Eirinshō Tokusetsukan." Image courtesy of An Ch'ang-mo.

(figure 12a), the upper half represents the precolonial period, with the past of Kyŏngbok Palace portrayed as dark and staid. The autumn leaves surrounding the private grounds contribute some color, but they are on the verge of falling to the ground, without anyone to appreciate their natural wonder. By contrast, the bottom section depicting the modern present and the future under Japanese rule is full of bright activity, as visitors enjoy the recently opened palace grounds. Green grass, blooming flowers, and an illuminated sky combine to produce an image of progress in which newly colonized Koreans are encouraged to participate. Tying together this assimilationist message of industry is a *kisaeng,* who literally straddles the premodern Korean past and the modern Japanese present. (This imagery was borrowed from a poster issued for the Tokyo Taishō Exhibition in 1914; see figure 12b.) The *kisaeng*'s colorful dress and extravagant headpiece stand in stark contrast to newer, simpler forms of dress and modern parasols more commonly used by *kisaeng* at various exhibition-related events, such as the citywide procession.[35] Promoters deliberately played up an essentially "traditional" image of *kisaeng* that would appeal to the libidinal sensibilities of her male viewers. With one arm seductively placed by her neck, this exoticized figure beckoned visitors with another outstretched arm, suggesting a transethnic dance that audiences could enjoy at the performance hall.[36] For their part, Japanese companies cashed in on *kisaeng,* whose images were reproduced in a number of commercial advertisements for such products as Beauty Cigarettes and Lion Toothbrushes. By the end of the event, expenditures on visits to high-end eateries where *kisaeng* entertained amounted to an estimated three hundred thousand yen, nearly half the total price spent on the exhibition itself![37]

The marketability of the exoticized *kisaeng* suggests the important, if unpredictable, role that recreation would play in advancing industry among newly colonized Koreans. So important were amusements that the Keijō Cooperative Committee (KCC), a semigovernmental support group, decided to double its initial allocation to one hundred thousand yen, accounting for nearly 20 percent of the total budget.[38] The importance of entertainment can also be seen in the space dedicated to recreational and commercial facilities, all of which produced needed revenue for the event. As figure 11a shows, display halls dominated the eastern part of the exhibition grounds, but amusement facilities occupied approximately one-third of Kyŏngbok Palace. Admission-based amusements included the aforementioned performance hall (fifteen to thirty sen), a Korean drama hall (ten to fifteen sen), a playground (one sen), a

FIGURE 12a. Promotional poster from exhibition of 1915.
Source: *Shisei 5 nen kinen Chōsen bussan kyōshinkai Keijō kyōsankai hōkoku* (Keijō: Keijō kyōsankai, 1916), plate 1.

horseshoe-throwing facility (five sen for ten throws), a sumo hall (five sen), a circus (ten to fifty sen), a wild animal zoo (ten sen), a labyrinth (ten sen), a georama (ten sen), and a mystery house (ten sen).[39] Other commercial facilities included food and beverage kiosks, stands where vendors sold a variety of memorial goods, and a series of rest stations sponsored by Korea's thirteen provinces.

Although officials welcomed entertainment as an integral part of the exhibition, they did so with both reservations and conditions. Matsuoka Kōki, former Agricultural and Commercial Affairs Minister,

FIGURE 12b. Promotional poster from exhibition of 1914.
Source: *Tōkyō taishō hakurankai jimu hōkoku (gekan)* (Tokyo: Tōkyō fuchō, 1917), plate between 818 and 819.

warned that if visitors failed to imbibe the ideological aim of this event, the promotion of colonial development through cheap labor, then the exhibition could easily devolve into festival revelry. He wrote about the desired relationship between the advancement of industry and the function of recreation as follows: "If people, as a reward for working hard, do not comfort their tired minds and tired bodies with recreation in a carefree and leisurely way, they cannot perform real labor. But, even the same recreation, if of the kind that disturbs social mores or causes damage to people's bodies, it should be avoided. What is really sought is recreation that has a purpose. The exhibition, which actually combines this kind of useful recreation and useful observation, is an interesting plan in that it advances knowledge while having fun."[40] Promoters thus conceived of entertainment as a recreational supplement to the dutiful and efficient performance of labor, rather than as a mere diversion. However, exactly how individuals engaged with amusements depended on a number of contingencies that officials like Matsuoka could not completely control; indeed, visitors had a remarkable degree of interpretive power. As An Sun-hwan, the Korean director of the KCC, reminded readers about the upcoming event: "The success or failure in accomplishing industrial development invariably lies with the people."[41]

Much as the spatial reconstruction of the palace grounds encouraged largely illiterate visitors to understand the recent colonial past as modern progress and adopt this ideology as their everyday ethic, the particular arrangement of displays in the exposition halls sought to induce similar ways of visualizing development.[42] The museological method, for example, methodically classified goods based on scientific standards, creating a product typology that allowed viewers to compare items along a recognizable and uniform scale. Officials capitalized on the flattening effect of this display technique in the Shinseikan (Simsegwan; literally, "hall to assess conditions") by extending its horizontal logic geographically to create a presentation of products from each of the thirteen provinces.[43] In contrast to the inherently spatializing effect of the museological method, the dichotomizing display technique played on a temporal logic. By juxtaposing an allegedly oppressive and unproductive precolonial Korean past with a supposedly liberating and productive Japanese colonial present and future, officials sought to convince viewers of the putative benefits of historical progress writ large. To this end, they filled display halls with statistical tables charting numerical developments and photographic images presenting visual examples of the inexorable move from premodernity to modernity. In both the museological and dichotomizing display methods, exhibition designers notably downplayed, and sometimes erased, the markedly uneven effects of Japanese rule. Instead, they mobilized the lure of modern development to induce participants to view the recent past as personally beneficial, rather than as an exploitative system of economic domination.

Officials showcased this ideological formula of colonial modernization in a final display method, which Chu Yun-jŏng has called a decontextualizing vision. Through this exhibitionary technique, they sought to abstract from their particular environments specific cultural traditions deemed unnecessary and harmful to material progress. The Korean shaman, for example, traditionally considered an active interlocutor with the divine and a healer of people's suffering, became an anachronistic object of scorn at the exhibition, positioned as a superstitious figure within the context of police surveillance and hygienic control. This treatment reflected an important goal of the Government-General: to replace healing practices performed by "traditional" shamans with biomedical techniques offered by "modern" hospitals.[44] Like the first two display techniques, this way of seeing encouraged viewers to concentrate on the benefits of industrial progress and to imagine their roles as wage laborers in advancing that trajectory of development. The repressive conditions of colonial rule clearly inhered in all three display techniques.

Despite elaborate exhibitionary efforts aimed at spreading the ideology of material assimilation, the colonial state struggled to ensure that spectators would focus their attention on display halls, as well as comprehend their contents in the ways intended by designers. Even official reports reveal that the Government-General had to rely on one hundred patrol officers to staunch unruly behavior that, in extreme cases, involved acts of theft. (That more than half of recorded arrests implicated ethnic Japanese—even though Korean visitors twice outnumbered their colonizers—certainly undercut the assumed superiority of the former.) Police officers also cited over sixty-four thousand instances of improprieties, including smoking, touching display items, trespassing onto off-limits areas, and urinating in public.[45] More important, most of these offenses occurred outside display halls, where visitors had strayed from the designated course to wander around the palace grounds or the city. Indeed, patrol officers explained that a major part of their daily work was dealing with lost children. They also mentioned trying to convince a provincial *yangban,* pictured in one newspaper cartoon with his hands uncomfortably placed over his crotch, to urinate in one of twenty-four public bathrooms, rather than venturing to Chongno to use a facility he had seen there.[46]

For those visitors who made it into the display halls, who could assist them in making stronger connections between exhibits of progress and attitudes of industry? Officials did place a limited number of guides in display halls to answer questions about specific items. However, newspaper reports suggest that guides found themselves unengaged by most visitors, receiving only occasional requests made by special guests. Even the *Keijō nippō* could not help but parody the inactivity of guides, if only to remind them of the important role they played in fostering a learning environment. One cartoon illustration showed a male guide slouching on a bench with a farcical caption (daily salary + bonus = [money] until the New Year), suggesting the pecuniary concerns of exhibition workers. The text accompanying this cartoon also pointed to the limited role that guides played:

> Wearing a hat, collar, and wristband made of scarlet-colored woolen cloth and a brown-colored handlebar moustache below his nose, a guide peers over a group of exhibition-goers from behind. Only fifteen or sixteen people a day ask me to do my job. The most [inquiries] in one day was fifty, but with four guides [in this building], all of us are suffering from idleness. . . . The most trouble I encountered was someone asking me to take him to a display or guiding someone to the VIP room in the Kyotae Hall.[47]

In the end, most Koreans were left to their own devices to make the connections desired by colonial officials. Although authorities urged visitors to carry a pen and paper to study the displays and to voice their questions and concerns, the lack of effective intermediaries made this educational project largely self-dependent.[48]

To better facilitate attendees' ability to visualize colonial "progress," exhibition organizers used local cooperative committees to encourage Korean elites, especially those living in rural areas, to see the exhibition in groups led by tour guides. In general, officials made conscious efforts to attract the peninsula's overwhelmingly agricultural population, who, in contrast to the country's much smaller urban population, possessed fewer opportunities to interact with the objects of industry promoted at the exhibition. Notably, during the first forty-eight days of this fifty-one-day event, almost 70 percent of 790,000 total admissions were made by individuals residing outside the capital city. Newspaper reports referred to most participants of group visits as local notables *(yuji;* J: *yūshi),* that is, male landowners who doubled as rural leaders.[49] Using honorary membership in local cooperative committees—surely, a symbol of privileged status—as an incentive, the Government-General urged these men to visit Keijō as part of a short-term training aimed at making them cultural intermediaries. Through displays of the latest farm technology, officials encouraged rural elites to draw connections between objects of progress and their use as instruments of agricultural efficiency and productivity. Having come to understand such connections, these local modernizers could, in turn, persuade the sharecropping classes below them to engage in similarly industrious improvements. According to this governing logic, bountiful harvests would benefit landholding farmers, their local societies, and the larger community. This logic, of course, obfuscated the markedly uneven benefits different groups would receive.

Although comprising less than 7 percent of total exhibition-goers, group visits formed the basis for most accounts penned in the *Maeil sinbo*—the government-controlled, Korean-language newspaper.[50] As expected, many of these accounts reproduced the official ideology of colonial industry. After visiting various display halls, one member of a tour group from Koyang, a village on the outskirts of Keijō, repeated the state's diffusionist goals by making the following vow: "When we return to the countryside, we must be the voice of advancement and effectively implement what we have seen this time, leading the many farmers of the village and creating a model for them."[51] In another, similarly worded article, a group leader from Hwanghae Province, Mr. Yi, recounted how he had been struggling to find a more efficient method to polish rice. Just then, a visit to the Machine Hall allowed him to witness the workings of a Japanese rice-refining machine, which, in his paternalistic phrasing, "even a single woman or child" could operate.[52] By "realizing" how a piece of machinery could reduce labor inputs and consequently increase net profits, Mr. Yi exemplified the type of thinking colonial officials hoped to instill. Whether or not they could afford a rice-polishing device, rural elites were lured by the possibility of increasing productivity and, hence, their own material well-being to adopt new techniques aimed at developing the local economy in unprecedented ways.

Despite the apparently seamless internalization of the objective display of industry illustrated by these examples, other writings reveal that local notables understood this event in ways that did not necessarily solidify this connection. Although the reasons for these incommensurabilities are complex, one significant factor was the novelty of the experience. Rural visitors—many of whom had never seen the royal capital, let alone an exhibition—seem to have understood their journey to Keijō in light of official trips made on a more local basis during the Chosŏn dynasty. In contrast to these horseback excursions, which typically included a visit to a local magistrate or sightseeing in a nearby rural area, most exhibition visitors made the journey to the colonial capital by means of the newly established railroad. If this new form of rapid transport did not sufficiently astonish them, they were overwhelmed by what they described as the splendor of Keijō and the newly reconstructed exhibition grounds, to which they responded with repeated expressions of *aigo* ("Wow!"). Although welcomed by officialdom and reiterated in the *Maeil sinbo,* their astonishment at the modern city and the exhibition grounds did not necessarily lead to "adequate" or "proper" scrutiny of the display halls. In fact, this posture of awe may have actually prevented that very scrutiny. As one Korean visitor recollected in a newspaper report, "Everyone just says how wonderfully splendid and great [the exhibition] is, but it appears that few people explain their excitement by systematically focusing on one aspect [of it]."[53]

Even individuals with a strong curiosity did not necessarily leave the event having successfully decoded the arrangement of display items as an object lesson in colonial industry. For example, the recollections of Mr. Chang, a local notable and tour guide from Kangwŏn Province, revealed that he mistook a water pump displayed in the Machine Hall for some kind of waterfall attraction *(p'okp'omul)*. According to his account, Mr. Chang took great pains in seeking to understand the function of this display item. However, the rapid pace with which he proceeded through exhibition halls prevented him from acquiring more than a surface knowledge of this particular gadget. Likening this shallow experience to that of licking a watermelon without being able to eat it *(subak kŏt halkki),* he lamented that the majority of visitors also failed to imbibe the message of colonial industry, in spite of their wish to become beneficiaries of its enriching possibilities.[54] Just weeks before the end of the exhibition, Tokutomi Sohō, the founder of the *Keijō nippō,* offered a similar metaphor to critique the superficiality of the event, which he argued had only a "daubing effect" (J: *tomatsuteki sayō*) on Koreans.[55]

Even as such self-congratulatory accounts sought to close the gap separating the alluring displays of "progress" and their polysemous reception by individual visitors, they also reveal the considerable difficulties faced by tour guides in disseminating knowledge to their followers. These accounts repeatedly criticized members of groups for misbehaving, making commotion inside the display halls, and failing to exert adequate self-control. The burdensome task of guiding a diverse group of visitors to view numerous display items within a limited time frame challenged tour guides to keep individuals on the authorized tour route.[56] Even when visitors followed instructions and stayed with the group, they frequently found the allotted time insufficient, as suggested by Mr. Chang's account mentioned above. To remedy this problem, Mr. Chang recommended that his entourage break up into small groups and take turns closely examining each display hall. Another approach was taken by Mr. Yi, the guide from Hwanghae Province, who encouraged visitors to focus their attention on a limited number of items rather than seeking more effective ways to cover all of the displays. Bringing the question back to the self-governing individual, he urged visitors to pick a useful item and actively demand answers from their tour guide. "If group leaders and tour guides are unable to understand the things inside people's minds," he asked, "how can they provide satisfying explanations to each person?"[57]

A subset of group visitors for whom interactions with guides proved especially critical in making connections with colonial industry was school children, more than twenty-three thousand of whom visited the palace grounds as part of teacher-led tour groups. Officials considered students "individuals possessing new attitudes" and thus model exhibition-goers.[58] With pencil and paper in hand, students spent time viewing the display halls, taking notes on what they observed. Their teachers, in turn, used the students' impressions of the exhibition as material for classroom education, and the colonial government requested that they report the results of this education in the form of statistical data.[59] Although none of these official records remains, the *Keijō nippō* does provide fragmentary evidence of school visits, like one made by a group of Korean common school students from Hwanghae Province. As expected, this report indicates that they showed a particularly strong interest in various models, charts, and pictures, but fails to explain how they understood these displays in their own terms. The students of Keijō's Sakurai Common School provide a slightly more revealing glance into children's subjectivities, although likely from the perspective of Japanese children.[60] According to an article summarizing comments made in their notebooks, students described a display of cotton trees and a whale exhibit as "unusual," the excavated cavity of a coal mine as "surprising," and the model of Suwŏn's forests as "beautiful." However, these words of enthusiasm did not necessarily mean that they mastered lessons of industrial progress, at least not at the exhibition itself. Echoing the experience of Mr. Chang, one student recorded the "waterfall" (in actuality, a water pump) as the most interesting attraction. As the student quizzically remarked, "That water never seems to go down!"[61]

Even celebratory reports about older students with greater knowledge suggest interpretive difficulties due to the same logistical obstacles that challenged adult groups. An article on the visit of six hundred female students from Keijō Women's High School reported that they appreciated various products showcased at the Shinseikan. They also enjoyed displays featuring the ports of Inch'ŏn and Pusan and various statistical charts, each of which they "investigated comparatively." The oft-repeated expression "comparative investigation" suggests that these students engaged in officially sanctioned ways of seeing. However, their teacher concluded his comments with reservations about the ability of students to effectively digest the message of industry when challenged by an overwhelming number of display items to see within just three hours. He wrote with some frustration, "Due to the large number [of display items], they cannot be viewed in a relaxed way because one tries to see all of them at once."[62]

Although few of the displays targeted a female audience per se, organizers did encourage women to attend the exhibition, particularly in their capacities as mothers expected to nurture the next generation of productive youth. On September 17, for example, the KCC sponsored a special event, Ladies' and Children's Day, at which admission-paying women received free cosmetics and their children paper whales and picture postcards.[63] These giveaways drew a record crowd of nearly 14,000 Koreans and 14,620 Japanese, a number far exceeding the average daily attendance of just over nine thousand Koreans and sixty-five hundred Japanese.[64] Discussions in the media suggest that women spent more time entertaining their children in the recreational area than viewing objects of colonial industry in display halls. To accommodate the large number of visitors, organizers opened the area around the Kyŏnghoe Pavilion as a rest area for mothers and their children, whom they served tea and sweets and even allowed to use the swings for free. Children could also enjoy a number of reduced-rate attractions designed to please youngsters, including girls' dancing and theatrical performances.[65] Throughout their visit, women were encouraged to perform a gendered division of labor as nurturing mothers, rather than focusing on displays of colonial industry like their husbands.

Female presence at the former palace grounds also reflected official efforts to promote a classed role for Korean women as efficient housewives. The Home Exhibition, held concurrently with the Industrial Exhibition (from September 11 to 26) at the offices of the *Keijō nippō* and *Maeil sinbo*, sought to transform women's attitudes about household work through domestic education, sanitary reform, and savings campaigns. For example, Cho Chung-ŭng, the Korean vice-director of the KCC, urged Korean women to abandon the anachronistic practice of turning away male visitors when their husbands were absent, a Confucian propriety now seen as an unproductive way to conduct household labor. To further increase domestic efficiency, Cho implored housewives to venture outdoors and shop during the day, a practice discouraged by precolonial conventions promoting the cloistering of female elites.[66] Through such self-governing reforms, exhibition ideologues encouraged Korean women to actively participate in the larger project of colonial industry as "good wives and wise mothers," a limited role defined by a system of patriarchy only strengthened by colonialism.[67]

Women's increased appearance in public at the exhibition had another effect, leading some men to use the colonized space of the former palace grounds less as an educational laboratory of industrial "progress" than as a marketplace for their own erotic pursuits. According to one sensational account, when a twenty-one-year-old Korean housewife from an upper-class neighborhood (Hyoja-dong) wandered around the palace grounds, a man in a Western suit pursued her fervently, chasing the woman all the way back to her home. Enamored of what he had seen at the exhibition, the persistent man proceeded to send one of his underlings to her residence ten times. With these visits, he hoped to persuade the married woman to leave her husband and elope with him, an offer she eventually accepted.[68] Although this story reveals little about the subjective experiences of female exhibition-goers, it does show how Korean women, not unlike the highly popular and exoticized *kisaeng*, were frequently targeted by men whose erotic and romantic desires distracted them from their expected roles as dispassionate observers of colonial industry.[69] Thus, in multiple ways, the exposition gave visitors the ability to impute different meanings to this commemorative event. Much as organizers had feared, the abundant opportunities to partake in amusement and consumption often overshadowed the exhibition's primary function as a pedagogical institution.

The transformation of the exhibition into a playground was especially conspicuous during the final two weeks, when officials organized a number of special event days. Even at ideologically named events such as Exhibition Success Day (which drew only 3,304 Japanese and 5,115 Koreans), visitors indulged in a variety of playful attractions, including the chance to win a free giveaway at the rice-cake-making competition, a tug-of-war game with prizes, and the employees' and performers' costume procession.[70] As a strategy to boost attendance, officials also offered free admission during the final three days, in the hope of enticing Keijō's poorest to view the exhibition.[71] Rather than using free admission to study colonial industry, the nearly 290,000 Koreans (and eighty-four thousand Japanese) who took advantage of the free admission spent their time enjoying a variety of popular attractions. Monkey Day (October 30), for example, drew record crowds of over ninety thousand Koreans (and almost twenty-three thousand Japanese) who found themselves mesmerized by a show featuring these adroit creatures walking on an elevated trapeze.[72] A semiofficial survey conducted after the exhibition also revealed that Koreans considered the following attractions most memorable (in descending order): the parade held at

Hanwŏn Palace, the fountain at Kwanghwa Gate, the stuffed whale, the gem stone in the pond, the miniature map of the peninsula, the circus, and the performances by humans and tigers.[73] The immense popularity of such attractions suggests that entertainment did not always complement the tedious task of viewing the displays by offering a respite from low-paid labor, as event promoters had hoped. Rather, they created a consumer-based, festival-like world, frustrating attempts to convince Koreans of the integral roles they should play as productive members of a modernizing economy.

Although the exhibition did not always effectively impart the ideology of material progress, it nonetheless produced some results in line with what organizers hoped. As the examples discussed above demonstrate, the exhibition functioned as a new public space that allowed Koreans of different regions, classes, sexes, and generations to create meanings from both the terms imposed upon them and those they brought into this contact zone. Some individuals did selectively respond to the suggestions of the displays, to the benefit of their own interests. The creation in 1916 of a popular night market along the commercial thoroughfare of Chongno is but one example of Korean-led projects to advance elements of "industry" in ways that elite organizers thought would enrich themselves while providing for their ethnic community.[74] In fact, the three prominent Koreans who spearheaded the plan to establish the Chongno night market, including the aforementioned Cho Chung-ŭng, had recently served on the KCC.[75] Using a system of licenses to manage the number and location of commercial stalls, municipal authorities required that merchants receive approval to conduct business from Chongno 2-chōme to Pagoda Park. With the exception of these regulations, the night market operated under unfettered conditions of commercial competition in which hundreds of Korean (and some Japanese) merchants battled to outsell one another.[76] So popular did this new form of evening business become that local officials had to extend the commercial area two additional blocks eastward from Pagoda Park.[77] The temporary stalls along this stretch, open every evening from the spring until the fall, featured sundry goods, food items, and writing utensils. Shirts, towels, soap, shoes, and children's products ranked among the most popular consumer goods.[78]

For the night market's consumers, the lure of personal consumption and various attractions also transformed this site into something new, a popular playground, but one without the edifying function of the exhibition. On opening night, thirty thousand visitors, a number far surpassing most daily admissions to the spectacle of 1915, reportedly enjoyed a festive procession of music, theatrical performers, and more than one hundred women from the city's *kisaeng* cooperatives. Clearly, these popular attractions mimicked those held at the recent exhibition. However, Korean organizers had no ulterior goal of encouraging the colonized masses to purposefully contribute to particular ways of visualizing industry. They simply created a playful site of commercial transactions that served the everyday needs of the city's colonized population while enriching themselves. Similarly, the petty merchants who lined the illuminated thoroughfare were there to eke out a living, not to support the purported "progress" of a colonial economy that continued to impoverish many of them.[79]

## INVESTMENTS IN "CULTURAL RULE" AT THE KOREA EXPOSITION OF 1929

As previously discussed, 1925 marks an important, if overlooked, turning point in the history of colonial Korea. In Keijō, at least, this year coincided with the completion of multiple monuments that would usher in a new phase of space- and place-making, in particular, the central administrative complex, built on the very site where, just ten years earlier, the Industrial Exhibition of 1915 had taken place. Together, these architectural displays of Japan's modernity left a strong imprint of the Government-General on the public landscape of a city whose residents were, as a result of colonial development, increasingly divided along both ethnic and class lines. Given these social tensions, which had been brought to a head in the March First Uprising of 1919 and continued to simmer throughout the 1920s, authorities redoubled their efforts at assimilation under the accommodationist policy of "cultural rule." While allowing a wider sphere of political activity for Koreans, this divide-and-rule strategy aimed at more effectively co-opting liberal-minded elites and, by extension, poorer residents who potentially leaned toward socialism, into the operation of capitalist power. Held behind the new Government-General building, the Korea Exposition of 1929, commemorating twenty years of colonial "progress," was one spectacular expression of cultural rule.

As early as 1921, officials began to discuss the possibility of holding another exposition to commemorate the fifteenth anniversary of Japanese rule and to celebrate the long-awaited unveiling of the Government-General's new administrative complex. As before, their goal for the event in 1926 was twofold: first, to introduce the world to the goods of Korean culture and the productive capabilities of its twenty million inhabitants; and, second, to transform people's consciousness by promoting industrial education.[80] They envisioned a huge event with a total budget of three million yen. However, the colonial state encountered budgetary obstacles almost from the start, forcing the government to postpone the event until 1929. Meanwhile, times of severe economic retrenchment forced officials to solicit additional sources of financial support.[81] In other words, they quite literally sought public investments in cultural rule.

In addition to the expected 1.43 million yen (56 percent) outlay, the Government-General's plan relied on funds from provincial governments and the Keijō municipal government for 130,000 yen (9 percent) and 250,000 yen (17 percent), respectively. Even with these additional sources of income, planners still required another 250,000 yen (17 percent), a sum they hoped to garner through daily admissions and a limited number of private donations.[82] Based on visitor numbers at previous expositions, organizers optimistically predicted that between two and three million would participate in the commemoration of 1929. Conservatively calculating two million visitors each paying twenty sen, they could expect to collect four hundred thousand yen in admission fees. Organizers also estimated an additional two to three hundred thousand yen in commercial sales and miscellaneous income.[83]

Mobilizing large crowds of visitors to pay their way into the exposition required another kind of investment from local elites, whom planners counted on to popularize the event among poorer Koreans. Building on techniques used during the exhibition in 1915, the Government-General exploited a vast network of regional institutions, delegating promotional tasks to officially sanctioned organizations. For example, the KCC, the most important of these organizations, sold tickets, postcards, and guidebooks to commercial boards and other local organizations. This organization also took charge of managing exposition commerce and recreation as well as facilitating travel to and tours of the capital city. In turn, the KCC called on a like-minded class of nearly 350 businessmen, deliberative councilmen, and neighborhood administrators (including more than one hundred Koreans) to support its efforts.[84] For local elites, membership in regional organizations like the KCC stood as a symbol of their privileged status. At the same time, semiofficial organizations allowed colonial power to more effectively reach the subaltern population and convince them to buy into the Government-General's underfunded project of cultural rule. To elicit popular support for the upcoming commemoration, members of the KCC and other local planners used a variety of modern media. Their advertising campaign included preevent celebrations such as automobile, costume, and lantern processions, song and poster competitions, and the publication and distribution of promotional materials. For example, guidelines for the poster competition, the winner of which would receive a two-hundred-yen prize, encouraged contestants to "promote Korea's industrial development and cultural advances as well as display Korean matters in both the colony and the metropole."[85] In the end, KCC promoters chose the design of a colonized resident from Keijō as the first prize winner, a symbolic decision echoing attempts to reward exemplary Korean "investments" in the exposition.[86] The winning poster foregrounded the Kyŏnghoe Pavilion, one of few remaining structures from Kyŏngbok Palace, suggesting its primacy on the exposition grounds. However, in the background lurked the new Government-General building, reminding visitors of the ultimate source of political authority in colonial Korea.

The media techniques of the KCC not only encouraged the colonized population to become self-regulating agents of capitalist development, but also targeted Japanese business and government interests to invest in the exposition and the colonial economy it would so spectacularly display. For example, Mitsukoshi, the most profitable Japanese department store in Keijō, responded by printing its logo on wrapping paper that notified consumers of the upcoming event.[87] That Mitsukoshi and other private institutions engaged in advertising campaigns in tandem with the KCC demonstrates the success of the Government-General in aligning the goals of colonial governance with those of commercial profit. In fact, efforts to solicit investments from Japanese organizations reached as far as the metropole, whose commercial boards and local government organizers were urged to sponsor their own display halls. To this end, a number of Keijō officials traveled to Tokyo, Osaka, and Kyoto, whose own expositions had already prominently featured Korea pavilions. In addition to these important cities, government officials and business leaders in Nagoya and Fukuoka also decided to fund special exhibition halls at an individual cost of four to five hundred thousand yen.[88] The Korea Exposition became so important in Tokyo and Osaka that local elites established their own cooperative committees to cash in on the colonial commemoration. Working with the KCC, these organizations publicized the upcoming exposition by issuing promotional train tickets and hanging event posters in highly visible places.[89] According to a colonial official who visited the metropole in the spring of 1929, these efforts quickly produced a "Korean fever," particularly among Japanese living in the western part of the country, who could most easily cross the straits on their way to the peninsula. To facilitate travel, the Government-General negotiated with railroad and ferry companies to offer discounts of more than 20 percent.[90] As a result, inflated predictions held that approximately three hundred thousand Japanese tourists would soon visit Keijō, using exposition displays of progress to familiarize themselves with a Korea slowly industrializing under colonial auspices.[91] Despite the early optimism of organizers and the KCC, by the time colonial officials managed to garner the necessary funds for the exposition, the Government-General, faced with an expanding recession, could only manage to contribute eight hundred thousand yen for a celebration whose total budget had already been reduced from three million to less than 1.5 million yen.[92] So severe had the economic situation become by the late 1920s that construction on display halls and other facilities did not begin until months before the exposition gates opened in the fall.

Efforts to encourage visitors to invest in the enriching logic of the event also colored the spatial and aesthetic design of the event grounds. Eschewing the exhibition of 1915's approach of deploying Western architectural styles to flaunt Japan's modernity, designers of the commemoration in 1929 resurrected a vanishing form of "Korean" palace architecture to better convince colonized visitors of their inclusion in Japan's multiethnic empire.[93] In addition to enticing Koreans to view the exposition as an ineluctable example of colonial development, this representational strategy also aimed to satisfy the desires of metropolitan tourists and expatriate settlers for both exotic spectacle and capitalist investment.[94] As with its role in city planning, the new Government-General building occupied a dominant position on the event grounds. To highlight this symbol of colonial authority, designers decided to relocate the main gate to the east side of Kyŏngbok Palace, brushing aside criticisms from Korean elites and even some Japanese intellectuals about the historical violence this measure represented. As Hong Kal has shown, the spatial manipulation of the Kwanghwa Gate led to the destruction of the palace's north-south axis, while also creating a new event corridor. As a result, the relocated palace gate, one anchor of this east-west corridor, continued to serve as the main entry point to the exposition of 1929, while the Kyŏnghoe Pavilion came to function as the western anchor.[95] As figure 13 shows, these two palace structures were the aesthetic inspiration for the dis-

FIGURE 13. "Pure Korean style" of exhibition corridor in 1931. Source: "Shisei 20 nen kinen Chōsen hakurankai ehagaki." (Image courtesy of An Ch'ang-mo.)

play halls lining the new event corridor, all of which were constructed in what the media called a "pure Korean style." Despite its superficiality, this gesture of including native culture aimed to demonstrate the important, if subordinated, position that the peninsula and its inhabitants played in the material progress of the empire.[96] Although they bragged about the authenticity of this style, even intrepid designers agreed that the shapes and proportions of these buildings were, in fact, new.[97] Further, as colonized critics were quick to condemn, the purported "Koreanness" of the display halls lining the main corridor belied their status as reproductions of palace structures destroyed under early colonial rule. In the end, this imperialist aesthetic may have been most successful at beckoning Japanese tourists to gaze at Korean culture as an anachronistic and exotic form of spectacle.[98]

The "Korean-style" halls of the main corridor touted various advancements made during the nearly twenty years of Japanese rule, encouraging visitors to place themselves within this ineluctable narrative of progress. For example, the North Industrial Hall featured developments made in Korean agriculture, forestry, and maritime goods, while the South Industrial Hall displayed products created by the colony's light industries, handicraft enterprises, and mining businesses. These buildings were followed by the Socioeconomics Hall, which exhibited graphs and charts championing reforms made in finances, while the Rice Hall

highlighted the important role that this crop played in the imperial economy. Like its predecessor in 1915, the exposition of 1929 also featured
a building where organizers displayed products from each of the peninsula's thirteen provinces. Together, these exhibits encouraged colonized
spectators and Japanese visitors to draw comparisons between different
Korean locales. This way of seeing not only allowed individuals from
comparatively less productive areas to imagine ways of catching up with
their more "industrious" neighbors, but also encouraged other exposition-goers to consider themselves as playing integral roles in the development of the colonial economy.

To represent the multiethnic nature of material assimilation, designers
included a number of aesthetically distinct display halls representing other
parts of the empire. Thus, as visitors made their way around the Kyŏnghoe
Pavilion, they encountered a series of buildings displaying "progress" outside the Korean peninsula. The first of these was the Naichikan (Metropolitan Hall), a large building constructed in a distinctly "Western" style.
Referring to the metropole, this building featured products from each of
Japan's prefectures and introduced Koreans to the ultimate source of the
empire's strength. Other halls constructed in the same Western style (i.e.,
the Civil Engineering, Architecture, and Communications Halls) highlighted advances made during the previous twenty years of colonial rule
and housed items associated with those developments. (They thus stood in
marked contrast to the Korean display halls, which exhibited only the
colony's primary goods and the tools used to produce them.) Along the
way to the recreational area, visitors could explore buildings exhibiting
representative items from several metropolitan cities (i.e., Osaka, Kyoto,
Tokyo, Nagasaki, and Nagoya) and individual prefectures (i.e., Nara and
Hokkaidō). The event also featured halls from each of Japan's overseas
holdings, including Karafuto, Taiwan, and Manchuria-Mongolia; the
South Seas was the only exception to this display of the empire.[99]

Also interspersed among the display halls of the empire were buildings
representing the peninsula's thirteen provinces. Unlike the "Korean"
halls, which colonial planners designed, local residents actively participated in creating a self-image for these provincial buildings.[100] With the
exception of the South P'yŏng'an Hall, these buildings were constructed
in a modernist style not unlike those representing metropolitan locations,
suggesting that the colony and its inhabitants could compete with the
more developed parts of the empire. Rather than relying on "traditional"
architectural forms, designers of the North Kyŏngsang Province Hall, for
example, drew on the latest styles of exposition architecture, which com-

FIGURE 14. Modernist style of North Kyŏngsang Province Hall. Source: *Chōsen hakurankai kinen shashinchō* (Keijō: Chōsen sōtokufu, 1930), 59.

bined overlapping rings with ornate window panels (figure 14). The modernist style of these buildings stood in contrast to the distinctly "Korean style" of architecture created to represent the Shinseikan, where goods from the colony were displayed. It also reflected local residents' enterprising activities, including special days when each province promoted regional products. By encouraging these efforts, officials thus sanctioned a carefully constructed image of a Korea whose culture remained "traditional" but whose society and economy had become "modern" after twenty years of Japanese rule.

Although exposition designers succeeded in representing the peninsula in these complimentary terms, even the residents of Keijō were not uniformly invested in its future development. Given the financial difficulties overwhelming the event by early 1929, the KCC was forced to engage in a last-minute fundraising campaign, one that highlighted the ethnic and class biases of colonial industry. From the beginning, the campaign was divisive. Some KCC members voiced concerns that most Koreans lacked the resources to make substantial contributions.[101] For their part, vocal critics in the Keijō Deliberative Council assailed the KCC's attempts to extort money from the colonized population. So

concerned was one Korean councilman, Sŏng Song-nok, that he proposed canceling the fundraising campaign all together. Two more optimistic councilmen, Kim Sa-yŏn and Han Man-hŭi, suggested a reduction in the unrealistic amount (250,000 yen) officials hoped to collect
from already impoverished Koreans.[102]

Meanwhile, popular suspicions of the KCC's fundraising scheme,
actively exposed by the Korean-language press, undercut official
attempts to convince poorer individuals to invest in the upcoming exposition. An article published in the *Tonga ilbo,* for example, reported
that a selfish KCC member had used donations to host a private party.[103]
Worse yet, accusations emerged that local agents were forcing Koreans
to make contributions. According to a report published just weeks
before the event, two South Chŏlla Province officials in Sunch'ŏn visited
a forty-four-year-old man named Kim Pu-ho, a local landlord. When
they requested a contribution, Mr. Kim refused, responding that he
could not spare the extra funds. At this point, the two officials tried to
convince him to acquiesce, but their efforts only provoked Mr. Kim to
respond with violence, which resulted in his arrest.[104] This dramatic
example underscores the heavy-handed methods officials used to solicit
donations, efforts that discouraged even middle-class Koreans from
contributing precious funds during harsh economic times.

Despite ongoing opposition, the KCC continued its fundraising
efforts, calling on neighborhood administrators and parish leaders to
promote their own campaigns.[105] Still, the KCC proved unable to elicit
sufficient funds from individual contributors, and, as a result, was
forced to turn to local businesses and metropolitan enterprises with
strong interests in the colonial economy. For instance, the Korea Bank
and the Development Bank, two important financial institutions based
in the capital, each promised to donate twelve thousand yen to the fundraising campaign. Officials also squeezed twenty thousand yen from
Keijō Electric, the company that ran the city's streetcars. Discussions
ensued to enlist Mitsui Bussan and Mitsubishi, both large transnational
corporations with offices in Korea, to contribute thirty thousand yen
each.[106] To meet their goal, the head of the KCC even traveled to Tokyo
in the summer of 1929 to secure a large donation from the Central
Korea Association, a metropolitan organization comprising former
colonial bureaucrats and prominent businessmen.[107]

Failure to elicit financial support from most Koreans also meant that
officials had to rely on income derived from exhibition-goers, many of
whom were mobilized as part of group tours. Even after the event began

on September 12, organizers continued to agonize over revenue from ticket sales. Just twenty days before the exposition ended on October 31, officials admitted that less than 75 percent of the one million visitors that they needed to attract to finance the event had, in fact, attended. Fearing that admissions might decrease during the final three weeks, they even considered extending the exposition in order to meet their quota, an anxious proposal referenced in an official newspaper that typically championed high attendance rates as a way of quantifying the event's popularity.[108] In the end, organizers obviated the need for an extension by drawing a large number of countryside groups. From the outset, event promoters had predicted that nearly half of an estimated seven hundred thousand rural exposition-goers would visit Keijō as part of tours. This figure more than tripled that of the eighty thousand who attended the exhibition in 1915 as members of tour groups.[109] To facilitate nearly three hundred thousand group visitors for the exposition in 1929, the colonial state relied on intermediary organizations like the KCC, which transported large numbers of people from the countryside at tightly scheduled intervals. According to one preevent estimate, an average of sixteen thousand railroad travelers would pass through Keijō Train Station each day during the exposition, an increase of nearly ten thousand passengers over an ordinary day in the capital city.[110] As a result of these coordinated efforts, officials managed to exceed their initial expectations, drawing more than 1.1 million paid admissions and a total of nearly 1.5 million visitors.[111]

Even as cultural rule sought to saturate the fabric of colonial society more deeply with a multiethnic ideology of material progress, it also created a new political space for Korean writers to critique the social unevenness and cultural violence of this governing program. Nationalist commentators of this conservative persuasion excoriated officials for callously forcing indigent peasants to finance a costly exposition, even while unabashedly distancing themselves from these "ignorant" subalterns by touting their own "enlightened" credentials. Moreover, they criticized organizers for failing to ensure that Korean merchants and innkeepers, individuals who had proactively invested in this event, would benefit from the onetime influx of tourists. Themselves members of the nascent middle class, these writers expressed their own stakes in the exposition and thus actively embraced the enriching possibilities of Japan's modernity. Yet in spite of their outward enthusiasm, not all elite visitors wholeheartedly bought into the incorporative logic of material assimilation. As a result, their responses to displays of the

Korean economy and their nation's cultural traditions reveal countervailing resentments of colonial subordination that ranged from witty satire to melancholic outrage. Essentially, these commentators, without aiming to overturn the economic system as their leftist counterparts had advocated, sought a larger portion of its wealth, first for themselves, but ultimately for their colonized nation.

While the Government-General publicized attendance statistics as a demonstrable indication of the exposition's popularity, nationalist accounts from Korean-language newspapers took great pains to reveal the coercive underside of this mass mobilization campaign, one that disproportionately burdened colonized peasants, especially those living at a considerable distance from the capital city. For example, the *Tonga ilbo* reported that local officials in North Kyŏngsang Province were visiting various townships several times a day, compelling residents to visit Keijō. Despite tearful complaints against such forms of intimidation, more than two thousand inhabitants of Sangju eventually acquiesced.[112] Another troubling account alleged that township heads in the same province were forcing residents to pawn clothing and dishware to pay for their visit.[113] Such coercion became a source of increasing stress for Korean peasants, whose plight bourgeois writers used to wage a nationalist indictment of the event. As these critics were quick to publicize, the trip to Keijō required not only fees for admission and attractions, but also travel and lodging costs as well as spending money. According to one concerned report, combined expenses amounted to as much as twenty yen. Referencing KCC figures predicting seven hundred thousand visits from rural Koreans, this nationalist critic calculated that exposition-related expenditures would further drain the countryside of at least one million yen. Given that peasant households paid between fifty and seventy yen in taxes each year, the additional squeeze of attending this commemoration accounted for as much as 40 percent of total tax expenditures, a situation reminiscent of shrine contributions forced on impecunious Korean residents by Japanese parishioners. So financially burdensome was a visit to the exposition that tax bureau officials themselves began to worry whether the peasantry could afford their upcoming dues.[114]

Thus, Korean elites decried the celebration of 1929 as a costly, Japanese-centered event that would further impoverish the colonized masses. In one *Tonga ilbo* editorial, the bourgeois authors agreed that expositions generally produce some material benefits, but argued that individuals below the middle classes could not enjoy the fruits of such events. In particular, they bemoaned that poor peasants were being convinced to take out usurious loans to attend the event. This risky investment, they feared, would only further accelerate emigration to the metropole and to Manchuria, already heavily populated sites of a working-class diaspora. Reviving Confucian morality as a critical resource, they faulted officials for failing to provide Koreans with an ethical policy of welfare: "It is moral conduct for the rich [to sacrifice] their opulence for the sake of the masses, but [doing the same] with the wealth of the poor will lead to their bankruptcy."[115] Or, as another editorialist put it, aiming his words at an ameliorative solution: "The ideal of politics should be to avoid creating one hundred beggars, rather than producing ten rich people."[116] Although most of these public critiques implicitly equated the rich with Japanese (but which also included native landlords) and the poor with Koreans, other nationalist commentators made even more explicit associations between the event's upper-class interests and the colonizing nation. Yun Ch'i-ho (1865–1945), for example, a privileged Korean man who frequently wrote disparagingly of the colonized masses, upbraided organizers for creating an unfair burden. As he wrote in his diary:

> The whole show is a show of the Japanese, by the Japanese, and for the Japanese. Its objective is to advertise Korea—its resources and attractions— to the Japanese to induce them to come over and to help themselves. The poor Koreans are made to foot the bills for running the exposition. Coming between two famine years with the price of rice unhulled at six sen per mal [approximately 18 liters], the Koreans of the provinces can't afford to bear this squeeze-dry policy. With the autumn taxes coming no sooner than this exposition closes, the Japanese land grabbers and usurious moneylenders will grow fat to the bursting point.[117]

In addition to decrying how the event skewed wealth distribution toward the metropole, Korean critics denounced the exposition for funneling peasants' already scarce resources into the showcase capital. In particular, they feared that farmers, deemed incapable of properly regulating their material desires, would squander money borrowed from financial cooperatives and loan sharks on expensive items they could not afford. Again using Confucian rhetoric to caution against the specter of extravagant consumption, these pundits also pointed out the hypocrisy of the Government-General's long-standing efforts to encourage the colonized masses to save and produce, rather than spend and consume.[118]

Furthermore, writers dreaded that the dazzling displays in the commercial district of Hon-machi would lead reckless Korean consumers to purchase expensive items at Mitsukoshi and other Japanese department stores, thereby threatening the livelihood of Korean businesses along Chongno.[119] And in fact, a number of commercial establishments in the northern village fell into bankruptcy due to unforeseen market changes caused by the upcoming exposition. Seeking to profit from future increases in demand, some Korean merchants, not unlike their impoverished rural counterparts, took out large sums of money from banks or loan sharks in order to purchase additional goods, stocking their shelves with up to ten times what they normally carried. However, an unexpected shortage of customers forced four major commercial houses to close their doors even before the event began, throwing the Korean merchants of Chongno into what one alarmist report called a "great panic."[120] A number of Korean inn owners also struggled to capitalize on the exposition when designated groups of rural tourists failed to stay at their appointed facilities. In response, five representatives of the Korean inn owners' association filed a complaint with the KCC, demanding immediate compensation for their losses.[121] Their complaint, published in the local Japanese-language newspaper, read as follows: "As for the exposition, we have [each] paid two yen for association fees, one yen for advertising fees, and fifty sen for signboards—a total of 3.5 yen. Ten days have passed since the opening of the exposition, but . . . only two inns have customers, while the other forty establishments do not have a single customer. They have just paid the 3.5 yen, which is meaningless."[122] As this objection suggests, the KCC had mobilized Korean inn owners to work on its behalf, insisting that they join an association and pay organizational fees. However, their investments in the exposition, like those of the Chongno merchants, had not necessarily paid off, leaving many Koreans in the service industry with debts they struggled to repay.

It is worth noting that other Korean participants did succeed in taking advantage of the exposition for their own personal ends. The "female guard," approximately six hundred of whom the KCC hired for two months to serve as tour guides, is a good example. Two-thirds of the female guards chosen for employment were Korean, ostensibly so that they could communicate with the large number of Korean-speaking visitors to the exposition.[123] As colonized employees, they also served as a symbol of native labor incorporated into the multiethnic market of the Japanese empire. To qualify for employment as a guard, officials required that women possess a common school diploma, be between the ages of sixteen and thirty, and have a healthy body.[124] Given this focus on their young age and healthy figures, it is little wonder that the media represented these women in highly sexualized terms, referring to them as princesses and associating them with the eroticized café waitress.[125] For example, in a cartoon appearing in the Korean section of a popular metropolitan newspaper, a female guard sits next to a display booth, the contents of which she explains to approaching visitors. However, rather than observing the items on display, the men in the cartoon are instead drawn to this exposition worker, whom they surround and ogle as an object of sexual attraction. As the accompanying caption reads: "At a certain display hall, there has been a sudden increase in young, male spectators. Even middle-age men go there every day. One might think that there is an unusual item on display. It turns out that these men are going to catch a glimpse of pretty girls, the female guard princesses. Can you believe it?"[126]

Yet female guards also took advantage of this sexualized environment to pursue their own material and erotic interests. For example, some of the guards became known as "kiss girls," reportedly selling pecks on the cheek for fifty sen each, with only two needed to quickly double their daily salary. In addition to moneymaking, the kissing business opened up new opportunities for young women to pursue their own romantic desires, much to the chagrin of organizers. According to highly critical newspaper reports, a number of female guards used their position at the exposition to meet attractive "modern boys." Some of them even absconded, taking their male companions on tours around the event grounds. Others made prior dates, unabashedly indulging in love talk with men in front of spectators.[127] Although clearly objectified by male visitors and harshly condemned in the press, kiss girls managed to both sell and experience desire, transforming the event grounds from a pedagogical laboratory into an erotic marketplace.

Other bourgeois exposition-goers, who also embraced the event's enriching and liberating possibilities, continued to prioritize ethnicity over class, gender, generation, or region as the most useful category with which to wage a nationalist critique of this Japanese-dominated event. Their writings highlight the economic inequalities and aesthetic violence of cultural rule as well as its inherent limitations as a divisive strategy of colonial governmentality. For example, a commentary penned by Kim Ki-gon, an exhibitor from Hamhŭng, the capital of South Hamgyŏng Province, recounted the sense of disappointment he felt as a potential beneficiary of the exposition. In his first impressions of the event of 1929, Mr. Kim found the buildings "spectacular," the decorations "dazzling," and the grounds "expansive." However, when he observed the contents of the display halls, Mr. Kim was disenchanted by what he described as their "scantiness" and "repetitiveness." Having visited the Rice Hall, he also criticized designers for failing to choose display techniques that effectively exhibited different forms of this staple and that properly highlighted local variations between products. As a result of his own experience, Mr. Kim predicted that peasants might be awed by the splendor of the exposition grounds, but that they, like he, would ultimately return to their villages without a solid impression of the display items. However, Mr. Kim did welcome modern advances in agricultural productivity, hoping to use them to promote local products, and he even went so far as to propose display techniques that would produce better results. For example, he recommended that future events exhibit products in separate buildings, rather than packing them into a single hall. Praising the usefulness of statistics, he also called on officials to produce more scientific and detailed materials to accompany the items on display. This measure would allow serious spectators like himself to obtain the information necessary to compete with rivals and thereby increase profits.[128]

If Mr. Kim criticized the exposition for its inability to produce benefits for Koreans with direct investments, the journalist Yu Kwang-yŏl disapproved of the inferior position that the Korean economy continued to occupy within the Japanese empire. In spite of its name, the "Korea Exposition," Mr. Yu argued, had not been created for the sake of Koreans. Therefore, he preferred to call it the "Exposition for the Japanese in Korea." By displaying Korea's agricultural products, the event of 1929 encouraged large capitalists from the metropole to invest in the peninsula. According to Mr. Yu's nationalist critique, these foreign investments relegated the colonized population to the position of primary suppliers who could no longer control the direction of their country's development. What Korean agricultural products officials did put on display paled in comparison to the mining, forestry, and industrial interests controlled by foreign investors. As Mr. Yu wrote of this inequality, "Koreans should, of course, be the protagonists at the Korea Exposition but, instead, the Japanese have become the protagonists, inverting the [relationship between] host and guest."

Mr. Yu's critique not only reflected Korea's inferiority vis-à-vis the metropole, but also disclosed the peninsula's lagging position within the imperial economy. When he visited the Taiwanese Pavilion, for example, he discovered that the bananas eaten in Korea during the summer months were actually imported from this tropical island. In another hall, Mr. Yu observed grazing sheep from the Mongolian tundra and Manchurian soybean lees and chestnuts that Korean peasants consumed in large quantities. Linking these products to the shifting trajectory of the imperial economy, Mr. Yu anxiously predicted that Manchuria and Mongolia would surpass Korea in terms of livestock and agricultural production, while the metropole would continue to monopolize industrial power. This scenario left the peninsula's economy somewhere in the middle as a "half-agricultural, half-industrial state" where the labor of colonized Koreans would be exchanged to promote Manchurian agriculture and Japanese industry. Based on this assessment, Mr. Yu concluded that the myriad products exhibited in display halls only functioned to promote the uneven operation of the imperial economy.[129]

Such critiques of the exposition as promoting Japanese economic domination also spilled over into the cultural sphere in harsh condemnations of the violent destruction of Kyŏngbok Palace and its inauthentic reconstruction. In one account, the participants—a newspaper reporter (K) accompanying a well-educated, bourgeois man (Mr. S) and his wife (Mrs. S)—told the story of their visit to this event in the form of a satirical dialogue.[130] After entering the former palace grounds, the reporter K explained to Mr. and Mrs. S that he could not understand why Japanese newspapers bragged about the "pure Korean style" of exposition architecture. In response, Mr. S also questioned the authenticity of event buildings, which he understood as having been modeled after a Japanese style of architecture found at Nagoya and Himeji castles. Making direct reference to the strategic repositioning of Kwanghwa Gate as the exposition's main entrance, he continued his critique of the inauthentic "Japanization" of Korean palace architecture. In particular, Mr. S described the structure of this important Korean landmark as irrevocably despoiled, having been reconstructed with a "Japanese-style turret." Aghast at the deplorable fate of Kwanghwa Gate, he responded to the other extant palace monument, the Kyŏnghoe Pavilion, with "immeasurably deep emotions." Gazing at the Kyŏnghoe Pavilion, which he described as basking in the morning sun, he could not help but "be full of melancholy" for this building's irretrievable past.

The group's displeasure with the Japanization of native palace architecture also explains how they skipped or made only brief stops at display halls along the Korean corridor, creating a route considerably different from that recommended by the KCC. Even at other halls, they found the displays unappealing, disappointing, or trivial. For example, in the Hall of Hygiene, constructed to promote "modern" health reforms and discourage "traditional" folk remedies, the group came upon a sign that read, "Those under twenty years of age may not enter," under which stood a throng of people waiting to see what stood behind a black curtain. Pushed through the crowds into a small display room, Mr. S. discovered the private parts of diseased female specimens infected with gonorrhea and syphilis.[131] Disgusted by the sight, Mrs. S, complaining of head pains, urged the group to proceed to the Reference Hall, only to be disappointed by the main attraction, a robot. Answering Mrs. S's question about why the robot's ears moved mechanically like those of a cow, the reporter caustically proclaimed, "That is a sign that [Japan] has not yet moved beyond an infantile science." Disappointed with material progress ostensibly made during twenty years of Japanese rule, the group also found themselves repelled by the Metropolitan Hall and decided to bypass this important structure altogether. As Mr. S put it curtly, "Let's skip this one. There cannot be anything [special] to see."

Following brief visits to various regional halls and entertainment attractions, the group finally returned to the Korean corridor, only to find the exhibits in these buildings poorly designed and thus unable to attract even the best-educated viewers. Mr. S described the display techniques in the Education, Arts, and Handicrafts Hall as so complex that they prevented spectators from focusing on any one thing. When discussing a revolving statistical exhibit, for example, he criticized organizers for creating a time-consuming display for which no one had the patience to wait. The reporter agreed, predicting that ineffective exhibition techniques would discourage visitors from taking the time to observe easier-to-view displays. The group found similar problems in the Socioeconomics Hall. Even Mr. S, who had majored in political economy at a private Japanese university, struggled to decipher arcane displays of statistical advancements. In response, the reporter criticized this building for its unambiguous ideological bent, boldly referring to it as the "hall for the promotion of assimilation."

Laughing, the three exposition-goers left the Socioeconomics Hall for brief stops at the Industrial Halls and the Rice Hall, the most important colonial displays of Korean "progress." Although Mrs. S expressed excitement at finally seeing goods made by Koreans in the North Industrial Hall, Mr. S tempered her enthusiasm by reminding the group of Korea's weak economic position within the empire. More specifically, this political economy expert informed his wife that the value of imports to the colony outnumbered Korean production by two or three times, a figure he substantiated with detailed import statistics. A similar scenario occurred in the South Industrial Hall, where the group observed a model farm sponsored by an official agency promoting agricultural improvements. Mr. S questioned this display of idealized village life from the point of view of its inhabitants, the colonized peasantry, repeating oft-cited criticism of poor harvests and mentioning various human disasters associated with the countryside's rapid development. Mrs. S also upbraided officials for the Rice Hall's inability to gain the peasantry's attention. According to her evaluation, the only redeeming part of this hall was a collection of products made from this glutinous staple, all displayed under a Japanese sign that read, "the power to produce goods." In typical fashion, the reporter agreed with Mrs. S, commenting how more effective display techniques could have convinced colonized visitors that their investments in the exposition would produce concomitant rewards.

Held amid a worldwide depression, the Korea Exposition perhaps best exposed the harsh realities and practical limits of cultural rule. That various classes, ages, sexes, and regions of Koreans engaged with the palace grounds of 1929 in considerably different ways, as had been true at the exhibitions of 1907 and 1915, suggests the highly uneven rewards of material assimilation, despite its universalist promise of enhancing everyone's well-being. Even middle-class Korean elites who eventually embraced the enriching possibilities offered by the exposition of 1929 continued to lament the weak position occupied by their colonized nation, most of whose destitute inhabitants failed to benefit from the ideology of development so carefully exhibited in the display halls. According to their nationalist critiques, reckless outlays at this commemoration by poorer Koreans, in turn, tended to go toward luxury items at the city's department stores, leaving small-scale and local merchants to suffer. For them, the event revealed the insidious ways that material assimilation tended to redistribute already scarce resources in the direction of more wealthy investors, especially Japanese business interests. However, individual engagements with colonial industry, like that pursued by the kiss girl, also uncover how Koreans of various backgrounds rearticulated the meaning and even reoriented the function of a powerful place aimed at convincing them to buy into subordinated roles in the imperial economy.

# CHAPTER 4

# Civic Assimilation

*Sanitary Life in Neighborhood Keijō*

As the previous chapter showed, the Government-General used expositions and other mass media to inculcate industriousness, which, organizers hoped, would serve as the basis for continuing to subordinate the
peninsula's economy to metropolitan interests. Although officials succeeded in displaying an ideological message of "progress," the temporary nature of such events and their festival-like atmosphere prevented
most Korean viewers from adequately cultivating the attitudes and
practices necessary to support this colonial project. Meanwhile, the limited reach of Seoul Shrine and its festivals, as chapter 2 illustrated,
meant that officials could not rely on the imperial house to create a
united spirit of "Japaneseness" based on loyalty. As they worked to fill
this gap with an influential complex of their own design (Korea Shrine),
the Government-General also attempted to promote practical ethics
with which the city's residents could contribute to—or, at least, not
obstruct—the health of the colonial city.

This chapter focuses, then, on the promotion of *eisei/wisaeng,* or
what Ruth Rogaski has aptly rendered as "hygienic modernity" in her
study of the Chinese treaty port Tienstin.[1] Although not necessarily
envisioned as such by its government architects, the encouragement of
Koreans to identify with Japanese-dictated norms of modern life in the
area of hygiene, while never fully embraced by all residents, became an
increasingly powerful mechanism of colonial subjectification. To illus-
trate the mediating role played by what I am calling civic assimilation,

this chapter focuses on the Korean-populated neighborhoods of Keijō, an important meeting point for colonial policies of public health and existing healing practices. By mobilizing the colonized population to participate in semiannual cleanups, hygiene exhibitions, and other media events led by sanitation cooperatives, officials sought to create an organic connection between the health practices of individual Koreans and the overall salubrity of their surrounding communities, beginning locally with the family, neighborhood, and city, extending outward to include the state, and ultimately encompassing the entire empire. Although these reforms produced some verifiable results, a number of obstacles prevented the implementation of civic assimilation. Perhaps most obstructive in this regard was the decision to utilize an intrusive police force to impose Japanese standards of hygienic practice on the colonized masses, whom authorities assumed responded best to authority but who learned to parry interventions through various forms of everyday resistance. Only through the activities of cultural nationalists, also eager advocates of hygienic modernity, did officials begin to cure Keijō's ill repute as the empire's "diseased city," even though the colonial state continued to privilege the health of Japanese settlers over most Koreans. Meanwhile, the colonized underclass, most of whom eschewed biomedical treatment and relied instead on herbal remedies and other unsanctioned techniques of healing, remained the despised object of liberal sympathy in the bourgeois campaigns of both Japanese imperialists and Korean nationalists. The common linguistic idiom "same bed, different dreams" *(tongsang imong;* J: *dōshō imu)* perhaps best captures this ironic and perilous situation, one whose origins lie in the imperial politics of the turn of the century.

## TWO COMPETITIVE HEALTH REGIMES ON THE PATH TO ANNEXATION

Indeed, the hygienic regime of the early colonial state grew out of biopolitical challenges facing two governing authorities during the final decades of the Chosŏn dynasty. Against a backdrop of recurring outbreaks of contagious disease, Japanese officials struggled to protect the health of Hanyang's growing expatriate population, whose numbers increased from fewer than one hundred in 1885 to more than 170,000 by 1910. At the same time, Korean modernizers mounted increasingly intrusive, if only partially effective, efforts to reform the allegedly unhygienic practices of the city's underclass population.[2] Each group attempted to harness the health of the urban body to its own sanitary regime as part of a larger bid for political power over the peninsula.

Ad hoc health policies aimed at protecting Japanese expatriates only slowly came to include resident Koreans, the latter seen primarily as an etiological threat to the well-being of the former rather than as self-governing subjects worthy of improved welfare. In the summer of 1895, just months after the Sino-Japanese War ended, a cholera outbreak from the Korean-populated part of the city penetrated the confines of the Japanese settlement. In response, affluent expatriates pooled five hundred yen to construct a temporary quarantine facility, the forerunner of Junkain Hospital.[3] In spite of these makeshift measures, the outbreak of contagious diseases, reoccurring in the summers of 1902 and 1904, continued to pose a regulatory problem. To combat the scourge, representatives of the Japanese settlement took additional measures, establishing waste disposal sites at the South Gate and outside the East Gate, installing excrement disposal buckets in Korean homes, ending the indiscriminate disposal of excreta on city streets, and having waste collected by designated laborers. At a meeting of settlement associations from across the peninsula in 1904, expatriate leaders decided to further systematize sanitation by conducting semiannual cleanups in Japanese neighborhoods and encouraging Koreans to do the same.[4]

A more systemic approach to urban hygiene began in 1905, when the settlement association, now under the legal aegis of the Residency-General, launched a system of sanitation cooperatives.[5] Adopted from metropolitan organizations, sanitation cooperatives functioned as intermediaries linking the policy goals of the protocolonial state to the hygienic conditions of local society. Like their counterparts in Meiji Japan, the leaders of Korea's sanitation cooperatives focused on promoting household and personal hygiene as well as conveying basic notions of public health. They also worked closely with the police to ensure that residents participated in semiannual cleanups, and they subjected symptoms of contagious disease to biomedical inspection and treatment.[6] Sanitation cooperatives thus occupied a central position in what Ambo Norio has called a "dual surveillance structure."[7] On the one hand, this regulatory system allowed itinerant doctors and police officers to turn an outside, medical gaze upon potentially uncooperative residents. On the other hand, it also facilitated a popular, inside gaze by relying on local leaders to monitor the sanitary practices of uncooperative neighbors.

When put into practice, this dual surveillance structure did not necessarily function as effectively as its official creators might have hoped, even among the city's Japanese residents. In 1909, when yet another cholera outbreak took the lives of over one thousand residents, settler leaders of sanitation cooperatives used their supervisory role to make door-to-door visits among Japanese expatriates, warning them about the epidemic and urging them to take hygienic precautions.[8] Although some inhabitants heeded their exhortations, other, "incredibly apathetic individuals," to quote one chastising newspaper account, ignored their own ailments or refused to take advantage of cooperatives' services. Worse yet, some medical officials failed to provide treatment to symptomatic individuals.[9] And finally, angry at the lack of official remuneration for leaders, settler elites waged a campaign to abolish the system of cooperatives. Although they did not fully succeed, their efforts did weaken the system: in fact, only twenty-three sanitation cooperatives were functioning when the colonial state took over in 1910, and not until the settlement's political dissolution in 1914 did that figure grow to nearly fifty.[10]

Meanwhile, in the northern village, Korean modernizers struggled to institute an autonomous program of neighborhood sanitation. While the Residency-General encouraged local leaders to implement hygienic reforms, it feared public health measures that might undercut its authority. This dynamic is perhaps best seen in the fate of the Hansŏng People's Association, an organization in Seoul founded under the leadership of Yu Kil-jun (1856–1914) in October 1907, just months after passage of the second protectorate treaty. A reformer with close connections to Meiji-style enlightenment projects, Yu hoped to use this organ to promote self-government along the lines of the Japanese settler association. Like sanitation cooperatives, the association paid close attention to issues of public health, establishing hygiene divisions in many of its branch offices.[11] However, the Residency-General quickly depoliticized the association, forcing it to concentrate on pro-Japanese activities.[12] Later, during the cholera outbreak in 1909, the protectorate government used its central office to instruct members of the disease prevention committee.[13] Thus, an increasing powerful protocolonial state not only promoted its own settler-centered program of public health, but also hindered Koreans from establishing themselves as intermediaries between state and society.

In order to reach the Korean population of Keijō, the Residency-General created its own direct, forceful, and instrumental policy of sanitary rule through the Seoul Sanitation Association (SSA). Bypassing local professionals and residents, this organization established its

authority from above. It was, in fact, the Japanese crown prince Yoshihito (1879–1926) and the future Taishō emperor (r. 1912–26) who
helped found the SSA when he visited the peninsula in 1907. Reportedly
"troubled" by recent outbreaks of cholera and "deeply concerned"
about the sanitary conditions of Korea, Yoshihito donated thirty thousand yen to launch a more systematic and wide-ranging sanitization,
one that occupied an astronomical portion (85 percent) of the city's
budget![14] With its headquarters located in the City Police Board and
branch offices established in police stations throughout Keijō, the SSA
worked with the hygiene police to collect and dispose of human excrement. It also took charge of collecting garbage, dredging sewers, and
installing public bathrooms. To improve the overall salubriousness of
the urban environment, the SSA planted rows of white willow trees,
seen by officials as the purifying "lungs" of the city, along Keijō's thoroughfares.[15] In response to the recurrence of cholera and other contagious diseases, the SSA also led campaigns to build a quarantine hospital and regulate the hygienic conditions of butcher houses. However,
this draconian system of reform, led by police officers, was not well
received.[16] Furthermore, its heavy-handed approach differed from ones
implemented in metropolitan cities, where doctors and other professionals could check the arbitrary power of the police. (After 1907,
Korean officials did accompany Japanese police doctors in promoting
the benefits of hygienic modernity, but only as linguistic intermediaries.) Meanwhile, the blatant overpricing of biomedical treatments and
forced inoculations created a deep sense of popular distrust, leading
some residents to believe that the police were trying to poison, rather
than heal, them.

To finance its projects, the SSA, whose duties the Keijō municipal
government eventually assumed in 1914, received largesse from both
the Japanese metropole and the Great Han Empire. A monthly service
fee (eight sen for Japanese, two sen for Koreans) provided additional
funding to support its wide-ranging activities. But in practice, this
monthly system severely disrupted existing practices of sanitation, both
for fertilizer merchants (who survived by converting human feces into
agricultural fertilizer) and Keijō residents. Nationalist reporters were
quick to censure these developments, urging Koreans to compete with
the profit-driven motives and heavy-handed tactics of Japanese interests. Contradicting colonialists' claims that the city's unsanitary conditions resulted from unhygienic Koreans, one critic explained the situation as follows: "In former days, Korean fertilizer merchants collected

excrement every day. However, because Japanese sanitation companies come around to collect once every ten or twenty days, shit piles up like mounds in and around people's houses and, therefore, popular resentment is widespread. . . . Hitherto, Korean fertilizer merchants gathered human waste everyday without charging people a single penny; however, after establishing so-called sanitation companies, a fee of two chŏn is levied on every room."[17]

According to other reports, many Koreans, especially the city's large indigent population, failed or refused to pay this fee, leading to heavy fines (up to five yen) and indiscriminate detentions (for as long as ten days). As a stopgap measure, the SSA hired destitute Koreans at low wages (one-third those of Japanese laborers) to carry out the dirty work of waste collection, rather than be forced to pay the sanitation fee.[18] Meanwhile, the police made intrusive home visits, threatening residents by confiscating food in lieu of the sanitation fee.[19] Some reports even mentioned that Japanese officers beat Koreans who offered to pay for a less fortunate friend or family member.[20] A newspaper article captured the violence underlying this project as follows: "the dunning threat [of sanitation fees] is more pressing than a falling meteor; even chickens and dogs [around the house] cannot be at peace due to the financial demands of police officers."[21] For Korean waste collectors, the Japanese monopolization of night soil also meant a loss of profits; for their countryside consumers, it resulted in a lower supply of fertilizer at higher prices. As one nationalist critic wrote not long before annexation:

> The Japanese take advantage of this opening to use their fertilizer companies to collect human excrement within the city walls and sell it at a high price to farmers outside the city walls. In this way, Koreans' excrement is put in the hands of the Japanese. As a result, the profit produced by hundreds and thousands of bushels of human fertilizer enters the hands of the Japanese. . . . Alas, if our brethren fail to understand business competition in this age of business competition and stand by idly, they will perish and meet their death.[22]

So disruptive was the new sanitation system that, in 1909, the SSA allowed displaced Korean fertilizer merchants to use its equipment to provide night soil to desperate farmers.[23] This measure aimed to placate the former, while reincorporating them into a colonial system of urban sanitation that continued to face a number of regulatory problems.

Even after officials assumed control over institutional reforms, they had far less success in modifying the attitudes of individuals Koreans, whose own hygienic practices also had an impact on the city's sanitary conditions. Disturbed by the deleterious consequences of inadequate lavatory facilities in Korean homes, the SSA attempted to reform the habits of the (semi)colonized population by making individuals publicly participate in their own self-surveillance and self-regulation. To this end, officials installed a number of public facilities throughout the city (seventy-nine by 1913), particularly in the northern village. However, seeing these facilities was not necessarily believing in or cooperating with the norms of colonial hygiene. In fact, some Koreans treated public bathrooms in ways that diverged greatly from the desired outcomes of the new sanitary regime. The SSA's own report described these tactics with a typically superior tone: "Koreans—who, from the beginning, lacked knowledge of health and who have not developed a sense of civic morality—sometimes break down the bathroom door, steal it, and use it as firewood for underground heating in their homes. They try to defecate in urinals, urinate outside of cesspools, and use public toilets as if they were the property of their own families."[24] The *Maeil sinbo* also reported that Koreans uprooted the willow trees recently planted to serve as the city's lungs. Such practices suggest that Koreans struggled to procure an adequate supply of firewood to heat their homes, a pressing economic concern that undercut expectations that they should adhere to unfamiliar and stringent notions of hygienic propriety. To deter such behavior and induce "proper" hygienic practices, officials resorted to harsh tactics, whipping offenders and punishing them with a three to four yen fine.[25]

Rather than recognize Koreans' economic concerns, the SSA resorted to a colonial discourse created by Okita Kinjō, Usuda Zan'un (1877–1956), and other Japanese pundits whom I have elsewhere called "popular ethnographers" to understand their behavior.[26] These amateur travel writers used specific elements of Korean culture—the native folksong Arirang, for example—to argue that an insular form of clanism had prevented the emergence of civic consciousness, including sanitary self-regulation. To these Orientalist discourses, the SSA added the power of numbers to explain and define Koreans' behavior.[27] From detailed tables enumerating the monthly quantity of excrement collected and the city's population, the SSA quantified Korean bodies and their feces, transforming the many individuals comprising the category of colonized Korean into a singular image centering on their unhygienic practices.

According to the SSA's narrative, verbal exhortations by the hygiene police led to knowledge of public health among Keijō's Korean population, resulting in a reduction of the sanitary force from 473 in 1909 to 287 in 1914.[28] While self-congratulation adorns many documents in the colonial archive, it is important to approach such statements critically, treating them not simply as a reflection of the politicized reality they purport to describe but also as "technologies of rule."[29] Indeed, if one follows the number of police officers and gendarmes (which remained about the same during the 1910s), Keijō's police and military officer-to-resident ratio (which outnumbered that of Tokyo by almost four to one), and numerous and unprecedented minor regulations instituted during the 1910s,[30] one can conclude that Koreans' continued evasion of Japanese sanitary impositions actually required an increasingly sophisticated formula of coercive and persuasive measures in order to produce the kind of everyday civic morality colonial officials hoped would lead to civic assimilation.

## CREATING AN EVERYDAY CIVIC MORALITY IN EARLY KEIJŌ

Once it gained full control over the peninsula in 1910, the Government-General transferred authority over hygienic matters from the Korean Home Ministry's Sanitary Bureau to its own Police Supervisory Board.[31] Although the police lacked the knowledge to implement a system of public health, colonial officials predictably justified this administrative reorganization in terms of a "differing state of affairs," a reference to the allegedly low level of civilization exhibited by Koreans in comparison to their Japanese counterparts.[32] Under this logic of racial difference, the hygiene police took far-reaching license to limit personal freedoms in the name of "protecting the 'common benefit' of the 'people.'"[33] This innocuous language echoed the egalitarian ideology of the emperor's benevolent gaze (J: *isshi dōjin; ilsi tong'in*), but the sanitary system clearly privileged Japanese settlers over colonized Koreans. Meanwhile, officials encouraged the latter to become self-regulating subjects of hygienic modernity, but without the state's commitment to improving their personal or collective welfare. For their part, most Koreans submitted to police authority only when it impinged on their lives, engaging in an everyday politics of evasion and concealment that quietly undercut rule by sanitation.

Such dynamics were perhaps best manifested in neighborhood clean-ups, hygienic rituals formally institutionalized in 1912. Led by the police in the fall and spring, these semiannual events called on Koreans (and Japanese) to become active, if subordinate, agents of the official program for sanitary reform. Detailed requirements included tidying in and around one's home, exposing household items to the sun's sanitizing rays, and airing out dampened *tatami* mats (but not unremovable Korean-style flooring). They also demanded that residents clean and conduct repairs on wells, toilets, and sewage ditches, facilities thought to carry waterborne illnesses. Unspecified stipulations allowed inspecting officers and cooperative leaders wide latitude to impose other regulations related to excrement and trash removal.[34] These regulations not only aimed to produce objectively "clean" streets and "tidy" homes, but also encouraged inhabitants to make subjective connections between their own health and that of their local communities. At a lecture held in 1910, Yamane Masatsugu (1857–1925), a government doctor, explained this connection according to a well-known Meiji maxim: "Because hygiene means making one's body healthy, if each individual citizen exerts him- or herself, it is only natural that the state will become rich and its army powerful."[35] Although many Koreans would struggle to understand, let alone accept, this imperialist logic, government authorities required that they support the police's sanitizing mission by becoming active participants in neighborhood cleanups. Intruding into the realm of what they called individual hygiene, police officers thus persuaded and, more often than not, coerced residents to become self-regulating individuals capable of ensuring their own health and, by extension, that of the surrounding community.[36]

Insofar as these sanitary regulations all concerned the home and the area around it, Korean women, especially those of the relatively small middle class, came to play a particularly important role in fostering an everyday civic morality.[37] Colonial officials went as far as to call the realm of individual hygiene the principal occupation of housewives, urging them to take special care of food preparation, household cleaning, and laundering tasks. As one *Maeil sinbo* editorial reminded bourgeois women, "If housewives neglect warnings about food and drink and they dispose of rancid items, not only will all household members become sick, but they may unexpectedly lose their lives."[38] Underlining the life-and-death importance of household sanitation, the authors urged middle-class women to refrain from delegating these tasks to servants, who presumably lacked the "proper" knowledge to practice sanctioned forms of hygiene. This exhortation points not only to gender-based but also to class-based assumptions about individual hygiene as practiced by the otherwise undifferentiated category of Korean. In the spring of 1914, for example, the *Maeil sinbo* reported that the lowest rung of society, the homeless, continued to endanger Keijō's sanitary conditions. Although aggressive policies to remove makeshift shelters from the streets had shown signs of success, these "uncouth" individuals, as the editorial called them, still posed a considerable threat to the productive capacity of the city and its diverse residents.[39] The practice of individual hygiene and, by extension, the health of the urban habitat depended on a rudimentary understanding of public health, knowledge that some Korean women and most of the lower classes did not possess.

Although difficult to gauge from official records, the critical conjunction between sanitary knowledge and hygienic practice yielded mixed results. The presence of the colonial police and local officials conducting semiannual sanitizations began to condition residents to a collective rhythm of cleaning. As expected, government reports described Koreans as submitting to official directives, suggesting that they fell in line with state dictates.[40] And in fact, police officers often described the colonized population as cooperative in contributing their physical labor to sanitization projects, though resistant to financial demands. By contrast, comparatively wealthy Japanese settlers preferred to spend pocket change to install household trash cans and purchase sanitary food containers, rather than follow orders to sweep in front of their homes.[41] Whatever ethnic-based cultural differences may have existed, the threat of financial sanctions, rather than self-regulation, seems to have served as the primary motivation for Korean compliance with the sanitary guidelines. Thus warnings about the monetary cost of noncompliance frequently appeared in the *Maeil sinbo* as cautionary tales.[42] For example, a report in 1913 described the ill fate of Cho Chŏng-sŏk, a food and beverage vendor in Hyejŏm-dong who disposed of dirty water onto the street in front of his store and unsanitary waste into the sewage system. In response, the police levied a heavy fine of three yen, a sum nearly forty times the monthly sanitation fee![43] Another article from 1913 mentioned ten individuals whom the military police summoned and strictly admonished for not adequately cleaning; those still unwilling to comply were forced to pay a one yen fine.[44]

Further evidence that Koreans did not necessarily internalize hygienic attitudes comes from newspaper reports suggesting that residents carried out sanitary tasks simply to avoid police pressure. Thus, they might quickly tidy up the area around the house before police officers arrived for inspection, giving officials fewer reasons to further intrude into the home. When police officials left, however, garbage and waste reportedly accumulated until residents participated in the next semiannual cleanup.[45] As one newspaper article lamented, "Even families above the so-called middle class only [tidy up] in spring and autumn when cleanups are conducted."[46] In other words, hygienic practice, which should have begun with the cleansing of homes and worked its way outward into the social world, instead addressed the need for official approval by creating the outward appearance of sanitary propriety.

Conscious of such evasions, officials began to mobilize local elites to ensure that working-class Koreans more willingly embraced individual hygiene. For example, an article from the fall of 1913 recounted how Koreans living in Chŏngsŏn-bang, the city's central district, cleaned the area in front of their homes, but failed to expose various household items to the air and sun. As a result, the police mobilized local leaders, who patrolled their neighborhoods and admonished residents to follow sanitary regulations. Local elites also exhorted residents to cultivate hygienic ethics by carrying out occasional house cleanings, especially before semiannual cleanups, to satisfy standards monitored by the hygiene police.[47] Similarly, a *Maeil sinbo* editorial from earlier that year attempted to motivate Korean residents to treat sewage properly. This article revealed that officials had made numerous efforts to ensure the sanitary conditions of Keijō's sewers, but struggled to control the water that entered homes. Rather than awaiting police instructions, Koreans were urged to appreciate the "relationship of interests" between themselves and their surrounding communities so that unsafe water did not pollute sewers.[48]

Together, these exhortations point to ongoing fears that the southern village would be harmed by the allegedly unhygienic conditions of the northern village. A good example of this fear is found in a critique from 1916 by a Japanese policeman in charge of Chongno and its colonized residents. As he wrote, "If one tries to take a walk in [these] Korean neighborhoods, around the buildings there is a ghastly amount of blue- and yellow-colored, foul-smelling phlegm with blood vessels mixed in— so much so that there is nowhere to step."[49] Not only did Chongno supposedly reek of spit, but, worse yet, this bodily fluid had infested the southern village due to Koreans' frequent movement across the city's ethnic divide. In response, the police chief entertained the idea of installing additional sanitation facilities, such as roadside saliva receptacles, as well as providing supplemental police warnings. In the end, however, he concluded that imparting better hygienic ethics was the most effective way to resolve the problem. Like other popular ethnographers, the policeman based his recommendation on Orientalist explanations of culture, namely, that a stuffy life on the *onddol*, combined with chain smoking and spicy foods, produced a high level of saliva in Koreans and thus their frequent need to expectorate. Reiterating the ideology of civic morality, he called on them to abandon these unhealthy practices and adopt officially sanctioned methods of discharging phlegm. Only through these methods of self-regulation, he concluded, could the police possibly succeed in its sanitizing mission, one that continued to consume a larger part of Keijō's annual budget than any city in the metropole.[50]

The biggest obstacle to imparting hygienic ethics and thus operationalizing civic assimilation was the lack of effective intermediaries between a repressive yet weak state and the marginalized constituency over which it ruled. Throughout the 1910s, the Police Supervisory Board, the organization entrusted with hygienic matters, could only respond in makeshift ways to the city's health problems due to an unknowledgeable and impatient staff, a situation that took an uneven financial and human toll on its residents. In order to improve Keijō's sanitary facilities, the board created a temporary commission for sanitation, consisting of police, military, and municipal officials as well as leaders of the local Japanese medical association. In addition to constructing and repairing sewers, its members followed in the footsteps of the SSA by expanding the number of public toilets and quarantine hospitals. In line with police inspections, they also encouraged Koreans to cultivate hygienic ethics by keeping their homes and surrounding areas adequately clean. One report on the commission went so far as to explain its very creation as a "domestic cure" for the poor structure and layout of native homes, a situation that its members considered the root cause for the ongoing spread of contagious diseases.[51]

Another problem was the inability of government officials to effectively monitor homes where Koreans concealed ailments from the unpleasant gaze of the police. Conscious of these practices of evasion, the temporary commission for sanitation ordered the medical association to ensure that native "students of medicine" *(ŭisaeng;* J: *isei)*—the official term designating unlicensed Korean clinicians as subordinates of doctors trained in Western medicine *(ŭisa;* J: *ishi)*—report individuals hiding their symptoms.[52] From the perspective of ailing Koreans, informing officials of one's symptoms often meant a handcuffed separation from family members and an isolating quarantine in a government hospital that used unfamiliar treatments. Furthermore, most of the colonized population abhorred the prospect of dying outside of their homes, which were not only more comfortable but the only place the spirits could visit and propitiate them in the afterlife.[53] As a result, most students of medicine tended to side with their Korean clients and offer them herbal remedies, a practice Japanese officials deemed ineffective but that may, in fact, have cured epidemics.[54] According to one alarmed report from 1917, these native clinicians did not even believe in dysentery, typhoid fever, or other contagious diseases against which Koreans had comparatively strong resistance.[55] As a result, the over three hundred students of medicine in early Keijō—although encouraged to study and distribute Western medical treatments[56]—failed to report their clients, some of whom allegedly lived with a contagious disease for three or four years without perishing.[57] Meanwhile, the colonial medical system remained woefully underdeveloped, consisting of only two schools, which produced fewer than one hundred graduates annually by 1920. As of 1923, fewer than eleven hundred doctors trained in Western medicine were available to treat a population of seventeen million, a ratio more than fifteen times lower than that of the metropole.[58] Moreover, Japanese settlers, although a statistical minority, comprised the vast majority of patients seeking their services, as the colonized population tended to frequent native clinicians, who were themselves not yet committed to the uneven and alienating regime of colonial hygiene.[59]

Although Koreans tended to opt out of Japanese-dominated institutions of public health whenever possible, the ongoing scourge of disease and death created conditions that forced them to cooperate with the state. In 1916, yet another outbreak of cholera swept the peninsula, taking the lives of more than 1,250 individuals.[60] With little time to respond, colonial officials created temporary sanitation cooperatives throughout Keijō, including in the northern village. For example, the Chongno police chief divided his precincts into seventeen districts, appointing a director and deputy to each. After summoning these officials and more than one hundred additional functionaries, he instructed them on the purpose of these emergency organizations, demanding that they serve as local arms of state power.[61] The police's aggressive response to the cholera outbreak of 1916 was also expressed in newspaper discussions aimed at mobilizing the city's denizens to battle the epidemic. Describing the desired response to the disease as "military conduct during a war," one article summoned the 240,000 residents of Keijō to "wake up and put on their armor."[62] In this way, the city's sanitation cooperatives came to function as "brigades," to borrow another military term used in the press. As one newspaper article boldly declared, "the establishment of sanitation cooperatives is our weapon!"[63] On the one hand, this militarized rhetoric aimed to create greater unity between official policies of health and popular responses to bodily hygiene. On the other hand, it underscores the highly coercive conditions under which the police promoted sanitation cooperatives, the institutional mechanism designed to forge this connection. The emergency conditions of the cholera outbreak in 1916 did increase the chances that Koreans (and Japanese) would obey official standards of hygienic propriety, responses that likely saved many lives. However, these same conditions had the unintended effect of undercutting state goals of promoting a self-generated knowledge of hygienic ethics.

Meanwhile, the cholera outbreak in 1916 provoked colonial officials to introduce popular lectures and innovative media to better inculcate the everyday ethics of hygienic modernity. Hygiene lectures as such were not new. Since the 1880s, temple clergy, local elites, and medical professionals had used these lectures to reach the uneducated masses of Meiji Japan with state-sanctioned information on public health.[64] In colonial Korea, mention of similar activities appears as early as the late protectorate period, although descriptions of the lectures reveal the overwhelmingly strong presence of the state in organizing them, if not carrying them out.[65] From 1912, the Police Supervisory Board began to institute lectures on hygiene for officers and gendarmes stationed throughout the peninsula.[66] In addition to these police-led efforts, authorities began to deploy a limited number of medical professionals to reach the public with the official message of hygienic modernity. In the fall of 1913, the *Maeil sinbo* reported that Nakajima Noboru, the Japanese police chief of the East Gate district, organized a popular hygiene lecture for his precinct's residents. Having received numerous reports of sanitary negligence on the part of local Koreans, Nakajima invited Yamane Masatsugu, a high-ranking Japanese physician, to speak to more than two thousand men and women. After playing a phonographic recording instructing the audience on the tenets of public health, Yamane proceeded to discuss more practical matters of hygienic ethics, including methods of disposal for household trash and human waste.[67]

During the height of the cholera epidemic in 1916, officials experimented with a new version of the hygiene lecture which came to define efforts to sanitize early Keijō. Rather than summoning Koreans to a specified place, frequently in or around a police station, authorities instead used automobiles to canvass the city, appearing in neighborhoods with instructions on how to deal with the deadly disease (see figure 15).

FIGURE 15. Caravan offering roadside hygiene lectures. Source: *Keijō nippō*, Sept. 27, 1916.

Sponsored by official newspapers, these roadside hygiene lectures were held at twenty locations along Chongno, twelve locations in Hon-machi, and eight sites in Yongsan. Through these itinerant methods, officials could reach a large segment of the city's Korean (and Japanese) population, especially those whose class, sex, or age prevented them from reading sanitary advice printed in the colonial press. As one newspaper article suggested, "The ear is quicker than the eye. Even a person who is busy must be able to listen to a lecture for twenty or thirty minutes, including women and children."[68] Although fragmentary, some reports suggest that these methods of imparting knowledge bore fruit during the epidemic in 1916. In addition to the nearly sixty thousand Koreans the roadside lectures attracted, another eighty thousand received written instructions on preventing the spread of the disease.[69] Even if one does not accept the conclusion that Koreans gratefully bowed and applauded, the automobile caravans and walking units did make effective use of the city's street network, conveying the rudiments of hygienic morality in straightforward and comprehensible ways.

In addition to the communicative use of the human voice as part of neighborhood hygiene lectures, colonial officials had, by the epidemic in 1916, also begun to appeal to the visual senses of Korean audiences by using other new technologies. Such methods included slide shows with official commentary. Like hygiene lectures, slide shows date back to the protectorate period when both Japanese and Koreans deployed this technology to impart hygienic knowledge to their targeted audiences. As early as 1907, a group of Korean elites, for example, made a slide show for government, business, and health officials.[70] In 1909, the Japanese police summoned more than four hundred Chongno spectators to a four-day presentation on personal hygiene at the local police station. Slides for this event dealt with problems such as household cleaning, potable water for cooking, and the installation of chamber pots.[71] The protectorate government also experimented with less intimidating locations, using Pagoda Park, a site more comfortably embedded in Koreans' everyday lives, to make slide presentations.[72]

Efforts to bring personal hygiene to a level both easily comprehensible and at least minimally interesting to Korean viewers continued throughout the 1910s and early 1920s, although authorities struggled to keep the audience's attention through this medium alone.[73] As a solution, event organizers began to intersperse more amusing attractions into didactic slide discussions. In April 1920, for example, police officials staged such a spectacle at the Umigwan, a one-thousand-seat theater located in Chongno. To keep audiences entertained, they used the latest visual technology—silent film, for example—as well as more established attractions, such as dancing by *kisaeng* and musical performances. At this particular gathering, an official from the Government-General began by explaining slides about hygiene. This presentation was followed by two didactic films on typhoid fever, one of which featured the disinfection of an ill person's home. Although Koreans occasionally applauded at scenes they found interesting, organizers found that audiences did not tolerate extended explanations of disease prevention. To regain their attention, they arranged for eight "beautifully dressed" *kisaeng* to perform a Western dance. After this crowd-pleasing event, officials took advantage of Koreans' second wind to make another slide presentation, this time on cholera. However, before delving too far into preventive measures, Koreans were treated to yet another attraction, a violin performance, followed by another film. Given that the audience was packed, lighthearted entertainment as part of hygiene presentations seems to have been a successful strategy. However, this concession may have diluted the message of everyday civic morality, transforming it into a considerably less ideological form of mass entertainment.

## "SAME BED, DIFFERENT DREAMS": DIAGNOSING AND CURING THE MALADIES OF A COLONIAL CITY

Even as the colonial state continued to target primarily the Korean population with its hygienic gospel, government officials and medical professionals encountered information that called into question their logic of civic assimilation. With medical reports published in monthly journals like the municipal government's *Seoul Digest (Keijō ihō)*, health authorities only had to look at the most recent statistics to realize that, ironically, Japanese settlers, whose numbers increased from just over sixty-five thousand in 1920 to more than 150,000 by 1940, contracted contagious diseases at a surprisingly higher rate than their supposedly less hygienic Korean counterparts. Comparing these statistics to those of other major cities in the Japanese empire, colonial officials struggled to find the causes and cures for Keijō's reputation as the empire's "diseased city." The discovery of colonizers' susceptibility to illness only led to an increasingly unequal distribution of public resources toward the already well-endowed southern village where expatriates predominated.

Meanwhile, Korean elites used newly established newspapers like the *Tonga ilbo* and *Chosŏn ilbo* to question the ethnocentric representations and partisan policies advanced by their Japanese counterparts. These nationalist critics posited Keijō as an intrinsically discriminatory city, using the common language and practice of *eisei/weisaeng* to challenge colonialist claims about the causal relationship between the city's sanitary infrastructure and the hygienic knowledge of its colonized residents. Firm believers in the benefits of Western medicine, their bourgeois views of the Korean underclass, depicted as considerably less hygienic and thus in dire need of reform, echoed similar charges by colonialist pundits. Yet even as they shared the "same bed" of hygienic modernity with their colonizers, Korean elites produced "different dreams," those of a more equitable future. For example, although they enthusiastically encouraged their poorer counterparts to submit their bodies to investigative pathology rather than conceal symptoms of disease, nationalist critics did not countenance the offensive presence of the hygiene police among local residents. Marshaling statistics from official publications, Chŏn Sŏng-uk—a Korean representative in the metropolitan council and an active member of Seoul Shrine's parish organization—captured this differing vision by promoting what he called "self-governance" *(chach'i;* J: *jichi)*. This catchword, recycled from Meiji debates about protecting local autonomy in the face of an authoritarian state, aimed to reclaim control over the administration of public health and the redistribution of related resources toward the relatively neglected northern village. Refuting racist claims about Koreans' unhygienic nature, critics like Chŏn used a common epistemological framework to demonstrate how class stood as the primary determinant of the high mortality rate among poorer Koreans. In particular, they challenged the essentializing logic underwriting racialized depictions of the Korean masses (and lower-class Japanese) as intrinsically dirty.[74] Instead, these writers highlighted the relatively low levels of education and wealth, both products of colonialism, as causes for ethnic differences in hygienic practices between Japanese and Koreans and for variations in the sanitary endowments of Keijō's ethnic enclaves. Citing recent government statistics, cultural nationalists also called on officials to institute more egalitarian policies of sanitary welfare for underclass Koreans who, although deemed uncivilized like their Japanese counterparts, stood to benefit most from such reforms.

During the 1920s, colonial officials began to examine the sanitary conditions of Keijō in a more comprehensive and systematic fashion, drawing on recent developments in medical sciences, investigatory statistics, and other forms of modern administration. They set out to quantify the salubrity of this diseased city as a means of ensuring the health of its inhabitants, especially the growing population of Japanese settlers.[75] Reports published throughout 1920s and into the 1930s increasingly detailed public health concerns, such as the number of contagious disease outbreaks and deaths by ailment and ethnicity. In one of the first such reports, which covered the period from 1914 until 1921, authorities discovered that Japanese residents consistently contracted illnesses at a considerably higher rate than colonized Koreans.[76] In 1919, for example, 776 Japanese succumbed to contagious diseases, including 294 cases of typhoid fever, 190 cases of dysentery, and 169 cases of typhus. By contrast, only two hundred Koreans fell sick from 119 cases of typhoid fever, twenty-one cases of dysentery, and twenty-one cases of typhus. In another report on the spread of dysentery in 1922, the author, a sanitary expert from the city government, discovered a similar etiological pattern, although he struggled with only limited success to identify its primary cause.[77] Disaggregating the disease by region, age, and ethnicity, he found that the incidence of dysentery had increased nearly ten times in comparison to the previous year (1921). Furthermore, he reported that nearly 50 percent of those afflicted inhabited the southern village, while less than 25 percent of those who contracted dysentery resided in the northern village. Based on these statistics, he conjectured that the disease first spread among the Japanese in Honmachi, who then passed it on to the colonized of Chongno. He attributed the lower infections among Koreans to their stronger resistance.[78] Seeking to further understand this phenomenon, he provided some guesses as to its possible causes. Of the eighty-seven people he examined, exposure to other family members or neighbors accounted for the highest ratio of contraction (45 percent). Another 36 percent reportedly contracted the disease after eating food or drinking beverages. Only 4 percent became infected due to the unsanitary conditions of waste receptacles.

Although Japanese officials presided over an increasingly large volume of epidemiological information, they struggled with little success to track the source and pathway of infections. Such was the conclusion of an anonymous report published in the fall of 1924 that detailed the incidence of contagious diseases between 1914 and 1923. According to this investigation, only nine of fifty-seven districts with five or more outbreaks were known to be populated by a high percentage of

Koreans, whereas other disease-prone districts were inhabited almost entirely by Japanese. Although this finding repeated the results of previous investigations, the author abandoned oft-cited explanations for this disturbing phenomenon, such as population density and transportation frequency, which failed to explain how the relatively "unhygienic" Korean neighborhoods of Keijō continued to record fewer incidences of contagious diseases than the city's more "sanitary" Japanese neighborhoods. However, the author was unable to provide a more credible explanation and thus concluded with a blunt statement that simply blamed the elusive nature of biomedical science: "I think that contagious disease is, by its very nature, something fickle."[79]

As government officials struggled to explain disease scientifically, Japanese pundits remained focused on the cultural particularities of "unhygienic" Koreans as the cause of epidemics, despite their enviable ability to ward off infections more effectively than purportedly more hygienic expatriates.[80] A sensationalist report published in 1928, for example, argued that Koreans' bodily practices had changed little since 1910. Although household toilets discouraged some privileged Koreans from disposing human waste on the streets, many continued to collect urine in chamber pots, often kept indoors on the *ondol* (underground heating system).[81] According to this colonialist account, sanitary conditions only began to show signs of improvement with the establishment of Japanese rule, although even these efforts failed to transform Keijō into what the author called a "cultured city." As a result, the showcase capital continued to experience a disproportionately high incidence of contagious diseases. The author excoriated the colonized population for continuing to defecate indiscriminately as well as for washing clothes and food in polluted waterways. Although recognizing Koreans' relatively high resistance to contagious diseases, he refused to consider local practices that might have helped prevent future outbreaks among Japanese settlers. Introducing the theory that garlic consumption aided Koreans in warding off illness, the author agreed that this food was good for the stomach and the bowels. Despite its medicinal benefits, garlic produced such a foul smell that this pundit could hardly imagine Japanese consuming it, lest they lower themselves to the "inferior" status of other East Asians. As he condescendingly wrote, "If Japanese begin to eat this [food], they will be expelled [from the category] of civilized people as a race just like Chinese and Koreans who emit a foul smell."

Making only oblique references to inadequate facilities in the northern village, reports in Japanese-language newspapers also tended to fault Koreans for failing to improve their "unhygienic" habits and thus aid in their own civic assimilation. In the summer of 1925, a bout of typhoid fever hit, infecting a large number of residents, particularly those living in densely populated parts of the city. To remedy the problem, the author of one *Keijō nippō* article advocated preventive measures closely associated with the modern planning movement. Calculating twenty-four neighborhoods with less than seventeen square meters of space per person, he proposed expanding these cramped living quarters by four times, reducing the possibility that the sick spread the disease among family members and neighboring residents.[82] Subsequent newspaper articles identified other deficiencies in the city's sanitary infrastructure as possible causes for the spread of typhoid fever. One report disclosed that only 123,000 of the city's three hundred thousand residents (41 percent) had access to potable drinking water, without specifying that most tap-water drinkers were likely Japanese. While implicitly revealing ethnic-based discrepancies in sanitary facilities, the author ultimately faulted the colonized masses for continuing to use polluted water. He also lambasted these "ignorant Koreans" for hiding their diseases, upsetting the efforts of police officers to make medical inspections.[83] Once again, government authorities proposed instituting measures to improve hygienic knowledge among Koreans, which they continued to view as woefully insufficient.[84]

Even as Japanese publications continued to upbraid Koreans, officials gradually recognized deficiencies in Keijō's sanitary facilities as an undeniable explanation for the diseased city. Amid the deadly outbreak of typhoid fever in 1925, the mayor, Mano Seiichi, comparing Keijō's "civilized infrastructure" to that of metropolitan cities, publicly announced his dissatisfaction with the capital's system of public health. Admitting his frustration with past efforts, he wrote: "We have made substantial efforts thus far, but as a government administrator, the results are not as evident as efforts we have put into the extremely simple work of sanitation."[85] Pledging seven hundred thousand yen in annual funding, the mayor vowed to make the improvement of public health his administration's number one priority. This plan included a renewed commitment to completing the city's sewer system, for which the government had already spent an astronomical 1.25 million yen.[86] Although Korean critics of Keijō's ethnocentric policies welcomed this development, less than one-third of colonized Koreans, most of whom were poor and thus dependent on well water, could afford to become beneficiaries of the city's fee-based water supply system.[87]

Moreover, the system of well water upon which most Korean residents continued to rely remained polluted due to ongoing problems of waste disposal, further straining the city's comparably high yearly expenditure (four hundred thousand yen) for such services.[88] According to detailed statistics from 1923, sanitation officials managed to collect only just over half of the daily output of excrement (340,937 liters). As a result, a large part of the remaining waste (160,547 liters) filtered into waterways and thus increased the spread of diseases, especially among Korean users.[89] In response, the mayor attempted to collect more human waste and convert it into fertilizer, but the company charged with this task struggled to keep up with the growing population and resultant increases in excrement production.[90] By 1931, Keijō's four hundred thousand residents produced 432,936 liters of human waste per day, an increase of 91,999 liters from 1923. Sanitation companies did manage to dispose of a slightly larger amount (245,330 liters as compared to 180,390 liters in 1923), but the quantity it failed to dispose actually increased more sharply (from 160,547 liters in 1923 to 187,606 in 1931), aggravating the problem of disease-carrying flies.[91] As residents regularly suffered from the adverse effects of epidemics, Mano's administration continued to spend more than half of its annual budget on curing the diseased city.[92] Moreover, unlike metropolitan cities benefiting from a broader base of taxpaying residents, the colonial regime managed a large underclass of colonized residents, more than half of whom could not afford public levies.[93] As the mayor put it in 1925, "Keijō's population is said to be three hundred thousand; however, because poor Koreans constitute two-thirds of it, [Keijō] is no different than cities of the metropole with one hundred thousand people in terms of the individual's actual capacity."[94]

While financial limitations undercut government attempts to develop Keijō's sanitary infrastructure, ongoing deficiencies in public facilities, such as lavatories, and their alleged misuse continued to plague efforts to rid Keijō of its reputation as the empire's diseased city. According to a report published in 1923, the large number of residents (three hundred thousand) using the relatively small number of toilets (seventy) left these public facilities in a chronic state of disarray, despite two daily cleanings by a ten-person staff. Worse yet, this report alleged that Korean residents continued to steal doors for firewood as well as light bulbs and toilet seats for use at home. Explaining these practices as evidence of their low level of "civic morality," the city's moral training corps took it upon themselves to remedy the problem. Using the third

Sunday of each month, the corps borrowed cleaning tools from the city government and spent two hours sanitizing public toilets.[95] Although serving as proactive agents of the colonial state, the group did little to improve the conditions of Keijō's public toilets because Koreans allegedly stared in bewilderment at corps members as they sanitized lavatories and even dirtied them during regular cleanups.[96]

The inability of many Koreans to afford private toilets and basic cleaning utensils posed an equally, if not more, significant liability to the city's sanitary infrastructure than the misuse of public facilities. In response, the government allocated an annual sum of 250 yen to the purchase of chamber pots, thirty-seven hundred of which was distributed between 1913 and 1928. During this same period, officials also spent fifteen thousand yen to provide thirty-six hundred dustbins to "unhygienic" households for trash collection.[97] Despite these efforts, a high proportion of homes and businesses still lacked these basic sanitary amenities. According to a detailed survey published in 1932, just over 50 percent of Keijō households owned their own dustbins, leaving more than forty thousand homeowners without any form of waste collection. Although almost 80 percent of households citywide could boast "sufficient" toilet facilities, areas populated by a high concentration of Koreans registered more dismal statistics. Only 42.7 percent of households in the East Gate area, for example, had adequate toilet facilities, as compared to 95.5 percent of Hon-machi households. Chongno, by contrast, registered a relatively high 79.8 percent, but over one thousand Korean households in the northern village had either "deficient" facilities or no toilet at all.[98] Even Korean merchants along Chongno lacked such facilities, prompting local police officers to demand that they immediately install toilets or submit a form explaining why they could not comply with this regulation. To assess damage caused by deficient toilet facilities, local police officers conducted an emergency survey of popular customs. During a four-day investigation in early July 1932, they recorded 144 instances of public defecation and urination in addition to 165 cases of indiscriminate trash disposal.[99] Although refraining from accusing the colonized population of engaging in such "wayward" behavior, the Korean-language press also voiced concern about the inadequacy of basic sanitary facilities in the northern village, citing it as a major cause for the large accumulation of waste on its city streets.[100]

Responding to such inequities in the distribution of public resources, Korean writers, having once served as public health leaders in the waning years of the Chosŏn dynasty, reentered a Japanese-dominated debate on hygienic modernity during the 1920s and early 1930s. Invoking Confucian notions of benevolence shown by superiors toward their subordinates, nationalist writers pointed to Japanese officials' failure to provide adequate facilities as the main cause for the unhealthy practices of some (but not all) Koreans. This bold reversal in the causal relationship between hygienic knowledge and sanitary infrastructure can be seen in an article published by the *Chosŏn ilbo* in 1921 with the pointed subtitle "Urging Keijō's Sanitation Division to Wake Up." Although recognizing road expansions and other improvements made to the city's outward appearance, the author condemned planners for failing to remedy more pressing problems for the colonized population, such as overcrowding and housing shortages. Absolving Koreans of responsibility for deficiencies in Keijō's sanitary infrastructure, this critic argued that inhumane living conditions caused by colonialism had led naturally to the accumulation of human waste and trash on city streets, in front of homes, and in areas of heavy foot traffic. Although he joined colonialist pundits in bemoaning these conditions as unhygienic, he denied that they reflected any inherent shortcoming of Koreans. Instead, he held the government responsible for failing to provide adequate facilities. When the same author turned to a discussion of desirable solutions, he again invoked precolonial notions of Confucian benevolence. In contrast to Japanese critics' focus on self-improvement, this modern-day sage-king placed the central responsibility on colonial authorities to persuade Koreans that the government was, in fact, committed to improving their health and not simply that of settlers. To this end, he encouraged officials to make more effective use of the sanitation fee. In particular, he urged them to invest this tax in improving the public health of Korean neighborhoods, rather than spending a high proportion of it to vaccinate disease-prone expatriates. Such gestures would, he hoped, instill greater faith in their subaltern counterparts, inducing them to more fully embrace new bodily practices.[101]

Although they encouraged the poor to adopt hygienic improvements as their own personal mantra, nationalist writers continued to challenge popular perceptions of Koreans as intrinsically dirty, positing ethnic-based class distinctions as the root of the problem. For example, the author of an article published in 1928 in the *Tonga ilbo* grudgingly agreed with Japanese pundits that the health practices of the colonized underclasses were far less developed than those of Japanese settlers. However, he assertively dispelled the notion of Koreans' inherent inferiority as an example of malicious propaganda. Like other Confucian-inspired critics of colonial negligence, the author blamed poor hygiene on officials' failure to provide adequate educational opportunities. To bolster his argument about ethnically determined class distinctions, he offered examples of middle-class Koreans like himself who practiced a level of hygiene on par with that of their bourgeois Japanese counterparts and demanded that Koreans not be considered intrinsically unhygienic. Whatever differences existed between Japanese and Koreans were, in sum, attributable to varyings levels of education and income.[102]

Even as they questioned essentialized distinctions between Japanese and Koreans, nationalist writings on the intolerably poor state of health in the northern village reinforced a bounded sense of ethnic categories and fixed residents to a single place in the city's social geography. Revealing the more complicated realm of interactions between Japanese and Koreans or the internal differences within each of these ethnic communities might have undercut nationalists' most pressing claim: to promote a healthier living space for their community. The publication of carefully researched exposés detailing inequities in municipal services was a particularly salient way in which their critiques enhanced the alluring "power of topography," as Akhil Gupta and James Ferguson have described the reification of space into mutually exclusive culture-areas.[103] A report published in the *Tonga ilbo* in 1923 presents a revealing, if hyperbolic, example of how nationalist discourse on hygienic modernity neatly cordoned off Keijō's spaces into ethnic enclaves. In this article, the author claimed that a "national boundary" *(kukgyŏng)*, as he put it in the starkest of geopolitical terms, still separated the residential worlds of Japanese and Koreans, especially in terms of their differing sanitary conditions. Downplaying class, sex, and other dynamics dividing these ethnic communities, he argued that the colonized population continued to suffer from deficient roads and sewers as well as infrequent human waste and trash collection services. He even went so far as to accuse the government of concealing these imbalances from the public and ignoring criticisms by concerned Koreans like himself.[104]

To promote a more egalitarian distribution of public resources, Korean-language newspapers began to wage a counterdiscourse of numbers against self-serving framings of Keijō as the empire's diseased city, using state-generated statistics to identify and publicize ethnic-based inequalities. For example, an article published in 1924 in the *Tonga ilbo* with the condemning title "An Example of Discrimination between the North and South" demonstrates how the Korean population of one district in the northern village far outnumbered that of a district in the southern village where Japanese settlers tended to reside. Although the district in the northern village produced a slightly greater volume of excreta and a considerably higher quantity of trash than the district in the southern village, a larger number of laborers and their carts collected trash and human waste from the Japanese settlement. Given such inequalities, the author doubted that the government would ever commit itself to improving the sanitary conditions of neighborhoods inhabited by the colonized population. As he wrote pessimistically, "Even if the budget increases by one hundred million yen or if one hundred million yen is spent on carts and laborers, Koreans [living] in the northern village will receive no benefits whatsoever."[105]

Korean nationalists also aimed attacks at the mayor's avowed campaign to prioritize sanitation, deriding it as a veiled policy to favor Japanese settlers. One editorial published in 1925 in the *Chosŏn ilbo* challenged the city government's neglect of the colonized population by exposing considerable deficiencies in waste collection, quarantine hospitals, public toilets, and sewage treatment, all of which the author urged the mayor to remedy.[106] Other critics lambasted his administration for funneling Korean taxpayers' money into measures aimed primarily at vaccinating disease-prone Japanese settlers. Rather than faulting impoverished Koreans for their inability to afford taxes, as the mayor had, nationalists instead focused on the numerical predominance of Keijō's colonized population, demanding that they receive a more equal share of services. Citing the most recent statistics from 1925, one article established that Japanese settlers comprised only eighty thousand of the city's 410,000 residents, or less than 20 percent of the population.[107] Nevertheless, officials continued to favor this overrepresented group at the expense of Koreans, provoking one nationalist critic to assail the mayor's sanitation policy as nothing more than a self-defense policy for the Japanese.[108]

In criticizing the colonial biases of hygienic modernity, Korean writers used official statistics to prove another point often overlooked by Japanese accounts, which had compared the diseased city of Keijō to more healthy metropolises throughout the empire. That is, even as Japanese settlers continued to contract contagious diseases at a higher rate than the colonized population, these ailments took a far greater toll on Koreans, many of whom refused to accept or could not afford effective treatments. According to a report written in 1927 by Pan Pok-ki, the

Korean Vice-Director of the Severance Hospital, Korea had one of the highest mortality rates of any country in the world. Basing his discussion on statistics for the period between 1917 and 1921, he showed that, whereas Japan, England, and the United States experienced annual death rates of 2.38, 1.48, and 1.4 percent, respectively, the peninsula's mortality rate of 2.43 percent was almost 0.7 percent higher than the average of these imperial powers.[109] In terms of death caused by disease, the colonized population experienced a relatively high rate of mortality, particularly among Korean children. One report estimated that infant mortality claimed the lives of nearly 25 percent of live births during the 1920s, whereas the rates for Japan (15 percent), Germany (10 percent), France (8 percent), and England (7 percent) remained considerably lower. Writing in 1930, Chŏng Sŏk-t'ae, a Korean physician, lamented that Korea posted the highest death and infant mortality rates among civilized nations, connecting these alarming figures to the ailing health of his colonized nation.[110] Seeking to inspire officials to take ameliorative measures, the *Tonga ilbo* actively publicized similarly disturbing statistics. An article from 1928, for example, reported that only 507 Koreans had contracted contagious diseases during the first ten months of that year, as compared to nearly four times as many Japanese (1,954), yet the colonized continued to die at a combined rate of 11 percent, a figure nearly 2.5 times higher than that of their colonizers. In fact, almost half of Koreans infected with scarlet fever, the most deadly ailment in 1928, passed away, whereas only 15 percent of infected Japanese succumbed to the disease.[111]

As regards the causes of and remedies for high mortality rates among Koreans, nationalist critics placed ultimate blame on the government for failing to provide the needed educational opportunities and medical facilities for the impoverished. To be sure, many nationalist authors continued to fault poor Koreans for concealing their ailments and refusing to submit them to biomedical cures. As one *Tonga ilbo* editorialist wrote: "To prevent typhoid fever, first, [receive] a vaccination shot; second, disinfect water, fruits, vegetables, and other foods and beverages; third, quarantine oneself from diseased individuals. In the unfortunate case of contraction, of course, immediately receive treatment from a doctor. For the sake of one's family and the general public, enter a hospital with facilities for contagious diseases without hesitating. If an individual is disobedient and conceals one's disease, this [behavior] will be reviled as selfishness that disregards one's family and the public."[112] Employing the language of hygienic modernity frequently used by Japanese officials and popular pundits, this writer stressed the responsibility of individuals. However, most nationalist writers continued to emphasize the unequal socioeconomic conditions under which most Koreans dealt with epidemics. The colony's relatively high mortality rate, according to one critic, stemmed from significant limitations in Koreans' access to public health, including a shortage of hospitals and a lack of money for medicine.[113] Another editorialist, responding to the outbreak of smallpox in 1932, diagnosed the problem by connecting three interrelated factors—ethnicity, class, and education—while still relying on the government for recourse. As he proposed: "We must first cure poverty. If that is accomplished, then eliminating ignorance and sickness will not be difficult. It is impossible to cure the nation's poverty with the folk remedies of diligence and frugality. Only through measures of state management will that happen."[114] Although most Korean writers did not analyze the structural conditions of the health problem with such acumen, they did actively foreground material discrepancies between colonizers and the colonized in order to promote progressive changes in the city's sanitary infrastructure and thereby develop Koreans' hygienic knowledge and practice. As one editorialist explained about the continually high mortality rate: "Although one cause is because Koreans' level of civilization has yet to develop and because [they] lack a notion of hygiene, the main cause is due to deficient sanitation facilities [provided] by city administrators and supervisory authorities."[115]

The formula of "same bed, different dreams" that characterized overlapping discourses of public health also captures neighborhood sanitation projects under two intersecting yet competitive campaigns. Through hygiene expositions, itinerant lectures, and other communication techniques, the Government-General and its local proxies continued to use sanitary reforms as a tactic of cultural rule aimed at binding the bodily practices of neighborhood Koreans to the sanitizing prerogatives of the colonial state. Alongside these government programs, a group of dedicated Korean nationalists promoted their own cultural movement in Keijō and elsewhere throughout the peninsula. Embracing hygienic modernity as one of its pedagogical mantras, this movement drew on many of the same institutions and media used by their colonialist counterparts to advance their goal of strengthening the national body. In this way, instilling a rudimentary knowledge of public health capable of protecting the colonized population from the deadly spread of germs brought the "differing dreams" of Korean nationalists and Japanese colonialists into the "same bed" of neighborhood campaigns.

While enabling competing visions of the Korean social body, these two initiatives combined to narrow definitions of healing practices outside the increasingly hegemonic parameters of hygienic modernity.

As part of his program of cultural rule, Governor-General Saitō Makoto (r. 1919–27, 1929–31) attempted to lay the foundations for a more hegemonic, less coercive form of administration.[116] By instituting a new program to "enlist the populace in police duties, while bringing the police deeper into the daily lives of the populace" (J: *keisatsu no minshūka, minshū no keisatsuka*), officials hoped to improve the police's reputation among the Korean population. It also encouraged colonized elites to more actively participate in disciplinary organizations at the neighborhood level, such as the aforementioned sanitation cooperatives. To this end, the mayor issued a directive in 1921 ordering that the leaders of neighborhood associations also serve as heads of cooperatives. Although created from above, sanitation cooperatives operated through the management of local elites to whom the colonial state delegated the responsibility for advising local residents on hygienic requirements. Residents were, for example, expected to

(1) conduct cleanings of the street and the areas around one's home;
(2) maintain a suitable dustbin and be sure to collect trash in that bin;
(3) clean and repair drains in one's home and nearby ditches;
(4) install a clean toilet, and ensure that feces and urine do not seep into the ground;
(5) report illnesses to the police station; and
(6) follow instructions about hygiene and contagious disease prevention.[117]

As Korean cooperative leaders sought to implement these regulations, they encountered noncompliance from their constituents, a situation requiring them to issue repeated verbal and written warnings. At one of the first meetings of cooperative leaders, for example, city officials announced a new campaign to lower the incidence of water- and insect-borne diseases, urging neighborhood representatives to cooperate in keeping Keijō's water supply clean. In particular, they urged local intermediaries to admonish residents to refrain from disposing of dirty water and trash into ditches and to take time to clean these waterways.[118] In spite of these warnings, lower-class inhabitants continued to throw waste into waterways and disobey other cooperative regulations. According to an article published in 1928, so much trash had accumulated in the already shallow ditches of Keijō that water from the Ch'ŏnggye Stream no longer flowed from one end of the city to the other. To remedy the problem, government officials once again called on local Korean leaders to admonish underclass residents about matters of waste disposal. At times, the situation became so grave that cooperative leaders had to make household visits with printed instructions, warning residents to use dustbins for eliminating trash.[119]

But as the Korean leaders of sanitation cooperatives began to lend greater administrative support to state projects, they quickly discovered that the lower classes could not afford the membership fee (ten sen), leaving them with inadequate finances to care for local residents. Rather than opt out of this inequitable system of neighborhood welfare, they demanded greater public resources to support their efforts. For example, at a meeting of the Keijō Municipal Council in April 1923, one influential leader, the aforementioned Chŏn Sŏng-uk, raised the issue of insufficient funds, announcing that many unpaid Korean neighborhood administrators could not fully assume the cost of managing their districts. Part of the problem, as another councilman explained, was that Korean administrators, in contrast to wealthy Japanese who volunteered their services, lacked the personal finances to support their constituents. To remedy the situation, Chŏn, complaining that colonized representatives functioned as lowly servants, requested that officials remunerate them appropriately.[120] Despite initial opposition, his argument convinced the mayor, who agreed to provide each neighborhood administrator with a monthly stipend of five yen.[121] This precedent set the stage for the city government to allocate an additional five yen per month to support the underfinanced activities of sanitation cooperatives. This "victory" for neighborhood elites helped strengthen the state's relationship with them, creating a more direct connection to the cooperatives.[122]

With greater financial support "to enlist the populace in police duties," Korean sanitation cooperatives gradually took on sanitizing tasks that had up to then been managed by patrolmen, but tried to implement them in less offensive ways. Before the establishment of the Central Association of Sanitation Cooperatives (CASC) in June 1925, police officers had posted notices on households announcing the specific date and time of semiannual cleanups. Following inspections, patrolmen hung further notices on doors signifying which households had achieved a satisfactory level of cleanliness. In the summer of 1925, the Korean cooperative leaders, although they remained under police supervision, convinced officials to allow them to conduct the semiannual cleanups. Over several years, they worked especially hard to modify those practices that most offended Korean sensibilities, especially the humiliating custom of posting notices announcing the results of household inspections. Instead, they simply reported the results of satisfactory cleanings to police officials, who agreed to rely on these local functionaries for trustworthy information. The municipal councilman Chŏn, who also served in the CASC, referred to this achievement, instituted in 1930, as the second of five stages toward hygienic self-governance. Success in this phrase suggests how colonized elites, seeking a greater role in administering state powers, hoped to redirect those powers for nationalist ends.

As Korean leaders negotiated the terms of their cooperation with the police, they continued to struggle with poor neighbors who refused to comply with the increasingly intrusive regime of sanitary surveillance. As mentioned above, local administrators rewarded residents who dutifully carried out their hygienic responsibilities during semiannual cleanups by not attaching a notice on their door. However, they continued to pin red warnings on households that failed to follow sanitary regulations, an ostracizing sign of communal disapproval. To ensure that noncompliant individuals met official standards, members of sanitary cooperatives also made special home visits. Only when residents acquiesced did neighborhood representatives remove the red notices. During the third phase of this process of hygienic self-governance, Chŏn hoped to soften surveillance measures by relying almost completely on local residents to follow the rules themselves. After this stage, a civilized style of sanitary operations, as he described it, would emerge, one wherein the specter of contagious disease naturally induced individuals to carry out necessary precautions. By 1931, however, lower-class Koreans had yet to fall in line with Chŏn's five-stage model.[123]

In the meantime, sanitation cooperatives provided important relief for the poorest residents. For example, neighborhood leaders used membership fees to conduct disinfections of toilets, dustbins, and sewer ditches during the spring and summer months. In a similar way, CASC leaders provided indigent residents with relatively inexpensive (two-yen) chamber pots to encourage hygienic forms of excretion and flypaper to catch disease-carrying insects. When a downtrodden member of their community became ill, cooperative leaders also made consolatory visits to afflicted households, providing family members with food and arranging for free medical consultations as well as inexpensive drugs. In some cases, particularly generous neighborhood elites even contributed money to provide poorer neighbors with medical supplies, thus positioning themselves as upstanding substitutes for a negligent colonial state.[124] In the event that these interventions failed to prevent the death of a sick patient, local leaders arranged funeral ceremonies. At first, they typically gathered donations (ten to twenty sen per family) from neighbors to pay for cremations, but such fund-raising activities often consumed community leaders for as much as a week. Fearing that the diseased corpse posed an ongoing threat to the health of other residents, local officials, working with the city government in what had now become a symbiotic relationship, arranged for a physician to certify the death and have the body immediately cremated at no cost to residents. In this way, the leaders of sanitation cooperatives worked in coordination with government authorities to fill the gap between the ideal of a uniformly healthy community of imperial subjects and the reality that the poorest struggled to adhere to official prescriptions of hygienic modernity.

In addition to managing neighborhood activities, Korean cooperative leaders also became active supporters of public media, such as films, exhibitions, and even plays, all of which they hoped to use to promote a more egalitarian form of sanitary welfare.[125] Regularly announced by the *Tonga ilbo* as complements to its own pedagogical activities, these popular events drew crowds into parks, squares, and schools. By supporting these events, however, neighborhood leaders also enabled the colonial state to further target Koreans as objects of medical surveillance, as officials used these civic sites to monitor the health of the colonized masses by conducting medical inspections and offering free vaccinations.

The popular events that took place during the second half of 1922 are a good example of these efforts. With the hot months of summer quickly approaching, officials began to worry about the possibility of yet another epidemic. Due to an unexpected outbreak of smallpox, the police had conducted preventive health inspections of Korean homes, where they found many inhabitants suffering from the ailment. To ensure that more residents take necessary precautions, government authorities organized hygiene lectures and an accompanying film at various locations throughout the city, including Pagoda Park. When the film and series of hygiene lectures took place in June, officials used the opportunity to further monitor the health of approximately ten thousand attendees by conducting onsite examinations and vaccinations.[126] Sanitary experts also issued written instructions about household cleaning, trash disposal, dietary health, and contagious outbreaks. They even distributed ten thousand free flyswatters and exterminating chemicals to use against disease-carrying insects, offering a monetary award for individuals who put these devices to best use.[127] At other times, government authorities mobilized Korean cooperative leaders to distribute promotional posters reading, "Do not drink cold water," "Do not buy unwashed vegetables," and "Do not overeat or overdrink."[128] These posters were hung in places where people tended to congregate and where contagious diseases were easily transmitted, such as bath houses, theaters, barbershops, markets, schools, and companies, as well as bus and train stations.[129]

To further enlist Koreans in officially sanctioned practices of sanitation and to prepare them for semiannual cleanups, government authorities also organized two campaigns in the summer and fall of 1922, both of which the *Tonga ilbo* promoted as a supplement to its own campaigns of cultural nationalism.[130] First, taking advantage of a traveling hygiene exhibition sponsored by the Osaka-based pharmaceutical company Jintan, city officials arranged for that firm to present a number of charts and displays on contagious diseases, along with seven guides to explain items to spectators. Drawn by the lure of free admission and the controversial display of a female corpse infected with a sexually transmitted disease, more than three thousand spectators attended the Jintan exhibition during the morning hours of the first day (July 23).[131] Second, in October, Government-General officials, working with their counterparts in the Kyŏnggi Prefectural Office and with the Korean Red Cross, allocated twenty-five hundred yen to host another hygiene exhibition.[132] Like its predecessor, this event featured specimens, charts, and pictures on matters of individual hygiene as well as on contagious and venereal diseases. To capture the audience's attention, organizers also presented a series of films during the evening hours, offering free admission to both attractions.[133] Although government authorities sponsored the event, the *Tonga ilbo,* in whose pages cultural nationalists critiqued public health under Japanese rule, promoted this exhibition as an opportunity for Koreans to learn about hygienic modernity. As one reporter explained, "There are explanations attached [to the display items] so that even an average person [*pot'ong saram*] can understand clearly. This is a very much needed exhibition to promote hygienic attitudes."[134]

More than a decade later, the *Tonga ilbo* was still endorsing government-led exhibitions and films, as persistent outbreaks of disease continued to endanger its Korean constituency. In 1933, for example, the Government-General, the city government, and the government of

Kyŏnggi Province jointly hosted a major event called the Disease Prevention Exhibition, which featured sixteen buildings displaying over twelve thousand items.[135] Held from August 9 to 15, the exhibition coincided with the usual summertime disease warnings, during a year in which an unprecedented number of inhabitants suffered from deadly ailments.[136] In addition to displaying instructional items, organizers used the meeting grounds of Susong Common School, a public institution attended mostly by Koreans residing in nearby Chongno, to offer free physical examinations as well as inspections of food and drink.[137] A host of other activities, part of a newly established disease prevention week, took place outside of the exhibition grounds, bringing the event's lessons into the neighborhoods and homes of residents. To uncover Koreans still hiding illnesses from the police and cooperative leaders, groups of inspectors made home visits, providing free medicine to indigent Koreans. For its part, the CASC hired fifty laborers to disinfect toilet facilities, enforcing this particular regulation of the semiannual cleanup. Exhibition officials also organized a special fly-catching day to encourage residents to exterminate contagion-carrying insects. In addition, police officers worked in coordination with local agents to clean streets, disinfect wells, and dispose of trash. An emergency cleanup team also mobilized the members of each neighborhood to cooperate in administering other sanitary regulations associated with semiannual cleanups.[138]

Although impossible to evaluate from the perspective of colonized spectators, the exhibition and related events—which drew nearly eighty thousand people, most of them Korean—seem to have had some immediate, if not longer-lasting, effects in terms of the self-regulation of their bodily health. According to congratulatory reports published both in the Korean-language press and in official documents, viewers gained a renewed appreciation for the gravity of deadly infections at a time when more than seven hundred people had succumbed to illness during Contagious Disease Prevention Week.[139] Moreover, a number of upstanding Koreans went out of their way to accompany sick neighbors to local police stations, and some especially good Samaritans even escorted them to emergency consultation rooms where they could receive immediate treatment, both unusual practices, given that many lower-class individuals refused to submit themselves to impersonal methods of quarantine.[140] In this way, the Contagious Disease Exhibition of 1933 and the week-long program of sanitary events seem to have finally drawn wary Koreans into the regime of sanitary rule, especially through the agency of some self-regulating individuals.

Although bourgeois leaders of Korean society lent tacit and sometimes active support to these local campaigns of cultural rule, they also mobilized the power of hygienic modernity to capture the interest of the lower classes in their own programs of nation building. In 1932, just one year before the Contagious Disease Prevention Exhibition, the CASC held its own series of hygiene campaigns in the city's Korean neighborhoods, beginning in late April with a film on the prevention of communicable illnesses. Organizers conducted the first screening at Susong Common School, where the exhibition of 1933 would take place; later, they showed the film at Pagoda Park and Sajik Park, two nearby sites frequented by Koreans.[141] In addition to providing disease-prevention instructions, the film functioned as a promotional device for a CASC-sponsored hygiene exhibition that was held from May 2 until May 7. This event coincided with the annual spring cleanup, now administered by sanitation cooperatives in the northern village. To encourage lower-class residents to become knowledgeable agents of hygienic reform, the CASC presented a series of awards at the exhibition to Koreans who most faithfully followed sanitary regulations to clean toilets, sewers, kitchens, and dustbins.[142] Such efforts reveal increasing "faith" that the colonized population could become agents of their own self-regulation, even as both Japanese and Korean agents subjected them to strict enforcement.

Whereas government officials aimed to discipline subaltern bodies to ensure the health of their privileged Japanese counterparts, Korean elites sought to instill hygienic knowledge as a way of promoting cultural autonomy and national development. Their projects took a variety of forms, the most notable of which was the traveling hygiene lecture. Organized by medical students, these events took advantage of specialized knowledge that a small but influential group of Korean doctors had acquired from colonial institutions of higher learning, such as Keijō Medical School.[143] Ambitious young doctors used their vacation to present colloquial lectures and slide shows on the importance of individual health. To capture audience attention, organizers included musical performances and other forms of entertainment, turning these lectures into popular events like the above-mentioned exhibitions. Through these attractions, Korean medical practitioners sought to teach the colonized masses that advancing hygienic knowledge and practice was essential to their own health and that of the colonized nation.

Sponsored by the *Tonga ilbo,* the first hygiene lecture had taken place in the fall of 1921, when eight members of the newly established Keijō Medical School Club, an organization comprising students and their friends, fanned out into the countryside, visiting cities that included Suwŏn, Taejŏn, Taegu, and Pusan. Although their lectures did not target Keijō residents, they set a pattern for events that came to include the city's colonized population. At all of these events, speakers stressed the close linkage between the development of personal hygiene and the advancement of national health. As the opening line to a *Tonga ilbo* report boldly pronounced, "A country's level of civilization can be described based on the hygienic attitudes of the general populace. In fact, it is no exaggeration to say that the rise and fall of the nation depends upon it."[144] In tours of regional cities, Korean medical students emphasized the cultural bonds linking the colonized population as an ethnic group in search of autonomy. At the same time, they acknowledged considerable deficiencies in popular knowledge that endangered the advancement of a healthy national body. Lecturing in Taegu about the problems of uneducated Koreans, one member explained the situation as follows: "Because our Korean brethren have insufficient knowledge, they lack a conception of hygiene. As a result, once a contagious disease begins to emerge, they cannot cope with it. If we want to live together, we must develop hygienic attitudes and constantly warn each other, rather than ignore public health."[145] The narrative describing their activities presented these elite lecturers as the proverbial heroes of the nation who, out of loyalty *(ch'ungsŏng ŭro)*, devoted themselves to saving the benighted masses, encouraging them to improve their everyday hygienic practices.[146] In this way, Keijō doctors sought to downplay the Japanese empire as the object of Koreans' obedience, even as they used the shared agenda of hygienic modernity to lure the colonized masses into their own nation-building project.

As the decade progressed, Korean medical students continued to make regular visits to the countryside, exhorting rural inhabitants to follow their example and devote themselves to the health of the colonized nation.[147] At the same time, they also began to target the residents of Keijō, who, while benefiting from greater exposure to hygienic modernity than their counterparts outside of the showcase capital, continued to suffer at a disproportionate rate.[148] Offering practical information to the urban masses, a group of Korean graduates and students of the Keijō Medical School created the Association of Neighbors *(Yurinhoe)*. Of their many activities, members regularly offered lectures on issues such as the prevention and treatment of contagious diseases. Their activities clearly overlapped with those of sanitation cooperatives; yet while seeming to acquiesce to the regime of hygienic rule, Korean medical students, some of whom had participated in the March First Movement, sought to maintain a critical distance from the colonial government by promoting their own nationalist agenda.[149] The chosen site for their lectures—the Ch'ŏndogyo hall in Kyŏng'un-dong—reflects this nation-centered stance. A driving force behind the March First Movement, Ch'ŏndogyo, a nativist religion that grew out of the Tonghak uprisings of the late nineteenth century, continued to play an important part in the cultural movement of the 1920s, sponsoring publications such as *Kyebyŏk (Creation)*. The topics of the students' lectures—"On National Hygiene" and "Colonial Korea Seen through Medicine," for example—closely reflect the perspectives of the organization hosting their events.

Korean medical students, like colonial officials, sometimes drew on popular forms of entertainment and new audio-visual materials to lure large audiences to events that would communicate their message. In the spring of 1924, for example, they organized a hygiene event featuring a vocal soloist and a violin performance. They also screened a film showing scenery of Kŭmgangsan, a sacred mountain that Yi Kwang-su and other cultural nationalists sought to reclaim from the intrusive projects of Japanese tourist agencies.[150] These attractions drew a large crowd of approximately six hundred Koreans, including two hundred women. Impressed by the turnout, one jubilant report pronounced the event a success, concluding that the hygienic attitudes of lower-class Koreans had improved dramatically.[151] These lectures were so popular that the Association of Neighbors took their event to the neighboring city of Inch'ŏn. Even rain did not keep away crowds who, although likely attracted by amusements, stayed for serious lectures with titles such as "Medicine and Its Relationship to Law" and "Civilization and Hygiene." As before, organizers interspersed lectures with entertainment, including performances by an orchestra, a violinist, a mandolin player, and a solo vocalist.[152] Employing techniques advanced by the colonial government, Korean doctors used the large turnout to provide free consultations, allowing medical specialists to further assess the health of the population. Having successfully attracted crowds in Keijō and Inch'ŏn, zealous lecturers attempted to visit other regional cities, but the police suddenly intervened, forbidding them from making further excursions. Undeterred in their mission, eager medical students succeeded the following year (1925), presenting hygiene lectures to hundreds of Koreans throughout the peninsula.[153] As late as 1930, the Association of Neighbors, sponsored by the *Tonga ilbo*, continued to organize popular events in order to enlist the colonized masses in the perilous project of building a healthy nation under foreign rule.[154]

Although cultural nationalists managed to redeploy techniques developed by the colonial government to fit their own ends, they found themselves at a serious disadvantage in terms of the goals they could achieve under ongoing conditions of colonialism. Civic assimilation, especially as it developed under cultural rule, allowed and even encouraged a certain degree of rearticulation and redeployment by Korean elites. However, as time wore on, Japanese authorities gradually replaced cultural-rule strategies with more forceful and centralized measures aimed at curing the diseased city once and for all. Faced with yet another epidemic in 1935, the deadliest since 1928, colonial officials announced a new campaign to transform an enlarged Keijō into what they now called a "hygienic city."[155] As part of this campaign, they began to institute a controversial tax, borrowed from the metropole, which levied an income-based fee on all households for waste collection.[156] Rather than providing an equitable redistribution of such services as Korean nationalists had demanded, authorities instead required that all residents contribute money to finance the Government-General's reforms. In addition to forcing Koreans to shoulder the financial burden of Keijō's sanitary problems, they also reinstituted harsh measures, some reminiscent of the 1910s, to more effectively ensure that the populace followed hygienic regulations. Under the Waste Disposal Ordinance of 1936, for example, officials made household cleaning an unquestionable duty of all imperial subjects. Rather than simply relying on sanitation cooperatives to persuade residents to follow semiannual cleanup regulations, the city government now dispatched groups of cleanup teams to sanitize households of noncompliant individuals, forcing them to pay for associated costs.[157] By 1937, the year in which Japan entered protracted hostilities with China, the ability of local actors to rearticulate the terms of civic (and other forms of) assimilation thus began to narrow, as urban residents edged closer to a new era of life. It is to this period of Keijō's wartime past that the following chapter turns to explore unprecedented transformations in the city's spatiality.

# CHAPTER 5

# Imperial Subjectification

*The Collapsing Spaces of a Wartime City*

With the onset of the Asia-Pacific War, the spaces of Keijō and their relationship to late colonial Korea and Japan's expanding empire changed in dramatic and unprecedented ways. As scholars of urban planning have showed, the decision to incorporate suburban areas into the city more than tripled its size. As a result, the population swelled from approximately 375,000 in 1936 to over 1.1 million by 1942, making "Great Keijō" one of the seven largest cities in the Japanese empire.[1] Meanwhile, the exigencies of wartime mobilization produced equally, if not more, significant transformations in the qualitative landscape of late colonial Korea, now subsumed as a more integral, if still subordinated, part of an increasingly unified geobody. In what follows, I argue that this transformation took shape through two interrelated processes: first, the collapsing of sacred sites both old and new along various spatial scales; and second, an expansion, albeit markedly uneven, in the consciousness of colonized Koreans (and Japanese settlers) as loyal subjects of the wartime empire. From the most familiar to the most distant, these concentric circles of identification began at the level of the home and the city, radiating outward to include other sacralized sites on the Korean peninsula. New connections within this region of Japan's multiethnic empire, what wartime officials now called the "outer territory" (J: *gaichi; oeji*) rather than an overseas colony, extended further afield to encompass the "inner territory" (J: *naichi; naeji*), a term that replaced references to the metropole, and these connections also came to include recently won footholds on the Asian continent.[2] Such transformations in both the nomenclature and topography of the empire reveal that Koreans, as Takashi Fujitani has argued, were included to an unprecedented degree in the biopolitical concerns of the state[3]—if only, I would add, as hurriedly enumerated and insufficiently trained bodies to participate in the war effort.

These transformations in the lived spaces of wartime Keijō and the empire now intimately surrounding them can best be understood as a central function of and driving force behind *kōminka (hwangminhwa),* or what I will describe in this chapter as a highly choreographed and skillfully negotiated process of "imperial subjectification." As discussed in previous chapters, assimilation, in its various spiritual, civic, and material forms, had served as a central, if vague, ideology during the first twenty-five years of Japanese rule. With the outbreak of war in 1937, imperial subjectification began to subsume assimilation as a new, homogenizing principle of the late colonial regime. This principle demanded that all subjects, and the colonized population in particular, offer themselves as loyal servants of the emperor.[4] Despite its egalitarian rhetoric, imperial subjectification was an inconsistent and alienating project. Specifically, Korean subjects faced a markedly unequal burden in demonstrating their allegiance to a system that continued to privilege Japanese settlers in both material and symbolic ways. Because of these ongoing disparities, the collapsing of ethnic distinctions produced a surprisingly wide range of responses, not all of which conformed to the equalizing rationality of the wartime regime.

To be sure, many Koreans—particularly young students, military recruits, and others with livelihoods closely tied to state power—read the imperial oath, bowed before Shintō shrines, and engaged in other mandatory practices of loyalty, some with an astonishing degree of enthusiasm. In contrast, as scholars of a nationalist bent have showed, Protestant Christians, although a statistical minority, aggressively challenged the Government-General's stance on the nonreligious nature of Shintō reverence by refusing to worship at shrines, a practice they understood to be an unacceptable of form of idolatry.[5] Other Koreans engaged in less visible, but equally significant, forms of opposition to what I will call the "Shintōization" of their households, such as failing to say prayers before miniature shrines (J: *kamidana*) or discarding Ise amulets (J: *taima*). And still others, when forced to perform reverence for the imperial house, found subtle and personally comforting methods of subversion. For example, some performed Confucian forms of ancestor worship, such as the deep bow *(k'ŭn chŏl)*, rather than Japanese rituals associated with Shintō. That the colonial state, in turn, used these unconventional practices of emperor worship as propagandistic fodder for its Pan-Asian ideology of coprosperity makes locating and analyzing resistance to the wartime project of differential incorporation that much more difficult.

To foreground the micropolitics of imperial subjectification, this chapter emphasizes the centrality of performance, a particular kind of practice that aimed to convince relevant audiences of its validity. On the one hand, this notion of performance explains the hyperbolic practices of reverence conducted by colonized Koreans at the sacralized sites of Japan's wartime empire. On the other hand, it demonstrates how government officials assessed these practices according to a late colonial rationality that I will characterize as essentially enumerative. That is to say, the wartime regime used statistical increases in the performance of loyalty as a convenient substitute for qualitative changes that officials could not ultimately control. As Shintō critics were quick to indicate, however, closer ethnographic inspection of Koreans' allegedly reverent practices revealed a far messier and less comforting reality of imperial subjectification.

## WARTIME KOREA IN THE EMPIRE'S SACRED TOPOGRAPHY

In 1940, near the midpoint of the Asia-Pacific War, the Japanese empire celebrated its twenty-sixth-hundredth birthday. In the ideology of the prewar period, Emperor Jimmu, a descendant of the Sun Goddess Amaterasu, began to rule his subjects in 660 BCE, and his line purportedly remained unbroken through the reign of the current monarch, Hirohito (1926–89). By the outbreak of war in 1937, almost every ethnic Japanese living in the inner territory had already forged a close, if still imperfect, relationship to this official story of the imperial nation-state, a story that had been propagated through compulsory education and frequent spectacles.[6] The eleven thousand events held across the Japanese archipelago in 1940 provided them further opportunities to visit and to discuss sacred sites as part of what Kenneth J. Ruoff has described as "codifying the empire's foundational moment."[7] By contrast, most Koreans, fewer than 20 percent of whom had attended state-run common schools, had received far less exposure to the mythical places associated with Japan's imperial history, to say nothing of having actually visited them. Of the more than 1.2 million labor brigade "volunteers" who, in 1940, visited Kashihara (the place of Jimmu's enthronement), for example, only 4,676 (0.4 percent) hailed from the peninsula, most of them likely ethnic Japanese of the middle class.[8] The colonized population was thus only beginning to experience how the empire's sacred sites were to function in mobilizing them to participate in what was being touted as a "holy war."[9]

Given this context, the estimated two thousand events that took place across the peninsula as part of the celebrations in 1940 afforded Koreans unprecedented opportunities to expand their consciousness as subjects of an increasingly unified polity. However, their encounters with the equalizing rhetoric of the wartime regime produced unforeseen contradictions and irresolvable dilemmas. Even as a select group of markedly Korean representatives appeared as "reverent" protagonists in these events, the highly censored media ironically tended to highlight the unquestioned loyalty of Japanese settlers as the primary model of imperial subjectification, thus undermining the idea that ethnicity was a fully collapsible category. Curiously, the wartime state also resorted overwhelmingly to the "national language" (Japanese) and to its mouthpiece publication, the Keijō nippō, as the primary medium to instruct largely illiterate and linguistically unassimilated Koreans in officially sanctioned ways of feeling about the celebrations in 1940.

Attended by more than 1.3 million people during most of September and October, the Great Keijō Exposition was perhaps the most impressive of these events, especially in its ability to compress the sites of the empire's sacred topography onto one spectacular space.[10] For this epochal celebration, officials chose a suburban location at a considerable distance from Kyŏngbok Palace, the most common location for previous expositions. Designers used a developing area near Wangsimni as a new site onto which they could inscribe the futuristic mottos of the wartime period, all of which encouraged colonized subjects to forge closer relations with the imperial house. At the center of the main exposition corridor, they erected a tower "uniting the eight corners of the world under one roof" (J: hakkō ichiu; p'algoeng il'u), a wartime slogan referring to Jimmu's consolidation of the realm during the Nara period (710–94). This tower was a half-sized replica of the thirty-seven-meter monument recently erected in Miyazaki (ancient Hyūga), the place where, according to official legend, Amaterasu's grandson, Ninigi, descended from heaven and where the Japanese imperial line dwelled for three generations until Ninigi's great-grandson, Jimmu, journeyed

FIGURE 16. Exposition tower uniting eight corners of world under one roof. Source: Ko Kyo-maeng, ed., *Chōsen Daihakurankai no gaikan* (Keijō: Keijō nippōsha, 1939), 20.

eastward toward his new power base in Yamato.[11] Although most Korean (and Japanese) visitors had never visited the Miyazaki tower in southeastern Kyūshū, the exposition replica embodied a novel attempt to rewrite the history of the peninsula as a central part of Japan's empire (see figure 16). The tower's unifying mantra similarly interpolated visitors as integral, if still subordinated, members of this ancient community, rather than as part of a separate and independent polity.

Once inside the Imperial History and Colonial Rule Commemoration Halls, the front anchor of the main corridor, visitors encountered a series of visual displays that further explained the empire's twenty-six-hundredth anniversary in terms of "uniting Japan(ese) and Korea(ns) as one body" (J:

*naisen ittai; naesŏn ilch'e*), another wartime slogan aimed at harnessing the complex history of Korea to a triumphant story of Japan's imperial past, present, and future.[12] Large dioramas transported visitors to sacralized sites on the peninsula, encouraging the colonized population to associate these places with the fate of "their" warring empire. One such site was Puyŏ, the last capital of the Paekche Kingdom (18 BCE–660 AD). Officials had recently designated this historic location as the home of a mammoth new shrine and a youth training facility, part of a grandiose (but failed) project to reconstruct Puyŏ as a Shintō city.[13] In order to highlight the purported, if spurious, connection between ancient "Japan" and the other states of the three kingdoms of "Korea," they chose four Japanese monarchs from this period as the shrine's deities.[14] The plan to worship these deities clearly tipped the balance of "uniting Japan(ese) and Korea(ns) as one body" in favor of the former, whose allegedly unbroken line of leaders figured as the heroic protagonists. The diorama of Puyŏ allowed spectators who could not afford the trains, buses, and planes facilitating wartime tourism to make a virtual tour of this recently inaugurated shrine, located in South Ch'ungch'ŏng Province at a distance of approximately 150 kilometers from the capital city. The *Keijō nippō,* the exposition's primary sponsor, functioned as a prescriptive guide for visitors' sentiments, encouraging spectators to feel "an affinity with the highly esteemed Japanese emperor" when viewing this sacred site. But with the exception of some prominent pro-Japanese supporters, most Koreans with only a basic education likely associated Puyŏ with indigenous traditions, making this mawkish exhortation difficult to accept.[15] And for illiterate and uneducated Koreans who composed the vast majority of exposition visitors, such a rarefied symbol of wartime ideology would have been virtually indecipherable.[16] A similarly scripted diorama of Korea Shrine, another important node in the empire's compressed topography, also encouraged colonized visitors to actively express reverence for the imperial house, regardless of what they might have felt for the enshrined deities (Amaterasu and the Meiji Emperor). Staged as a successful example of "uniting Japan(ese) and Korea(ns) as one body," this particular display showed a Korean family engaged in a Japanese-style bow before a Shintō priest.[17] This idealized presentation of reverence aimed to collapse the physical space between this simulacrum of Korea Shrine and the real site, especially for rural and lower-class Koreans who had few opportunities to visit Namsan.

If Shintō shrines formed one constellation of sacred sites displayed at the exposition of 1940, the deadly battlefields of China formed another, a heroic one with which officials hoped the colonized population would more closely associate. To this end, display halls sponsored by the armed forces, located at the rear anchor of the main corridor, brought an otherwise distanced and bloody conflict into one central site. For example, the Heroic Deeds Hall functioned as a temporary version of the Yūshūkan, a war memorial museum associated with Yasukuni Shrine that displayed a wide range of personal articles from deceased soldiers.[18] Items exhibited at this hall included swords, binoculars, and approximately three hundred portraits of soldiers who had recently perished in famous battles, including the Nanking Massacre (1937–38). To further acquaint potential recruits and their families with soldiers' "heroic deeds," designers exhibited bloodstained military uniforms, highly charged symbols of patriotism that allowed viewers to experience the second Sino-Japanese War as it progressed.[19]

Even as exposition designers sought to emphasize the peninsula's increasingly close connections to the battlefront, ethnic Japanese continued to dominate the symbols that officials could display as successful examples of imperial subjectification. As a result, colonized visitors struggled to find their likenesses represented as valiant soldiers. And in truth, only a miniscule number of Koreans had recently entered the military as part of the new system of applicant-based recruitment (J: *shiganhei; chiwŏnbyŏng*). In 1938, the late colonial regime had made the unprecedented decision to accept highly qualified Korean recruits into the military as a preliminary experiment in conscription. However, ongoing suspicions of Koreans' loyalty delayed the implementation of conscription until late 1944, less than a year before the war ended. As a result, before 1944, officials enlisted only 16,830 Koreans from a total of 808,000 applications (2.1 percent), nearly 70 percent of which were filed after Japan's bombing of Pearl Harbor in late 1941.[20] So, an otherwise triumphant article on the exposition's armed forces halls embarrassingly revealed that only twenty-two (0.2 percent) of those 12,600 peninsulars who had lost their lives in the war were of Korean descent.[21] Even if designers had included all of these deceased soldiers, their portraits would still have constituted less than 10 percent of those displayed. Instead, to highlight this symbolically important minority, officials went out of their way to invite bereaved families and newly recruited Koreans to special celebrations, such as Imperial Army Appreciation Day.[22] Meanwhile, the *Keijō nippō* and other media used sentimental terms to prescribe how officials expected viewers to respond to these military displays. Ironically, however, newspaper reports did this only through the privileged position of colonizers. As one otherwise resounding article noted, "Whatever [display] appears before one's eyes strikes the heart with pride. And as long as one is *Japanese,* one cannot help but overflow with excitement."[23]

Given the experiential distance still separating most Koreans from actual combat, the armed forces buildings were instrumental in encouraging colonized men and male youth to imagine themselves as imminent participants in far-flung battles and for Korean women and female children to see themselves as dedicated supporters from the home front.[24] For example, the Friends of the Military Rationing Hall drew on the gustatory and tactile sensations of military combatants stationed in China, exposing visitors to the wartime systems of food and clothing rations. At this hall, designers displayed charts seeking to prove the nutritional superiority of tofu, sprouted rice, and other Japanese rations as compared to the milk and meat consumed by their enemies, whom one article degraded as "smelly Westerners."[25] Domesticating an originally foreign food, exposition employees also demonstrated the process of baking bread on the warfront, distributing four thousand Asian-style buns to visitors who wanted to try a staple consumed by their military counterparts. Meanwhile, a trip to the Outdoor Display of Military Weaponry provided visitors with the opportunity to view aircrafts, tanks, and rapid-fire cannons used to wage battles. Here, members of the armed forces offered spirited lectures about the awesome capabilities of these armaments. They especially targeted youngsters, the next generation of male soldiers and their female supporters who visited the exposition as part of class field trips, or what the media often described with the militarized term "troops of schoolchildren."[26] These mandatory visits allowed the media to display throngs of bodies filling the event grounds as a quantitative substitute for the highly incomplete and uneven project of wartime mobilization.[27]

A similar framing of patriotic youth and their enthused supporters took center stage at two other media celebrations of 1940. Both the sacred torch relay and the school tour of the inner territory used the spectacular movement of imperialized bodies along a scripted route of Shintō shrines to pull closer together the empire's sacred sites. The former bore an uncanny resemblance to the captivating opening of the Olympics in 1936, when Hitler orchestrated a course from Athens to Berlin. Although the war forced Tokyo to forfeit its bid to host the first Olympics outside of the West, government officials devised an equally impressive torch relay for the empire's twenty-six-hundredth-anniversary celebration. In this distinctly Pan-Asian event, staged to end on National Foundation Day, fifty-six children (forty-one Korean and fifteen Japanese) from the peninsula's thirteen provinces took turns shuttling a sacred flame from Ise Shrine, the highest-ranking Shintō complex on the Japanese mainland, to Korea Shrine, its counterpart atop Namsan.[28]

Coverage in the *Keijō nippō* both described noteworthy details about the torch relay and told audiences how to feel about a novel spectacle that most Koreans (and even some Japanese) might not have associated with the imperial house. Perhaps fearing what participants, spectators, and readers might say, the highly censored media afforded them remarkably few opportunities to express their feelings about this celebration, especially the masses of poorly educated Koreans, the most anxiously targeted objects of wartime mobilization. Even before the *Kōan-maru* pulled into the port of Pusan on February 3, the *Keijō nippō* triumphantly asserted that various road repairs and surveys made by local residents had laid the groundwork for Ise's sacred flame to purify the hearts of procession onlookers.[29] Similarly grand claims about the successfully "imperialized" subjectivities of spectators filled subsequent reports. At Tongnae, a neighboring spa town in South Kyŏngsang Province where the first torch handoff took place, a Japanese reporter dispatched to cover the 560-kilometer relay described deep emotions swirling around this spectacle. So entranced were the audiences that even farmers and merchants braved several hours of bitingly cold weather to welcome the procession. As expected of a highly choreographed celebration, Japanese flags could also be seen fluttering in front of houses in the most remote villages. The reporter framed these seemingly self-generated practices of loyalty as "proof" that Koreans' reverence was on the rise, although without ever once quoting the impressions of individual spectators. Rather than exposing their invariably complex and diverse emotions, he preemptively concluded that the "true spirit of the imperial nation" emitted from the sacred flame was making a profound impression on all twenty-three million inhabitants of the peninsula.[30]

Yet the *Keijō nippō*'s featured stories and images of the torch relay's homogenizing triumphs ironically proved that not all communities received the sacred flame with the same level or practice of reverence, even among ostensibly compliant Koreans. On the one hand, when the relay passed through a small village in North Kyŏngsang Province, forty students from the local common school and their Japanese principal reportedly followed the procession for almost eight kilometers, their own youthful bodies becoming an exemplary model of loyalty for

FIGURE 17. Korean men "revering" sacred flame. Source: *Keijō nippō*, Feb. 6, 1940.

other villagers. On the other hand, the elderly Korean villagers featured in figure 17, although similarly trumpeted as a successful case of imperial subjectification, seem to be engaging in a halfhearted and contrived practice of veneration, perhaps staged for propagandistic effect. These men, some dressed in clothing associated with the former *yangban* class, are casually sitting on the ground, rather than standing in austere veneration of the sacred flame. One article asserted that they prostrated themselves in loyalty, but such practices were certainly not captured by this image, which shows only a few of them lowering their heads. The hyperbolic claim that the men "trembled with divine inspiration" is also belied by the fact that many of them failed to remove their horsehair hats *(kat)*.[31] As discussed in chapter 2, Shintō priests and other colonialist pundits frequently criticized this practice as a sign of insincerity. The *Keijō nippō* also reached dubious conclusions about Koreans engaging in Confucian-style practices of ancestor worship, displaying it as a legitimate, if anomalous, substitute for imperial loyalty. One such account featured the remarkable story of an elderly Korean who, despite his blindness, prostrated before the scared flame, a practice causing the members of the procession to weep.[32] Another report mentioned that on its way to Ch'ŏn'an, an A-frame carrier, a clear reference to a Korean peddler, similarly kowtowed before the sacred flame.[33]

Even as the late colonial government attempted to recuperate these nonconventional practices as successful examples of differential incorporation into the imperial polity, the Keijō nippō still preferred to feature Japanese settlers and Japanese-dominated organizations as substitutes for Korean subjects and as models of loyalty. When the torch relay passed through Kŭm'osan (North Kyŏngsang Province) on February 5, for example, Kiyama Kensaku, an elderly expatriate from Aomori Prefecture who worked as a local sake brewer, reportedly cried when he saw the sacred flame. So moved was Kiyama that he donated numerous barrels of alcohol made from chestnuts, a substitute for rice, which remained scarce from the previous summer's drought.[34] In a similar article, the media reported that students at Keijō's Nandaimon Common School, attended primarily by settler children, had raised enough money selling empty bottles and cans, scrap paper, and recycled rubber to contribute nearly two hundred kilograms of pinewood for the closing ceremony, in which the head priest of Korea Shrine installed the sacred flame from Ise.[35] To further disseminate the culture of the imperial house among Koreans, local youth groups received branches of firewood to light subsidiary flames, which they used to boil rice, make celebratory rice cakes, and distribute among neighbors. Following this missionary practice, the Keijō branch of the Patriotic Woman's Association, another Japanese-dominated organization, used sparks from the sacred flame to prepare twenty-six hundred rice cakes for wounded soldiers convalescing in a local hospital.[36] All in all, the reporting on self-generated gestures of imperial subjectification privileged expatriates, suggesting that the torch relay as a whole had a far greater impact on Japanese settlers than colonized Koreans.

If that event aimed to expose the underimperialized masses to the distant symbols of the Japanese royal family, then the school tour of 1940 allowed a select group of twenty-nine youngsters from the peninsula to visit the inner territory's most sacred sites, a privilege only the middle classes—again, mostly Japanese settlers—could usually afford.[37] Official choreographers hoped not only that this tour would expand their consciousness of the empire's sacred topography, but also that it would spread the spirit of divine reverence and ancestor worship among less fortunate Koreans on the home front.[38] The Government-General's head of political affairs explained this missionary role as follows: "By making visits to Kashihara Shrine, the Imperial Palace, and Yasukuni

Shrine, you will strongly acquire the essence of the Japanese spirit and the Japanese culture. After your trip, you must work to convey those impressions to your common school friends and to members of your family, thereby inspiring all students on the peninsula to realize ever so more [their status] as imperial subjects."[39] Equipped with military uniforms, Prussian-style backpacks, and heavy-duty water bottles, the members of this tour were frequently described by the wartime media as "little warriors," an injunction to the colony's youth to prepare themselves for the war.

During their ten-day trip, the students were treated as local celebrities, showered with gifts, and, most important, admired for their contagious, if still insufficient, sense of loyalty. Before they boarded the *Kōan-maru*, the same vessel that had transported the sacred flame from Shimonoseki to Pusan just two months earlier, throngs of students from Pusan appeared to greet Cho Ch'ang-su, their local Korean representative, presenting him with fruits and sweets for the journey across the straits.[40] Later, after boarding a train from Fukuoka to Osaka, the group began to perform synchronized practices of reverence that brought them ever closer to the spiritual epicenter of the wartime empire. For example, the *Keijō nippō* reported that at exactly 10:15 AM on the morning of April 26, the students joined the emperor in a ceremonial bow directed at Yasukuni Shrine, the Tokyo complex honoring soldiers who had died in Japan's modern wars. They also observed a moment of silence for recently deceased soldiers with a continent-based tour group, a reverent scene that impressed passengers as a timely example of "Korean-Manchurian unity."[41] At one point during their visit to Osaka, Matsui Kutarō (1887–1969), a popular major general in the imperial army, spotted the student group in their military garb and, once again, lavished them with praise.[42]

Yet even as they were celebrated, encounters with residents of the inner territory painfully reminded the students of their relative inferiority as imperial subjects. For example, in a special Japanese-Korean conference with twenty-four Osaka students, Han Sin-su, a resident Korean attending a local school, encouraged his peers living in the outer territory to follow his footsteps and become "good Japanese," an ethnocentric code word for loyalty. Aimed at both ethnic Japanese and Koreans, this exhortation underscored the long-standing view that life on the peninsula had diminished the reverence of settlers, to say nothing of the colonized.[43] To prove themselves, the tour group stood up and recited the imperial oath, a shorter version of the Imperial Rescript on Education that colonial officials had specifically created for Koreans in late 1937.[44] Although instituted as part of a homogenizing project of imperial subjectification, this oath, recited almost exclusively by the colonized population as a supplemental demonstration of their loyalty, marked even these peninsular representatives as categorically distinct from their inner-territory counterparts.

Similarly hyperbolic performances of reverence took place throughout their tour, inspiring both real and imagined audiences to match their frenzied sense of loyalty. At the first sacred site of their tour, Kashihara Shrine, the head representative from Kangwŏn Province, Furukawa Jun'ichi, led the students in reiterating their allegiance to the Japanese empire. Never hesitant to engage in totalizing rhetoric, the *Keijō nippō* claimed that their "ringing voices" pierced the silence of this sacred complex and, in the process, became the collective voices of all students on the peninsula.[45] On the afternoon of April 27, the group reached Ise, the sacred shrine dedicated to Amaterasu. Following a ceremonial bow performed before the outer shrine, the location of the agriculture and industry god (Toyouke), the group recited the imperial oath. After a six-kilometer journey to the inner shrine's sacred precincts, they genuflected before Amaterasu and then recited the imperial oath for a second time. Once they reached Tokyo on April 29, the group made their way to the imperial palace, the spiritual epicenter of the wartime empire. In front of the two-tiered bridge, the place where millions of ethnic Japanese had come to pay their respects to the modern emperor, the students sang the national anthem and, once again, recited the imperial oath (see figure 18).[46]

Despite the tiring repetition of these expressions of loyalty, media reports suggest that the peninsula-based students gained an adequate appreciation for the imperial cause only when they came in contact with what the *Keijō nippō* described as "the real portrait of divine Japan." As one article stated, "It was the first time [for them] to know the honor of [being] a real imperial subject."[47] In both of these phrases, the reporter emphasized the "real" or "true" version of loyalty that most colonized Koreans (and some expatriate Japanese) had allegedly failed to embody, despite the never-ending performance of statements and practices required of them. Indeed, in a rare interview with the wartime media, two of the Korean students, Pak Sŭng-gŏl and Kwŏn O-hŭng, themselves concluded that their ritual practices at Ise finally came to produce the "Japanese spirit," suggesting an Ise visit as necessary for acquiring that level of loyalty. Strictly adhering to the event's official

FIGURE 18. Korea-based students bowing before Imperial Palace (Tokyo). Source: *Keijō nippō*, May 2, 1940.

purpose, they vowed to convey this spirit to underimperialized class-mates after their return.[48]

When the students toured Yasukuni Shrine, whose annual grand festival and Hirohito's birthday celebration coincided with their visit, crowds reportedly cleared the way for these celebrities to make yet another recitation of the imperial oath. Unaware of but impressed by this colony-specific practice, Japanese onlookers bombarded the accompanying newspaper reporter with questions about it.[49] On the following day, spent in part visiting various government ministries, Tokyo officials offered still ambiguous assessments of their loyalty. On the one hand, they reiterated the group's superiority in this regard even when compared to some residents of the inner territory. On the other, they suggested the inadequacy of loyalty among most Korea-based students, as if peninsular life had made them less reverent than subjects with more frequent and direct access to the empire's sacred topography.[50]

## MILITARIZED NAMSAN AS SPIRITUAL EPICENTER

The Shintō shrines of Namsan figured as an important node in all of the Korea-related celebrations of 1940. Within the city, Namsan also came to function as the spiritual epicenter of late colonial Keijō. As early as the summer of 1936, the Government-General began to pass new regulations to yoke hundreds of local shrines to the colony's most important Shintō monuments.[51] With the passage of these regulations, officials elevated Seoul Shrine (as well as Pusan's Ryūtōsan Shrine) to the status of a small, national shrine, situated just below the higher-ranking Korea Shrine (as well as Puyŏ Shrine).[52] At the same time, the late colonial state placed other, lower-ranking shrines under its managerial purview by unifying Shintō practices, including the conduct of festival celebrations, the content of priests' prayers, and the salary and clothing worn by clergymen. Through these homogenizing regulations, authorities transformed local shrines into more effective sites of wartime mobilization.

Interventions into the everyday operation of Seoul Shrine's parish organization led to the gradual militarization of the grand festival, a strategy aimed at spotlighting the sacred grounds of Namsan, rather than the rowdy streets of Keijō. After the onset of war, the festival procession continued to form a central part of the shrine's celebrations but was transformed by the Government-General into a means of rallying residents in support of military hostilities. To curtail what they now overwhelmingly disapproved of as the excessive display of festival play, the managers of late colonial spirituality replaced forms of entertainment that might lead to unruly behavior with new, austere forms of Shintō reverence that conformed more closely to state goals. In this way, they transformed a long-standing urban spectacle into another expression of the military battles already enveloping nearby China and that would soon extend into the Pacific.

Just three months after the outbreak of the second Sino-Japanese War in July 1937, colonial officials began to modify the city's autumn festival to reflect the somber mood of the wartime empire. The Government-General's Bureau Chief for Home Affairs, the department that oversaw Shintō, issued a new set of regulations exhorting inhabitants "to avoid unnecessary expenses and to practice frugality [instead]." These regulations included reducing expenditures on customary offerings, such as sumo wrestling, martial arts, flower arrangement, and the tea ceremony. Other playful practices, such as the float display and costume procession, were prohibited altogether from the festivities of 1937.[53] As one newspaper article reminded residents, "This year, the imperial army is moving righteous forces forward, and at a time when they are arduously fighting in northern China and Shanghai—arduously fighting and experiencing numerous [human] sacrifices—we must carry out a heartfelt autumn festival with those hardships in mind."[54]

The militarization of the imperial palanquin, the most important symbol of the annual procession, is a good example of how battlefront hostilities came to dominate the late colonial festival. Before 1937, the shrine's parish organization had granted the honor of pulling the palanquin to wealthy Japanese merchants and other influential members of the expatriate community. However, with the onset of the war, the Government-General mandated that influential settlers yield this privilege to military forces. These included the peninsula's reserve army and defense groups as well as armed units of middle-school students and youth groups, individuals who could more effectively imbue onlookers with reverence for their warring empire. In 1938, newspaper reports claimed that an incredible one hundred thousand people, approximately one-seventh of Keijō's total population, gathered on the streets as the militarized procession made journeys into newly incorporated parts of the city.[55] Yet, even after nearly three decades of assimilation, it is not clear that the draw was exclusively about imperial reverence. To be sure, parish leaders and other local proxies of the wartime state had mobilized large numbers of festival participants. However, procession organizers continued to include military music from the former Chosŏn court and an ancient-style Korean procession. Described by the *Keijō nippō* in the multiethnic language of "local flavor," these markedly Korean attractions might also explain why so many colonized residents ventured onto the streets to see this well-established, if recently modified, ritual.[56]

The new slogan of "Japan(ese) and Korea(ns) as one body" led wartime officials to introduce new cultural forms directing festival-goers' attention to the imperial house. During the autumn festival of 1941, for example, residents first witnessed the *Urayasu no mai,* a formal dance performed by ringing ritual bells in the shape of the three imperial regalia, each representing a primary virtue of the Japanese monarch (sword = valor, mirror = wisdom, and jewel = benevolence).[57] Created by the Imperial Household Agency in 1940 as part of the twenty-six-hundredth-anniversary celebrations, this popular attraction presented the outward appearance of an ancient Shintō ritual in the novel guise of modern emperor worship. Not unlike festival performances conducted by *geisha* and *kisaeng* before 1937, the dance featured nine attractive women selected from a local high school, an honor they were not allowed to refuse.[58] Another new attraction to the festival celebration of 1941 was the warrior procession, which was granted the privilege of pulling the imperial palanquin that year. This special procession was fittingly described by the *Keijō nippō* as "leading the prayers for the nation's future prosperity."[59] Thereafter, the warrior procession always appeared in front of the portable shrine, a clear sign that the emperor and his military forces predominated in this urban spectacle.[60]

During this period, authorities also created new military- and emperor-centered activities on Namsan and relocated older forms of festival entertainment to this solemn site. As early as 1937, officials used the autumn festival to organize a ceremony at Korea Shrine to pray for continued good fortunes in the war. Held simultaneously at 3 PM on October 19 at shrines throughout the empire, this annual prayer event aimed to unite the hearts and minds of the colony's subjects with their counterparts elsewhere. Namsan visitors also enjoyed Japanese fencing, sumo wrestling, sword dancing, and poetry writing, Shintō offerings performed in front of the shrine grounds, rather than on the city streets.[61] Following the festival, during the remainder of 1937, Namsan hosted more than five hundred military celebrations, the majority of which Japanese settlers organized in coordination with government and Shintō officials.[62] Later, in 1939, state officials unveiled a seventeen-meter imperial subject oath tower at the base of Korea Shrine to attract further attention from the colonized masses. Made possible by one hundred thousand yen in "donations" from schoolchildren across the peninsula, this tower, which housed 1.4 million copies of their handwritten oath, aimed to prove that Koreans were "voluntarily" supporting the war effort.[63] Such shrine-centered activities, including bowing in front of the oath tower, only increased as the war progressed, especially after Japan's control over the Pacific dwindled following the battle of Midway in June 1942.

If the city's militarized festival celebrations and the imperial subject oath tower did not adequately condition residents to consider Namsan the city's spiritual epicenter, then the specter of death associated with a new Shintō shrine did.[64] Built in close proximity to the military base at Yongsan, Seoul Nation-Protecting Shrine functioned as a local version of Yasukuni Shrine. As early as 1885, Keijō's expatriate population had begun to participate in yearly celebrations for Yasukuni's annual festival and in memorial services dedicated to fallen soldiers. Shintō priests had also memorialized approximately five thousand Japanese expatriates (simultaneously enshrined at Yasukuni) in triannual services.[65] The onset of hostilities in 1937 and the desire to mobilize soldiers from the colony finally convinced the Government-General to systematize these memorial services and establish facilities on the peninsula to administer them, resulting in the creation of two Yasukuni satellites, one in Keijō and the other in Ranam, a military port city on the northeastern coast of Korea.[66]

Although largely orchestrated by government and military officials, the emergence of Seoul Nation-Protecting Shrine was presented by the wartime regime as a popular manifestation of imperial subjectification. To this end, they created a shrine support association and housed it in the Government-General's Domestic Affairs Bureau.[67] This organization lobbied metropolitan organizations for nearly one-fourth of the funds necessary to construct the shrine. Members also led a peninsula-wide campaign to gather the remaining funds through donations that would underscore subjects' voluntary consciousness.[68] Once construction on the new Keijō complex began in the summer of 1940 with a highly symbolic one-week labor brigade of the Governor-General and more than twenty-six hundred officials, more than sixty thousand students, members of neighborhood associations, and military personnel followed suit over the next three years, offering their physical labor to help build the shrine.[69] Another self-congratulatory report announced that a collection box placed at the entrance of the Great Korea Exposition's Heroic Deeds Hall elicited more than 730 yen in donations. Although these contributions amounted to an average of less than fifteen yen among the nearly twenty-five thousand daily visitors, the author triumphantly wrote that this collective donation exemplified the Pan-Asian solidarity of the wartime empire.[70] Whether forced or voluntary, these individual and collective efforts were repeatedly framed in the media as successful examples of imperial subjectification.[71]

Although it is nearly impossible to capture the complex subjectivities behind such acts, even a skeptical reading of these highly scripted accounts suggests that some residents did actively participate in their own transformation as imperial subjects. However, as with the celebrations in 1940, the *Keijō nippō* tended to spotlight Japanese settlers over colonized Koreans. For example, an article from 1940 enthusiastically reported that 150 individuals, including a sickly fifty-four-year-old man, demonstrated the same level of loyalty as their deceased kin by performing labor for the new nation-protecting shrine.[72] Another article congratulated Ōkuma Chūjirō, a local member of a popular sect of shrine Shintō, Tenrikyō, for donating five hundred yen to the new monument. The same piece also lavished praise on Ōkubo Satoko, a Keijō expatriate who pawned her own personal belongings to gather funds for a contribution of nearly three hundred yen.[73]

Perhaps more than any other activity associated with late colonial Namsan, the installation of fallen soldiers at Seoul Nation-Protecting Shrine helped advance imperial subjectification, at least among Japanese settlers. As Takahashi Tetsuya has argued for Yasukuni, these solemn events transformed the suffering of surviving family members, particularly women and children, into national glory.[74] This process of "emotional alchemy" began in the summer of 1943 when Shintō clergy, facing an escalating number of deaths, invited approximately six hundred relatives of fallen soldiers to attend the shrine's first installation ceremony.[75] When the shrine was finally unveiled during a major, three-day celebration in late November of that year, officials had already installed 7,447 souls, including those of 549 newly recruited Korean soldiers.[76] To honor family members who had lost relatives in the war, government officials called on neighborhood patriotic units and local businesses to welcome these individuals as living heroes. On all-expense-paid trips to the capital, bereaved family members wore red ribbons pinned to their lapels, which entitled them to seats on crowded buses and streetcars and free rides anywhere in the city.[77] Their stay also coincided with a special reception at the people's hall, where photographers captured portraits of them as honorable bereaved families.[78] The Keijō branch of the Greater Japan Women's Association, an organization established in 1942 to assist male soldiers on the warfront, played an especially important part in these family visits as the gendered face of the late colonial state. In late 1943, this organization welcomed approximately fifteen hundred out-of-town guests being honored at the new shrine. Dressed in the baggy *monpe* pants worn by women during the war, members of this association greeted visitors at the train station, carried luggage to their appointed inn, and met them for morning and evening meals. They even joined these venerated nation-protecting mothers and wives for a special tour of the capital, including visits to famous sites such as Ch'anggyŏng Garden, home to the city's zoo.

Another instance of "emotional alchemy" took place in late March 1944 when twenty-five orphaned children participated in another all-expense-paid trip to Keijō to honor their deceased fathers as nation-protecting gods.[79] Such visits were featured prominently in the late colonial media, whose sentimental rhetoric functioned as a mobilizing technology in its own right. According to one account, Tsuruzaki Tome, a common school student from Kwangju, was so impressed with Ch'angdŏk Palace and the Secret Garden (Piwŏn) that she returned to bed that night thanking her deceased father for allowing her to make this once-in-a-lifetime visit (rather than mourning him). For Iseki Sonae, a student from Kyŏnggi Province, receiving special sweets delivered from the Japanese empress at a special ceremony held at the Government-General building was the highlight of her trip; indeed, that the imperial house displayed such concern for orphans made the pain of her father's loss more palatable. According to a similarly aestheticized account, such "benevolent" gestures made Shimizu Kayoko, another visitor, all the more "happy" to become a wartime orphan.

Although written in the "national language" and featuring Japanese children, this article was published in a Korean woman's magazine, where it encouraged colonized mothers to selflessly part with their male partners and relatives.[80] The orphans' seemingly cheerful, if restrained, answers to a series of highly scripted questions also aimed to hearten children whose fathers might soon enter the battlefield with no guarantee of ever returning home. To accomplish this feat, the interviewer first confirmed that each of the nine participants was in good spirits after his or her father's death. As expected, the orphaned children responded with uniformly affirmative responses, rather than offering countervailing examples of the pain that their fathers' deaths likely caused. The aforementioned Tsuruzaki Tome reported that her six brothers and sisters were all living happily. That three of her male siblings had subsequently entered the military and that her older sister paid a visit to Yasukuni Shrine only further supported this "fact." Then the reporter solicited accounts of the orphans' visits. Yoshimoto Teruo, a student in Kunsan, responded that he felt overjoyed to visit Seoul Nation-Protecting Shrine, where he was finally reunited with his father. Other orphans were so moved that they could reportedly see the faces of their dead fathers when they looked into the shrine's sacred mirror, one of the three imperial regalia. Emotional responses of this variety allowed readers to better appreciate the "benevolence" so often attributed to the Japanese emperor, the man who stood at the center of an increasingly deadly war.

The media's elaborate efforts to highlight the imperialized subjectivities of younger individuals with close connections to military service were complemented by its important role in convincing the public of the growing success of official attempts to mobilize the colonized masses to show reverence for the imperial house.[81] Government officials rarely conducted interviews with those compelled to worship at Namsam. Perhaps fearful of what they would find beneath the façade of reverence, the late colonial state preferred to rely on increases in visits as its primary means of tracking, publicizing, and thereby heightening the loyalty of largely undifferentiated shrine-goers, indexing change in statistical (quantitative) rather than ethnographic (qualitative) terms. The official formula promoted in the newspapers was quite simplistic: aggregate growth in shrine visits denoted greater reverence.

Before the outbreak of hostilities with China in 1937, shrine authorities had quantified visitors to Korea Shrine by ethnicity. Such categorizations suggest that the Government-General invested bureaucratic energy in distinguishing under-"assimilated" Koreans from their "loyal" Japanese counterparts. Although the media did not place a rhetorical focus on elevated shrine visits until the late 1930s, prior statistics reveal deep ethnic-based discrepancies.[82] In 1926, officials recorded more than 301,000 Japanese visits to this new Shintō complex. Although the colonized population continued to far outnumber Japanese settlers, shrine authorities recorded approximately 172,000 visits made by Koreans during the same year. That is to say, despite their statistical underrepresentation as part of the colony's total population, Japanese accounted for nearly two-thirds of shrine visits in 1926, whereas Koreans composed just over one-third.

Official statistics show that shrine visits made by both ethnic groups continued to grow throughout the late 1920s and early 1930s, the result of increasingly aggressive policies of spiritual mobilization.[83] By 1936, Japanese made nearly 830,000 visits to Korea Shrine, a figure 2.75 times higher than that of ten years earlier. For their part, Koreans doubled their shrine visits to approximately 341,000 in the same year. However, over this ten-year period, the proportion of visits made by Koreans actually decreased to slightly less than 30 percent of total visits; and during the early 1930s, that figure dipped well below 20 percent. At the same time, the number of individual visits made by Koreans—perhaps a more reliable indicator of imperial reverence than statistics for mandatory visits as part of school, company, or military groups—remained remarkably low.[84] For example, in 1934 and 1936, not one member of the colonized population visited Korea Shrine as part of New Year celebrations. By contrast, 193 and 299 Japanese endured the cold to pay their respects to Amaterasu and the Meiji Emperor.[85] These statistics demonstrate that large segments of colonized Koreans and many Japanese settlers continued to remain alienated from this Shintō complex.

Just as the Government-General began to enforce visits to shrines as a civic duty of all imperial subjects, officials stopped tracking visitors' ethnicity.[86] Although the amalgamated category of "Japanese-Korean" *(naisenjin;* K: *naesŏn'in)* clearly embodied the late colonial ideology of imperial unity, this new practice of enumeration made it nearly impossible to determine the proportion of each ethnic group in the total wartime statistics. In 1936, official documents recorded nearly 1.2 million visits to Korea Shrine; that number exceeded two million the following year. By 1942, authorities boasted more than 2.6 million annual visits, an increase of more than 710,000 from ten years earlier. Only in tracking group visits to Korea Shrine—the category that officials could more effectively control—did the wartime state continue to note ethnicity. Not surprisingly, Koreans made up the majority of group visits. In 1930, the colonized population accounted for approximately 80 percent of group visits to the shrine; by 1943, that figure increased to nearly 100 percent![87]

The *Keijō nippō* used numerical increases in shrine visits as media performances aimed at convincing the public that imperial subjectification was advancing apace. Examples of this type of enumerative rationality can be found as early as 1935, the year in which the Government-General launched a new spiritual campaign to shore up communal solidarity by superimposing Japanese Shintō onto Korean religions, including shamanism.[88] In an article published in June of that year, the author boasted that the number of monthly visits to Korea Shrine had grown to nearly one hundred thousand, almost half of which were made by the colonized population. Furthermore, he claimed that the daily average of three thousand visits during the first half of 1935 marked an unprecedented record since the shrine's establishment in late 1925. In a rare comment made at the end of this triumphant article, the author also boasted of an important qualitative change: whereas most Koreans had entered the shrine gate with a "sightseeing feeling" up to that point, they now performed bows in front of the shrine. This shift—the author concluded boldly, if without evidence—signified increasingly internalized sentiments of loyalty.

In the fall of 1936, a *Keijō nippō* report described how another government campaign, National Spirit Promotion Week, helped advance loyalty to the wartime state. Held every year during the second week of November, this campaign featured a special shrine visitation day as its opening event.[89] Although newspaper reports used the astronomical figure of 33,600 visits to declare this day a "great success," nearly 92 percent of shrine-goers participated as members of 145 groups. That only 636 Koreans and 2,124 Japanese made individual shrine visits suggests that even mass campaigns like National Spirit Promotion Week could not elicit colonized (or colonizing) subjects without a considerable mix of persuasion and coercion.[90] In spite of these problems, the late colonial state continued to act as if such visits derived from internalized sentiments of loyalty. A newspaper report from the fall of 1937, for example, claimed that the record-breaking growth in shrine visits since the outbreak of the war accurately reflected the self-awareness of Koreans who were "burning with the single color of devotion."[91] By the end of 1939, the *Keijō nippō* reported that an average of nearly sixty-seven hundred individuals made visits to Korea Shrine every day, a sign that these ethnically undifferentiated masses supported the war. The article suggested that the two million shrine visits made during 1939 meant that the 750,000 inhabitants of Keijō, from infants to the sick, visited the shrine three times each in that year.[92]

Even as the media promoted growth in shrine visits as the primary criteria for gauging imperial reverence, this enumerative rationality was threatened by the specter of statistical decreases, especially as war fever cooled off. Even official figures reveal that aggregate numbers of visits to Korea Shrine dropped from a high of nearly 2.7 million in 1938 to just over 2.1 million in 1940.[93] Although not widely publicized, internal police reports also exposed deep-seated concerns about maintaining high numbers. In one such report, the author alerted officials to a notable drop in visits to Korea Shrine, from 265,733 in April 1941 to 188,125 in May. The number of visits in May 1941 paled in comparison not only to April but to those made in May of the previous year (213,657).[94] Even in a month when the number of shrine visits increased, police reports, although suggesting that "thoughts of reverence" were gradually on the rise, expressed anxieties that visits by the educated classes had, ironically, decreased.[95] It took the attack on Pearl Harbor and war with the United States in late 1941 to bring a record-breaking 316,490 individuals to Korea Shrine during the month of December, including nearly thirty thousand residents of Keijō who attended a special service to pray for future success in battles.[96] As before, the late colonial media touted these numerical increases as tangible signs that even momentary lapses in shrine visits could not derail the upsurge in support for the war.

Shintō priests, however, rarely accepted these media performances at face value. Concerned about Shintō's spiritual foundations, these clergymen seriously questioned the governing rationality of the Government-General, arguing that persistent forms of coercion undercut official claims that numerical increases in shrine visits should be understood as reflecting growth in Korean reverence. In 1936, Achiwa Yasuhiko published an article in the Government-General's monthly bulletin in which he cited the most recent statistics for shrine visits, showing a steady increase from 403,550 in 1931 to 937,588 in 1935. Like government officials, he predicted that these figures would only increase in the future. However, as a Shintō priest, what concerned him more than the numbers was the attitude of shrine-goers, who, he argued, "probably did not climb those 375 [sic] stone steps of their own volition." Most came as members of groups, he pointed out, and were mechanistically guided by leaders. So troubled was Achiwa with this level of coercion that he likened colonized visitors to Korea Shrine as cows being pulled to pray at Kōzenji, a famous Kyoto temple established in the thirteenth century. Directing his critique at the superficial rationality of enumeration, he concluded, "It is absolutely meaningless to make shrine visits without recognizing the existence of divine spirits."[97] Other Shintō officials continued to remind Koreans that the enshrined deities were, in fact, the ancestors of the Japanese empire and not "some hypothetical gods."[98]

Later, in the summer of 1940, Achiwa wrote another article that questioned using numerical increases in visits as evidence for growth in reverence. By this time, the boom in shrine visits recorded during 1938 and 1939 had subsided, convincing Achiwa that most visits had, once again, become mere formalities. As before, he argued for "quality over quantity," suggesting that one's attitude toward the deities far outweighed in importance the number of instances that one prayed before them. In particular, he criticized imperial subjects for failing to worship on nonfestival occasions or when they had no business to conduct with clergy. He also decried visitors who appeared before the shrine in unseemly clothes, using their ragged appearance as an excuse for not praying. Attentive to the psychology of shrine visitors, Achiwa harshly criticized this practice as an unpardonable "impropriety."[99] And in 1943, Suzukawa Genshō, another high-ranking priest at Korea Shrine, regretfully wrote that many Koreans still tended to make visits to Namsan in an overly formalistic way or did so with great reluctance.[100] Using Korean-language publications to chastise under-"imperialized" readers, Suzukawa described such individuals as "apathetic" in terms of their understanding of Shintō rituals.[101] Government studies on local festivals also discovered that the colonized population, although accustomed to bowing at these events, still did not clap before the gods, a standard practice designed to elicit the deities and gain their blessings.[102] Semiofficial reports revealed that even some Japanese settlers failed to perform purification rites according to official standards or contravened ritual propriety by praying after sunset or without disembarking from vehicles.[103] As one Shintō critic anxiously concluded about the insufficiently internalized sense of reverence implied by such practices and the nonautonomous nature of wartime shrine visits more generally: "No matter how much [we] lecture individuals about divine reverence or promote shrine visits, if individuals do not conduct [these practices] of their own volition, there is no use. And, unless that spirit penetrates all of their words and deeds, it is a falsehood. Rituals performed in front of the shrine are but one expression of that sense of reverence."[104]

## THE "SHINTŌIZATION" OF HOUSEHOLD LIFE

Although they criticized the state's logic of enumeration, priests did not oppose wartime mobilization. In fact, they became some of its strongest supporters, urging Koreans to more fully internalize sentiments of reverence. Indeed, intimate knowledge of shrine-goers' spiritual practices allowed the clergy to promote their own agenda. What I am calling the "Shintōization" of household life aimed to collapse the ritual practices of public shrines into the everyday activities of the private sphere, thus expanding residents' consciousness as imperial subjects. Led by shrine clergy in close cooperation with police officers, schoolteachers, and neighborhood leaders, this project included the mass distribution of shrine amulets and calendars, the installation of and prayer before miniature shrines, and the daily performance of ritual bows toward Tokyo's imperial palace. Although never nearly as successful as the mass mobilizations of visits to Namsan, the gradual penetration of shrine culture into wartime homes pushed the operational limits of imperial subjectification and altered the topography of sacred space in new ways. Naturally, however, even when officials could rely on a local network of proxies subjecting homes to unprecedented forms of surveillance, they could not ensure that the colonized population voluntarily embraced the cult of the Japanese emperor as the supranational head of their family clans.

From the late 1930s, priests began the mass circulation of official calendars and shrine amulets, which were distributed directly from Ise Shrine, the most simple and inexpensive way of Shintōizing Korean households. The amulets were to be placed next to the home's miniature shrine. Shintō officials considered these amulets actual seals of the imperial house, symbolic emblems of Amaterasu herself. As such, they expected that imperial subjects would treat Ise amulets as sacred objects of respect, praying before them morning and night.[105] The single-page official calendars contained everyday information for imperial subjects, including important festival dates. Like other local institutions, Seoul Shrine complemented Ise's official calendar with its own, a version of which for 1938 lists more than fifty annual celebrations and seven monthly rituals. A Shintōizing device itself, this calendar contained a convenient reminder exhorting parishioners to post it next to the miniature shrine, the spiritual focal point of wartime homes. Other local shrine publications provided residents with detailed instructions on how to memorialize one's ancestors and celebrate family milestones, such as births, admissions to school, and weddings.[106] Through these calendars, officials hoped to synchronize the daily rhythm of imperial subjects around the common practice of household rituals.

Statistics on the distribution of Ise amulets demonstrate significant growth in Korea over the course of the war. Predictably, official accounts, deploying the same enumerative rationality used to track shrine visits, repeatedly heralded these increases as a demonstrable sign that imperial subjectification was progressing with great success. For example, a publication in 1941 reported that the number of Ise amulets distributed in Korea increased from fewer than seventy-five thousand in 1936 to more than 1.25 million by 1940.[107] Similarly, a document presented to the Diet in late 1944 triumphantly predicted that number to exceed three million by year's end, a more than fortyfold increase from 1936.[108]

Even as government authorities continued to vaunt these aggregate increases, shrine officials voiced their concerns that amulet distribution in Korea lagged behind other parts of the empire. In 1939, one priest embarrassingly admitted that whereas nearly 60 percent of households in the inner territory used Ise amulets, and Taiwan registered amulets in 37 percent of homes, the proportion of households on the peninsula that possessed one remained at less than 5 percent.[109] Even by the end of the war, the three million amulets boasted by some government authorities still only covered about 20 percent of the total number of households in Korea, a proportion 3.5 times less than that of Taiwan.[110] Meanwhile, although the number of official calendars distributed during the war remains unclear, extant records suggest that their dissemination across the peninsula lagged even further behind other parts of the empire, the result of different understandings attributed to this object among most of the colonized population.[111]

Like police reports on occasional decreases in shrine visits, wartime accounts by Shintō priests and neighborhood leaders exposed fluctuations in the distribution and use of Ise amulets. In 1939, one clergyman revealed that the number of amulets, although generally on the rise, had actually decreased from eighty thousand in 1937 to seventy-five thousand in 1938. He thus remained skeptical about correlating these depressed figures with the efficacy of imperial subjectification. As he anxiously wrote, "Although the number of groups, school students, and other shrine visitors is increasing dramatically, thoughts of reverence are not penetrating homes at nearly the same rate. Few are [those who] pray before the gods in the morning and at night."[112] Sŏk T'ae-u, an elite Korean member of the city's spiritual mobilization campaign, came to a similar conclusion regarding the attitudes of poorer Koreans. Writing in early 1940, Sŏk praised recent increases in the distribution of Ise amulets, but simultaneously lamented that even this figure paled in comparison to other parts of the wartime empire. Like his Shintō counterparts, he attributed these relatively low numbers to an "insufficient understanding" of the deities installed at Namsan's shrines.[113]

Due to a relative lack of shrines and clergymen, the method of Shintōizing homes on the peninsula involved a far more intrusive presence of state power than in the inner territory. These impositions undercut official hopes that loyalty would arise from the voluntary consciousness of most Korean subjects. Even otherwise upbeat authorities grudgingly recognized forced reverence as a significant, if not insurmountable, obstacle to imperial subjectification. In an article on Shintō practices, a high-ranking bureaucrat concurred with a Japanese tourist who astutely observed that coercion best explained the dramatic increase in Koreans' shrine visits and their possession of Ise amulets. Dismissing the governing logic that these outward signs offered empirical proof of loyalty, he argued that most Koreans were engaging in traditional practices of acquiescence aimed at placating officials. Furthermore, he suggested that they reverted to noncompliance when state proxies did not enforce ritual performances.[114] Subsequent accounts only confirmed this disturbing conclusion. In 1941, a high-ranking priest complained that although they visited Namsan numerous times each month, few Koreans spent any time praying in their homes.[115] As late as 1944, another writer lamented the frequency with which the colonized population treated Ise amulets carelessly or with irreverence.[116]

Facing perennial difficulties in Shintōizing household life, wartime officials called on school staff, shrine clergy, and neighborhood leaders to advance this missionary project.[117] In addition to talking about household rituals in the classroom, teachers used home visits to survey the extent to which each student's family practiced these rituals and, where necessary, to provide additional on-site instruction. Older students were also expected to provide guidance to junior classmates in perfecting daily bows toward the imperial palace, a ritual youngsters could then practice with family members. For their part, Shintō clergymen presented lectures, distributed written materials, and even projected films familiarizing Koreans with household rituals.[118]

Although not sufficiently recognized by most scholars of the late 1930s and early 1940s, who have simplistically understood this period as one of cultural "erasure" (malsal),[119] late colonial officials actively sought to recuperate nonstandard practices of emperor worship within a multiethnic polity that they hoped would outlast the war. In all of these media, priests worked to more fully merge Shintō practices of imperial reverence with Confucian rituals of ancestor worship, arguing that the former should be understood as an extension of the latter. In a Korean-language article published in early 1943, for instance, Suzukawa Genshō reminded readers of their own venerable custom of revering spirit tablets before ancestral shrines. To be sure, he recognized considerable differences between these clan-centered practices and those of emperor worship. For example, he noted that ancestor worship was generally limited to the heads of yangban households and only practiced on a few occasions throughout the year. In the end, however, Suzukawa remained confident that Koreans would overlook these differences of kind and frequency, accepting deities representing the imperial house as their own familial ancestors.[120]

Controversial for their alleged collaboration with the wartime regime, some Korean intellectuals also came to enthusiastically embrace this position. Yi Kwang-su (1892–1950) is perhaps the most infamous of these "pro-Japanese" writers.[121] Although previously associated with cultural nationalism, Yi penned "The Spirit of Bowing" ("Chŏl hanŭn maŭm") just a year before the war ended. This essay, designed to reach and convince even the most poorly educated Koreans, was written in the vernacular han'gŭl syllabary with the didactic tone of a schoolteacher. Yi argued that revering one's familial ancestors and the god of heaven and earth (ch'ŏnji shinmyŏng) should be yoked to local expressions of loyalty for the imperial house. To make this equation palatable to unconvinced readers, Yi deployed a wide range of Confucian examples representing Korean traditions, for example, children filial to their parents and subjects loyal to their lord. In the end, these long-standing forms of veneration were subordinated to modern rituals honoring the

Japanese emperor. As he pithily advised, "Revere the nation's gods *before* doing ancestor worship; bow to the emperor *before* paying respect to one's ancestors."[122] Likely aware of popular resistance to this ideological formulation, he exhorted the colonized population to abandon their reservations about venerating a foreign ruler and to concentrate, instead, on the purportedly shared tradition of ancestor worship. To this end, Yi strategically referred to the Japanese emperor with the indigenous term for monarch *(imgŭm-nim)* and portrayed him as a Korean-like figure who also prayed before his primal ancestor, Amaterasu, a figure doubling as the nation's great deity *(nara ŭi k'ŭn sin)*. Yi thus encouraged the Korean masses to forge their primary ancestral identification with the imperial house, whose symbolic presence increasingly permeated the intimate confines of household life.

Perhaps the best way to gauge the effectiveness of these Shintōizing proposals is to examine the installation of and practice before miniature shrines, described in various late colonial publications as the spiritual center of the home. Indeed, without these miniature facsimiles of larger shrines, conventionally placed in the alcove *(J: tokonoma)* of Japanese homes, the everyday practice of household rituals centering on the imperial house would have remained incomplete. Even as shrine officials and their Korean supporters embarked on increasing the distribution of Ise amulets starting in the late 1930s, they quickly realized that most colonized homes still did not contain a proper place to worship them. Tsuda Setsuko, one of the most prominent female figures of the Green Flag League, a nongovernmental organization established to promote the policies of the wartime state, recounted an emotional discussion with a Korean youth that highlighted this situation. After watching various wartime films depicting Japanese homes with miniature shrines as their spiritual core, the youth experienced jealousy that his Korean counterparts lacked such "holy sites."[123] Given that this account was likely dramatized for ideological effect and part of a scripted archive regularly spotlighting such spectacular cases, it is difficult to discern the degree to which this individual's unfulfilled desire to "become Japanese" represented the actual sentiments of most wartime Koreans. Nevertheless, his sense of inadequacy had the practical effect of allowing the wartime state to make unprecedented interventions into the everyday lives of the colonized population, including installing inexpensive offertory shelves in "unpatriotic" households.[124]

Although installing miniature household shrines was a mandatory wartime duty, most of the colonized population remained noncompliant. This was likely due to the costs (ten to fifteen sen) of purchasing or constructing the shrines in addition to Koreans' long-standing reluctance to abide by official impositions on the private space of the home. Aware of the considerable architectural (and financial) obstacles to the construction of a new, dedicated space for miniature shrines in Korean households, officials made various exceptions that allowed these shrines to be placed in unconventional locations, such as the main floored room *(taech'ŏng)* or on the wall of an *ondol* (floor-heated) room.[125] Nonetheless, it took the determined presence of neighborhood patriotic units, the lowest-level agents of the wartime regime, to ensure that Koreans installed miniature shrines, a policy these government proxies earnestly began to enforce in early 1943.[126] Meanwhile, the official bulletin of the spiritual mobilization campaign continued to publish frequent exhortations. One telling article offered detailed instructions on how to build an inexpensive miniature shrine that, the author condescendingly asserted, even a fifth or sixth grader could follow.[127]

Even when local leaders did successfully persuade their neighbors to acquire miniature shrines, Shintō priests continued to complain that many individuals failed to properly worship before them. That their exhortatory articles continued to appear until the very end of the war suggests that the mere existence of a household shrine did not necessarily ensure that family members worshiped at it with internalized sentiments of reverence. As Suzukawa wrote in 1943, "If [Koreans] conduct ancestor worship and bow before the miniature shrine carelessly, then [such practices] have absolutely no meaning and are nothing more than a formality. Although this is just one form of ceremony, the bottom line is whether or not [it is performed] with sincerity."[128] Neighborhood patriotic units echoed priests' concerns, reminding the colonized population as follows: "The point is to respectfully worship the deities from [the bottom of] one's heart; it is a matter of one's spirit, not the form."[129] To avoid practices deemed insufficiently reverent to the imperial house, local Shintōizers could only urge Koreans to study and rehearse on their own. Priests even grudgingly accepted that the colonized population might conduct these practices according to what Suzukawa called "customary rituals," a term denoting the deep bow associated with clan-based ancestor worship. In spite of these inclusionary concessions, the more "Korean" the style of Shintō rituals became, the less likely it was that its practitioners would have associated them with the imperial house.

For this reason, the late colonial state and its local proxies continued to publish textual and visual materials highlighting Koreans who had actively adopted Japanese-style household rituals. Take, for example, the following photographic leaflet (figure 19), entitled "Conditions of an Imperializing Family," which portrays the ideal life of a bourgeois Korean home.[130] Distributed by neighborhood patriotic units to the ten families in their charge, the image in the upper right of figure 19 shows a Korean mother and her young son conducting officially sanctioned rituals before a miniature shrine, in front of which they have placed fresh offerings of food and a branch from a sacred evergreen tree.[131] To the right of the household altar, this model family has also posted a copy of an official calendar, reminding themselves of important festival dates. In the center of the leaflet, the Korean mother is shown raising a Japanese flag in front of the home, an outward sign of her loyalty for the wartime empire. Together, these images underscore the important role played by "patriotic mothers" in instructing their young children to become loyal subjects of the emperor.[132] In the image to the lower left, the four members of this bourgeois family relax on *tatami* mats covering the floor of a Japanese-style room, rather than on the heated flooring common to most nonelite Korean houses. Yet another sign of this Korean family's "imperialization" is the transistor radio, one medium through which the wartime state disseminated timely information.[133]

Given the intense censorship of the late colonial media and the radically circumscribed conditions in which wartime Koreans could articulate their views, it is difficult to ascertain with any certainty how the colonized population responded to the project of Shintōizing their homes. However, in addition to widespread resistance to the installation of miniature shrines, fragmentary evidence points to their frequent misuse as well as the casual discarding of Ise amulets and official calendars. Part of the problem, as suggested above, seems to have been architectural. The concessions that allowed Koreans to install miniature shrines in the main hall or in an *ondol* room created unexpected obstacles to acceptable household practice. In an article published in early 1941, Suzukawa discussed the proper placement of the miniature shrine. On the one hand, he encouraged residents to install them in a clean place, but one that would not discourage family members from making morning and evening prayers. On the other hand, if placed in a frequently inhabited part of the home, the miniature shrine might be subjected to unnecessary commotion. Since most Korean homes lacked closets, family members could easily leave bedding and other miscellaneous items to pile up in a disorderly fashion near the shrine, an "impropriety" intimated by the author's convoluted instructions for household rituals.[134]

FIGURE 19. Leaflet promoting household worship. Source:
*Shashin hōdō, tatakao Chōsen* (Osaka: Asahi shimbunsha,
1945), 36.

More concrete, if equally fragmentary, accounts of Koreans living
outside Keijō suggest more conscious forms of resistance toward the
Shintōization of their homes, even though household surveillance was
generally less severe and shrine supporters (Japanese settlers) were
more concentrated in the capital city. Even a leader of a neighborhood
patriotic unit in rural Hwanghae Province was accused of mistreating
one of the two shrine amulets he received in 1941, placing it on a shelf
for bedding in a storage room. Although he did rest the other amulet

next to his miniature shrine, police officers inspecting his home in late May 1942 discovered that he continued to store haircutting instruments on top of the sacred shrine, a crime for which he was arrested and forced to resign his position.[135] In other, more rarely documented cases, Koreans engaged in even more overt forms of protest against the intrusion of public shrine culture into the everyday lives of their homes. In the fall of 1944, less than a year before the war ended, local officials conducted a survey of South Ch'ungch'ŏng Province. There, they found many rural families who responded to the imposition of amulet worship and other household rituals performed in front of miniature shrines with remarkably confrontational epithets, such as "[those are] Jap's evil spirits" *(oenom kwisin),* a shibboleth also repeated, if silently, by "worshipers" at Keijō's Shintō shrines (which will be discussed more below).[136] The irreverent treatment of Amaterasu and the imperial house as a menacing and distinctly foreign tradition suggests that few Koreans embraced these gods as shared objects of ancestral worship, despite elaborate efforts to Shintōize their homes.

## FROM WARTIME PERFORMANCES TO POSTCOLONIAL MEMORIES

From 1937 on, Koreans' performances of loyalty—whether at public shrines or in their households—quickly moved from a public practice that concerned individuals could still debate to a wartime imperative that few could oppose, at least outwardly. As Leo Ching has argued in his analysis of identity formations in wartime Taiwan, the challenge of becoming a loyal "Japanese" subject fostered overwhelming existential anxiety.[137] The same formulation might be applied to late colonial Korea as regards shrine worship, if understood as a highly scrutinized form of public performance. Obviously, the late colonial state could not possibly place every individual under perfect surveillance. Nevertheless, the perception of being seen placed a heavy burden on Koreans to make performances that would convince onlooking shrine officials of their reverence. When allowed to speak about those onerous visits in the highly censored media, most Koreans eagerly expressed internalized subjectivities that mirrored expected practices of loyalty.[138] Less common but perhaps more representative are accounts of shrine performances that also satisfied Namsan's "public eyes" but in far less enthusiastic and "imperialized" ways. These subtle and personally comforting methods of subversion ranged from subtly disguised Confucian rituals of ancestor worship to the enactment of silent forms of protest against the Japanese emperor.

One example of an ambivalent shrine performance appears, astonishingly, in a propagandistic newsreel produced by the late colonial state. As discussed above, wartime officials frequently summoned Keijō's residents to the militarized grounds of Namsan to participate in celebrations of battlefield victories, hoping thereby to expand their consciousness of the empire's topography. A series of newsreels was filmed at such events, including "Korea, Our Rear Base" ("Chosŏn, uri ŭi hubang").[139] That this particular newsreel featured, among other things, the fall of Hankou (October 25, 1938) suggests that it dates to late 1938 or early 1939, when shrine visits reached an all-time high: in October 1938 alone, officials tallied a record-breaking 452,882 visits to Korea Shrine, meaning that nearly fifteen thousand people came to this sacred complex each day. In one segment, the viewer sees such a crowd labeled with two different captions, "From the home front, under the Japanese spirit" and "Praying before the deities for continued luck in the fortunes of war."

To underline the increasingly compressed topography of the sacralized empire, this segment begins and ends with images of Tokyo's imperial palace, to which all subjects were, at the sound of a siren, mobilized to bow in unison every morning during the wartime period. At the beginning of the segment, a picture of the palace's two-tiered bridge is shown, followed by a shot of a chrysanthemum, the symbol of the Japanese monarchy, with a caption that reads, "The Imperial Will is all the more solidified." The last scene shows a photographic image of the same bridge, across from which is printed the imperial oath, creating a direct link between the spiritual epicenter of the inner territory and the everyday lives of peninsular subjects. The caption for this image is the oft-repeated wartime slogan "Japan(ese) and Korea(ns) as one body." Rhetorically, then, this series of images emphasizes imperial subjectification as a process of cultural homogenization where practices of imperial reverence are exalted as the primary mechanism of wartime identification. In addition to numerous scenes of ethnically indistinguishable groups paying their respects in unison, the newsreel also features visits by individual Koreans, including a young woman performing a Japanese-style bow as a voluntary gesture of loyalty.

However, even in this propagandistic newsreel documenting the ostensible success of imperial subjectification, not all Koreans performed their reverence in the same way. Exemplary in this regard is the brief

FIGURE 20. Korean-style bow before Shintō shrine. Source: Stills from newsreel, "Chosŏn, uri ŭi hubang" (1939), in *Palgul toen kwagŏ, ne bŏnjjae: Kosŭpilmop'ondŭ, palgul yŏngsang moŭm* (Seoul: Korea Film Archive, 2009).

scene of an elderly Korean man engaging in what appears to be a household practice of ancestor worship in front of Korea Shrine. As mandated by Shintō clergy, the man has removed his hat at this sacred site, but he has also removed his rubber shoes as he performs a Confucian-style prostration on an indoor mat (see figure 20). Although likely included to demonstrate the multiethnic "tolerance" characteristic of Japan's wartime empire, this nonstandard practice of reverence alerts us to the multiple meanings that Koreans of different sexes, generations, classes, regions, and religions undoubtedly attributed to Shintō worship.

From this last scene, one can only guess at the subjectivity undergirding this Korean man's bow, as thousands like him labored to convince critical onlookers of their commitment to the imperial house. The wartime recollections of Kim Chae-jun (1901–87), a well-known theologian interviewed in 1985, forty years after liberation, provide one final example of how Koreans of different backgrounds anxiously "performed" their loyalty. As a number of South Korean scholars have shown, the onset of forced shrine worship during the late 1930s caused an existential crisis for many Christians, one that reverberated into the postcolonial era. Many denominations considered bowing before Shintō shrines an act of idolatry, a blasphemy some particularly pious Koreans became martyrs to avoid. However, as Kim Sung-Gun has also demonstrated, Christians who refused to perform imperial rituals jeopardized the future of their mission-run schools.[140] Fearing government closure of the newly established Chosŏn Theological Seminary, where he was a twenty-nine-year-old professor, Kim Chae-jun consulted with his pastor, Ham T'ae-yŏng, about whether or not to comply with mandatory shrine visits. Ham convinced Kim and the students of the seminary to put aside their reservations and visit Korea Shrine, as he himself had decided to do. However, before they ascended the stairs leading to the shrine, Ham assured them that they could perform the external rituals necessary to satisfy official demands while still retaining their inner beliefs. As Kim recalled, Ham told him how he would overcome his anxieties when praying before gods he did not want to revere: "May you swiftly chase away these Japanese demons *(kwisin)* and replace them with a Christian church. And may we quickly regain our independence."[141]

# After Empire's Demise

*The Postcolonial Remaking of Seoul's
Public Spaces*

In previous chapters, I have shown how the spectacular modifications of public space by the colonial state and their contestations by local residents played a crucial role in the development of society and culture in Keijō and, by extension, other areas of colonial Korea affected by the capital's remarkable, if highly uneven, transformations. The partial upgrading of the city's thoroughfares in radial and block forms (chapter 1), the establishment of Namsan's Shintō monuments and urban festivals as sites of reverence (chapter 2), the re-creation of the private grounds of Kyŏngbok Palace into a public classroom promoting material "progress" (chapter 3), and the use of neighborhood activities to produce an everyday civic morality centered on hygienic modernity (chapter 4) were just some of the many spatial interventions that undergirded colonial rule. To be sure, government officials and local proxies controlled the project of transforming Keijō from the royal capital of an extinguished dynasty into a modern city of the Japanese empire, aiming to reorient Koreans' attitudes from an allegedly parochial loyalty to clans and the ethnonation to an expanded identification with a multiethnic polity (chapter 5). However, the everyday practices of nonelite actors, the majority of Korean society, determined the degree to which overlapping modalities of assimilation—spiritual, material, and civic— could penetrate the fabric of Keijō and thus the consciousness of its residents. As a result, these contested experiments of colonial governmentality, especially those implemented before 1937, remained highly piecemeal and makeshift in their subjectivizing effects. That poorer Koreans and other marginalized individuals refused to invest financial or emotional resources in the highly discriminatory rationality of the Government-General also reveals the limited reach of Japanese rule. Both the structure and agency of colonial society thus produced considerable discrepancies between the arterial ostentation of the city's modern infrastructure and the capillary frailty of its wretched alleyways. Although wartime mobilization necessitated a more thorough program of imperial subjectification to overcome these fissures, the biopolitical rationality of the late colonial regime could not but inherit the disabling fractures of the previous era. When read both along and against the archival grain, the frenetic enumeration of inadequately trained Korean bodies called upon to make overcompensated demonstrations of loyalty for the empire stand out as dramatic reminders of this long-standing and largely insurmountable problem of rule.

Much as the Government-General sought to displace the spatiality of the precolonial city of Hanyang/Hwangsŏng after 1910, Korea's new leaders ventured to remake Seoul into a proud symbol of an autonomous nation-state, albeit one that quickly divided into two rival regimes as a result of the Cold War. In contrast to the thirty-five-year history of Keijō explored thus far, the city's postcolonial reconstruction commenced immediately after liberation with the virtual erasure of Namsan's Shintō shrines, the most palpable and foreign symbol of wartime mobilization. However, the project to decolonize the city's public spaces, although certainly not carried out continuously or with the same intensity after 1945, will continue until at least until 2030, when the current phase of restorations on Kyŏngbok Palace, the site of the former Government-General building (demolished in 1995), are complete. Considered together as temporal bookends of a nearly century-long project, these two sites demonstrate that the intangible legacies of Keijō's spaces have remained very much alive in the changing landscape of contemporary Seoul, even though the physical manifestations of Japanese rule have been largely removed. Moreover, official projects to replace these monuments with ones befitting a liberated (but still divided) peninsula have uncannily followed the Government-General in even more thoroughly subjectifying South Koreans as anti-Japanese and anticommunist subjects, while silencing their complex and unresolved colonial pasts.[1]

The immediate destruction of Namsan's Shintō shrines resulted from the unlikely convergence of Koreans who sought to raze the powerful symbols of forced emperor worship and Japanese officials who hoped to protect the dignity of these besieged sites. As was true throughout post-liberation Korea, anti-Japanese activities in Seoul broke out quickly following the end of the war, as agitated organizers posted handbills encouraging residents to "Burn Korea Shrine and Seoul Shrine!"[2] Given such threats, Shintō priests met with Japanese officials the day after liberation (August 16) and decided to remove Japan's deities before Koreans sullied them, a practiced followed at shrines throughout the peninsula.[3] Despite these defensive measures, threats against Namsan continued into early September, forcing Japanese merchants to close their shops early and stay in during the dangerous hours surrounding nightfall. Worse yet, Japanese officials continued to find placards encouraging Koreans to burn down Korea Shrine as well as discarded bottles filled with gasoline, the likely catalyst for such incendiary actions.[4]

At this juncture, former shrine priests decided to preempt the retaliation of agitated Koreans by demolishing Korea Shrine of their own accord. But this project, begun on September 7, took nearly a month to complete because of negotiations between the now defunct Government-General and the United States Army Forces in Korea (USAFIK). At stake was how to redefine Namsan for the postcolony, a project, once again, directed from above. In their discussions, Shintō priests emphasized the nonreligious, civic character of shrines. This ideology, used during the colonial period to compel Koreans of all faiths to worship before Korea Shrine, now aimed to satisfy Americans' insistence on religious freedom. By contrast, Japanese settlers, some of whom opposed repatriation to the home islands, appealed to the USAFIK's desire to separate church from state as a way of regaining control over Seoul Shrine as a religious institution.[5] In the end, American authorities privileged the official ideology of Shintō as nonreligion. Such complicity allowed Japanese officials both to downplay the violence of wartime shrines and to dismiss ongoing reprisals against them. For example, Nukaga Hironao (1877–1961), the late colonial priest of Korea Shrine, even described shrines as the property of Japanese and thus irrelevant to Koreans.[6] With US support, he could rest assured that the spiritual complex over which he had presided was razed on Japanese terms, thereby preserving the dignity of former colonizers. Ultimately, this denouement also pleased prodemolition Koreans, although they themselves played a less definitive role in its demise. Nevertheless, by early 1946, enthused journalists conveyed their joy at visiting a music school that temporarily occupied part of this site, where students now sang patriotic Korean songs to the accompaniment of a piano.[7]

Even as Seoul's Shintō shrines all but disappeared within months of liberation, the colonial past continued to wield a strong influence over both Namsan's built environment and the practices of its visitors. For example, the former grounds of Korea Shrine temporarily became home to the Presbyterian Theological Seminary, the dream of some, if not many, Christians who were forced to visit Namsan lest the wartime state close their churches and schools.[8] Although their plan to construct a church in place of the shrine did not come to fruition, Korean Christians continued to visit Namsan as a religious refuge, especially during the springtime festival of Easter. As early as 1947, believers began to gather at this site for a predawn worship ceremony. Although distinct in its doctrinal content, this ritual bore an uncanny resemblance to Shintō practices recently performed at this very same place.[9] For example, thousands of Christians endured rain on April 1 to attend the Easter ceremony of 1956. After ascending Namsan, they prayed before a large cross and listened to an American brass band, a sign of the United States's lingering military presence after the Korean War.[10] In following years, Korean residents of Seoul and American soldiers stationed in nearby Yongsan often joined hands to celebrate Easter atop Namsan, now a Christianized place of this postcolonial city.[11]

Despite the persistence of some religious overtones, monuments promoting anti-Japanese nationalism came to dominate this site. These monuments virtually silenced Namsan's colonial-period meanings, while simultaneously reinscribing them through a simplistic narrative of resistance. Perhaps most emblematic of this ghostly presence are memorials dedicated to An Chung-gŭn (1879–1910), the nationalist patriot who, in 1909, killed the first Japanese Resident-General, Itō Hirobumi (1841–1909).[12] Even South Korea's first leader, Syngman Rhee (Yi Sŭng-man [r. 1948–60]), although known at the time more for his political connections to the United States, where he had resided for most of the colonial period, sought to align himself with the history of anticolonial nationalism, having served in the short-lived Independence Club (1896–98) and in the early stages of the Shanghai Provisional Government (1919–48). Capitalizing on yearly celebrations of the patriot's death on March 26, which conveniently overlapped with President Rhee's own birthday, his administration oversaw the erection of a 9.1-meter bronze statue of An in front of the Sung'ŭi Women's Middle School in 1959, an area of western Namsan where a Buddhist temple (est. 1932) dedicated to Itō used to sit.[13] A much larger statue of Rhee himself, unveiled in 1955 to celebrate his eightieth birthday, had been raised atop central Namsan in the very place where, until just ten years earlier, Korea Shrine was located. This uncanny but powerful strategy of displacement and replacement aimed to present President Rhee as his country's only "king" in the wake of the Japanese empire's downfall and the concomitant demise of Korea's besmirched royal family.[14] To more closely link his own personal authority to the collective history of his citizen-subjects, the groundbreaking and unveiling ceremonies for the statue, measuring a towering eighty feet (28.4 meters) to commemorate each year of his life, symbolically coincided with National Foundation Day (October 3) and Liberation Day (August 15), respectively.[15] Although President Rhee used this ostentatious statue to ensure his own reelection in 1956, the monument was razed just four years later when the student leaders of the 1960 revolution brought an end to his corrupt first republic.[16] Although he too resorted to a cult of personality, the military dictator Park Chung-hee (Pak Chŏng-hŭi [r. 1961–79]) and his supporters avoided personifying Namsan with their administration and instead relied on the subjectifying power of the more popular nationalist symbol of An Chung-gŭn, whose bust was designated a national memorial in 1967 and subsequently moved to the former site of Korea Shrine (and Rhee's statue).[17] Later, in 1970, the relocated statue of An was joined by a museum dedicated to the same patriot.[18] Significantly remodeled and expanded in 2010 to celebrate the centennial of his death, this popular site is visited by thousands of schoolchildren and adult citizens every year.[19] In this way, a monument once symbolizing Japanese rule was eventually replaced by memorials promoting anticolonial resistance in the form of martyrdom.

But the removal and replacement of Korea Shrine could not completely erase the spectral presence of the former Shintō monument. In fact, Namsan became the source of considerable controversy when Japanese diplomats visited Seoul after 1945. Such was the case with Yatsugi Kazuo, a special envoy sent by Prime Minister Kishi Nobusuke (1896–1987) in 1958 to begin discussions to normalize Japanese–South Korean relations. While in Seoul, Yatsugi met with President Rhee over outstanding issues from the colonial period, including atrocities committed against Koreans during the Asia-Pacific War. This visit produced few concrete results beyond a vague apology by Yatsugi, a gesture subsequently repeated by various Japanese authorities.[20] More spectacular was the outcry when, on the morning of May 20, Yatsugi took a car up to Namsan, ostensibly to snap a picture of the recently erected statue of President Rhee. Korean newspapers lambasted Yatsugi, charging that he certainly knew this site as the erstwhile home of Korea Shrine, the Shintō monument associated with the colonial violence for which he had just expressed his regrets. Although Yatsugi denied any such knowledge, his cheerful facial expression, as one dubious report described his photogenic pose, suggested that he took delight in experiencing the environs of this former shrine, even after Namsan had been transformed into a site of civic nationalism.[21]

Later, in the early 1980s, Namsan gained renewed attention amid an escalating strain between Seoul and Tokyo over depictions of the colonial period in Japanese school textbooks.[22] The first flash point in the so-called textbook controversy was a visit to Seoul during the summer of 1982 by Mitsuzuka Hiroshi (1927–2004) and Mori Yoshirō (1937– ). Both members of Japan's Liberal Democratic Party (LDP) and councilmen on the textbook controversy committee, Mitsuzuka and Mori met with South Korean parliamentarians to resolve tensions. Although little progress was made, Kim Yŏng-gwan (1931–2010), a member of the National Party, took the opportunity to accompany Mitsuzuka and Mori to Namsan. Redirecting the burden of civic worship onto the LDP politicians, Kim encouraged Mitsuzuka and Mori to visit the An memorial, before which they reportedly "bowed" (ch'ambae; J: sampai). One critical report in the Chosŏn ilbo then denounced this seemingly reverent practice as nothing but a show, questioning whether their bow before An's statue reflected a serious commitment to resolve the textbook controversy. Much as government officials and Shintō priests had doubted the internalized loyalties of formerly colonized Koreans, this article expressed serious reservations about what likely went through the minds of Mitsuzuka and Mori when they bowed before the statue—perhaps that An was not a patriotic martyr, but instead a criminal assassin.[23]

Over time, however, the anticolonial monuments of Namsan did work to change the attitudes of some visitors, a trend Korean newspapers eagerly reported. According to an article on a group of twelve thousand Japanese youngsters who toured South Korea in 1984 as part of school trips, these middle and high school students were most impressed by the An memorial and his towering bust. The report triumphantly quoted the remarks of one female student from a Hiroshima women's high school, which were part of an essay contest: "There is no mention in Japanese textbooks of the fact that the patriot An Chung-gŭn went so far as to sacrifice his life by killing Itō Hirobumi, the symbol of an invading country, or other cruel acts that Japan committed. At the An Chung-gŭn Memorial Museum, I was shocked to see graphic images of Japanese soldiers killing Koreans and of the [missing part of his] left ring finger, which An cut off while imprisoned at the Lushun Jail."[24] Although perhaps reflecting the view of only some Japanese visitors, this student's comments suggest that the memorial was beginning to produce its intended effects, which were the result of refashioning public spaces first developed under Japanese rule.

If, by the 1980s, Presidents Rhee and Park had successfully reconstructed Namsan into a recreational and educational site promoting anticolonial (and anticommunist) nationalism, the Kyŏngbok Palace grounds took far longer to re-create into a place that South Korean leaders, if not the general populace, could call their own. Part of the problem was the presence of the Government-General building, the colonial monument that continued to obstruct a view of the palace. For decades, South Korean leaders struggled to meet the high cost of removing this embarrassing monument. Postwar destitution—epitomized by heavy financial aid from the United States, South Korea's Cold War ally—hamstrung President Rhee, who knew the continued presence of the building was a national disgrace but failed to destroy or relocate it.[25] Meanwhile, the press chafed at calls for the building's destruction, fearing that a new administrative complex would far exceed South Korean coffers and contravene a long-term plan to rebuild the war-torn capital into a symbol of an independent nation-state. Critics also suggested that anticolonial and nationalist arguments favoring demolition would logically require officials to destroy *all* buildings used to dominate the formerly colonized population, a mandate they found both farcical and impractical when compared with the option of reusing them to promote the interests of South Korean citizens.[26] Given the building's recent history as a site promoting industrial "progress," its postcolonial custodians refashioned the decrepit palace grounds into a powerful symbol of anticommunist development.[27] This widely accepted trajectory of capitalism stood in stark contrast with the particularity of Japanese spirituality, which had made Namsan impossible to reclaim as something even remotely (South) Korean.

Adopting pragmatic approaches to bolster their authority, President Rhee and his successors, imitating strategies developed under Japanese rule, deployed state pageantry to transform the Government-General building into their own Capitol Hall (1948–86), which became a frequent staging ground for anticommunist activities.[28] Perhaps only during the protests of 1960 and 1986, when prodemocracy advocates stoned police officers and broke complex windows, did this site become the successful locus of antigovernment protests, which eventually ousted both Syngman Rhee and Chun Doo-hwan (Chŏn Tu-hwan [r. 1980–88]).[29] Before the emergence of civil society during the 1990s, early postcolonial leaders, policing possible uprisings with military force, groomed Kyŏngbok Palace to host elaborate national ceremonies. As early as 1949, President Rhee used this site to celebrate the one-year anniversary of South Korea's constitution.[30] These festivities continued into the 1950s, as did annual commemorations of Liberation Day, the Gregorian New Year, and National Foundation Day.[31] At these events, audiences participated in collective rituals of citizenship, such as military music, patriotic songs, anticommunist speeches, and shouts of *manse!* (hooray!).[32] Not unlike the expositions held here in 1915 and 1929, these celebrations included familiar forms of entertainment, such as decorated streetcars and buses, free admission to city palaces, and VIP cocktail parties hosted at the Kyŏnghoe Pavilion.[33] Capitol Hall also functioned as a site for President Rhee and his supporters to memorialize the spirits of the 170,000 souls who had enabled their country's liberation, which encouraged crowds to support their country's anticommunist militarism.[34] A former lieutenant in the Japanese imperial army, General Park Chung-hee, expanded these nationalistic trends. In 1966, for example, he ordered the widening of Sejongno, which was formerly Kōkamon (Kwanghwamun) Boulevard, but was quickly renamed to honor Chosŏn's most revered king, Sejong (r. 1418–50).[35] In the following year, he used this symbolic thoroughfare to review the country's armed forces and a display of their latest weapons. A tradition first instituted by President Rhee during the late 1950s, this spectacular event was attended by local politicians, foreign dignitaries, overseas Koreans, and more than one hundred thousand onlookers.[36]

During the late 1960s, Kyŏngbok Palace and its environs underwent a more thorough "Koreanization" as President Park revived venerated figures from the Chosŏn dynasty to build further support for the martial prowess of his anticommunist regime.[37] One such figure was Yi Sun-sin (1545–98), the navy admiral who defended the peninsula against Toyotomi Hideyoshi's invasions of the 1590s.[38] So invested was President Park in resurrecting the memory of this national hero that he donated the funds necessary to create in his honor a 6.4-meter statue, which was unveiled in 1967 and is still standing today.[39] Seeking to rally the nation's energies, he also oversaw the pseudorestoration of the Kwanghwa Gate in 1968. Relocated to the front of the former Government-General building but still not aligned with the palace grounds, the gate was built in a more durable, ferroconcrete style, a choice that rankled some critics who favored a traditional wooden form.[40] To promote his authority, President Park violated other protocols of authenticity by using his own vernacular *(han'gŭl)* calligraphy for the gate's new signboard, rather than relying on Chinese characters, the elite language of precolonial literati.[41] Although neither its location nor its style adhered to Chosŏn precedents, the semirestored Kwanghwa Gate did reduce the portion of the former Government-General building visible to visitors as they looked at the palace grounds from the statue of Yi Sun-sin. Upon entering Capitol Hall, visitors found other symbolic modifications, part of a three-trillion-wŏn project to repair the dilapidated structure and to Koreanize its internal aesthetics. Most emblematic was the replacement of chrysanthemums, a symbol of the Japanese imperial house, with South Korea's national flower, the *Hibiscus syriacus*.[42] Although he was unable to afford the 7.7 trillion wŏn necessary to replace this monument, President Park successfully refashioned the palace grounds into a potent instrument of mass mobilization, one that softened his ruthless developmental autocracy.

After Park's reign, when some began to advocate seriously for its costly demolition, arguments favoring the creative reuse of the former Government-General building as the National Museum (1985–96) once again prevailed, if only temporarily.[43] In this incarnation, the palace grounds, once the site of colonial expositions, continued to function as an educational center, but one now aimed at inculcating what one official called a "master consciousness" *(chuin ŭisik)*. As he explained, "By creating a museum from a building that is the historic symbol of the nation's suffering, we will convey the regretful lesson of losing [our] sovereignty and of being invaded by a foreign country."[44] To this end, landscape architects removed all of the grounds' cherry trees and replaced them with trees indigenous to the peninsula.[45] Following President Park's example, museum designers further Koreanized the building's floor plan by filling in two open courtyards that, according to a new but powerful urban legend, colonial officials had constructed to form the first Chinese character *(il;* J: *nichi)* for the word *Japan (ilbon;* J: *nippon).*[46] To be sure, modernist architects designed most buildings of this European style in a similar shape, and few visitors would have possessed the top-down vision necessary to decode this subliminal message. However, critics conveniently overlooked these facts, decrying the building's structure as unforgiving proof that their former colonizers had intentionally inscribed their own country's name into the palace's landscape.[47] Around the same time, sensational reports began to spread about the nearby discovery of twenty-five iron stakes piercing Mount Pukhan, which the media interpreted as a Japanese scheme to disrupt the city's spiritual energy.[48] Disregarding postcolonial strategies aimed at re-refashioning the palace grounds (and the contemporaneous project that paved over another geomantic landmark, the Ch'ŏnggye Stream), this new narrative of anticolonial nationalism claimed that the former Government-General building, together with Mount Pukhan and City Hall, formed the Chinese characters spelling "Great Japan," an indication of the country's ongoing domination by its former colonizer. Some pundits even went so far as to decry this invasion as a symbolic embodiment of sexual violence inflicted upon the uterus of the motherland, a nationalistic view that overlapped with growing, but similarly patriarchal, criticisms of the so-called comfort women system.[49]

Given these influential, if problematic, critiques, the work of various authoritarian regimes to transform the former Government-General building into a national symbol of capitalist development—and, indeed, anticommunism, since South Korean leaders also used Kyŏngbok Palace against their northern rivals to claim legitimacy over a peninsula once united under the Seoul-based Chosŏn dynasty—could not, in the long run, outlast growing complaints about its Japanese origins. Even during its short tenure as the National Museum, prodemolitionists decried that the building was drawing ten thousand more Japanese tourists than Korean visitors, tourists they worried came to recall its former colonial splendor, rather than to appreciate the impressive art collection.[50] With the fiftieth anniversary of liberation approaching, the civilian and democratically elected administration of Kim Yŏng-sam (r. 1993–98) used the growing consensus around Japan's geomantic invasion and other traditionalist metaphors to remove this lingering symbol of colonialism as a way of "preserving the nation's spirit."[51] Although some cultural heritage conservationists preferred to relocate the building and save its function as an educational facility, Kim carefully manipulated opinion polls to "prove" that most citizens favored its demolition.[52] With shallow support, Kim took advantage of the fiftieth anniversary of liberation to make razing the former Government-General building a cause célèbre. Its iconic dome was finally removed (and is today preserved at the Independence Hall in Ch'ŏn'an), and, to further dramatize the spectacle, state choreographers replayed the radio broadcast of Emperor Hirohito's surrender speech, rekindling the euphoria of August 15, 1945. Capitalizing on the latest audio-visual technologies, KBS broadcasted this event across the peninsula, allowing citizens to participate in the nationalistic folklore of the Kim regime.[53]

But even since the physical removal of this symbolic manifestation of Japanese rule, the site's deeply entrenched colonial history has continued to haunt the long-term restoration of Kyŏngbok Palace, which has been strategically recast as a public embodiment of the (South) Korean nation, rather than as the private residence of Yi dynasty kings. Perhaps the most obvious continuity can be found in the troubled search for the palace's authenticity amid a "Chosŏn renaissance." With this term, I mean to convey how selective elements of Korea's last dynasty, which was previously considered a primary cause for the peninsula's slide into Japanese rule, were positively reimagined as the basis for national identity and international tourism in contemporary South Korea. Just as colonial officials struggled to infuse the grounds with a "pure Korean style" to serve their own interests at the exposition of 1929, South Korean leaders have found it challenging to produce an authentic version of the site, whose precolonial history was also shrouded in ignominy.[54] For example, the first phase of palace restorations, undertaken between 1996 and 2010 at an astronomical cost of 180 trillion wŏn, began with restoring the Kwanghwa Gate to its original position and aesthetic form. This plan required moving the gate 3.5 degrees in a westerly direction and 47.5 feet to the south so that it lined up with the palace's initial north-south orientation, rather than with the axis of the recently demolished Government-General building, and re-creating a wooden gate, a choice that, as mentioned above, President Park had eschewed due to high costs and fears of flammability.[55] However, the signboard for the Kwanghwa Gate generated a cacophonous debate about what calligraphic inscription originally adorned this splendid monument. Clearly, President Park's *han'gŭl* letters failed to represent the classical Chinese letters that would have emblazoned a late-fourteenth-century gate. But until its partial reconstruction during the late nineteenth century, the palace, largely destroyed by Hideyoshi's invasions of the 1590s, had lain in ruins, making it nearly impossible to discover the original inscription. Given this uncertainty, some officials favored collecting two characters (and doctoring another one) written by King Chŏngjo (r. 1776–1800), who was known for backing several artistic projects related to painting and calligraphy. Quickly, however, critics charged that a Chosŏn monarch would never have penned such a sign, while others claimed that this king too uncannily resembled South Korea's current president, Roh Moo-hyun (No Mu-hyŏn [1946–

2009]). In the end, government authorities, even as they realized the semifabricated nature of their final decision, settled on using extant photographs to digitally reproduce a version of the signboard from 1865 written by the high-ranking military official Yim T'ae-yŏng (1791–1868).[56]

Although the restoration of Kyŏngbok Palace (as of 2010 officials have rebuilt about 40 percent of palace structures destroyed under Japanese rule) has forced architects to reference its late-nineteenth-century form, the Chosŏn renaissance surrounding it has focused on particular monuments in Korean history known for anti-Japanese nationalism, of both premodern and modern vintages. King Sejong—credited with establishing the vernacular syllabary (ironically, the very linguistic form eliminated from the new Kwanghwa Gate)—has become a particularly important figure, symbolizing the peaceful and literary traditions of the dynasty's premodern "golden age." To lend an aura of authenticity to the palace and its environs, state choreographers have experimented with various methods of memorializing this famous sage-king. For example, when the new Hŭngnye Gate was unveiled in 1999 (the original had been destroyed by colonial officials in 1916 to accommodate the new Government-General building), media promoters elaborately recreated Sejong's coronation ceremony. Staged every Saturday for more than two months, the spectacular pageant attracted throngs of South Koreans who witnessed approximately 340 individuals dressed in formal court attire. To more effectively attract foreign tourists, officials even presented versions of this "traditional" ceremony with English and Japanese translations; after the show, tourists were allowed to take commemorative photographs with colorfully dressed participants.[57] A decade later, in 2009, authorities unveiled a 6.7-meter bust of Sejong in the center of the newly remodeled Kwanghwa Gate Plaza, surrounded by stones marking important dates of the Chosŏn period. This monument to King Sejong, who embodies the dynasty's cultural accomplishments, complements the older statue of Yi Sun-sin, who, by contrast, reminds visitors of its martial achievements. A small museum beneath the plaza recalls the national contributions of both revered figures.[58]

If these monuments reference the period before Hideyoshi's invasions, other dimensions of palace pageantry have foregrounded the Great Han Empire, long considered the cause of dynastic decline and Japanese colonization, but increasingly understood as a modernizing regime in its own right.[59] These ceremonies have especially spotlighted Kojong, whom officials elevated from king to emperor in 1897 in order to reassert the nation-building power of the throne in a perilous age of imperial competition. In 2003, for example, state choreographers used the restoration of the palace's main hall (Kŭmjŏngjŏn) to re-create the monarch's ascension ceremony, a spectacular event attended by approximately thirty-eight thousand visitors.[60] The public had celebrated this ceremony at the Ring Hill Altar (Wŏn'gudan), which was constructed in the closing years of the nineteenth century as part of a nation-building project aimed at recentering monarchical authority on Kyŏng'un Palace (present-day Tŏksu Palace), rather than the ill-fated Kyŏngbok Palace. Although using Kyŏngbok Palace to re-create Kojong's ascension failed to recognize this new locus of power, the creative memorialization of the Great Han Empire sought to correct the peninsula's slide into colonization. Such interpretive license offered powerful symbols of (South) Korean autonomy and wealth in the globalized world of the twenty-first century. Most recently, the Yi Myŏng-bak administration has designated the entire two-kilometer stretch from Kyŏngbok Palace to the South Gate as the symbolic thoroughfare of the state. Explicitly likening this thoroughfare to Paris's Champs-Élysées—a metaphor recycled from colonial planners—Yi's architectural policy planning committee has deployed these nationalized symbols of the Chosŏn period to boost citizens' confidence in what it called the country's "proud history."[61]

These gestures of South Korea's Chosŏn renaissance, like the continued prominence of anticolonial and anticommunist monuments on Namsan, point to an ongoing engagement with the ghostly presence of Seoul's colonial spaces nearly seventy years after liberation from Japanese rule. Yet the current custodians of these sites have produced narratives of national progress that consciously bypass the ravages of the (post)colonial period. Although effective in mobilizing South Koreans against Japanese denials about the past and their northern rival, for instance, none of the monuments atop Namsan specifically alludes to the complex history of spiritual assimilation and imperial subjectification. To be sure, the statue and memorial museum clearly reference the violent history of Korea's colonization. However, they do so without acknowledging the geohistorical significance of the very place on which they presently sit, the former site of Korea Shrine. This silencing has made it difficult for uninitiated visitors to acquire knowledge of Namsan's recent past, knowledge that might lend itself toward a praxis of postcolonial justice. To offer just one example of how this might happen: rather than serving as a quintessential symbol of anticolonial resistance that in fact predates the period of Japanese rule, Namsan might also function as a common ground from which to continue opposing the illegitimate deification of twenty-one thousand Koreans (and, for that matter, twenty-eight thousand Taiwanese) who perished during the Asia-Pacific War and whose remains are still "incarcerated" at Yasu-kuni Shrine in Tokyo.[62]

The absence of the former Government-General building has produced a similarly narrow counterpolitics of silencing. Even as the ongoing "restoration" of Kyŏngbok Palace seeks to further erase the disgraceful memories of that once-powerful structure, the glorification of Chosŏn's main palace as the basis for South Korea's anticolonial and anticommunist identity has ironically reasserted the centrality of Japanese rule and its postcolonial legacies. By redirecting the attention of South Korean and international visitors to the aesthetic splendor and imagined glory of a unified peninsula under Yi dynasty kings, the period immediately preceding Japanese rule, it privileges a historical periodization determined by Japanese imperialism. Further, although the grounds are no longer the private and sacred residence of Yi family kings, a focus on re-creating what architects are calling the "cultural lifestyle" of another 254 buildings slated for restoration during the second phase (2011–30) encourages visitors to identify with the lion-ized traditions of courtly life.[63] Still quietly referencing uses of the grounds first developed during the period of Japanese rule and later inherited by the regime after 1945, Kyŏngbok Palace today stands as a public site of profit-oriented tourism, promoting an independent vision of a nation once showcased as an integral part of the Japanese empire. In this way, the architects of postcolonial South Korea—joined by academic historians, popular writers, and entertainment gurus—are substituting "authentic" re-creation for a thoughtful engagement with Korea's twentieth-century history. As in the past, these efforts may well succeed in erasing the physical remnants of Japanese rule (and South Korean authoritarianism), but they will not necessarily silence the historical memories that continue to haunt these hypernationalistic sites. For that process of decolonization to run its course, the respatial-izing agents of South Korea need the courage to reexamine the con-tinuous remaking of Seoul's public sites during the twentieth century. They must also be willing to transform them in ways that open up, rather than close off, a dialogue about the contested meanings they hold for individuals who have inhabited and will continue to inhabit those lived spaces.

. . .

That the country may be moving in this direction is evidenced by two recent restorations, both of which juxtapose an older colonial structure with a new, future-oriented building rather than simply replacing the former with the latter. The first is Seoul Train Station, unveiled in 2004 to accommodate the country's new high-speed rail system, KTX. Rather than razing the old station, still a gathering spot for the homeless, planners spent four years restoring this structure, now used as a cultural space.[64] Officials also retained part of the old city hall, which was completed in 1926 by the Japanese, but has long since been too small to house Seoul's growing administration. Like the train station, the old city hall, or at least what remains of it, now functions as cultural space with a library and museum. Its plaza is used for various festivals and popular events, including a performance in 2012 of Psy's "Gangnam Style" that drew eighty thousand fans! As for the newly unveiled city hall, most people understand Yu Kŏl's thirteen-story glass structure as a tidal wave subsuming the old city hall, although the architect reportedly intended to evoke in a contemporary design the eaves of a traditional Korean house.[65] Whatever the interpretation, such novel projects suggest that Seoul's public spaces may finally be overcoming their colonial past by recalling, rather than silencing, that tumultuous history. However, more than 75 percent of Koreans now feel that the new city hall clashes with both the old city hall façade and Tŏksu Palace, Kojong's former residence.[66] This statistic reveals the ongoing difficulties of reconciling past and present in a way that satisfies the diverse inhabitants that such lived spaces seek but have only rarely represented.

# Notes

*A list of the Korean and Japanese publications cited and the abbreviations used in the notes is found at the beginning of the bibliography.*

## INTRODUCTION

1. Unless noted otherwise, East Asian terms are romanized in Korean. However, some terms denoting Japanese rule—Keijō, for example—are given in their original linguistic form.

2. Ogasawara Shōzō, ed., *Kaigai jinjashi (jōkan)* (Tokyo: Kaigai jinjashi hensankai, 1953), 73.

3. As he once explained, "By production of truth I mean not the production of true utterances, but the establishment of domains in which the practice of true or false can be made at once ordered and pertinent." Michel Foucault, "Questions of Method," in *Essential Works of Foucault, 1954–1984*, vol. 3, *Power,* ed. James D. Faubion (New York: New Press, 2000), 230.

4. Korean church membership statistics from 1937 include 281,939 Presbyterians, 109,963 Roman Catholics, 54,654 Methodists, in addition to 10,445 Holiness adherents, 8,688 Episcopalians, 6,387 Soldiers of the Salvation Army, and 5,096 Seventh Day Adventists. Sung-Gun Kim [Kim Sŏng-gŏn], "Korean Christianity and the Shinto Shrine Issue in the War Period, 1931–1945: A Sociological Study of Religion and Politics," PhD diss., University of Hull, 1989, 205. Although Christians accounted for less than 3 percent of the colonized population (approximately twenty-two million) at the time, their anti-Japanese activities have been the subject of much postcolonial research. For these studies, see Kim Sŭng-t'ae, ed., *Han'guk kidokkyo wa sinsa ch'ambae munje* (Seoul: Han'guk kidokkyo yŏksa yŏn'guso, 1991); and Kim Sŭng-t'ae, *Sinsa ch'ambae kŏbu hangjaengjadŭl ŭi chŭng'ŏn: Ŏdum ŭi kwŏnse rŭl igin saramdŭl* (Seoul:

Tasan kŭlbang, 1993); as well as Han Sŏk-hŭi, *Nihon no Chōsen shihai to shū kyo seisaku* (Tokyo: Miraisha, 1990).

5. For more on the city's place in the tourist industry, see Hyung Il Pai [Pae Hyŏng-il], "Navigating Modern Seoul: The Typology of Guidebooks and City Landmarks," *Sŏulhak yŏn'gu* 44 (Aug. 2011): 1–40.

6. Kim Paek-yŏng, *Chibae wa konggan: Singminji tosi Kyŏngsŏng kwa cheguk ilbon* (Seoul: Munhak kwa chisŏngsa, 2009); and Jun Uchida, *Brokers of Empire: Japanese Settler Colonialism in Korea, 1876–1945* (Cambridge, MA: Harvard University Asia Center, 2011).

7. Michel Foucault, "Governmentality," in *The Foucault Effect: Studies in Governmentality*, ed. G. Burchell, C. Gordon, and P. Miller (London: Harvester Wheatsheaf, 1991), 87–104; and Foucault, *Security, Territory, Population: Lectures at the Collège de France, 1977–78* (New York: Palgrave Macmillan, 2007).

8. Takashi Fujitani, *Race for Empire: Koreans as Japanese and Japanese as Americans during World War II* (Berkeley: University of California Press, 2011).

9. One notable exception is Chen Peifeng, *"Dōka" no dōshō imu: Nihon tōchika Taiwan no kokugo kyōikushi saikō* (Tokyo: Sangensha, 2001).

10. As scholars of invented traditions have suggested, even these seemingly "Japanese" practices of spiritual cultivation, far from being indigenous to the archipelago, emerged as functional equivalents of nation-building strategies adopted by Meiji elites, partly as a way to compete with other modern empires. On these practices, see Stephen Vlastos, ed., *Mirror of Modernity: Invented Traditions of Modern Japan* (Berkeley: University of California Press, 1998).

11. Komagome Takeshi, *Shokumichi tekikoku Nihon no bunka tōgō* (Tokyo: Iwanami shoten, 1996), esp. 2–27.

12. On the precarious effects of commodifying colonial labor power, see Ken C. Kawashima, *The Proletarian Gamble: Korean Workers in Interwar Japan* (Durham: Duke University Press, 2009). See also Mark Driscoll, *Absolute Erotic, Absolute Grotesque: The Living, the Dead, and the Undead in Japan's Imperialism, 1895–1945* (Durham: Duke University Press, 2010).

13. See, for example, E. Patricia Tsurumi, *Japanese Colonial Education in Taiwan, 1895–1945* (Cambridge, MA: Harvard University Press, 1977). Kwŏn T'ae-ŏk takes a similar approach to colonial Korea in Kwŏn, "1910 nyŏndae ilche ŭi Chosŏn tonghwaron kwa tonghwa chŏngch'aek," *Han'guk munhwa* 44 (Dec. 2008): 99–125; and Kwŏn, "1920–1930 nyŏndae ilche ŭi tonghwa chŏngch'aeknon," in *Han'guk kŭndae sahoe wa munhwa III: 1920–1930 nyŏndae 'singminjijŏk kŭndae' wa han'gugin ŭi taeŭng* (Seoul: Sŏul taehakkyo ch'ulp'anbu, 2007), 3–37. On how the common schools of colonial Korea supplemented—and, at times, replaced—the role that more ubiquitous Shintō shrines played in the metrople, see Hiura Satoko, *Jinja, gakkō, shokuminchi: Gyaku kinō suru Chōsen shihai* (Kyoto: Kyōto daigaku gakujustsu shuppankai, 2013).

14. For a pioneering study of this variety, see Mark R. Peattie, "Japanese Attitudes toward Colonialism, 1895–1945," in *The Japanese Colonial Empire, 1895–1945*, ed. Ramon H. Myers and Mark R. Peattie (Princeton, NJ: Princeton University Press, 1987), 80–127; and, more recently, Mark E. Caprio,

*Japanese Assimilation Policies in Colonial Korea, 1910–1945* (Seattle: University of Washington Press, 2009). In Japanese, see Komagome, *Shokumichi tekikoku Nihon no bunka tōgō;* and Oguma Eiji, *"Nihonjin" no kyōkai: Okinanwa, Ainu, Taiwan, Chōsen shokuminchi shihai kara fukki undō made* (Tokyo: Shin'yōsha, 1998).

15. Dipesh Chakrabarty, *Provincializing Europe: Postcolonial Thought and Historical Difference* (Princeton, NJ: Princeton University Press, 2000), 3–11.

16. This observation draws on Leo Ching's insistence that assimilation is best understood as "the ideology par excellence for concealing the gap between political and economic discrimination and cultural assimilation." Ching, *Becoming "Japanese": Colonial Taiwan and the Politics of Identity Formation* (Berkeley: University of California Press, 2001), 104.

17. For these tendencies, see Michael Kim, "The Colonial Public Sphere and the Discursive Mechanism of *Mindo*," in *Mass Dictatorship and Modernity,* ed. Michael Kim, Michael Schoenhals, and Yong-Woo Kim (London: Routledge, 2013). On association in French colonial thought and practice, see Raymond F. Betts, *Assimilation and Association in French Colonial Theory, 1890–1914* (New York: Columbia University Press, 1960); and Gwendolyn Wright, *The Politics of Design in French Colonial Urbanism* (Chicago: University of Chicago Press, 1991).

18. This approach draws on Timothy Mitchell, "Society, Economy, and the State Effect," in *State/Culture: State-Formation after the Cultural Turn,* ed. George Steinmetz (Ithaca, NY: Cornell University Press, 1999), 76–97.

19. Thomas Blom Hansen and Finn Stepputat, eds., *States of Imagination: Ethnographic Explorations of the Postcolonial State* (Durham: Duke University Press, 2001), 5.

20. This method follows what Michel Foucault once called an "ascending analysis of power." Foucault, "Two Lectures," in *Power/Knowledge: Selected Interviews, and Other Writings, 1972–1977,* ed. Colin Gordon (New York: Pantheon, 1980), 99.

21. Partha Chatterjee, *The Nation and Its Fragments: Colonial and Postcolonial Histories* (Princeton, NJ: Princeton University Press, 1993), 14–34. A similar dichotomy between colonial and metropolitan forms of rule is found in Ranajit Guha, *Dominance without Hegemony: History and Power in Colonial India* (Cambridge, MA: Harvard University Press, 1988).

22. David Scott, "Colonial Governmentality," *Social Text* 43 (Autumn 1995): 193. For a study applying this approach, see Peter Redfield, "Foucault in the Tropics: Displacing the Panopticon," in *Anthropologies of Modernity: Foucault, Governmentality, and Life Politics,* ed. Jonathan Xavier Inda (London: Blackwell, 2005).

23. Barry Hindess, "The Liberal Government of Unfreedom," *Alternatives: Global, Local, Political* 26, no. 2 (April-June 2001): 107. See also Sven Opitz, "Government Unlimited: The Security Dispositif of Illiberal Governmentality," in *Governmentality: Current Issues and Future Challenges,* ed. Ulrich Bröckling, Susanne Krausmann, and Thomas Lemke (New York: Routledge, 2010).

24. On the political positioning of Japan's colonies, see Edward I-te Chen, "The Attempt to Integrate the Empire: Legal Perspectives," in Myers and

Peattie, eds., *The Japanese Colonial Empire*, 240–74; and Yamamoto Yūzo, *Nihon shokuminchi keizaishi kenkyū* (Nagoya: Nagoya daigaku shuppankai, 1992), 3–62.

25. Gary Wilder, *The French Imperial Nation-State: Negritude and Colonial Humanism between the Two World Wars* (Chicago: University of Chicago Press, 2005). In a similar way, the stalled debate over Korea's colonial modernity has tended to alternate between studies that emphasize one of these forces at the expense of the other. See, for example, Gi-Wook Shin and Michael Robinson, eds., *Colonial Modernity in Korea* (Cambridge, MA: Harvard University Press, 2001); Do Myoun-hoi [To Myŏn-hoe], "The Implications of Colonial Modernity without Colonialism," *Korea Journal* 44, no. 2 (Summer 2004): 189–209; and Younghan Cho [Cho Yŏng-han], "Colonial Modernity Matters?," *Cultural Studies* 26, no. 5 (2012): 645–99. For one possible solution, see Tani Barlow, "Debates over Colonial Modernity in East Asia and Another Alternative," *Cultural Studies* 26, no. 5 (2012): 617–44.

26. I draw this observation from Stephen Legg, *Spaces of Colonialism: Dehli's Urban Governmentalities* (Oxford: Blackwell, 2007).

27. For a genealogy of this historiographic issue, see Tae-hern Jung [Chŏng T'ae-hŏn], "Two Korea's Perceptions of the 'Colonial Modernity' since 1945," *International Journal of Korean History* 2 (Dec. 2001): 193–219.

28. On the role of the police in colonial Korea, see, for example, Matsuda Toshihiko, *Nihon no Chōsen shihai to keisatsu: 1905 nen-1945 nen* (Tokyo: Azekura shobō, 2009). For a pioneering study that introduced examples of disciplinary power in colonial Korea, see Kim Chin-gyun and Chŏng Kŭn-sik, eds., *Kŭndae chuch'e wa singminji kyuyul kwŏllyŏk* (Seoul: Munhwa kwahaksa, 1997).

29. Se Hoon Park [Pak Se-hun], "Care and Control: Colonial Governmentality and Urban Social Policy in Colonial Seoul," in *East Asia: A Critical Geography Perspective,* ed. Wing-Shing Tang and Fujio Mizuoka (Tokyo: Kokon shoin, 2010), 112–32.

30. I borrow this term from Tania Murray Li, *The Will to Improve: Governmentality, Development, and the Practice of Politics* (Durham: Duke University Press, 2007), 13.

31. Henri Lefebvre, *The Production of Space* (Oxford: Blackwell, 1991), 39 (emphasis in original).

32. The qualitative distinction between "categories of analysis" and "categories of practice" is outlined in Pierre Bourdieu, *The Logic of Practice* (Stanford: Stanford University Press, 1992).

33. Mary Louise Pratt, *Imperial Eyes: Travel Writing and Transculturation* (London: Routledge, 1992), 7.

34. Mizuno Naoki, ed., *Seikatsu no naka no shokuminchi shugi* (Kyoto: Jinbun shoin, 2004); Yŏnse taehakkyo kukhak yŏn'guwŏn, ed., *Ilche ŭi chibae wa ilsang saenghwal* (Seoul: Hyean, 2004); Kong Che-uk and Chŏng Kŭn-sik, eds., *Singminji ŭi ilsang, chibae wa kyun'yŏl* (Seoul: Munhwa kwahaksa, 2006); and Kang Yŏng-sim, ed., *Ilche sigi kŭndaejŏk ilsang kwa singminji munhwa* (Seoul: Ihwa yŏja taehakkyo ch'ulp'anbu, 2008).

35. As critics of postnationalism have suggested, recent scholarship on colonial Korea has tended to place a disproportionate emphasis on the center and

the city over the periphery and the rural, not to mention having a privileged focus on modern developments at the expense of colonial violence. See, for example, Itagaki Ryūta, "'Shokuminchi kindai' o megutte: Chōsenshi kenkyū ni okeru genjō to kadai," *Rekishi hyōron* 654 (2004): 35–45; and Cho Kyŏng-dal, "Bōryoku to kōron: Shokuminchi Chōsen in okeru minshū no bōryoku," in *Bōryoku no heichi o koete: Rekishigaku kara no chōsen,* ed. Suda Tsutomu, Cho Kyŏng-dal, and Nakajima Hisato (Tokyo: Aoki shoten, 2004). For a wide-ranging analysis of Japanese colonial cities, see Hashiya Hiroshi, *Teikoku Nihon to shokuminchi toshi* (Tokyo: Yoshikawa kōbunkan, 2004); and the *Korea Journal*'s special issue on the making of modern Korean cities, *Korea Journal* 48, no. 3 (Autumn 2008). On the countryside in colonial Korea, see Matsumoto Takenori, *Chōsen nōson no "shokuminchi kindai" keiken* (Tokyo: Shakai hyōronsha, 2005).

36. Gabrielle M. Spiegel, *Practicing History: New Directions in Historical Writing after the Linguistic Turn* (New York: Routledge, 2005), 17 (emphasis in original).

37. See, for example, Nicholas Thomas, *Colonialism's Culture: Anthropology, Travel, and Government* (Princeton, NJ: Princeton University Press, 1994).

38. For more on colonial censorship, see Kyeong-Hee Choi [Ch'oe Kyŏng-hŭi], *Beneath the Vermillion Ink: Japanese Colonial Censorship and the Making of Modern Korean Literature* (Ithaca, NY: Cornell University Press, forthcoming).

39. Ann L. Stoler, "Colonial Archives and the Arts of Governance," *Archival Sciences* 2 (2002): 87. Because of this close connection to colonial power and its linguistic medium (Japanese), most South Korea–based academics have not made adequate use of the *Keijō nippō,* at least until recently. Although now reprinted and available online, the newspaper's ongoing status as a digitally unsearchable resource is another reason for its scholarly neglect. My own research was conducted through a meticulous, year-long examination of the microfilm version.

40. For an exploration of these approaches, see ibid., 87–109.

41. Andre Schmid has made a similar point for the preceding era in Schmid, *Korea between Empires, 1895–1919* (New York: Columbia University Press, 2002). I borrow the term "hygienic modernity" from Ruth Rogaski, *Hygienic Modernity: Meanings of Health and Disease in Treaty-Port China* (Berkeley: University of California Press, 2004).

42. As he explains, these are "naïve knowledges, hierarchically inferior knowledges, knowledges that are below the required level of erudition or scientificity." Michel Foucault, *"Society Must Be Defended": Lectures at the Collège de France, 1975–76* (New York: Picador, 2003), 7.

43. Sonja M. Kim, "Contesting Bodies: Managing Population, Birthing, and Medicine in Korea, 1876–1945," PhD diss., University of California, Los Angeles, 2008, 82.

44. On the March First Movement, see Frank Baldwin "Participatory Anti-Imperialism: The 1919 Independence Movement," *Journal of Korean Studies* 1 (1979): 123–62. For a compelling account that places this movement into a broader global history, see Erez Manela, *The Wilsonian Moment: Self-*

*Determination and the International Origins of Anticolonial Nationalism* (Oxford: Oxford University Press, 2007).

45. For one work on the urban dimensions of these changes, see Pak Se-hun, *Singmin kukka wa chiyŏk kongdongch'e: 1930 nyŏndae Kyŏngsŏngbu ŭi tosi sahoe chŏngch'aek yŏn'gu* (Seoul: Han'guk haksul chŏngbo, 2006).

46. Uchida, *Brokers of Empire.* For studies of colonial Korea which also foreground the role played by Japanese settlers, see Helen J.S. Lee, "Writing Colonial Relations of Everyday Life in Senryu," *Positions: East Asia Cultures Critique* 16, no. 3 (Winter 2008): 601–28; and Nicole Leah Cohen, "Children of Empire: Growing up Japanese in Colonial Korea, 1876–1945," PhD diss., Columbia University, 2006.

47. For more on the precolonial history of the Japanese settler community, see Kimura Kenji, *Zaichō nihonjin no shakaishi* (Tokyo: Miraisha, 1989); and Peter Duus, *Abacus and the Sword: The Japanese Penetration of Korea, 1895–1910* (Berkeley: University of California Press, 1995), 245–423.

48. For more on this dynamic, see Todd A. Henry, "Assimilation's Racializing Sensibilities: Colonized Koreans as *Yobos* and the '*Yobo*-ization' of Japanese Settlers," *Positions: Asia Critique* 21, no. 1 (Winter 2013): 11–49.

49. Ching, *Becoming "Japanese,"* 91.

50. See, for example, the essays in Kim Sŭng-t'ae, *Han'guk kidokkyo wa sinsa ch'ambae munje;* and Kim Sŭng-t'ae, *Sinsa ch'ambae kŏbu hangjaengjadŭl ŭi chŭng'ŏn.*

51. For one industry's place in these developments, see Carter J. Eckert, *Offspring of Empire: The Koch'ang Kims and the Colonial Origins of Korean Capitalism, 1876–1945* (Seattle: University of Washington Press, 1996).

## 1. CONSTRUCTING KEIJŌ

1. Gyan Prakash, *Another Reason: Science and the Imagination of Modern India* (Princeton, NJ: Princeton University Press, 1999).

2. Kaesŏng did, however, briefly become the Chosŏn capital again from 1398 to 1400. On the complicated process of selecting and establishing Hanyang, see Hong-key Yoon [Yun Hong-gi], *The Culture of Fengshui in Korea: An Exploration of East Asian Geomancy* (Lanham, MD: Lexington Books, 2006), 231–40; and Yoshida Mitsuo, *Kinsei Souru toshi shakai kenkyū: Kanjō no machi to jūmin* (Urayasu: Sōfūkan, 2009), 16–25. Before the Chosŏn period, Korean dynasties also maintained various smaller capitals. Koryŏ kings, for example, administered three such cities, including one in Hanyang, or what was also called Namgyŏng (literally, southern capital) at the time.

3. The following discussion is based on Im Tŏk-sun, "Chosŏn ch'ogi Hanyang chŏngdo wa sudo ŭi sangjinghwa," in *Sŏul ŭi kyŏnggwan pyŏnhwa,* ed. An Tu-sun (Seoul: Sŏulhak yŏn'guso, 1994), 43–55; Qinghua Guo, *Chinese Architecture and Planning: Ideas, Methods, Techniques* (Stuttgart: Axel Menges, 2005), 147–56; and Ko Tong-hwan, "Chosŏn ch'ogi Hanyang ŭi hyŏngsŏng kwa tosi kujo," *Chibangsa wa chibang munwa* 8, no. 1 (2005): 52–89.

4. During the colonial period, this stream became an imagined, if not real, boundary separating the historic center of Korean royal authority in the northern village and the Japanese upstart regions of the southern village.

5. Ko Dong-hwan [Ko Tong-hwan], "The Characteristics of the Urban Development of Seoul during the Late Chosŏn Dynasty: With a Focus on the Changes in Urban Structure," *Seoul Journal of Korean Studies* 10 (1997): 95–123. By the late eighteenth century, the extramural population of merchants and other social groups nearly matched that of Hanyang's official residents who lived within the city's walls. For other important works on the city's commercial development, see Ch'oe Wan-gi, *Hanyang: Kŭ kot esŏ salgo sipta* (Seoul: Kyohwasa, 1997); Ko Tong-hwan, *Chosŏn hugi Sŏul sang'ŏp paldalsa* (Seoul: Chisik sanŏpsa, 1998); and Ko Tong-hwan, *Chosŏn sidae Sŏul tosisa* (Seoul: T'aehaksa, 2007).

6. For more on the *chung'in,* see Kyung Moon Hwang [Hwang Kyŏng-mun], *Beyond Birth: Social Status in the Emergence of Modern Korea* (Cambridge, MA: Harvard University Press, 2004).

7. For an overview, see Kim Do-hyung [Kim To-hyŏng], "Introduction: The Nature of Reform in the Taehan Empire," in *Reform and Modernity in the Taehan Empire,* ed. Kim Dong-no, John B. Duncan, and Kim Do-hyung (Seoul: Jimoondang, 2006), 1–34.

8. According to Yi, the plan also included other elements of a modern urban infrastructure, such as sewers, electricity, waterworks, streetcars, railroads, an industrial district (in Yongsan), and city market (around the South Gate). For more on this project, see Yi, "Seoul's Modern Development during the Eighteenth and Nineteenth Centuries" and "The Leaders and Objectives of the Seoul Urban Renovation Project of 1896–1904," in *The Dynamics of Confucianism and Modernization in Korean History* (Ithaca, NY: Cornell University Press, 2008). For a comparative analysis of Hwangsŏng and Tokyo during this period, see Yi, "Meiji Tok'yo wa kwangmu Sŏul: Kŭndae tosi ro ŭi chihyangsŏng kwa kaejo sŏngkwa pigyo," in *Han'guk, ilbon, "sŏyang,"* ed. Watanabe Hiroshi and Park Ch'ung-sŏk (Seoul: Ayŏn ch'ulp'anbu, 2008).

9. Similar problems of self-definition characterized the Korean flag and other national symbols. For more on this history, see Andre Schmid, *Korea between Empires, 1895–1919* (New York: Columbia University Press, 2002), 55–100.

10. Kim Kwang-u, "Taehan cheguk sidae ŭi tosi kyehoek: Hansŏngbu tosi kaejo saŏp," *Hyangt'o Sŏul* 50 (1990): 115. On the history of this district (Chŏngdong), see Kim Chŏng-dong, *Kojong hwangje ka sarang han chŏngdong kwa tŏksugung* (Seoul: Pal'ŏn, 2004); and An Ch'ang-mo, *Tŏksugung: Sidae ŭi unmyŏng ŭl anko cheguk ŭi chungsim e sŏda* (Seoul: Tongnyŏk, 2009).

11. On these concessions, see Peter Duus, *The Abacus and the Sword: The Japanese Penetration of Korea, 1895–1910* (Berkeley: University of California Press, 1995), 134–68.

12. No In-hwa. "Taehan cheguk sigi ŭi Hansŏng chŏngi hoesa e taehan yŏn'gu: 'Kwangmu kaehyŏk' kwa migukch'ŭk igwŏn ŭi ilyangt'ae," *Idae sawŏn* 17 (Dec. 1980): 1–27.

13. Min Suh Son [Son Min-sŏ], "Enlightenment and Electrification: The Introduction of Electric Light, Telegraph and Streetcars in Late Nineteenth Cen-

tury Korea," in Kim, Duncan, and Kim, eds., *Reform and Modernity in the Taehan Empire*, 126–98.

14. Chŏn U-yong, "Taehan chegukki—ilche ch'ogi Sŏul konggan ŭi pyŏnhwa wa kwŏllyŏk ŭi chihyang," *Chŏnnong saron* 5 (1999): 39–72.

15. On the rise and fall of the Independence Club, see Vipan Chandra, *Imperialism, Resistance, and Reform in Late Nineteenth-Century Korea: Enlightenment and the Independence Club* (Berkeley: Institute of East Asian Studies, 1988). See also Kim Do-hyung [Kim To-hyŏng], "Introduction: The Nature of Reform in the Taehan Empire," 22–27.

16. Chong Chinsok [Chŏng Chin-sŏk], "A Study on the *Maeil Sinbo* (Daily News): Public Information Policy of the Japanese Imperialists and Korean Journalism under Japanese Imperialism," *Journal of Social Sciences and Humanities* 52 (1980): 62, 70. The new colonial government also downgraded the position of the former capital, reducing its administrative area from approximately two hundred and fifty square kilometers to just over thirty-six square kilometers in 1914.

17. During the Chosŏn period, residents occasionally referred to Keijō with this same Korean name, Kyŏngsŏng. For more on the history of the city's nomenclatures, see Kim Paek-yŏng, *Chibae wa konggan: Singminji tosi Kyŏngsŏng kwa cheguk ilbon* (Seoul: Munhak kwa chisŏngsa, 2009), 264n105. On the movement of capitals in Japanese history, see Nicolas Fiévé and Paul Waley, eds., *Japanese Capitals in Historical Perspective: Place, Power and Memory in Kyoto, Edo and Tokyo* (London: Routledge, 2003).

18. Takashi Fujitani, *Splendid Monarchy: Power and Pageantry in Modern Japan* (Berkeley: University of California Press, 1996), 31–92; and Christine Kim, "Politics and Pageantry in Protectorate Korea, 1905–10: The Imperial Progresses of Sunjong," *Journal of Asian Studies* 68, no. 3 (2009): 835–59.

19. During the Great Han Empire, Kojong did follow historic precedents by working to establish a secondary capital in P'yŏngyang—the former center of Old Chosŏn (?–108 BCE), Koguryŏ (37 BCE–668 AD), and Koryŏ kings—in an effort to more closely align the beleaguered country with Russia, but which ultimately failed due to Japanese interference. For more on this project and the importance of *chung'in* and Protestantism in its development, see Eugene Y. Park, "The Phantasm of the Western Capital (Sŏgyŏng): Imperial Korea's Redevelopment of Pyongyang, 1902–1908," unpublished manuscript.

20. For more on this Meiji-style transformation, see U Tong-sŏn, "Ch'anggyŏngwŏn kwa Ueno kongwŏn kŭrigo Meiji ŭi konggan chibae," in *Kunggwŏl ŭi nunmul, paeknyŏn ŭi ch'inmok: Cheguk ŭi somyŏl 100 nyŏn, uri kunggwŏl ŭn ŏdi ro kassŭlkka?*, ed. U Tong-sŏn and Pak Sŏng-jin. (Seoul: Hyohyŏng ch'ulp'an, 2009), 202–37. On Ueno Park, see Thomas R. H. Havens, *Parkscapes: Green Spaces in Modern Japan* (Honolulu: University of Hawai'i Press, 2011), 28–32.

21. On the shifting nature of what he calls the "dual palace system," see Hong Sun-min, *Uri kunggwŏl iyagi* (Seoul: Ch'ŏngnyŏnsa, 2004).

22. For more on the fate of this palace, see Chŏng Chae-jŏng, *Sŏul ŭi munhwa yusa t'ambanggi* (Seoul: Sŏulhak yŏn'guso, 1997), 261–93; and An, *Tŏksugung*. On that of the Ring Hall, see Pak Hŭi-yong, "Chosŏn hwangje ŭi

aedalp'ŭn yŏksa rŭl chŭngmyŏng hada: Wŏn'gudan ŭi ch'ŏlgŏ wa Chosŏn hot'el ŭi kŏnch'uk," in U Tong-sŏn and Pak Sŏng-jin, *Kunggwŏl ŭi nunmul, paeknyŏn ŭi ch'inmok*, 48–85.

23. Ōta Hideharu, "Kŭndae han'il yangguk ŭi sŏnggwak insik kwa ilbon ŭi chosŏn singminji chŏngch'aek," *Han'guk saron* 49 (June 2003): 185–203. On the late-nineteenth-century reconstruction of Kyŏngbok Palace, see Cho Chae-ho and Chŏn Pong-hŭi, "Kojongjo kyŏngbokgung chunggŏn e taehan yŏn'gu," *Taehan kŏnch'uk hakhoe nonmunjip* 16, no. 4 (April 2000): 31–40; and Hong Sun-min, "Kojongdae kyŏngbokgung chunggŏn ŭi chŏngch'ijŏk ŭimi," *Sŏulhak yŏn'gu* 29 (Aug. 2007): 57–82.

24. Fujimori Terunobu, *Meiji no Tōkyō keikaku* (Tokyo: Iwanami shoten, 1990), 89–258.

25. Gotō Yasushi, "'Keijō' shiku kaisei (1912–1937) no tokuchō ni kansuru kenkyū," paper delivered at International Symposium on Urban and Architectural Histories under Colonial Rule in Asia, Academica Sinica (Taipei, Taiwan), Sept. 6–7, 2000, 11–12.

26. For urban reforms in Meiji Tokyo, see Ishida Yorifusa, *Nihon kindai toshi keikakushi kenkyū* (Tokyo: Kashiwa shobō, 1987), 51–106; and André Sorensen, *The Making of Urban Japan: Cities and Planning from Edo to the Twenty-First Century* (London: Routledge, 2002), 60–84. On early colonial Taipei, see Gotō Yasushi, "Nihon tōchika no taihoku jōnai no gaiku keisei ni kansuru kenkyū," *Dobokushi kenkyū* 18 (1998): 103–16.

27. *KS*, Nov. 15, 1907. Unless otherwise mentioned, the following discussion is based on *CSb*, October 5, 1911.

28. *CTK*, Sept. 1928, 54. On the settler occupation of the southern village, see Kim Chong-gŭn, "Sŏul chungsimbu ŭi ilbon'in sigaji hwaksan: Kaehanggi esŏ ilche kangjŏm chŏnhangi kkaji (1885 nyŏn-1929 nyŏn)," *Sŏulhak yŏn'gu* 20 (March 2003): 181–233; and Pak Ch'ang-sŭng, "Sŏul ilbon'in kŏryuji hyŏngsŏng kwajŏng: 1880 nyŏndae-1903 nyŏn ŭl chungsim ŭro," *Sahoe wa yŏksa* 62 (2002): 64–100.

29. The Japanese population of Yongsan increased dramatically from just thirty-five in 1897 to over ten thousand by 1910. On the development of this area, see Son Chŏng-mok, *Han'guk kaehanggi tosi sahoe kyŏngjesa yŏn'gu* (Seoul: Iljisa, 1982), 307–27; and Kim, *Chibae wa konggan*, 272–309.

30. *CSb*, May 24, 1912.

31. For this proposal, see Ōmura Tomonojō, *Keijō kaikoroku* (Keijō: Chōsen kenkyūkai, 1922), 278–81. On settlers' early struggles against disenfranchisement and their accusations of favoritism, see Jun Uchida, *Brokers of Empire: Japanese Settler Colonialism in Korea, 1876–1945* (Cambridge, MA: Harvard University Asia Center, 2011), 96–139. For a study of Seoul's settler institutions, see Yamanaka Mai, "Sŏul kŏju ilbon'in chach'i kigang yŏn'gu, 1885–1914," MA thesis, Catholic University (Seoul), 2001.

32. "Keijō Honmachi dōri no dōro kakuchō ni tsuite," *COM* 45 (Sept. 1, 1911): 48–51.

33. *CSb*, June 27, 1911. For a list of settlement road projects completed before 1912, see Kim, *Chibae wa konggan*, 279.

34. The following discussion is based on *CSb*, June 25, 1912. On Mochiji's career, see Kaneko Fumio, "Mochiji Rokusaburō no shōgai to chosaku," *Taiwan kingendaishi kenkyū* 2 (Aug. 1979): 119–28.

35. Yamaoka Gen'ichi, a Government-General technician, made similar points in *CK* 1, no. 4 (July 1913): 30–32. For the planning of Dairen (C: Dalian), see Koshizawa Akira, *Dairen no toshi keikakushi, 1898–1945* (Tokyo: Ajia keizai kenkyūjo, 1984); and Nishizawa Yasuhiko, *Zusetsu Dairen toshi monogatari* (Tokyo: Kawade shobō shinsha, 1999).

36. *CSb*, Sept. 8, 1912.

37. In designating Kōgane-machi for this plaza, Gotō Yasushi has suggested that Keijō officials might have been mimicking the efforts of Tokyo planners to transform Marunouchi into an administrative hub. However, given that they had already decided to move their headquarters from the Namsan area to Kyŏngbok Palace, this possibility seems unlikely. Gotō Yasushi, "Nihon tōchika 'Keijō' no toshi keikaku ni kansuru rekishiteki kenkyū," PhD diss., Tokyo Institute of Technology, 1995, 67. For the Marunouchi project, see Fujimori Terunobu, *Meiji no Tōkyō keikaku*, 259–304.

38. Expatriate leaders indefatigably pursued this project even after the colonial state dissolved the settlement's legal dissolution in 1914. *CSb*, May 21, 1913. On later activities to improve roads in the southern village, see *CTK*, June 1929, 49.

39. See, for example, *CTK*, Sept. 1924, 2.

40. Gotō, "Nihon tōchika 'Keijō' no toshi keikaku ni kansuru rekishiteki kenkyū," 67; and Yi Kyŏng-su, "Ilche sigi kyŏngsŏngbu ŭi karo chŏngbi kyehoek e ŭi han karo pyŏnhwa e kwanhan yŏn'gu," MA thesis, Yonsei University, 1990, 75.

41. On these proposals, *KN*, Feb. 20, 1916.

42. *KN*, Feb. 8, 1917. In the future, this bridge would serve as an important link for overland trade and transport moving southward and for traffic proceeding along the Han River toward the port city of Inch'ŏn.

43. Of the eight radial roads proposed in the plan of 1913, only two remained for future construction; one other remained, but did not form part of a symmetric radial road system. Gotō, "Nihon tōchika 'Keijō' no toshi keikaku ni kansuru rekishiteki kenkyū," 72–73.

44. *Chongnogu-ji* 2 (Seoul: Chongno-gu, 1994), 57. The number of roads slated for (re)construction increased to forty-seven in 1930, although only twenty-five were ever completed. See ibid. On the fate of Keijō's planning before 1920, see Kim Ki-ho, "Ilche sidae ch'ogi ŭi tosi kyehoek e taehan yŏn'gu: Kyŏngsŏngbu sigu kaejŏng ŭl chungsim ŭro," *Sŏulhak yŏn'gu* 6 (1995): 41–66.

45. Gotō, "Nihon tōchika 'Keijō' no toshi keikaku ni kansuru rekishiteki kenkyū," 67–71.

46. On this region, see the essays in *Ch'ŏnggyech'ŏn: Sigan, changso, saram* (Seoul: Sŏulhak yŏn'guso, 2001). For a literary treatment, see Pak T'ae-wŏn, *Ch'ŏnbyŏn p'unggyŏng* (Streamside sketches), a modernist novel serialized in the *CI* from 1936 to 1937.

47. Seo Hyŏn-ju [Sŏ Hyŏn-ju], "Chosŏnmal ilcheha Sŏul ŭi habu haengjŏng chedo yŏn'gu: Chŏngdonghoe wa ch'ongdae rŭl chungsim ŭro," PhD diss., Seoul National University, 2002, 133.

48. Gotō, "Nihon tōchika 'Keijō' no toshi keikaku ni kansuru rekishiteki kenkyū," 190.

49. On neighborhood transformations in the southern village, see Yang Sŭng-u, "Namch'on ŭi p'ilji chojik tŭksŏng kwa pyŏnhwa," in *Sŏul namch'on: Sigan, changso, saram* (Seoul: Sŏulhak yŏn'guso, 2003), 37–71.

50. Countering nationalist accounts of ethnic segregation, one scholar has calculated that, in 1925 and 1935, 37 percent and 47 percent of Keijō neighborhoods—mostly in the central and southern parts of the city, the location of commercial and government offices—were places of considerable mixed residence. Kim Chong-gŭn, "Singminji Kyŏngsŏng ŭi ijung tosiron e taehan pip'anjŏk koch'al," *Sŏulhak yŏn'gu* 38 (Feb. 2010): 43–59.

51. *MS*, July 10, 1912.

52. *MS*, Nov. 17, 1912.

53. For more on these accusations, see Henry, "Sanitizing Empire: Japanese Articulations of Korean Otherness and the Construction of Early Colonial Seoul, 1905–19," *Journal of Asian Studies* 64, no. 3 (Aug. 2005): 643–53.

54. *MS*, July 10, 1912.

55. *MS*, Oct. 25, 1911. For more on these racialized accusations, see Henry, "Assimilation's Racializing Sensibilities: Colonized Koreans as *Yobos* and the 'Yobo-ization' of Japanese Settlers," *Positions: Asia Critique* 21, no. 1 (Winter 2013): 11–49.

56. *MS*, Aug. 24, 1913.

57. Yi Chong-min, "Keihanzai no torishimari hōrei ni miru minshū tōsei: Chōsen no baai o chūsin ni," in *Shokuminchi teikoku nihon no hōteki kōzō*, ed. Asano Toyomi and Matsuda Toshihiko (Tokyo: Shinsansha, 2004), 338–47.

58. *MS*, Nov. 17, 1912.

59. Linked to a growing network of intramural trade during the late Chosŏn dynasty, these stalls continued to flourish well into the early twentieth century, despite aggressive attempts to remove them by the Great Han Empire.

60. *KS*, Oct. 10, 1910. For more on the meanings of illumination, see Son, "Enlightenment and Electrification."

61. *MS*, Nov. 17, 1910. Arguments such as these continued, sporadically, until the opening of night markets, first along Taihei Boulevard in 1914 and subsequently along Chongno in 1916.

62. Matsui Shigeru, *Jichi to keisatsu* (Tokyo: Keigansha, 1913), 830.

63. Ibid., 846.

64. *COM*, March 1, 1915, 830.

65. On metropolitan women in Japan's empire, see Barbara Brooks, "Reading the Japanese Colonial Archive: Gender and Bourgeois Civility in Korea and Manchuria Before 1932," in *Gendering Modern Japanese History*, ed. Barbara Molony and Kathleen Uno (Cambridge, MA: Harvard University Press, 2005).

66. *Sŏul 20 segi konggan pyŏnch'ŏnsa* (Seoul: Sŏul sijŏng kaebal yŏn'guwŏn, 2002), 392.

67. Kang Sin-yong, "Kankoku ni okeru kindai toshi kōen no juyō to tenkai," PhD diss., Kyoto University, 2004, 56.

68. *MS*, June 28, 1914.

69. On the involvement of Korean (and Japanese) businessmen in these state-led projects, see Carter J. Eckert, *Offspring of Empire: The Koch'ang Kims and the Colonial Origins of Korean Capitalism, 1876–1945* (Seattle: University of Washington Press, 1991); and Uchida, *Brokers of Empire.*

70. Sorensen, *The Making of Urban Japan,* 108, 110. For a detailed discussion of these urban planning components and their implementation in post-Kantō earthquake Tokyo, see ibid., 114–33.

71. For examples of the "warped modernity" school as they relate to city planning, see Son Chŏng-mok, *Ilche kangjŏmgi tosi kyehoek yŏn'gu* (Seoul: Iljisa, 1990); and Yi Myŏng-gu, "Han'guk kwa ilbon ŭi tosi kyehoek chedo ŭi pigyo punsŏk e kwanhan yŏn'gu: Chosŏn sigaji kyehoengnyŏng kwa ilbon (ku) tosi kyehoekbŏp ŭl chungsim ŭro," PhD diss., Seoul National University, 1994.

72. Two important studies that have emphasized the contentious nature of colonial planning include Kim, *Chibae wa konggan;* and Pak Se-hun, *Singmin kukka wa chiyŏk kongdongch'e: 1930 nyŏndae Kyŏngsŏngbu ŭi tosi sahoe chŏngch'aek yŏn'gu* (Seoul: Han'guk haksul chŏngbo, 2006).

73. For a study plotting the institutions and laws of Japanese urban planning within the context of European traditions, see Watanabe Shun'ichi, *"Toshi keikaku" no tanjō: Kokusai hikaku kara mita nihon kindai toshi keikaku* (Tokyo: Kashiwa shobō, 1994). On the Euro-American traditions of modern planning, see Anthony Sutcliffe, *The Rise of Modern Urban Planning, 1800–1914* (New York: St. Martin's Press, 1980).

74. Gotō later became mayor of Tokyo and, following the Great Kantō earthquake of 1923, head of the Imperial Capital Reconstruction Board. For more on his career, see Yukiko Hayase, "The Career of Gotō Shimpei: Japan's Statesman of Research, 1857–1929," PhD diss., Florida State University, 1974.

75. For his detailed reports, see *KI* 8 (May 1922): 6–10; *KI* 9 (June 1922): 8–10; and *KI* 10 (July 1922): 4–12. On his views of city planning in Korea, see *CTK,* Sept. 1925, 19–26.

76. Inspiration for this approach derives, in part, from Andre Schmid, "Colonialism and the 'Korea Problem' in the Historiography of Japan: A Review Article," *Journal of Asian Studies* 59, no. 4 (Nov. 2000): 951–76.

77. *KI* 9 (July 1922): 6–7.

78. *KN,* Sept. 6, 1921.

79. Ikeda Hiroshi, URA director and Gotō Shimpei's loyal underling at City Hall during the early 1920s, described the family-city of Tokyo as the "driving force sustaining the essence of the national body." *TK,* Feb. 1921, 16–18. On the role of Ikeda in Japan's planning movement, see Watanabe, *"Toshi keikaku" no tanjō,* 169–86.

80. Uchida, *Brokers of Empire,* 143–87, 262–304; Yun Hae-dong, "Colonial Publicness as Metaphor," in *Mass Dictatorship and Modernity,* ed. Michael Kim, Michael Schoenhals, and Yong-Woo Kim (London: Routledge, 2013). On the Keijō Municipal Council, see Son Chong-mŏk, "Irŭnba 'munhwa chŏngch'i' ha esŏ ŭi tosi chibang chedo yŏn'gu: Kyŏngsŏngbu hyŏbŭihoe rŭl chungsim ŭro," *Hyangt'o sŏul* 50 (1991): 125–94.

81. *KN,* Sept. 1, 1920.

82. *CTK,* June 1924, 1–3.

83. For a metropolitan iteration, see, *TK*, Feb. 1921, 16–18. See also Se Hoon Park [Pak Se-hun], "Care and Control: Colonial Governmentality and Urban Social Policy in Colonial Seoul," in *East Asia: A Critical Geography Perspective*, ed. Wing-Shing Tang and Fujio Mizuoka (Tokyo: Kokon shoin, 2010), 124–26.

84. *KI* 19 (May 1923): 1; and *KI* 22 (Aug. 1923): 1.

85. On these policies, see Yamamoto Tsuneo, *Kindai nihon toshi kyōkashi kenkyū* (Tokyo: Reimei shobō, 1972).

86. *KI* 20 (June 1923): 1.

87. *Chōsen doboku jigyōshi* (Keijō: Chōsen sōtokufu, 1937), 309–24.

88. The flood in 1925 resulted in approximately four hundred deaths or injuries and more than forty-six million yen in property damage. For responses to this disaster, see Jong-Geun Kim [Kim Chong-gŭn], "Colonial Modernity and the Colonial City: Seoul during the Japanese Occupation, 1910–1945," PhD diss., University of Cambridge, 2013, 211–54.

89. Unless noted otherwise, the following discussion is based on Kim, *Chibae wa konggan*, 385–433. For an English-language version, see Kim Baek Yung [Kim Paek-yŏng], "Ruptures and Conflicts in the Colonial Power Bloc: The Great Keijo Plan of the 1920s," *Korea Journal* 48, no. 3 (Autumn 2008): 10–40.

90. *TI*, Oct. 15, 1922.

91. For KCPRA's inaugural statement, see *Dai-Keijō* (Keijō: Chōsen kenkyū kai, 1925), 9–12.

92. Pak Se-hun, "1920 nyŏndae Kyŏngsŏng tosi kyehoek ŭi sŏnggyŏk: 'Kyŏngsŏng tosi kyehoek yŏn'guhoe' wa 'tosi kyehoek undong,'" *Sŏulhak yŏn'gu* 15 (Sept. 2000): 187–88. For a list of key members as of 1925, see ibid., 186.

93. Their advisory position is reflected in their later meeting place, the municipal government. Unless noted otherwise, the following discussion is based on *KI* 39 (Feb. 1925): 4; and *Keijōfu toshi keikaku yōran* (Keijō: Keijōfu, 1939), 2–3.

94. For list of survey subjects, see *KI* 42 (June 1926): 10.

95. Kim, "Ruptures and Conflicts in the Colonial Power Bloc," 18–21.

96. *Keijō toshi keikaku kuiki setteisho* (Keijō: Keijōfu, 1926), 7.

97. Ibid., 176.

98. Ibid., 201. For a list of proposed expanded and newly constructed roads, see ibid., 203–23.

99. Son, *Ilche kangjŏmgi tosi kyehoek yŏn'gu*, 146.

100. *KN*, June 15, 1927.

101. *KN*, June 14, 1925.

102. Son, *Ilche kangjŏmgi tosi kwajŏng yŏn'gu* (Seoul: Iljisa, 1996), 567–83.

103. *KI* 62 (Dec. 1926): 27–29; and *CTK*, Oct. 1926, 9–10.

104. *KI* 62 (Dec. 1926): 17–18.

105. *KN*, Oct. 21, 1926; and *KI* 62 (Dec. 1926): 50–51.

106. *KI* 62 (Dec. 1926): 225; and *CTK*, July 1928, 34–35. By contrast, Korea Shrine served as the city's geographical center.

107. See, for example, Son, *Ilche kangjŏmgi tosi kwajŏng yŏn'gu*, 520–60; Kim Chŏng-dong, *Nama innŭn yŏksa, sarajinŭn kŏnch'ungmul* (Seoul: Taewŏnsa, 2000), 183–252; and Hŏ Yŏng-sŏp, *Chosŏn Ch'ongdokbu: Kŭ ch'ŏngsa kŏllip ŭi iyagi* (Seoul: Han'ul, 1996).

108. For their missives, see, respectively, "Ushinawaren to suru ichi Chōsen kenchiku no tame," *Kaizō*, Sept. 1922, 22–29; and "Sōtokufu shinchōsa wa rokotsu sugiru," *CTK*, June 1923, 17–19. An English translation of the former appears in Wm. Theodore de Bary, Carol Gluck, and Arthur E. Tiedemann, eds., *Sources of Japanese Tradition, Abridged*, vol. 2, *1868 to 2000* (New York: Columbia University Press, 2006), 144–47.

109. *KN*, April 30, 1925.

110. Sunyoung Park [Pak Sun-yŏng], tr., *On the Eve of the Uprising, and Other Stories from Colonial Korea* (Ithaca, NY: Cornell University Press, 2010), 162–64. On the trope of disease in colonial literature, see Christopher P. Hanscom, "Modernism, Hysteria, and the Colonial Double Bind: Pak T'aewŏn's *One Day in the Life of the Author, Mr. Kubo*," *Positions: Asia Critique* 21, no. 3 (Summer 2013): 607–36.

111. Park, *On the Eve of the Uprising*, 160.

112. Sorensen, *The Making of Urban Japan*, 122. On the development of this system in the metropole, see Ishida Yorifusa, "Nihon ni okeru tochi kukaku seiri seidoshi gaisetsu, 1870–1980," *Sōgō toshi kenkyū* 28 (1986): 45–87.

113. *KI* 59 (Oct. 1926): 14.

114. *Keijō toshi keikaku chōsasho*, 251–52.

115. *Keijō toshi keikaku chōsasho*, plates in between pages 270 and 271.

116. *KI* 71 (Aug. 1927): 14.

117. *Keijō toshi keikaku chōsasho*, 254–55.

118. *KI* 66 (March 1927): 34.

119. For Naoki's writings, see *KN*, Dec. 27, 1928; and *KN*, Jan. 17, 19–20 and 23–27. The following discussion is based on *Chōsen doboku kenchiku kyōkai kaihō* 133 (March 1929): 11–12.

120. Sorensen, *The Making of Urban Japan*, 125–31.

121. *CTK*, July 1926, 4; and *CTK*, June 1932, 55.

122. On these wartime projects, see Son, *Ilche kangjŏmgi tosi kyehoek yŏn'gu*, 281–300.

123. For an explanation of the BL and its application to Keijō, see *CTK*, April 1929, 32–34.

124. *KN*, June 24, 1926. During the late 1920s and early 1930s, organized groups of renters did, however, struggle to protect their right to subsistence against rapacious landlords through the colonial police and court systems, albeit with little success. For more on these local politics, see Yŏm Pok-kyu, "1920 nyŏndae huban—30 nyŏndae chŏnban ch'aji, ch'again undong ŭi chojikhwa yangsik kwa chŏngae kwajŏng," *Yoksa wa sahoe* 73 (March 2007): 75–105.

125. *KN*, Feb. 6, 1926.

126. *TI*, June 24, 1926. See, for example, *CTK*, April 1929, 17–20.

127. *TI*, Feb. 26, 1927.

128. *TI*, March 5, 1927.

129. *TI*, March 8, 1927. For more on the local politics of urban problems, see Kim Yŏng-mi, "Ilche sigi tosi munje wa chiyŏk undong: Kyŏngsŏng chiyŏk sŏngbuk-dong ŭi sarye rŭl chungsim ŭro," in *Han'guk kŭndae sahoe wa munhwa III: 1920–1930 nyŏndae 'singminjijŏk kŭndae' wa han'gugin ŭi taeŭng* (Seoul: Sŏul taehakkyo ch'ulp'anbu, 2007).

130. *KN*, March 4, 1929. For a draft of the BL regulations as of late 1928, see *KN*, Nov. 24, 1928.

131. *TI*, April 1, 1927.

132. *KN*, March 4, 1929. On this controversy and proposals to move the shrine or convert it into a park, see Kim Tae-ho, "Ilcheha Chongmyo rŭl tullŏssan seryŏk kaldŭng kwa konggan pyŏnhwa: 1920 nyŏndae singmin kwŏllyŏk kwa kwijok seryŏk ŭi kwan'gye rŭl chungsim ŭro," *Sŏulhak yŏn'gu* 43 (2011): 1–54.

133. *KN*, May 28, 1926. On Sunjong's role in the protest of 1922, see Kim, "Ilcheha Chongmyo rŭl tullŏssan seryŏk kaldŭng kwa konggan pyŏnhwa," 27–29.

134. *TI*, Feb. 11, 1930.

135. The only road improvements made were in Moto-machi, the East Gate, and West Gate areas. *KN*, March 8, 1934.

136. According to the colonial census in 1925, Hyoja-dong consisted of 1,845 Koreans (87.7 percent) and 212 Japanese (12.3 percent). Son, *Ilche kangjŏmgi tosi kwajŏng yŏn'gu*, 372.

137. *TI*, Oct. 23, 1929. Revenue lost from the postponed BL reportedly amounted to 130,000 yen. *KN*, March 2, 1930.

138. *TI*, April 26, 1929 (emphasis mine).

139. Unless otherwise noted, the following discussion is based on *KN*, Sept. 21, 1932.

140. *TI*, March 17, 1933. For more on the merchants of Chongno, see Chŏn U-yong, "Chongno wa ponjŏng: Singmin tosi Kyŏngsŏng ŭi tu ŏlgul," *Yŏksa wa hyŏnsil* 40 (June 2001): 163–93.

141. Strolling (*bura bura suru* in Japanese) along the Ginza in Tokyo was referred to as *Ginbura*, while a promenade along Keijō's Honmachi Street was known as *Honbura*.

142. From the spring of 1935, officials further upgraded Chongno by installing roadside lights. *KN*, Nov. 7, 1934; and *KN*, Feb. 20, 1935.

143. On the passage of this Act and its effects, see Son, *Ilche kangjŏmgi tosi kyehoek yŏn'gu*, 177–212.

144. Kim, *Chibae wa konggan*, 428–29.

145. *KN*, March 8, 1934; and *KN*, May 14, 1935. For a study of city planning during this period, see Yŏm Pok-kyu, "1933–43 nyŏn ilche ŭi 'Kyŏngsŏng sigaji kyehoek,'" *Han'guk saron* 46 (2001): 233–83.

146. *KN*, Oct. 24, 1932.

147. According to one scholar, personal loyalties toward the Great Han Empire lingered among many Koreans at least until Kojong's elaborately staged funeral of 1919. For more on this history, see Christine Kim, "The King Is Dead: The Monarchy and National Identity in Modern Korea," PhD diss., Harvard University, 2004.

148. *KN*, Nov. 22, 1933.

## 2. SPIRITUAL ASSIMILATION

1. Until 1913, when it came to nominally include the city's Japanese and Korean communities, Seoul Shrine (J: *Keijō jinja; Kyŏngsŏng sinsa*) was called the Great Shrine of Namsan (J: *Nanzan dai-jingū; Namsan tae-sin'gung*). For

simplicity's sake, I will refer to this site as Seoul Shrine. As chapter 5 will explain, Seoul Nation-Protecting Shrine (J: *Keijō gokoku jinja; Kyŏngsŏng hoguk sinsa*), a satellite of the Tokyo-based Yasukuni Shrine, which memorialized the peninsula's fallen soldiers, was added to this complex in 1943.

2. On the role played by new conceptions of "religion," see Jason Ānanda Josephson, *The Invention of Religion in Japan* (Chicago: University of Chicago Press, 2012); and Trent E. Maxey, *The "Greatest Problem": Religion and State Formation in Meiji Japan* (Cambridge, MA: Harvard University Asia Center, 2014).

3. By contrast, the police monitored shamanism and other so-called pseudo-religions, which the colonial state considered superstitious threats to the social order. Yamaguchi Kōichi, "Shokuminchiki Chōsen ni okeru jinja seisaku to Chōsen shakai," PhD diss., Hitotsubashi University, 2006, 58–61, 87–90, and 95–96. On the Government-General's relationship to religions in early colonial Korea, see Henrik H. Sørensen, "The Attitude of the Japanese Colonial Government towards Religion in Korea, 1910–1919," *Copenhagen Papers in East and Southeast Asia Studies* 8 (1993): 49–69. For the separation of shrine and sect Shintō, see Helen Hardacre, *Shintō and the State, 1868–1988* (Princeton: Princeton University Press, 1989).

4. Hiura Satoko, "Chōsen jingū Ōharaishiki e no jidō seitō dōin: 'Sūhai' to 'shinkō' no aida," *Chōsenshi kenkyū ronbunshū* 46 (2008): 215–44.

5. In 1928, for example, the Home Ministry sent an investigative official, Miyaji Naoichi (1886–1949), a Tokyo Imperial University Professor of (Shintō) history, to the shrine in Keijō to survey the situation. Although the specific rationale for his opinion remains unclear, Miyaji concluded that colonial shrines did not require unification along the lines of those in the metropole. *KN*, Aug. 21, 1928. For more on this loose hierarchy of colonial shrines, see Chiba Masaji, "Tōa shihai ideorogii toshite no jinja seisaku," in *Nihonhō to Ajia*, ed. Niida Noboru hakushi tsuitō ronbunshū henshū iinkai (Tokyo: Keisō shobō, 1970), 297–318.

6. My argument contravenes conventional understandings of the two shrines as forming a seamlessly complementary relationship in which Korea Shrine functioned as the guardian center for the entire peninsula and Seoul Shrine operated as the capital city's guardian facility. For this view, see Suga Kōji, *Nihon tōchika no kaigai jinja: Chōsen jingū, Taiwan jinja to saijin* (Tokyo: Kōbundō, 2004); and Aoi Akihito, *Shokuminchi jinja to teikoku nihon* (Tokyo: Yoshikawa kōbunkan, 2005).

7. On efforts first promoted in the metrople, see Hardacre, *Shintō and the State*.

8. For these measures, see Andre Schmid, *Korea between Empires, 1895–1919* (New York: Columbia University Press, 2002), 72–78.

9. Yamaguchi, "Shokuminchiki Chōsen ni okeru jinja seisaku to Chōsen shakai," 42–43; and Aoi, *Shokuminchi jinja to teikoku nihon*, 58–59. On the other hand, the colonial government allowed private rites at Chongmyo, a Confucian shrine dedicated to past Chosŏn kings, to continue. On the transformation of this shrine's national rites and their relationship to the city's changing spatiality, see Ch'oe Sŏk-yŏng, "Hanmal ilche kangjŏmgi kukka cherye konggan ŭi pyŏnhwa," *Han'guksa yŏn'gu* 118 (2002): 221–47; and Kim Tae-ho, "Ilcheha

Chongmyo rŭl tullŏssan seryŏk kaldŭng kwa konggan pyŏnhwa: 1920 nyŏndae singmin kwŏllyŏk kwa kwijok seryŏk ŭi kwangye rŭl chungsim ŭro," Sŏulhak yŏn'gu 43 (2011): 1–54.

10. On the early colonial reorganization of the Korean royal house, see Christine Kim, "The King Is Dead: The Monarchy and National Identity in Modern Korea," PhD diss., Harvard University, 2004, 114–22; and Yi Yun-sang, "Ilcheha 'Chosŏn wangsil' ŭi chiwi wa iwangjik ŭi ki'nŭng," Han'guk munhwa 40 (2007): 315–42.

11. Kim Tae-ho, "1910 nyŏndae–1930 nyŏndae ch'o Kyŏngsŏng sinsa wa chiyŏk sahoe ŭi kwan'gye: Kyŏngsŏng sinsa ŭi unyŏng kwa han'gugin kwa ŭi kwan'gye rŭl chungsim ŭro," in Ilbon ŭi singminji chibae wa singminjijŏk kŭndae, ed. Yi Sŭng-il (Seoul: Tongbuk ayŏksa chaedan, 2009), 112.

12. On the transient nature of the early settler community, see Peter Duus, The Abacus and the Sword: The Japanese Penetration of Korea (Berkeley: University of California Press, 1995), 289–323; and Jun Uchida, Brokers of Empire: Japanese Settler Colonialism in Korea, 1876–1945 (Cambridge, MA: Harvard University Press, 2011), 35–95. For literary expressions of this phenomenon in the expatriate culture of the working classes, see Helen J. S. Lee, "Writing Colonial Relations of Everyday Life in Senryu," Positions: East Asia Culture Critiques 16, no. 3 (Winter 2008): 601–28.

13. On the intellectual roots of this theory, see Oguma Eiji, A Genealogy of Japanese "Self-Images" (Melbourne: Trans Pacific Press, 2002), 64–92. For the responses of Korean intellectuals, see Chŏng Sang-u, "1910 nyŏndae ilche ŭi chibae nolli wa chisikinch'ung ŭi insik: 'Ilsŏndongjoron' kwa 'munmyŏnghwa' ŭl chungsim ŭro," Han'guk saron 46 (Dec. 2001): 183–231.

14. As early as 1916, however, local clergymen, including the head priest of Seoul Shrine, Tanimura Yorinao, did begin to advocate using Shintō to assimilate colonized Koreans. KN, Oct. 17, 1917.

15. Keijō fu-shi (Keijō: Keijōfu, 1941), 3:181–86.

16. Kim, "1910 nyŏndae–1930 nyŏndae ch'o Kyŏngsŏng sinsa wa chiyŏk sahoe ŭi kwan'gye."

17. Aoi Akihito, "Chōsen no kyoryūmin hōsai jinja to chōsen sōtokufu no jinja seisaku: 'Shōchi' toshite no jinja keidai no keisei oyobi sono henyō to jizoku," Chōsen gakuhō 112 (July 1999): 103.

18. In order to promote reverence toward the Japanese imperial house, the Government-General refused to recognize Shintō shrines that did not revere Amaterasu. For more on these institutions, see Kurita Eiji, "Shokuminchika Chōsen ni okeru jinmei jinshi to 'tada no jinshi,'" in Nihon shokuminchi to bunka henyō: Kankoku, Kyobuntō, ed. Ch'oe Kil-sŏng (Tokyo: Ochanomizu shobō, 1994), 197–217; and Aono Masaaki, "Chōsen sōtokufu no jinja seisaku: 1930 nendai o chūsin ni," Chōsen gakuhō 160 (July 1996): 89–132.

19. Young Koreans did, of course, encounter mutually reinforcing lessons in imperial loyalty and filial piety, which formed the pillars of primary education in colonial classrooms. However, only 20 percent of school-aged children in 1933 attended common schools (pot'ong hakkyo; J: futsū gakkō). Attendance figures run slightly higher for urban areas, such as Keijō, and substantially higher for male students. By 1940, that figure more than doubled to nearly

50 percent. E. Patricia Tsurumi, "Colonial Education in Korea and Taiwan," in *The Japanese Colonial Empire, 1895–1945*, ed. Ramon H. Meyers and Mark R. Peattie (Princeton, NJ: Princeton University Press, 1982), 305. For more on the relationship between primary education and shrine worship, see Hiura Satoko, *Jinja, gakkō, shokuminchi: Gyaku kinō suru Chōsen shihai* (Kyoto: Kyōto daigaku gakujustsu shuppankai, 2013).

20. On creation of emperor-centered celebrations during this period, see Takashi Fujitani, *Splendid Monarchy: Power and Pageantry in Modern Japan* (Berkeley: University of California Press, 1998).

21. For more on the changing historical meaning of this Shintō complex, see Jonathan Reynolds, "Ise Shrine and a Modernist Construction of Japanese Tradition," *Art Bulletin* 83, no. 2 (June 2001): 316–41.

22. I borrow these terms from Nam-lin Hur [Hŏ Nam-lin], *Prayer and Play in Late Tokugawa Japan: Asakusa Sensōji and Edo Society* (Cambridge, MA: Harvard University Press, 2000).

23. Sonoda Minoru, "Festival and Sacred Transgression," in *Matsuri: Festival and Rite in Japanese Life* (Tokyo: Institute for Japanese Culture and Classics, Kokugakuin University, 1988), 36.

24. *KN*, Oct. 16, 1916.

25. *KN*, Oct. 19, 1917.

26. *KN*, Oct. 17, 1918.

27. See, for example, Son Chŏng-mok, *Ilche kangjŏmgi tosi kwajŏng yŏn'gu* (Seoul: Iljisa, 1996), 360–84. For a more nuanced view of residential patterns, one pointing to increasing instances of ethnic intermixing in both the southern and northern villages, see Namiki Naoto, "Shokuminchi kōki Chōsen ni okeru minshū tōgō no ichidan: Souru no jirei o chūshin toshite," in *Chōsen shakai no shiteki tenkai to higashi ajia*, ed. Takeda Yukio (Tokyo: Yamakawa shuppansha, 1997), 528–36; and Kim Chong-gŭn, "Singminji Kyŏngsŏng ŭi ijung tosiron e taehan pip'anjŏk koch'al," *Sŏulhak yŏn'gu* 38 (Feb. 2010): 1–68.

28. I thank Komagome Takashi for suggesting the bridge metaphor. On the cultural dimensions of these interactions, see Se-mi Oh [O Se-mi], "Consuming the Modern: The Everyday in Colonial Seoul, 1915–1937," PhD diss., Columbia University, 2008.

29. Concern over cultivating a sense of "native spirit" among the expatriate Japanese in Korea provoked frequent debate in colonial journals. See, for example, *COM* 75 (Oct. 1, 1913) and 105 (April 1, 1916).

30. *KN*, Oct. 17, 1917. The Japanese population of Seoul increased from 38,397 at the end of 1910 to 69,774 at the end of 1921 and to 97,758 at the end of 1931. In terms of the urban population by geographic origin, the numbers are highly varied; the highest percentage of residents (nearly 30 percent in 1921 and just over 28 percent in 1931) hailed from the island of Kyūshū.

31. On the development of the new middle class in the metropole, see David Ambaras, "Social Knowledge, Cultural Capital, and the New Middle Class in Japan, 1895–1912," *Journal of Japanese Studies* 24, no. 1 (1988): 1–33. For early colonial Korea, see Duus, *The Abacus and the Sword*, 324–63.

32. According to occupational statistics from 1907, "laborers" (10 percent), "geisha, waitresses" (3 percent), and the "unemployed" (3 percent) composed

16 percent of the settler population. If one also considers the ambiguous category of "miscellaneous" (18 percent) in this group, the percentage of lower-class settlers rises to more than one-third of expatriate Japanese. Uchida, *Brokers of Empire*, 67. For settler's occupational statistics from 1910 until 1940, see ibid., 68.

33. *Keijōjfu-shi* 3:179–81; and Kim, "1910 nyŏndae—1930 nyŏndae ch'o Kyŏngsŏng sinsa wa chiyŏk sahoe ŭi kwan'gye," 102, and 126–30.

34. *MS*, Oct. 17, 1918.

35. *Yun Ch'i-ho ilgi* (Seoul: Kuksa p'yŏngch'an wiwŏnhoe, 1968), 7:432.

36. On the *kisaeng*, see Kawamura Minato, *Kiisen: "Mono iu hana" no bunkashi* (Tokyo: Sakuhinsha, 2001). For a critique of Kawamura's work and an exploration of a more diverse range of issues relating to these women, see Yi Kyŏng-min, *Kisaeng ŭn ŏttŏk'e mandŭrŏjŏnŭnga: Kŭndae kisaeng ŭi t'ansaeng kwa p'yosang konggan* (Seoul: Sajin ak'aibŭ yŏn'guso, 2005).

37. A Japanese-language newspaper report on the status and living conditions of the *kisaeng* published less than six months after the annexation told readers that some of these women had already begun to learn Japanese to cater to their colonizers. This article even recommended that interested individuals apply at the *kisaeng* cooperative office located in Chongno. *CSb*, Jan. 19, 1911.

38. *KN*, Oct. 15, 1915.

39. For a discussion on the polyvalent meanings of Korean clothing during the colonial period, see Hyung-gu Lynn, "Fashioning Modernity: Changing Meanings of Clothing in Colonial Korea," *Journal of International and Area Studies* 12, no. 1 (Spring 2005): 75–93.

40. In addition to figure 8a and the bottom image of figure 9, another similar photograph can be found in *KN*, Oct. 20, 1920.

41. *MS*, Oct. 15, 1916; and Kim, "1910 nyŏndae–1930 nyŏndae ch'o Kyŏngsŏng sinsa wa chiyŏk sahoe ŭi kwan'gye," 125. In a rare discussion of the shrine festival published by one vernacular newspaper, the *Tonga ilbo* revealed that such disorder actually did break out in the fall of 1922, when a group of inebriated Japanese who had participated in that year's grand festival threw bricks through a Chongno storefront and violently confronted female employees who had looked down at them from the second story. Given that these women had not committed a ritual impropriety against the portable shrine, the owner of the Korean company aggressively responded to the attack, maintaining that his employees had been unduly mistreated for simply glancing at the rowdy group of Japanese passing their workplace. *TI*, Oct. 20, 1922; and Kim, "1910 nyŏndae–1930 nyŏndae ch'o Kyŏngsŏng sinsa wa chiyŏk sahoe ŭi kwan'gye," 125–26.

42. *KN*, Oct. 11, 1919. On this incident, see also *MS*, Oct. 12, 1919.

43. For one such photograph showing crowds looking down onto Kojong's funeral procession from the second floor balcony of a Chongo merchant house, see *Se ibang'in ŭi sŏul hoesang: Tik'usya esŏ ch'onggyech'ŏn kkaji* (Seoul: Sŏul yŏksa pangmulgwan yumul kwallikwa, 2009), 17.

44. *KN*, Oct. 30, 1919.

45. *COM* 215 (Oct. 5, 1925): 7.

46. *KN*, June 24, 1919. *Kokuheisha kankei tsuzuri* (Keijō: n.p., 1933), 66. I thank Aoi Akihito for providing me with this invaluable document.

47. *KN*, Oct. 17, 1919.

48. *KN,* Oct. 19, 1920.

49. *KN,* Oct. 17, 1921.

50. *KN,* Oct. 8, 1920.

51. On the place of Chongno in Korean nationalist movements during the colonial period, see Chang Kyu-sik, "Ilceha Chongno ŭi minjok undong kong-gan," *Han'guk kŭnhyŏndaesa yŏn'gu* 26 (Fall 2003): 71–91.

52. *KN,* Sept. 18, 1919.

53. *KN,* Oct. 6, 1922; and *KN,* Oct. 16, 1920.

54. *COM* 115 (Jan. 1, 1917): 60–62 and 67–68; *COM* 130 (April 1, 1918): 2–8. For more this debate, see Henry, "Assimilation's Racializing Sensibilities: Colonized Koreans as *Yobos* and the '*Yobo*-ization' of Japanese Settlers," *Positions: Asia Critique* 21, no. 1 (Winter 2013): 11–49.

55. *KN,* Oct. 15, 1924.

56. *KN,* June 26, 1925.

57. *KN,* Oct. 13, 1923.

58. *Yun* 1968, (Dec. 17, 1919). This figure remained under 17 percent in early 1937 and did not reach 30 percent until 1941. *KI* 186 (March 1937): 25; and Ogasawara Shōzō, ed., *Kaigai jinjashi (jōkan)* (Tokyo: Kagai jinjashi hen-sankai, 1953), 456.

59. See *KN,* Oct. 11, 1919.

60. See, for example, *TI,* Oct. 18, 1922.

61. On the process of the shrine's construction, see Aoi, *Shokuminchi jinja to teikoku nihon,* 28–62. When the Government-General decided to erect Korea Shrine atop Namsan, officials forced the custodians of the Kuksadang (literally, "shrine of the national preceptor")—a shamanic sanctuary that, since at least the late nineteenth century if not much earlier, drew the most important healers from across the land—to remove this structure, lest it overlook and thus dominate the new Shintō complex. Although not destroyed, the Kuksadang was subsequently repositioned at a lower elevation and at a considerable distance from Namsan on Mount Inwang. James Grayson, "The Accomodation of Korean Folk Religion to the Religious Forms of Buddhism: An Example of Reverse Syncretism," *Asian Folklore Studies* 51, no. 2 (1992): 199–217.

62. *KN,* April 6, 1916; and *KN,* Dec. 8, 1918.

63. *KN,* Dec. 11, 1918.

64. *KN,* Sept. 17, 1925.

65. *KN,* Sept. 26, 1925.

66. *KN,* Oct. 11 and 18, 1925.

67. Ogasawara, *Kaigai jinjashi (jōkan),* 446–48.

68. These numbers are based on statistics from 1921. For more details, see *KN,* Nov. 27, 1921.

69. *KN,* July 16, 1917; *KN,* Dec. 12, 1925; and *KN,* Nov. 27, 1921.

70. *KN,* March 30, 1926.

71. *KN,* May 4, 1926. For more on shrine's wedding facilities, see *CTK* 7, no. 5 (May 1928): 30–31.

72. *KN,* May 4, 1932.

73. On developments during the 1910s, see Suga, *Nihon tōchika no kaigai jinja,* 79–110.

74. For more on the so-called enshrinement debates, see Kim Ch'ŏl-su and Nomura Hiroshi, "Chōsen sōtokufu no shūkyo seisaku: 'Chōsen jingū' no setsuritsu o megutte," *Shakai gakubu ronshū* (Bukkyō daigaku) 31 (March 1998): 17–34; Kim Ch'ŏl-su, "Chosŏn ch'ongdokbu ŭi chonggyo chŏngch'aek: 'Chosŏn sin'gung chesin nonjaeng e nat'anan hwangminhwa imbo," *Uri sahoe yŏn'gu* 4 (1997): 66–114; Ch'oe Sŏk-yŏng, *Ilcheha musongnon kwa singminji kwŏllyŏk* (Seoul: Sŏgyŏng munhwasa, 1999), 101–28; and Suga, *Nihon tōchika no kaigai jinja*, 111–57.

75. *KN*, March 20, 1926; and *KN*, Aug. 21, 1928. Because Tan'gun had served as a nationalistic symbol of anticolonial resistance in religious organizations such as *Taejonggyo* (J: *Daishūkyo*), he was quickly co-opted and woven into a Japan-centered ideology of ancestral sameness, often appearing as Amaterasu's impish brother, Susanoo. On this strand of Tan'gun thought and practice, see Sassa Mitsuaki, "Kanmatsu ni okeru Dankunkyō 'jūko' to Dankun nashonarizumu," *Chōsen gakuhō* 180 (July 2001): 31–36; and Sassa Mitsuaki, "Shokuminchi Chōsen ni okeru dankunkyō enkaku to katsudō," *Chōsen kenkyūkai ronbunshū* 41 (Oct. 2003): 203–27. For a comparative account of anticolonial resistance by Tan'gun followers, see Hwang Min-ho, "Taejonggyo ŭi hang'il minjok undong," in *Ilcheha Kyŏnggido chiyŏk chonggyogye ŭi minjok munhwa undong* (Seoul: Kyŏnggi munhwa chaedan, 2001), 292–322.

76. *KI* 118 (July 1931): font plate. Later, during the early 1930s, they even mobilized female shamans—hitherto perceived as a serious threat to the social order and thus carefully policed as a superstitious "pseudoreligion"—to elicit popular support among uneducated Koreans, especially women. For an account of their charismatic activities at Seoul Shrine, see *Keijō jinja jingi geppō* 3, no. 6 (June 1941): 1. I thank Hiura Satoko for providing me with this rare source.

77. Like other imperial shrines in the metropole, Korea Shrine did, as of 1934, maintain a list of devotees, persons who affiliated themselves with this Shintō institution and regularly supported it through financial donations.

78. *KN*, Oct. 4 and 6, 1925.

79. *KN*, Oct. 15, 1925. With the exception of a short article on the first shrine athletic meet, the *Tonga ilbo*, the most widely circulated Korean-language daily, did not carry one single report on Koreans' participation in festival preparations.

80. For more on the cultural politics of Korea Shrine's inaugural festivities, see Todd A. Henry, "Keijō: Japanese and Korean Constructions of Colonial Seoul and the History of its Lived Spaces, 1910–37," PhD diss., University of California, Los Angeles, 2006, 406–20.

81. For more on the difference between group and individual visits of worship at Korea Shrine, see Namiki, "Shokuminchi kōki Chōsen ni okeru minshū tōgō no ichidan," 528–36.

82. The following discussion is based on Ogasawara 73. For another account describing Koreans' shrine practices as "onlooking" rather than "worshiping," see *COM* (April 1927): 25.

83. Only after 1934 did the number of annual Korean visitors increase, reaching 340,909 by 1936. However, even this elevated number still paled in comparison to the 828,314 Japanese who visited the shrine in 1936. Namiki, "Shokuminchi kōki Chōsen ni okeru minshū tōgō no ichidan," 548.

84. Ogasawara Shōzō, *Kaigai no jinja* (Tokyo: Shintō hyōronsha, 1933), 186, and 188–89.

85. According to official statistics from the mid- to late 1930s, no more than three Koreans ever made New Year's visits to Korea Shrine. By contrast, the average number of Japanese New Year's visitors between 1934 and 1939 was 283, a figure also curiously low, given that nearly 125,000 settlers had made Keijō their home by 1935. Namiki, "Shokuminchi kōki Chōsen ni okeru minshū tōgō no ichidan," 554–55.

86. *Chōsen dōhō ni taisuru naichijin hansei shiryō* (Keijō: Chōsen kenpeitai shireibu, 1933), 81–82. I thank Yi Sŭng-yŏp for providing me with this valuable document. For more on the racist underpinnings of the term "yobo" and its colonial variations, see Henry, "Assimilation's Racializing Sensibilities."

87. *KN*, Oct. 12, 1929.

88. *KN*, March 20, 1926.

89. *KN*, Oct. 18, 1926.

90. *KN*, Oct. 18, 1928.

91. Kōrei taidai shidaisho (Keijō: Keijō jinja, 1929), 5.

92. *KN*, Oct. 11, 1931.

93. *KN*, Oct. 16, 1931. Images from the late Chosŏn period suggest that this combination of a dark robe and a white collar was commonly worn by Korean officials in royal processions. See, for example, *Seoul through Pictures 1: The Modernization of Seoul and its Trials, 1876–1910* (Seoul: City History Compilation Committee of Seoul, 2002), 61.

94. For poetic invocations of this term, see Roald Maliangkay, "Them Pig Feet: Anti-Japanese Folksongs in Korea," in *Korea in the Middle: Positioning Korea*, ed. Remco Breuker (Leiden: CNWS Publications, 2007), 157–85.

95. Indeed, Kim Tae-ho has identified these Koreans as important members of the pro-Japanese Taishō Friendship Association. Kim, "1910 nyŏndae—1930 nyŏndae ch'o Kyŏngsŏng sinsa wa chiyŏk sahoe ŭi kwan'gye," 108. For more on this organization, see Chang Sin, "Taejŏng ch'inmokhoe wa naesŏn yunghwa undong," *Taedong munhwa yŏn'gu* 60 (2007): 361–92.

96. According to the official narrative, Chŏn's heart was completely changed by donning the ceremonial dress, allowing him to appreciate the shrine's "divine virtues." *Kōkoku jihō* 440 (Dec. 1931): 6.

97. *MS*, Oct. 19, 1928.

98. According to one scholar, more than 60 percent of Koreans living in cities (versus 40 percent in the countryside) during the 1930s fell within the category of the "poor," and an equal percentage of individuals residing in Seoul could not even afford to pay their taxes. Son, *Ilche kangjŏmgi tosi kwajŏng yŏn'gu*, 106.

99. *KN*, Oct. 18, 1933.

100. *KN*, Oct. 11, 1934.

101. *KN*, Oct. 17, 1935; and *MS*, Oct. 20, 1935.

102. *KN*, Oct. 19, 1935.

103. On these urban institutions, see Yun Chŏng-uk, *Shokuminchi Chōsen ni okeru shakai jigyō* (Osaka: Ōsaka keizai hōka daigaku shuppanbu, 1996); and Pak Se-hun, *Singmin kukka wa chiyŏk kongdongch'e: 1930 nyŏndae*

*Kyŏngsŏngbu ŭi tosi sahoe chŏngch'aek yŏn'gu* (Seoul: Han'guk haksul chŏngbo, 2006).

## 3. MATERIAL ASSIMILATION

1. Andre Schmid, *Korea between Empires, 1895–1919* (New York: Columbia University Press, 2002). On intellectuals' embrace of competition during this period, see also Vladimir Tikhonov, *Social Darwinism and Nationalism in Korea: The Beginnings, 1880s to 1910s* (Leiden: Brill, 2009).

2. Robert W. Rydell, *All the World's a Fair* (Chicago: University of Chicago Press, 1984). Following Rydell, many scholars have treated representations of colonized (or racially subordinated) peoples in metropolitan events, but far fewer have explored the staging of these events in the colony itself. For a review of this literature, see Lisa Munro, "Investigating World's Fairs: An Historiography," *Studies in Latin American Popular Culture* 28 (2010): 80–94. On expositions in colonial Korea, see Sin Chu-baek, "Pangnamhoe: Kwasi, sŏnjŏn, kyemong, sobi ŭi ch'ehŏm konggan," *Yŏksa pip'yŏng* 67 (Summer 2004): 357–94.

3. For more on these events, see Daniel Kane, "Korea in the White City: Korea at the World's Columbian Exhibition (1893)," *Transactions of the Korea Branch Royal Asiatic Society* 77 (2002): 1–58; and Kane, "Display at Empire's End: Korea's Participation in the 1900 Paris Universal Exposition," *Sungkyun Journal of East Asian Studies* 4, no. 2 (Aug. 2004): 41–66. On Korea's appearance in Japanese expositions, see Yi Kak-kyu, *Han'guk ŭi kŭndae pangnamhoe* (Seoul: K'ŏmyunik'eisyŏn puksŭ, 2010), 68–87.

4. On these efforts and the hosting of Korea's first exposition in Pusan (in 1906), see Yi, *Han'guk ŭi kŭndae pangnamhoe*, 60–68, and 87–100.

5. In contrast to the more costly expositions held after 1910, officials only allocated fifty-two thousand yen for this event, nearly half of which the Korean government shouldered. The grounds in 1907 also paled in size to colonial expositions held at Kyŏngbok Palace. *CSp*, Aug. 8, 1907.

6. On these overtures and their consequences, see Peter Duus, *The Abacus and the Sword: The Japanese Penetration of Korea, 1895–1910* (Berkeley: University of California Press, 1998); and Alexis Dudden, *Japan's Colonization of Korea: Discourse and Power* (Honolulu: University of Hawai'i Press, 2006). For a nationalist response, see Yi Tae-jin [Yi T'ae-jin], "The Annexation of Korea Failed to Come into Being: Forced Treaties and Japan's Annexation of the Great Han Empire," *Seoul Journal of Korean Studies* 18 (2005): 1–41.

7. *CSp*, May 12, 1907.

8. *CSp*, Sept. 1, 1907. One of the first scholars to treat the exhibition in 1907 has conjectured that Meiji-machi (Tonghyŏn) was chosen for its equidistant position between the South and East Gates, which the Department of Agriculture, Commerce, and Industry utilized to advertise products to incoming visitors. Mok Su-hyŏn, "Ilcheha pangmulgwan ŭi hyŏngsŏng kwa kŭ ŭimi," MA thesis, Seoul National University, 2000, 18.

9. *HS*, Sept. 7, 1907. This discrepancy stood in stark contrast to the ratio of objects produced by colonized Koreans (13,717, almost 35 percent), expatriate

settlers (3,917, nearly 10 percent), and metropolitan Japanese (8,300, over 20 percent) for the Industrial Exhibition of 1915. Hong Kal, "Politics of Visual Comparison: Notes on the Formation of Nationalism in the Colonial Exposition in Korea," *Tong asia munhwa wa yesul* 3 (2006): 235.

10. See, for example, *HS*, Sept. 11, 1907.

11. *CSp*, Sept. 1, 3, 4, and 7, 1907.

12. *CSp*, Sept. 10, 1907.

13. *HS*, Sept. 16, 1907.

14. *CSp*, May 25, 1907.

15. *CSp*, Nov. 7, 1907. Just two months earlier, the Japanese crown prince and future Taishō emperor, Yoshihito, had visited the exhibition on opening day, a similarly symbolic gesture of royal patronage. *CSp*, Sept. 12, 1907. For more on the Japanese uses of the Korean royalty during this period, see Christine Kim, "Politics and Pageantry in Protectorate Korea, 1905–10: The Imperial Progresses of Sunjong," *Journal of Asian Studies* 68, no. 3 (2009): 835–59.

16. *CSp*, Sept. 17, 1907.

17. *CSp*, Sept. 19, 1907.

18. *CSp*, Sept. 5, 1907.

19. *CSp*, Sept. 10, 1907.

20. *CSp*, Sept. 15, 1907.

21. Kim Tae-woong [Kim Tae-ung], "Industrial Exhibitions ('Gongjinghoe') and the Political Propaganda of Japanese Imperialism in the 1910s," *International Journal of Korean History* 3 (Dec. 2002): 183.

22. *HS*, Sept. 18, 1907.

23. See, for example, *HS*, Oct. 13, 1907.

24. *CSp*, Nov. 13, 1907.

25. *CSp*, July 13 and 23, 1908.

26. *CSb*, May 1, 1910.

27. For financial impediments to holding an early colonial exhibition, see *CSb*, July 3, 1912. On a settler-led initiative, see *CSb*, June 5, 1913.

28. *CSb*, Oct. 30, 1913.

29. *Shisei 5 nen kinen Chōsen bussan kyōshinkai hōkokusho* (Keijō: Chōsen sōtokufu, 1916), 1: 53. Hereafter this text is abbreviated *RCIE*.

30. Son Chŏng-mok, *Ilche kangjŏmgi tosi sahoesang yŏn'gu* (Seoul: Iljisa, 1996), 525–28. For a functional breakdown of the palace, see Hong Sun-min, *Uri kunggwŏl iyagi* (Seoul: Ch'ŏngnyŏngsa, 1999), 128–83.

31. Hŏ Yŏng-sŏp, *Chosŏn Ch'ongdokbu: Kŭ ch'ŏngsa kŏllip ŭi iyagi* (Seoul: Han'ul, 1996), 61.

32. *CSb*, July 6, 1914.

33. For more on the intrusion of Western-style architecture into Keijo's palace grounds, see Song Sŏk-ki, "Kunggwŏl e tŭlŏsŏn kŭndae kŏnch'ungmul," in *Kunggwŏl ŭi nunmul, paeknyŏn ŭi ch'inmok: Cheguk ŭi somyŏl 100 nyŏn, uri kunggwŏl ŭn ŏdi ro kassŭlkka?*, ed. U Tong-sŏn and Pak Sŏng-jin (Seoul: Hyohyŏng ch'ulp'an, 2009), 48–85.

34. *RCIE*, 1:54; and Yi Kyu-mok, "Sŏul ŭi tosi kyŏnggwan kwa kŭ imiji," *Sŏulhak yŏn'gu* 2 (March 1994): 154.

35. Yi Kyŏng-min, *Kisaeng ŭn ŏttŏk'e mandŭrŏjŏnŭnga: Kŭndae kisaeng ŭi t'ansaeng kwa p'yosang konggan* (Seoul: Sajin ak'aibŭ yŏn'guso, 2005), 150–54.

36. In this performance, one hundred *kisaeng* appeared on stage with flower-adorned hats and other Japanese dance accoutrements, masquerading themselves as metropolitan performers. Soon, however, these temporarily "Japanized" Korean performers removed part of their ethnic masquerade and suddenly revealed their identity as "real" *kisaeng*. *CSb*, March 30, 1915.

37. *MS*, Dec. 3, 1915.

38. In addition to twenty thousand yen from expected entrance fees, the Government-General donated thirty thousand yen, while private donations were to cover the remaining fifty thousand yen for recreation costs. *CSb*, May 22, 1915.

39. All prices are for adults. Among others, children, military personnel, and group visitors received discounts. *KN*, Sept. 11, 1915.

40. *CK* 3, no. 4 (April 1915): 6. A similar point is made in *MS*, April 17, 1915.

41. *MS*, March 3, 1915.

42. The following discussion is based, in part, on Chu Yun-jŏng, "'Chosŏn mulsan kongjinhoe' (1915) e taehan yŏn'gu," MA thesis, Academy of Korean Studies, 2002, 29–46. One scholar has persuasively argued that this verbal-visual connection also underwrote literary movements of the colonial period. For this view, see Theodore Q. Hughes, *Literature and Film in Cold War South Korea: Freedom's Frontier* (New York: Columbia University Press, 2012).

43. Although unable to substantiate her point empirically, Hong Kal has provocatively suggested that this display technique may have unintentionally produced a sense of comradeship among Korean spectators that allowed them to imagine themselves as national subjects of a colonized nation. Kal, "Politics of Visual Comparison," 217–49.

44. For more on this history, see Do-Hyun Han [Han To-hyŏn], "Shamanism, Superstition, and the Colonial Government," *Review of Korean Studies* 3 (2000): 34–54.

45. *RCIE*, 1:243–61, 273.

46. *KN*, Oct. 31, 1915; and *MS*, Aug. 28, 1915.

47. *KN*, Oct. 30, 1915.

48. See, for example, and *MS*, March 4, 1915.

49. For more on the relationship of these elites to the local government and their lower-class counterparts, see Matsumoto Takenori, *Chōsen nōson no "shokuminchi kindai" keiken* (Tokyo: Shakai hyōronsha, 2005); and Yun Hae-dong, *Chibae wa chach'i* (Seoul: Yŏksa pip'yŏngsa, 2006).

50. *RCIE*, 1:270–71. The *Maeil sinbo* increased in circulation to ten thousand copies for this event. *MS*, Aug. 26, 1915.

51. *MS*, Sept. 13, 1915. Similar comments are made in *MS*, Oct. 23, 1915.

52. *MS*, Sept. 18, 1915. Another such conclusion can be found in *MS*, Oct. 8, 1915, wherein the author, a native of the northern city of Hamhŭng, argues that by teaching local residents about their findings, the over one hundred members of this group could reach thousands, even tens of thousands, of followers.

53. *MS*, Sept. 16, 1915.

54. *MS*, Sept. 18, 1915.

55. *KN*, Oct. 17, 1915.

56. Colonial officials recommended six hours for groups to tour the grounds: an hour for each of the most important buildings (Buildings 1 and 2 and the Shinseikan), leaving three hours for the remaining display halls. *KN*, Sept. 26, 1915.

57. *MS*, Sept. 18, 1915.

58. *MS*, Sept. 20, 1915.

59. *RCIE*, 1:270.

60. Established in April of 1910, Sakurai Common School enrolled 1,041 students in 1915, most of whom came from wealthy Japanese families. *Keijō annai* (Keijō: Keijō kyōsankai, 1915), 95.

61. *KN*, Sept. 17, 1915.

62. *KN*, Sept. 16, 1915.

63. *KN*, Oct. 12, 1915.

64. *Shisei 5 nen kinen Chōsen bussan kyōshinkai Keijō kyōsankai hōkoku* (Keijō: Keijō kyōsankai, 1916), 161–68. Hereafter this text is abbreviated as *KCCR*. As discussed below, this daily average does not include the last three days, whose numbers are much higher due to the lure of free admission.

65. *KN*, Oct. 12, 1915.

66. *KN*, Sept. 22, 1915. According to one late-nineteenth-century account, only when their husbands returned home during the evening hours (8 PM–12 AM) did married women amuse themselves on the streets. Isabella Bishop, *Korea and Her Neighbors* (Seoul: Yonsei University Press, 1970), 47.

67. For more on this ideology, see Hong Yang-hee [Hong Yang-hŭi], "Debates about 'A Good Wife and Wise Mother' and Tradition in Colonial Korea," *Review of Korean Studies* 11, no. 4 (Dec. 2008): 41–60. For an overview of the Home Exhibition, see Yi, *Han'guk ŭi kŭndae pangnamhoe*, 162–67. On the event's display of middle-class Japanese homes, see Kim Myŏng-sŏn, "1915 nyŏn Kyŏngsŏng kajŏng pangnamhoe chŏnsi chut'aek ŭi p'yosang," *Taehan kŏnch'uk hakhoe nonmunjip* 28, no. 3 (March 2012): 155–64.

68. *MS*, Jan. 20, 1916.

69. The Performance Hall, where the *kisaeng* sang and danced, recorded an average of more than twelve hundred daily attendees. *KCCR*, 148.

70. *KN*, Sept. 26, 1915.

71. *KN*, Oct. 31, 1915.

72. *KN*, Oct. 30, 1915. For one of the few Korean commentaries making this connection between the colonial exhibition and imperial benevolence, see *MS*, Oct. 6, 1915.

73. *KCCR*, 168.

74. On how the exhibition inspired rural-based projects, see *MS*, Feb. 17, 19, and 20, 1916; and *Chōsen*, Jan. 1, 1916, 174–76.

75. *CSb*, March 4, 1915.

76. *KN*, July 23, 1916.

77. *MS*, July 7, 1916.

78. *KN*, July 23, 1916.

79. Such projects also allowed Korean elites like Cho to win the graces of the Japanese-dominated business world, wherein cooperation with the colonial state continued to remain paramount, even after liberalizing reforms made in wake of the March First Uprising in 1919. For more on these perilous connections, see Carter J. Eckert, *Offspring of Empire: The Koch'ang Kims and the Origins of Korean Capitalism, 1876–1945* (Seattle: University of Washington Press, 1991).

80. *KN*, May 6, 1921.

81. *KN*, March 12, 1922; and *KN*, April 29, 1922.

82. *KN*, May 10, 1928.

83. *KN*, Feb. 17, 1928.

84. Each member of the cooperative paid a fee ranging from five yen (for a regular membership) to five thousand yen (for an honorary membership). *KI* 93 (June 1929): 46. For a complete list of founding members, see *Chōsen hakurankai Keijō kyōsankai hōkokusho* (Keijō: Chōsen hakurankai Keijō kyōsankai hōkokusho, 1930), 1–7. Hereafter this text is abbreviated as *CHKYH*.

85. *KN*, Aug. 9, 1928.

86. *KN*, March 12, 1929. Thousands of copies of the winning poster were distributed throughout Korea to more than five hundred cafes, train stations, barbershops, and public baths; individual prefectures, commerce boards, and museums displayed posters in the metropole. *KN*, Jan. 31, 1929.

87. *KN*, March 12, 1929.

88. *KN*, Feb. 2, 1929.

89. *KN*, Jan. 31, 1929; and *KN*, May 16, 1929.

90. *KN*, Jan. 23, 1929.

91. *KN*, May 7, 1929. In the end, only 21,746 Japanese visited the exposition. *TI*, Nov. 4, 1929.

92. *KN*, March 27, 1928. For more on these budgetary woes, see *COM* 262 (Sept. 1929): 8–9.

93. On similar efforts to "protect" the dying natives of Hokkaidō, see Tessa Morris-Suzuki, "Becoming Japanese: Imperial Expansion and Identity Crises in the Early Twentieth Century," in *Japan's Competing Modernities: Issues in Culture and Democracy, 1900–1930*, ed. Sharon Minichiello (Honolulu: University of Hawai'i Press, 1998).

94. For the metropolitan fascination with the culture of colonial Korea, see A. Taylor Akins, *Primitive Selves: Koreana in the Japanese Colonial Gaze, 1910–1945* (Berkeley: University of California Press, 2010). On initiatives to industrialize the peninsula after 1919, see Eckert, *Offspring of Empire*.

95. Hong Kal, "Modeling the West, Returning to Asia: Shifting Politics of Representation in Japanese Colonial Expositions in Korea," *Comparative Studies in Society and History* 47, no. 3 (2005): 514–18.

96. To this end, officials also demanded that building materials from the peninsula and Korean contractors be used in the construction of the main exhibition halls. *KN*, July 7, 1929.

97. *CTK* 8, no. 9 (Sept. 1929): 13. See also ibid., 12.

98. According to one scholar, train stations were constructed in a similar "native design." On this trend, see Ahn Changmo [An Ch'ang-mo], "Colonial

Tourism in 1930s Korean Architecture: The Tradition of the Colonized and the Colonial Policy behind the Style of Railroad Station," *Journal of Southeast Asian Architecture* 7 (2004): 13–25.

99. In addition to these place-based display halls, the grounds also included a number of privately managed buildings sponsored by colonial newspapers (*Chōsen shimbun, Chōsen shōkō shimbun, Chōsen maicnichi shimbun*), large trading companies (Mitsui bussan, Mitsui, and Sumitomo), smaller commercial interests (Hirahara merchant house and Hachiman ironworks), and important colonial organizations (Chōsen stock-breading association, Chōsen maritime products association, and so on). For a full description of display halls and their contents, see Kim Yŏng-hŭi, "Chosŏn pangnamhoe wa singminji kŭndae," *Tongbang hakji* 140 (2007): 221–67. For another study of the exhibition from the point of view of visitors' visual experiences, see Chŏn Min-jŏng, "Ilche sigi Chosŏn pangnamhoe (1929 nyŏn) yŏn'gu: Chosŏn'in ŭi kŭndaejŏk sigak ch'ehŏm chungsim ŭro," Sŏnggyungwan University, PhD diss., 2003.

100. *KN*, Sept. 29, 1929.

101. *TI*, Jan. 1, 1929.

102. *TI*, April 4, 1929; and *OASFCA*, April 6, 1929.

103. *TI*, July 6, 1929.

104. *TI*, Sept. 8, 1929.

105. *CHKYH*, 90–92.

106. *OASFCA*, June 5, 1929.

107. *CHKYH*, 90, 92.

108. *MS*, Oct. 13, 1929.

109. *TI*, July 25, 1929. In the end, a total of 290,438 group visitors came to Keijō, in addition to 431,862 people as individual visitors of the exposition. Of these 612,300 visitors living in Korea, approximately 570,000 (93.1 percent) were Korean and 42,300 (5.9 percent) were Japanese. An additional 21,746 (3.4 percent) and 4,267 (0.007 percent) came from Japan and Manchuria, respectively, while the inhabitants of Korea made up 95.9 percent of total exposition-goers. Approximately sixty thousand Japanese, or less than 1 percent of total attendees, resided in the colony or hailed from the metropole. *TI*, Nov. 4, 1929.

110. *TI*, Nov. 2, 1928.

111. *TI*, Nov. 4, 1929.

112. *TI*, Sept. 17, 1929. For a similar account from South Kyŏngsang Province, see *CI*, Sept. 24, 1929.

113. *TI*, Sept. 21, 1929.

114. *TI*, Oct. 5, 1929.

115. *TI*, Sept. 18, 1929.

116. *TI*, Nov. 1, 1929.

117. *Yun Ch'i-ho ilgi* (Seoul: Kuksa p'yŏngch'an wiwŏnhoe, 1968), 9:239.

118. *CI*, Sept. 17, 1929. On the consumptive practices of colonial expositions, see Se-mi Oh [O Se-mi], "Consuming the Modern: The Everyday in Colonial Seoul, 1915–1937," PhD diss., Columbia University, 2008.

119. *Chōsen shisō tsūshin*, Oct. 7, 1929. According to one report, the number of daily visitors to Mitsukoshi ranged from five to eight thousand,

generating eight to ten thousand yen of revenue per day (an average of 1.23 yen per person). This report also mentions that Hwasin, the newly constructed department store in Chongno, also took in approximately ten thousand yen in daily profits. *KN*, Oct. 14, 1929. In contrast to large department stores, smaller-scale Japanese merchants seem to have benefited only slightly from the upturn in customers during the exposition, earning between five and six hundred yen per day. This income paled in comparison to the one thousand yen of daily income they received during the New Year period. By contrast, small-scale Korean merchants who successfully sold their wares only earned about three hundred yen per day. *KN*, Oct. 27, 1929.

120. *CI*, Oct. 6, 1929.

121. *KN*, Sept. 13, 1929. For more on the background of the so-called inn problem, see *KN*, Sept. 30, 1929.

122. *KN*, Sept. 22, 1929.

123. *KN*, May 19, 1929. By early August 1929, more than seven hundred Koreans had already made applications, and officials expected that number to increase to one thousand. *MS*, Aug. 8, 1929.

124. *MS*, July 11, 1929.

125. See, for example, *KN*, Sept. 13, 1929.

126. *OASFC*, Oct. 9, 1929.

127. *OASFCA*, Sept. 15, 1929. Unsettled by such encounters, officials responded by attempting to solve this "problem of public morals." Labeling kiss girls "deviant," they immediately fired three Korean female guards accused of selling pecks on the cheek. *TI*, Oct. 31, 1929.

128. *Sinmin* 53 (Nov. 1929): 36–37.

129. *Sinmin* 53 (Nov. 1929): 42–45. Korean writers often leveled similar critiques, lamenting that Japanese merchants had become the event's main beneficiaries. Ibid., 41. For other responses from colonized intellectuals, see Kim, "Chosŏn pangnamhoe wa singminji kŭndae," 255–59.

130. The following discussion is based on *Sinmin* 53 (Nov. 1929): 21–33. For the thoughts of Japanese visitors, see *COM* 263 (Oct. 1929): 119–23; and *COM* 264 (Nov. 1929): 111–17.

131. Discussions of this particular display also appeared in the Japanese media. In one newspaper cartoon, the caption warned readers that even visitors with a strong heart would likely not be able to eat for three days after seeing the diseased body parts. *OASFCA*, Oct. 11, 1929.

## 4. CIVIC ASSIMILATION

1. Ruth Rogaski, *Hygienic Modernity: Meanings of Health and Disease in Treaty-Port China* (Berkeley: University of California Press, 2004). The Japanese term *eisei* and its Korean counterpart, *wisaeng*, came to include an incredibly wide range of human activities, including those related to what is usually referred to in English as public health as well as to personal or individual hygiene. In this chapter, I have taken the liberty to translate the term as "hygiene," "sanitation," and "hygienic modernity" so that it fits the particular context, while at times leaving *eisei* and *wisaeng* in their original Japanese and

Korean forms. For an introduction to the meaning of *eisei* and its usages in modern Japan, see Abe Yasunari, "'Eisei' to iu chitsujo," in *Shippei, kaihatsu, teikoku iryō: Ajia ni okeru byōki to iryō no rekishigaku*, ed. Miichi Masatoshi, Saitō Osamu, Wakimura Kōhei, and Iijima Wataru (Tokyo: Tōkyō daigaku shuppan, 2001), 107–29; and Sakagami Takashi, "Kōshū eisei no tanjō: 'Dainihon shiritsu eisei kyōkai' no seiritsu to tenkai," *Keizai ronsō* 156, no. 4 (Oct. 1995): 1–27. On Korean engagements with *wisaeng* during the immediate precolonial period, see Pak Yun-jae, "Yangsaeng esŏ wisaeng ŭro: Kaehwap'a ŭi ŭihangnon kwa kŭndae kukka kŏnsŏl," *Sahoe wa yŏksa* 63 (May 2003): 30–50; and Shin Dongwon [Sin Tong-wŏn], "Hygiene, Medicine, and Modernity in Korea, 1876–1910," *East Asian Science, Technology and Society: An International Journal* 3 (2009): 5–26.

2. For more on these efforts, see Sonja Kim, "The Search for Health: Translating *Wisaeng* and Medicine during the Taehan Empire," in *Reform and Modernity in the Taehan Empire*, ed. Kim Dong-no, John B. Duncan, and Kim Do-hyung (Seoul: Jimoondang, 2006), 299–341.

3. *Keijōfu-shi* (Keijō: Keijōfu, 1936/1941), 2:606, 609, and 636. Hereafter this text is abbreviated as *KF*.

4. *KF*, 2:723–24, and 727.

5. *Keijō hattatsushi* (Keijō: Keijō kyoryū mindan yakusho, 1912), 151; and *KF*, 2:738.

6. Oguri Shirō, *Chihō eisei gyōsei no sōsetsu katei* (Tokyo: Iryō tosho shuppansha, 1981), 171–73.

7. Ambo Norio, *Minato Kōbe, korera, pesuto, suramu: Shakaiteki sabetsu keiseishi no kenkyū* (Kyoto: Gakujutsu shuppansha, 1989), 95.

8. On the cholera outbreak in 1909, see Pak Yun-jae, *Han'guk kŭndae ŭihak ŭi kiwŏn* (Seoul: Hyean, 2005), 202–12; and Sin Tong-wŏn, *Han'guk kŭndae pogŏn ŭiryosa* (Seoul: Han'ul, 1997), 408–9.

9. *CSb*, Sept. 24, 1909.

10. *Keijō hattastsushi*, 363; and *KF*, 2:891. For a list of sanitation cooperative leaders, see Kawabata Gentarō, *Keijō to naichijin* (Keijō: Nikkan shobō, 1910), 92–93.

11. Yun Hyŏng-gi, "Hansŏng puminhoe e kwanhan ilkocha'l," *Tonga yŏn'gu* 17 (1989): 620–21. For documents related to this organization, see Kim Yŏng-sang, "Hansŏng puminhoe e taehan koch'al," *Hyangt'o sŏul* 31 (1967): 3–47. On Yu's intellectual trajectory, see Koen de Ceuster, "The World in a Book: Yu Kilchun's *Sŏyu kyŏnmun*," in *Korea in the Middle: Korean Studies and Area Studies*, ed. Remco E. Breuker (Leiden: CNWS Publications, 2007).

12. Seo Hyŏn-ju [Sŏ Hyŏn-ju], "Ilchemal ilcheha Sŏul ŭi habu haengjŏng chedo yŏn'gu: Chŏngdonghoe wa ch'ongdae rŭl chungsim ŭro," PhD diss., Seoul National University, 2002, 96–97.

13. *CSb*, Oct. 19, 1909.

14. *Kanjō eiseikai jōkyō ippan* (Keijō: Kanjō eiseika, 1914), 1, 13–14. Hereafter this text is abbreviated *KEJI*. On Yoshihito's visit to Korea, see Hara Takeshi, *Kashika sareta teikokoku: Kindai nihon no gyōkōkei* (Tokyo: Misuzu shobō, 2001), 168–87.

15. On the role of roadside trees in Japanese city planning, see Shirahata Yōzaburō, *Kindai toshi kōen no kenkyū: Ooka no keifu* (Tokyo: Shibunkaku shuppan, 1995), 285–318.

16. Pak, *Han'guk kŭndae ŭihak ŭi kiwŏn*, 168–73 and 206–12. On the development of the hygiene police system prior to the annexation, see Pak, *Han'guk kŭndae ŭihak ŭi kiwŏn*, 168–75; and Sin, *Han'guk kŭndae pogŏn ŭiryosa*, 329–32.

17. *TMS*, Dec. 15, 1908. One hundred chŏn equals one wŏn.

18. *TMS*, June 26, 1909; and *KEJI*, 166.

19. *TMS*, April 3 and 22, 1909.

20. Sin, *Han'guk kŭndae pogŏn ŭiryosa*, 402.

21. *TMS*, Dec. 15, 1908.

22. *TMS*, Oct. 11, 1908.

23. Sin, *Han'guk kŭndae pogŏn ŭiryosa*, 401.

24. *KEJI*, 37.

25. *MS*, April 20, 1911.

26. Todd A. Henry, "Sanitizing Empire: Japanese Articulations of Korean Otherness and the Construction of Early Colonial Seoul, 1905–19," *Journal of Asian Studies* 64, no. 3 (Aug. 2005): 643–53. For scholarship on similar accounts, see Sonia Ryang, "Japanese Travelers' Accounts of Korea," *East Asian History* 13/14 (June/Dec. 1997): 133–52; and Helen J. S. Lee, "Voices of the 'Colonists,' Voices of the 'Immigrants': 'Korea' in Japan's Early Colonial Travel Narratives and Guides, 1894–1914," *Japanese Language and Literature* 41, no. 1 (April 2007): 1–36.

27. For this line of analysis, I borrow from Arjun Appadurai, *Modernity at Large: Cultural Dimensions of Globalization* (Minneapolis: University of Minnesota Press, 1996), 114–38.

28. *KEJI*, 87.

29. Ann Stoler, "Colonial Archives and the Arts of Governance: On the Content in the Form," *Archival Sciences* 2 (2002): 87.

30. Yi Chong-min, "1910 nyŏndae Kyŏngsŏng chumindŭl ŭi 'choe' wa 'bŏl' Kyŏngbŏmjae t'ongje rŭl chungsim ŭro," *Sŏulhak yŏn'gu* 17 (Sept. 2001): 95–128.

31. Pak, *Han'guk kŭndae ŭihak ŭi kiwŏn*, 330.

32. To provide officers with a rudimentary knowledge of disease detection and prevention, the board arranged for instructors to visit police stations and gendarmes, and also invited local officials to participate in courses held in its Keijō offices. *MS*, Jan. 14, 1912; Pak, *Han'guk kŭndae ŭihak ŭi kiwŏn*, 339; and *MS*, Oct. 3, 1913.

33. Shiraishi Yasunari, *Chōsen eisei yōgi* (Keijō: Nikkan insatsusho, 1918), 28.

34. Ibid., 205–6.

35. *MS*, Dec. 11, 1910.

36. For a categorized discussion of personal hygiene by a Korean author for a Korean audience, see *MS*, Feb. 15–17, 20, 22–24, and 26, 1918.

37. For more on the role of women in Korea's colonial modernity, see Theodore Jun Yoo, *The Politics of Gender in Colonial Korea: Education, Labor, and*

*Health, 1910–45* (Berkeley: University of California Press, 2008); and Sonja Kim, "'Limiting Birth': Birth Control in Colonial Korea," *East Asian Science, Technology, and Society: An International Journal* 2, no. 3 (2008): 335–59.

38. *MS*, July 25, 1911. On the gendered dimensions of house cleanings for Japanese, see also *KN*, Oct. 4, 1918.

39. *MS*, June 26, 1914.

40. *MS*, Sept. 10, 1912.

41. See, for example, *COM* 66 (Jan. 1, 1913): 30–32.

42. See, for example, *MS*, June 8, 1911.

43. *MS*, April 8, 1913.

44. *MS*, June 27, 1913.

45. *MS*, Sept. 26, 1916.

46. *MS*, July 6, 1920.

47. *MS*, Sept. 26, 1913.

48. *MS*, April 17, 1913.

49. *KN*, March 13, 1916.

50. *KN*, March 13, 1916; and *KN*, Dec. 28, 1919. For an official survey of the spitting problem, see *KI*, May 1916, 127–28.

51. *MS*, July 15, 1915.

52. *KI*, Dec. 1915, 127; and *KF*, 3:171–72. For more on students of medicine and their intermediary role in colonial medicine, see So Young Suh [Sŏ So-yŏng], "Korean Medicine between the Local and the Universal, 1600–1945," PhD diss., University of California, Los Angeles, 2006, 141–75; and Yŏnse tae-hakkyo ŭihaksa yŏn'guso, ed., *Han'ŭihak, singminji rŭl alt'a: Singminji sigi Han'ŭihak ŭi kŭndaehwa yŏn'gu* (Seoul, Ak'anet, 2008).

53. *COM* 124 (Oct. 1, 1917): 117–19.

54. Unless mentioned otherwise, the following account is based on *COM* 186 (May 9, 1923): 37–38.

55. On the hierarchical nature of the early colonial medical system, see Suh, "Korean Medicine between the Local and the Universal," 93–111; and Sin Tong-wŏn, "1910 nyŏndae ilche ŭi pogŏn ŭiryo chŏngch'aek: Han'ŭiyak chŏngch'aek ŭl chungsim ŭro," *Han'guk munhwa* 30 (Dec. 2002): 330–70.

56. *MS*, Oct. 17 and 20, 1917; Pak, *Han'guk kŭndae ŭihak ŭi kiwŏn*, 341–44.

57. *KI*, Dec. 1915, 127; and *KF*, 3:171–72.

58. Even in 1940, the ratio of patients to doctors of traditional medicine amounted to 3,604, whereas the figure for doctors of Western medicine was 11,800. Yi KKotme, "Ilban'in han'ŭihak insik kwa ŭiyak iyong," in Yŏnse tae-hakkyo ŭihaksa yŏn'guso, *Han'ŭihak, singminji rŭl alt'a*, 143.

59. In a North Ch'ungch'ŏng Province village with sixty-one households in 1940 (most of which were likely Korean), only 8.5 percent of all medical con-sults went to Western-style doctors, whereas 25.4 percent called upon traditional practitioners. Meanwhile, 19.4 percent of them purchased medicine based on self-diagnoses, 23.9 percent used locally available botanicals, 19 percent ignored their symptoms, and 3.9 percent relied on shamans and other magical cures. Yi, "Ilban'in han'ŭihak insik kwa ŭiyak iyong," 143–44. For responses by Koreans to open a hospital offering patients a wider choice of treatments, including Chi-nese medicine, see Park Yun-jae [Pak Yun-jae], "Anti-Cholera Measures by the

Japanese Colonial Government and the Reaction of Koreans in the Early 1920s," *Review of Korean Studies* 8, no. 4 (2005): 169–86.

60. *Taishō 9 nen korerabyō bōekishi* (Keijō: Chōsen sōtokufu, 1921), 9.

61. *KN*, Sept. 26, 1916.

62. *KN*, Sept. 20, 1916.

63. *KN*, Sept. 29, 1916.

64. On the process of translating the government's message to the Japanese public, see Abe Yasunari, "Densenbyō yobō no gensetsu: Kindai tenkanki no kokumin kokka, Nihon to eisei," *Rekishigaku kenkyū* 686 (1996): 15–31.

65. See, for example, *HS*, May 1, 1909.

66. *MS*, Jan. 14, 1912; and *MS*, Oct. 3, 1913.

67. The colonial press predictably reported Koreans' "great happiness" at hearing the lecture; however, considering that this article described Koreans as "struggling to get over the great impression" they took away from the phonograph, it is possible that the awe produced by this newfangled device may have muted the hygienic message it intended to convey.

68. *KN*, Sept. 26, 1916.

69. *KN*, Sept. 27, 1916.

70. *HS*, Jan. 14, 1907.

71. *HS*, May 1, 1909.

72. *HS*, Aug. 20, 1909.

73. *MS*, April 28, 1920.

74. For more the place of race in the everyday practice of Japanese colonialism, see Henry, "Assimilation's Racializing Sensibilities: Colonized Koreans as *Yobo*s and the '*Yobo*-ization' of Japanese Settlers," *Positions: Asia Critique* 21, no. 1 (Winter 2013): 11–49.

75. The population of Keijō increased from 181,829 in 1920 to 312,587 in 1935.

76. The only instance in which this pattern did not hold true was in 1920, when 1,340 Koreans contracted diseases as opposed to 1,164 Japanese. On the other hand, reports about Koreans hiding ailments suggest that statistics for the colonized failed to capture actual incidence of disease. *KI* 5 (March 1922): 13.

77. The following account is based on *KI* 9 (June 1922): 7–8.

78. A similar argument was made in *COM* 218 (Dec. 31, 1925): 44–46.

79. *KI* 36 (Oct. 1924): 4.

80. Unless noted, the following account is based on *COM* 244 (March 1928): 84–86.

81. Occasionally, sanitary officials also cited expatriates for failing to abide by official standards of hygienic behavior. When a sanitary authority visited the home of a Japanese suffering from dysentery, he found that the family kept excreta in its living quarters, infuriating the local police. *KN*, Oct. 12, 1932. As a result, Japanese homes also became targets for toilet reforms. See, for example, *CTK*, July 1927, 13–15.

82. According to his calculations, twenty-four neighborhoods averaged less than seventeen square meters, or just one-quarter of the ideal allocation. *KN*, June 24, 1925.

83. *KN*, July 3, 1925.

84. *KN*, Sept. 22, 1925. Strangely, one author did claim that hygienic knowledge among the colonized had spread considerably, which officials used as evidence to explain the "incredibly unusually phenomenon" that relatively few Koreans living in the unsanitary part of the city contracted the disease. *KN*, Dec. 12, 1925.

85. *KI* 46 (Oct. 1925): 2–3.

86. *KN*, Sept. 22, 1925.

87. Kim Yŏng-mi, "Ilche sigi tosi ŭi sansudo munje wa konggongsŏng," *Sahoe wa yŏksa* 73 (March 2007): 45–74. See also Hong Sŏng-t'ae, "Singminji kŭndaehwa wa mul saenghwal ŭi pyŏnhwa," in *Singminji ŭi ilsang, chibae wa kyun'yŏl*, ed. Kong Chae-uk and Chŏng Kŭn-sik (Seoul: Munhwa kwahaksa, 2006).

88. *KN*, Sept. 13, 1925.

89. *KN*, Aug. 29, 1923.

90. *KN*, Dec. 22, 1926. For the committee's report, see *KI* 48 (Dec. 1925): 28–29.

91. *TI*, March 26, 1931. For more on the fly problem, see *KI* 32 (June 1924): 12.

92. *KN*, April 1, 1928.

93. *COM* 313 (Dec. 1933): 89–91.

94. *KI* 46 (Oct. 1925).

95. *KN*, May 14, 1923.

96. *KN*, May 28, 1923.

97. *KI* 46 (Oct. 1925): 2.

98. *KI* 129 (June 1932): 17–18.

99. *KN*, July 15, 1932.

100. *TI*, May 31, 1932.

101. *CI*, June 2, 1921.

102. *TI*, Feb. 1, 1927.

103. Akhil Gupta and James Ferguson, "Beyond 'Culture': Space, Identity, and the Politics of Difference," *Cultural Anthropology* 7, no. 1 (Feb. 1992): 7.

104. *TI*, Dec. 7, 1923. For similar invocations of ethnic-based residential segregation as a nationalist strategy of reclaiming a more equal distribution of public resources, see Kim Chong-gŭn, "Singminji Kyŏngsŏng ŭi ijung tosiron e taehan pip'anjŏk koch'al," *Sŏulhak yŏn'gu* 38 (Feb. 2010): 36–43.

105. *TI*, March 23, 1924.

106. *CI*, Nov. 7, 1925.

107. *TI*, Dec. 21, 1925.

108. *TI*, Dec. 20, 1925.

109. *TI*, May 16, 1927.

110. Kim, "Limiting Birth," 239–40.

111. *TI*, Oct. 23, 1928. On preventative measures, see *KI* 47 (Dec. 1925): 5–8.

112. *TI*, June 27, 1931.

113. As a solution, this author recommended ten inexpensive measures, including not drinking cold water or eating raw food, putting trash in dustbins, and disinfecting toilets. *TI*, July 4, 1927.

114. *TI*, May 4, 1932.

115. *TI*, March 3, 1930. A similar argument was made in *TI*, April 20, 1933.

116. On this program, see Matsuda Toshihiko, "Nihon tōchika no Chōsen ni okeru 'keisatsu no minshūka' to 'minshū no keisatsuka': Shokuminchi ni okeru minshū tōgōsaku," *Jinbun ronshū* 33, no. 4 (1998): 27–70.

117. *TI*, June 12, 1921.

118. *TI*, June 16, 1921.

119. *TI*, June 28, 1921. See also *TI*, July 7, 1921.

120. *KI* 19 (May 1923): 4.

121. *KN*, April 2, 1923.

122. *TI*, July 7, 1924; and *TI*, April 2, 1925.

123. The final two stages involved promoting further independence from supervising police officers (stage four) and establishing administrative offices beyond the immediate purview of government authorities (stage five).

124. *TI*, July 7, 1921. For more on the guiding role of local elites, see Se Hoon Park [Pak Se-hun], "Care and Control: Colonial Governmentality and Urban Social Policy in Colonial Seoul," in *East Asia: A Critical Geography Perspective,* ed. Wing-Shing Tang and Fujio Mizuoka (Tokyo: Kokon shoin, 2010), 112–32. On the pharmaceutical industry in colonial Korea, see Suh, "Korean Medicine between the Local and the Universal," 198–237.

125. On the hygiene play, see *TI*, April 24, 1920.

126. *TI*, June 2 and 17, 1922.

127. *TI*, June 10 and 17, 1922; and *TI*, April 10, 1921.

128. *TI*, Aug. 10, 1926.

129. *KI* 44 (Aug. 1925): 28–29; and *TI*, Aug. 13, 1925.

130. The first government-organized hygiene exhibition took place in early July 1921. Held at Pagoda Park, this one-week event included five hundred displays on contagious diseases and other matters of public health as well as the presentation of related films. *KN*, June 22, 1921.

131. In the end, police officials insisted that this display be pulled on the grounds that it would "destroy civic mores." *KN*, July 23, 1922.

132. *KI* 19 (May 1923): 5.

133. *TI*, Sept. 28, 1922.

134. *TI*, Oct. 4, 1922.

135. *KI* 143 (Aug. 1933): 38.

136. *KN*, May 16, 1933.

137. *CI*, July 11, 1933.

138. *TI*, Aug. 3, 1933.

139. *CI*, Aug. 17 and 18, 1933.

140. *TI*, Aug. 17, 1933; and *KI* 143 (Aug. 1933): 38.

141. *TI*, April 23, 1932; and *CI*, April 23, 1932.

142. *TI*, May 1, 1932; and *KI* 29 (June 1932): 22.

143. Established in 1914, this school trained both Korean and Japanese students to become doctors in colonial Korea. For more on the school's establishment, curriculum, faculty, and students, see Yi Ch'ung-ho, *Ilche t'ongch'igi han'guk ŭisa kyoyuksa yŏn'gu* (Seoul: Han'guk charyowŏn, 1998), 139–228.

144. *TI*, March 16, 1921.

145. *TI*, March 23, 1921.

146. *TI*, March 18, 1921.

147. See, for example, *TI*, July 16, 1923.

148. As late as 1934, reports suggested that Keijō remained Korea's sickest city. *COM* 334 (Sept. 1935): 84.

149. On these students' participation in the March First Movement, see Yi, *Ilche t'ongch'igi han'guk ŭisa kyoyuksa yŏn'gu*, 178–88. Ming-Cheng Lo has discovered a similar political bent to the medical students of colonial Taiwan during this period. On their activities, see Lo, *Doctors within Borders: Profession, Ethnicity, and Modernity in Colonial Taiwan* (Berkeley: University of California Press, 2002), 51–83.

150. For more on the contested meanings of Mount Kŭmgang, see Ellie Choi, "Space and the Historical Imagination: Yi Kwangsu's Vision of Korea during the Japanese Empire," PhD diss., Harvard University, 2008, 190–234.

151. *TI*, June 9, 1924.

152. *TI*, June 28, 1924; and *TI*, July 3, 1924.

153. *TI*, July 7 and 24, 1925.

154. *TI*, Nov. 17, 1928; and *TI*, Nov. 16, 1930.

155. On the "hygienic city," see, for example, *COM* 360 (Nov. 1937): 74–75; and *COM* 373 (Dec. 1938): 34–35.

156. *KN*, Feb. 23, 1935. For efforts to mollify residents' "misunderstandings," see *CK*, May 1935, 12–16; and *KI* 164 (May 1935): 54–56.

157. *KN*, June 6, 1936.

## 5. IMPERIAL SUBJECTIFICATION

1. Son Chŏng-mok, *Ilche kangjŏmgi tosi kyehoek yŏn'gu* (Seoul: Iljisa, 1990), 177–252; and Yŏm Pok-kyu, "'1933–43 nyŏn ilche ŭi 'Kyŏngsŏng sigaji kyehoek,'" *Han'guk saron* 46 (Dec. 2001): 233–83.

2. For one innovative conceptualization of the "inner" and "outer" territory as they relate to the peninsula's diasporic population, see Hyun Ok Park [Pak Hyŏn-ok], "Korean Manchuria: The Racial Politics of the Territorial Osmosis," *South Atlantic Quarterly* 99, no. 1 (Winter 2000): 193–215. On the "regionalization" of Korea into a multiethnic empire at war, see Ch'a Sŭng-gi, *Pankŭndaejŏk sangsangnyŏk ŭi imgyedŭl: Singminji Chosŏn tamnonjang esŏ ŭi chŏnt'ong, segye, chuch'e* (Seoul: P'urŭn yŏksa, 2009); and Kate L. McDonald, "The Boundaries of the Interesting: Itineraries, Guidebooks, and Travel in Imperial Japan," PhD diss., University of California, San Diego, 2011, esp. 141–70.

3. Takashi Fujitani, *Race for Empire: Koreans as Japanese and Japanese as Americans during World War II* (Berkeley: California University Press, 2011).

4. For one astute explanation on the difference between "assimilation" and "imperialization," see Leo Ching, *Becoming "Japanese": Colonial Taiwan and the Politics of Identity Formation* (Berkeley: University of California Press, 2001), 89–132.

5. Examples of this type of scholarship include Kim Sŭng-t'ae, ed., *Han'guk kidokkyo wa sinsa ch'ambae munje* (Seoul: Han'guk kidokkyo yŏksa yŏn'guso,

1991); and Kim Sŭng-t'ae, *Sinsa ch'ambae kŏbu hangjaengjadŭl ŭi chŭng'ŏn: Ŏdum ŭi kwŏnse rŭl igin saramdŭl* (Seoul: Tasan kŭlbang, 1993).

6. On the origins of this system, see Carol Gluck, *Japan's Modern Myths: Ideology in the Late Meiji Period* (Princeton, NJ: Princeton University Press, 1985); and Takashi Fujitani, *Splendid Monarchy: Power and Pageantry in Modern Japan* (Berkeley: University of California Press, 1998).

7. Kenneth J. Ruoff, *Imperial Japan at Its Zenith* (Ithaca, NY: Cornell University Press, 2011), 4.

8. Ibid, 63, 201n17. The vast majority of these visitors resided in the nearby Kansai region, suggesting that geographic proximity and transportation access to imperial sites as well as local claims on them produced different meanings of the 1940 celebrations, even within the inner territory.

9. To be sure, essays on the twenty-six-hundredth anniversary written by Korean (and Japanese) children educated on the peninsula did demonstrate a considerable, if predictably rehearsed, knowledge of this past. For an analysis of their writings on the celebrations in 1940, see ibid., 30–32.

10. For a more detailed analysis of this event, see Henry, "Cheguk ŭl kinyŏm hago, chŏnjaeng ŭl tongnyŏ hagi: Singminji malgi (1940 nyŏn) Chosŏn esŏ ŭi pangnamhoe," *Asea yŏn'gu* 51, no. 4 (Winter 2008): 72–112.

11. Walter Edwards, "Forging Tradition for a Holy War: The *Hakkō Ichiu* Tower in Miyazaki and Japanese Wartime Ideology," *Journal of Japanese Studies* 29, no. 2 (Summer 2003): 294. On Miyazaki's place in the celebrations of 1940, see Ruoff, *Imperial Japan at Its Zenith*, 86–97.

12. On policies related to this ruling ideology, see Miyata Setsuko, *Chōsen minshū to "kōminka" seisaku* (Tokyo: Miraisha, 1991); and Ch'oe Yu-ri, *Ilche malgi singminji chibae chŏngch'aek yŏn'gu* (Seoul: Kukhak charyowŏn, 1997).

13. After Japan's attack on Pearl Harbor in late 1941, this four-year, 1.5 million yen project came to a screeching halt. For more on these aborted plans, see Son, *Ilche kangjŏmgi tosi kyehoek yŏn'gu,* 337–70. In the early postcolonial period, Puyŏ reemerged as a site of controversy when the architect Kim Su-gŭn (1931–86) proposed a national museum with a design similar to a Shintō shrine. Jung In Kim [Kim Chung-in], "Constructing a 'Miracle': Architecture, National Identity and Development of the Han River," PhD diss., University of California, Berkeley, 2008, 50–55.

14. Although the Yamato court supported Paekche against its neighboring rivals, ancient "Japan" maintained only marginal relations with Silla by briefly forming a military alliance with this kingdom, and possessed virtually no direct connection to Kogoryŏ, its strongest rival on the peninsula.

15. *KN*, Aug. 20, 1940. For some supportive gestures, see Son, *Ilche kangjŏmgi tosi kyehoek yŏn'gu,* 356–58. See also Hŏ Pyŏng-sik, "P'yehŏ ŭi kodo wa ch'angjo toen sindo," *Han'guk minhak yŏn'gu* 36 (June 2009): 79–105.

16. According to police statistics, less than 1 percent of peninsular residents (mostly Koreans) read Japanese-language newspapers as of early 1940. *Shisō ihō* 23 (June 1940): 84. I thank Itagaki Ryūta for bringing this document to my attention.

17. *KN*, Aug. 25, 1940.

18. For more on the controversies surrounding this museum, see Shaun O'Dwyer, "The Yasukuni Shrine and the Competing Patriotic Pasts of East Asia," *History & Memory* 22, no. 2 (Fall/Winter 2010): 147–77.

19. *KN*, Aug. 3, 1940.

20. Brandon Palmer, "Imperial Japan's Preparations to Conscript Koreans as Soldiers, 1942–1945," *Korean Studies* 31 (2007): 64. Despite delays in implementing conscription, an estimated 110,000 Koreans served in the military by the time of Japan's defeat. To boost the number of applicants, authorities also aggressively targeted colonized women, encouraging them to overcome their reservations about parting with male family members and to become nurturing supporters from the home front.

21. *KN*, Sept. 26, 1940.

22. *KN*, Oct. 8, 1940.

23. *KN*, Aug. 20, 1940 (emphasis mine).

24. Unless otherwise noted, the following discussion is based on *KN*, Sept. 29, 1940.

25. *KN*, Sept. 12, 1940.

26. *KN*, Sept. 14 and 29, 1940.

27. For more on these "numerical performances," see Henry, "Cheguk ŭl kinyŏm hago, chŏnjaeng ŭl tongnyŏ hagi," 101–6.

28. The idea of a torch relay linking the empire's most sacred shrines had been percolating in Japan since the late 1930s and functioned as a nationalistic alternative to the internationalist proposal connecting Europe and Asia for the games in 1940. Sandra Collins, *The Missing Olympics: Japan, the Asian Olympics and the Olympic Movement* (London: Routledge, 2007), 124–32. For an account situating the Shintō meanings of fire within a universal history of religions, see *KN*, Jan. 24 and 25, 1940.

29. *KN*, Jan. 29, 1940. For similar examples, see *KN*, Jan. 30, 1940; *KN*, Feb. 1, 1940; and *KN*, Feb. 3, 1940.

30. *KN*, Feb. 4, 1940.

31. *KN*, Feb. 6, 1940.

32. *KN*, Feb. 7, 1940.

33. *KN*, Feb. 8, 1940.

34. *KN*, Feb. 6, 1940.

35. *KN*, Feb. 7, 1940.

36. *KN*, Feb. 10, 1940.

37. One estimate suggests that only 2.5 percent of the colony's population visited Nara Prefecture, one of the most important centers for the celebrations in 1940. Ruoff, *Imperial Japan at Its Zenith*, 98. Other statistics reveal that, as of early 1940, less than 1 percent of peninsular residents had either visited or lived in the inner territory. *Shisō ihō* 23 (June 1940): 83–84.

38. *KN*, April 14, 1940.

39. *KN*, April 24, 1940.

40. *KN*, April 26, 1940.

41. For more on these precisely timed rituals, see Ruoff, *Imperial Japan at Its Zenith*, 57–61; and Hara Takeshi, "Senchūki no 'jikan shihai,'" *Misuzu* 521 (2004): 28–44.

42. *KN*, April 27, 1940.

43. On this view, see Henry, "Assimilation's Racializing Sensibilities: Colonized Koreans as *Yobos* and the '*Yobo*-ization' of Expatriate Settlers," *Positions: Asia Critique* 21, no. 1 (Winter 2013): 11–49.

44. *KN*, April 27, 1940. The oath for the junior age group read as follows: "1. We are subjects of the Great Japanese Empire; 2. We, in the unity of our minds, fulfill the duty of the loyalty and service to the Emperor; and 3. We endure hardships and become strong and good citizens." Quoted in Wi Jo Kang [Kang Wi-jo], *Christ and Caesar in Modern Korea: A History of Christianity and Politics* (Albany: SUNY Press, 1997), 65. On the oath's origins and dissemination, see Mizuno Naoki, "Kōminka seisaku no kyozō to jitsuzō: 'Kōkoku shinmin no seishi' ni tsuite no ichi kōsatsu," in *Kankoku heigō 100 nen o tō: 2010 nen kokusai shimpōjimu* (Tokyo: Iwanami shoten, 2011).

45. *KN*, April 27, 1940.

46. For more the modern creation of this site of loyalty, see Fujitani, *Splendid Monarchy*, 14–15, 32, 79–80, 132–33, and 147–48.

47. *KN*, April 30, 1940.

48. *KN*, April 29, 1940.

49. *KN*, May 1, 1940.

50. *KN*, May 1, 1940.

51. For a list of these regulations, see Yamaguchi Kōichi, "Shokuminchi Chōsen ni okeru jinja seisaku to Chōsen shakai," Hitotsubashi University, PhD diss., 2006, 129. The number of Shintō structures, including "lesser shrines," increased from approximately 350 in 1936 to nearly 1,150 by 1945. This wartime increase accounts for more than two-thirds of shrines constructed during the Asia-Pacific War.

52. For more on this process, see Suga Kōji, *Nihon tōchika no kaigai jinja: Chōsen jingū, Taiwan jinja to saijin* (Tokyo: Kōbundō, 2004), 159–201.

53. *KN*, Sept. 18, 1937.

54. *KN*, Oct. 6, 1937.

55. *KN*, Oct. 15 and 19, 1938.

56. *KN*, Oct. 17 and 19, 1939. Other Shintō events like the annual Inani festival, which included traditional music and *kisaeng* dancing, had a similar imperializing effect. In 1941, officials joyfully reported that these local attractions were drawing thousands of Koreans, who were making voluntary and heartfelt (rather than forced and superficial) bows before Inani Shrine, a satellite of Seoul Shrine. *Keijō jinja jingi geppō* 3, no. 6 (June 1941): 1.

57. *KN*, Oct. 17, 1941. For a discussion about how air raids affected city planning in wartime Keijō, see Son, *Ilche kangjŏmgi tosi kyehoek yŏn'gu*, 311–38.

58. *KN*, Oct. 19, 1941.

59. *KN*, Oct. 24, 1941. For a detailed discussion of this year's annual festival, see *Keijō jinja jingi geppō* 3, no. 10 (Oct. 1941): 2–5.

60. *KN*, Oct. 17, 1942.

61. *KN*, Oct. 16 and 19, 1937.

62. According to one scholar, Koreans only organized two of the 362 private ceremonies held during this period. Kim Kŭn-hŭi, "'Kōminka seisakuki' no jinja seisaku ni tsuite," *Nicchō kankeishi ronshū* (2003): 408–10.

63. Mizuno, "Kōminka seisaku no kyozō to jitsuzō," 104.

64. Unless mentioned otherwise, the following discussion is based on *Tairiku jinja taikan* (Keijō: Tairiku jinja renmei, 1941), 74–78.

65. For an account of this history, see "Shōkonsai ensoku taiyō," *KI* (May 1931), 50–51.

66. Whereas Ranam Nation-Protecting Shrine fell under the jurisdiction of Kangwŏn and North and South Hamgyŏng Provinces, Seoul Nation-Protecting Shrine covered the rest of the peninsula.

67. Aoi, *Shokuminchi jinja to teikoku nihon*, 261. For the support group's founding statement and regulations, see *Tairiku jinja taikan*, 83–87.

68. For a breakdown of these contributions, see *Tairiku jinja taikan*, 81–82.

69. *KN*, Aug. 12, 1940; and *KN*, Sept. 27, 1940.

70. *KN*, Oct. 24, 1940.

71. *KN*, Sept. 2, 1940; *KN*, Nov. 22, 1940; *KN*, March 25, 1941; and *KN*, July 22, 1943.

72. *KN*, Sept. 24, 1940.

73. *KN*, Oct. 25, 1940.

74. Takahashi Testuya, "The National Politics of the Yasukuni Shrine," in *Nationalisms in Japan*, ed. Naoko Shimazu (London: Routledge, 2006), 155–80. In Japanese, see *Yasukuni mondai* (Tokyo: Chikuma shobō, 2005), 11–59.

75. *KN*, July 22, 1943.

76. *Hantō no hikari*, Feb. 1944, 3. These 549 Koreans constituted only a small portion (about 2.5 percent) of those twenty-one thousand colonized souls currently installed at Yasukuni Shrine.

77. *KN*, Nov. 23, 1943.

78. *KN*, Nov. 23, 1943.

79. Unless otherwise noted, the following discussion is based on *Sinyŏsong*, May 1944, 24–25.

80. On the perceived threat of Korean women in wartime representations of empire, see Fujitani, *Race for Empire*, 347–61.

81. The colonial state was invested in presenting numerical increases in shrine visits to bureaucratic agencies in Tokyo in order to receive continuing support for its mobilization activities. In 1934, for example, the Japanese government awarded Korea Shrine seventy thousand yen, a relatively high figure when compared to the 20,500 yen received by Kashihara Shrine, the second-best-funded Shintō facility next to Meiji Shrine. Hiura Satoko, "Chōsen jingū ōharaishiki e no jidō seitō dōin: 'Sūhai' to 'shinkō' no aida," *Chōsenshi kenkyū ronbunshū* 46 (2008): 217–18, and 240.

82. The following discussion is based on statistics presented in Namiki Naoto, "Shokuminchi kōki Chōsen ni okeru minshū tōgō no ichidan: Souru no jirei o chūshin toshite," in *Chōsen shakai no shiteki tenkai to higashi ajia*, ed. Takeda Yukio (Tokyo: Yamakawa shuppansha, 1997), 548.

83. For a discussion of semicoercive summer visits to Korea Shrine made by school children, see Hiura Satoko, *Jinja, gakkō, shokuminchi: Gyakukinō suru Chōsen shihai* (Kyoto: Kyōto daigaku gakujustsu shuppankai, 2013), 155–63.

84. During the wartime period, the percentage of groups comprising total shrine visits actually increased from less than 42 percent in 1936 to over 51 percent by 1943. Hiura, *Jinja, gakkō, shokuminchi*, 127.

85. Namiki, "Shokuminchi kōki Chōsen ni okeru minshū tōgō no ichidan," 554.

86. The Government-General did retain the ethnic and racial categories of "Chinese" and "Westerners," although their combined totals accounted for less than 1 percent of shrine-goers throughout this period. Namiki, "Shokuminchi kōki Chōsen ni okeru minshū tōgō no ichidan," 548.

87. For these statistics, see Takatani Miho, "Shokuminchi Chōsen ni okeru jinja seisaku no tenkai to jittai," *Nicchō kankeishi ronshū* (2003): 367.

88. For more on this campaign and its development in Keijō, see Yamaguchi Kōichi, "Shokuminchi Chōsen ni okeru jinja seisaku: 1930 nendai o chūshin ni," *Rekishi hyōron* 635 (March 2003): 56–65; Kawase Takuya, *Shokuminchi Chōsen no shūkyo to gakuchi* (Tokyo: Seikyūsha, 2009), 181–222; and Ch'oe Sŏk-yŏng, *Ilcheha musongnon kwa singminji kwŏllyŏk* (Seoul: Sŏgyŏng munhwasa, 1999), 129–58. Unless otherwise mentioned, the following discussion is based on *KN*, June 9, 1935.

89. For a lecture broadcasted on the radio commemorating shrine visitation day, see *Bunkyō no Chōsen*, Dec. 1935, 40–46.

90. *KN*, Nov. 8, 1936.

91. *KN*, Oct. 17, 1937.

92. *KN*, Dec. 12, 1939.

93. Namiki, "Shokuminchi kōki Chōsen ni okeru minshū tōgō no ichidan," 548.

94. "Jikyokuka no minjō ni kansuru ken," in *Shisō ni taisuru jōhō* (13), *Keikidō keisatsu buchō*, June 30, 1941, 2. Official statistics from the shrine's annual report list 265,769 visits for April 1941, 186,943 for May 1941, and 213,657 for May 1940.

95. "Jikyokuka no minjō ni kansuru ken," in *Shisō ni taisuru jōhō* (13), *Keikidō keisatsu buchō*, Aug. 30, 1941, 2–3.

96. *KN*, Dec. 12, 1941.

97. *Chōsen* 250 (March 1936): 28–29. The shrine's main approach had 381 stairs.

98. *Katei no tomo* (Chōsenban), April 1941, 12.

99. *Sōdōin*, June 1940, 7–9.

100. *Sinsidae*, Jan. 1943, 46–47.

101. *Sinsidae*, Feb. 1943, 80.

102. *Torii* 8, no. 2 (Feb. 1, 1938): 7. For a fuller account, see the government-sponsored study by Murayama Chijun, *Burakusai* (Keijō: Chōsen sōtokufu, 1937).

103. *Rokki*, Oct. 1942, 45.

104. *Torii* 8, no. 1 (Jan. 1, 1938): 6. For another account criticizing the use of pressure to promote shrine visits, see *Torii* 8, no. 9 (Sept. 1, 1938): 3–5.

105. Encyclopedia of Shintō entry for "Jingū taima," http://eos.kokugakuin.ac.jp/modules/xwords/entry.php?entryID = 283, accessed on December 29, 2011; and *Torii* 5, no. 11 (Jan. 1, 1935): 2. See also *Kokumin sōryoku*, Dec. 1942, 40–41.

106. *Kokuhei shōsha Keijō jinja saijireki* (Keijō: Kokuhei shōsha Keijō jinja, 1938); and *Katei saiji no reikō* (Keijō: Kokuhei shōsha Keijō jinja, n.d.). I thank Mizuno Naoki for providing me with these rare documents.

107. *Tairiku jinja taikan*, 176. That figure remained below fifty thousand until 1935. Ch'oe, *Ilcheha musongnon kwa singminji kwŏllyŏk*, 156.

108. *Shōwa 19nen 12 gatsu Dai 86kai teikoku gikai sestsumei shiryō* (Tokyo: Fuji shuppan, 1994), 25; and Sai Kindō, *Nihon teikokushugika Taiwan no shū kyo seisaku* (Tokyo: Dōseisha, 1994), 183–84.

109. *Torii* 9, no. 2 (Feb. 1, 1939): 4. By the end of 1939, police statistics, part of a study analyzing the degree to which the manners and customs of peninsular inhabitants had been "Japanized," recorded that number at just over 20 percent. *Shisō ihō* 23 (June 1940): 82–83.

110. Sai, *Nihon teikokushugika Taiwan no shūkyo seisaku*, 183–84. For comparison of other policies, see Wan-yao Chou, "The Kōminka Movement in Taiwan and Korea: Comparisons and Interpretations," in *The Japanese Wartime Empire, 1931–1945*, ed. Peter Duus, Ramon Myers, and Mark Peattie (Princeton, NJ: Princeton University Press, 1996).

111. *Torii* 8, no. 4 (April 1, 1938): 10.

112. *Kokumin seishin sōdōin kōenroku* (Keijō: Keikidō shakaika, 1939), 46–47.

113. *Naisen ittai* 2 (Feb. 1940): 86.

114. *Torii* 8, no. 12 (Dec. 1, 1938): 2.

115. *Kokumin seishin sōdōin kōenroku*, 47.

116. *Kokumin sōryoku*, March 1, 1944, 26.

117. Unless otherwise noted, the following discussion is based on *Torii* 8, no. 8 (Aug. 1, 1938): 2–3. For more on the role of schools in distributing shrine amulets and other Shintō paraphernalia, see Hiura, *Jinja, gakkō, shokuminchi*, 203–40.

118. An example of these materials includes *Taima to kamidana: Katei no kamimatsuri kokoroe* (Keijō: Tairiku Shintō renmei, 1939?). Although advertised in *Torii* 9, no. 11 (Nov. 1, 1939): 8, I have been unable to locate a copy of this text.

119. See, for example, Ch'oe, *Ilche malgi singminji chibae chŏngch'aek yŏn'gu*.

120. *Sinsidae*, Jan. 1943, 47–48.

121. For a compelling account of his ideological "conversion" *(chŏnhwan; J:* tenkan), see Park Chan-seung [Pak Ch'an-sŭng], "Yi Kwang-su and the Endorsement of State Power," *Journal of Korean Studies* 19, no. 1 (Dec. 2006): 161–90.

122. *Sinsidae*, July 1944, 27 (emphasis mine). For more on Yi's writings in this wartime journal, see Watanabe Naoki, "Yi Kwang-su to 'Sinsindae,'" *Shokuminchi bunka kenkyū* 10 (July 2011): 46–61.

123. *Rokki* 5, no. 2 (March 1940): 13.

124. Although these efforts bore some fruit in the capital city, many Korean homes in other parts of the peninsula received shrine amulets but continued to lack a ritual shelf on which to place them. *Torii* 8, no. 1 (Jan. 1, 1938): 4.

125. *Kokumin sōryoku*, Jan. 1, 1941, 26; *Kokumin sōryoku*, Nov. 1941, 12; and *Keijō jinja jingi geppō* 3, no. 11 (Nov. 1941): 4.

126. *KN,* Jan. 24, 1943. For more on these organizations in wartime Keijō, see Yi Chong-min, "Tosi ŭi ilsang ŭl t'ong hae pon chumin saenghwal t'ongje: Kyŏngsŏngbu ŭi aegukban ŭl chungsim ŭro," in *Ilsaeng p'asijŭm chibae chŏngch'aek kwa minjung saenghwal,* ed. Pang Ki-jun (Seoul: Hyean, 2004), 415–53.

127. *Kokumin sōryoku,* March 1, 1944, 26–27. See also *Keijō jinja jingi geppō* 3, no. 11 (Nov. 1941): 2–5.

128. *Sinsidae,* Jan. 1943, 46–49.

129. *Kokumin sōryoku,* Dec. 1941, 46.

130. *Singminji Chosŏn kwa chŏnjaeng misul* (Seoul: Minjok munje yŏn'guso, 2004), 70.

131. Like the placement of miniature shrines, officials also made exceptions in terms of offerings Koreans could make to household deities, including using pine instead of evergreen. For more on these local variations, see *Kokumin sōryoku,* Dec. 1941, 47.

132. For more on this topic, see *Keijō jinja jingi geppō* 3, no. 11 (Nov. 1941): 5.

133. According to one scholar, "By 1940, the number of registered receivers hovered around the 200,000 mark and best estimates of radio distribution at the end of the colonial period are approximately 305,000 receivers (slightly more than 1 percent of the Korean population) in use." Michael Robinson, "Broadcasting, Cultural Hegemony, and Colonial Modernity in Korea, 1924–1945," in *Colonial Modernity in Korea,* ed. Shin Gi-Wook and Michael Robinson (Cambridge, MA: Harvard University Press, 1999), 57.

134. *Kokumin sōryoku,* Jan. 1, 1941, 26. For a similar account that considered two-story homes, see *Kokumin sōryoku,* Nov. 1941, 12.

135. Yamaguchi Kōichi, "Shokuminchi Chōsen ni okeru jinja seisaku to Chōsenjin no taiō: 1936–1945," *Jinmin no rekishigaku* 146 (Dec. 2000): 27.

136. Kim, "'Kōminka seisakuki' no jinja seisaku ni tsuite," 427.

137. Ching, *Becoming "Japanese,"* 91.

138. Although slightly predating the wartime period, see, for example, the two Korean student accounts published in *Torii* 3, no. 5 (May 1, 1933): 6.

139. These newsreels are available (with English subtitles) on the DVD *Palgul toen kwagŏ, ne bŏnjjae: Kosŭpilmop'ondŭ, palgul yŏngsang moŭm* (Seoul: Korea Film Archive, 2009).

140. Sung-Gun Kim [Kim Sŏng-gŏn], "The Shinto Shrine Issue in Korean Christianity under Japanese Colonialism," *Journal of Church and State* 39, no. 3 (Summer 1997): 503–22.

141. Pak Hyo-saeng and Sŏ Chong-min, "Yŏksa ŭi kilmok ŭl jik'in i wa hamkke: Changgong Kim Chae-jun paksa ŭi hoego," *Han'guk kidokkyosa yon'gu* 6 (1986): 6. I thank Kim Sŭng-t'ae, South Korea's foremost scholar of Christian resistance to colonial Shintō, for bringing this interview to my attention. For more on Kim, see Hwang Sung Kyu [Hwang Sung-gyu], ed., *The Life and Theology of Changgong, Kim Chai Choon* (Seoul: Hanshin University Press, 2005); and Hong Chi-mo, "Kim Chae-jun as Seen from the Perspective of Korean Conservative Theology," *Chongshin Review* 2 (October 1997): 5–35. Other accounts suggest that some, if not many, wartime Koreans were praying for national

liberation, rather than for a Japanese victory. Jun Uchida, *Brokers of Empire: Japanese Settler Colonialism in Korea, 1876–1945* (Cambridge, MA: Harvard University Asia Center, 2011), 393. For more on the late colonial phenomenon of anti-Japanese rumors and insubordination, see Yi Si-jae, "Ilchemal ŭi chosŏn'in yuŏn ŭi yŏn'gu," *Han'guk sahoehak* 20 (Winter 1987): 211–30.

EPILOGUE

1. In part, I borrow this framework from Michel-Rolph Trouillot, *Silencing the Past: Power and the Production of History* (Boston: Beacon Press, 1997).

2. Suga Kōji, *Nihon tōchika no kaigai jinja: Chōsen jingū, Taiwan jinja to saijin* (Tokyo: Kōbundō, 2004), 9. According to one estimate, departing Japanese officials counted 136 incidents of arson within just eight days after the official surrender on August 15. Of course, not every incident resulted in the total destruction of the 1,141 shrines that covered the peninsula by 1945. Even if each of these 136 incidents would have led to the destruction of one shrine, Koreans would still have demolished less than 9 percent of these sacred sites. Matsutani Motokazu, "Minami Chōsen ni okeru bei-senryōgun no shintō seisaku: GHQ/SCAP no shintō seisaku to sono hikaku no shiten kara," *Gendai Kankoku Chōsen kenkyū* 3 (Nov. 2003): 66. For a list of shrines Koreans destroyed in the immediate postliberation period, see Morita Yoshio, *Chōsen shūsen no kiroku* (Tokyo: Gannandō shoten, 1964), 112–13. For a semifictional account of Koreans' postliberation treatment of Shintō shrines, see Richard E. Kim, *Lost Names: Scenes from a Korean Boyhood* (Berkeley: University of California Press, 1998), 160–96.

3. Morita, *Chōsen shūsen no kiroku*, 109–11.

4. Nukaga Hironao, *Jinja shimpō*, Aug. 13, 1960, 111–18. I thank Aoi Akihito for providing me with this rare document. Japanese views of Koreans as unreliable and even dangerous, which were long-standing images produced during the colonial period, continued into the Asia-Pacific War as new images of them as disloyal and insubordinate, especially after 1941. For more on these views, see Yi Si-jae, "Ilchemal ŭi chosŏn'in yuŏn ŭi yŏn'gu," *Han'guk sahoehak* 20 (Winter 1987): esp. 226–28.

5. Interestingly, some Korean elites attempted to remove Amaterasu from Seoul Shrine's Japan-dominated pantheon and establish a memorial to the native deities installed there in 1929. However, by November 1945, a placard reading "Tan'gun Mausoleum" had been removed and was replaced with one announcing the Oriental School of Medicine, a public facility more palatable to postliberation Koreans. Morita, *Chōsen shūsen no kiroku*, 406. Unlike Korea Shrine, some dilapidated structures of the Seoul Shrine complex, used as an orphanage after the Korean War, probably survived into the late 1960s or early 1970s. I thank An Ch'ang-mo, whose tour of this site in 2005 helped me to confirm this silenced history.

6. Ibid., 404–6. For a comprehensive analysis of the shrine issue in postwar Japan and postliberation Korea, see Matsutani, "Minami Chōsen ni okeru bei-senryōgun no shintō seisaku," 64–77.

7. *Sŏul sinmun*, Feb. 21, 1946.

8. Donald Clark, "Protestant Christianity and the State: Religious Organizations as Civil Society," in *Korean Society: Civil Society, Democracy and the State,* ed. Charles K. Armstrong (London: Routledge, 2002), 184; and *CI,* April 23, 1946.

9. *CI,* April 23, 1946; *TI,* April 6, 1947; and *TI,* March 27, 1948. This popular tradition of worship continued well into the 1970s, if not later. *CI,* April 14, 1974.

10. *TI,* April 2, 1956.

11. *TI,* March 29, 1959.

12. Another project that fits this pattern is President Rhee's failed plan to place South Korea's National Assembly building atop Namsan. However, army engineers did remove the 381 stairs leading to the former Korea Shrine before Park Chung-hee scrapped Rhee's seven-billon-wŏn plan. *TI,* Feb. 25, 1959; *TI,* May 13, 1959; *TI,* Dec. 27, 1959; and *Kungminbo,* June 6, 1962. In the end, Park decided to use this former shrine site to construct a comprehensive cultural center, which included a library, greenhouse, aquarium, and national culture museum as well as sports and recreation centers. *CI,* Nov. 11, 1968.

13. The overlap of President Rhee's birthday and An's death might explain why Itō's assassination (on October 26) was not celebrated. Ideas to replace the Itō temple with An's statue emerged immediately after liberation, but were interrupted by national division and civil war. For more on the colonial meanings of the temple, see Mizuno Naoki, "Shokuminchi Chōsen ni okeru Itō Hirobumi no kioku: Keijō no Hakubunji o chūshin ni," in *Itō Hirobumi to kankoku tōchi,* ed. Itō Yukio and Yi Sŏng-hwan (Tokyo: Mineruba shobō, 2009).

14. Although occasionally claiming dynastic connections, President Rhee (Yi) dismantled the assets of the Yi family, turning their personal assets into cultural properties of the nation. On the ill fate of the royal house after liberation, see Christine Kim, "The Chosŏn Monarchy in Republican Korea, 1945–1965," in *Northeast Asia's Difficult Past: Essays in Collective Memory,* ed. Barry Schwartz and Mikyoung Kim (London: Palgrave Macmillan, 2010), 213–28. For a documentary chronicling this history, see Yi Sang-hyŏn, *Chosŏn ŭi nakjo* (Seoul: n.p., 2006). On President Rhee's efforts to deify himself through the same Chosŏn traditions he displaced, see Cho Ŭn-chŏng, "Yi Sŭng-man tongsang yŏn'gu," *Han'guk kŭndae misul sahak* 14 (2005): 75–113.

15. For more on the "traditional" clothing and nationalist pose of the Rhee statue, see Cho, "Yi Sŭng-man tongsang yŏn'gu," 88–93.

16. On the leadership behind the revolution in 1960, see Charles Kim, "The April 19th Generation and the Start of Postcolonial History in South Korea," *Review of Korean Studies* 12, no. 3 (September 2009): 71–99.

17. *TI,* Oct. 4, 1955; and *TI,* July 24, 1960. For more on statuary practices during Park's reign, see Chŏng Ho-ki, "Pak Chŏng-hŭi sidae ŭi 'tongsang kŏllip undong' kwa aegukjuŭi: 'Aeguk sŏnyŏl chosang kŏllip ŭiwŏnhoe' ŭi hwaldong ŭl chungsim ŭro," *Chŏngsin munhwa yŏn'gu* 30, no. 1 (Spring 2007): 335–63.

18. For more on the museum and postcolonial memorializations of An, see Yun Sŏn-ja, "Haebang hu An Chung-gŭn kinyŏm ŭi yŏksajŏk ŭiŭi," *Han'guk tongnip undongsa yŏn'gu* 34 (Dec. 2009): 123–60.

19. *CI*, Oct. 31, 1957; *CI*, Oct. 2, 1966; *CI*, April 27, 1976; and *CI*, Oct. 27, 1970.

20. For coverage by the South Korean press of this event, including statements by both parties, see *CI*, May 22, 1958. On these politics more generally, see Alexis Dudden, *Troubled Apologies among Japan, Korea, and the United States* (New York: Columbia University Press, 2008).

21. *TI*, May 5, 1958.

22. For more on this issue, see, for example, Lee Won-deog [Yi Wŏn-dŏk], "A Normal State without Remorse: The Textbook Controversy and Korea-Japan Relations," *East Asian Review* 13, no. 3 (Autumn 2001): 21–40.

23. *CI*, Aug. 26, 1982.

24. *CI*, May 11, 1985. For some limited commemorations of An in postwar Japan, see Yun, "Haebang hu An Chung-gŭn kinyŏm ŭi yŏksajŏk ŭiŭi," 139.

25. Changmii Bae [Pae Chang-mi], "The Symbolic Landscape of National Identity: Planning, Politics, and Culture in South Korea," PhD diss., University of Southern California, 2002, 128–130, 133, and 138–39. For President Rhee's financial dependence on the United States and his ability to manipulate American magnanimity, see Gregg Brazinsky, *Nation Building in South Korea: Koreans, Americans, and the Making of a Democracy* (Chapel Hill: University of North Carolina Press, 2007), esp. 13–40.

26. *CI*, March 17, 1954; and *CI*, April 19, 1959.

27. In 1945, only thirty-six of the approximately three hundred original buildings remained standing. Jong-Heon Jin [Chin Chong-hŏn], "Demolishing Colony: The Demolition of the Old Government-General Building of Chosŏn," in *Sitings: Critical Approaches to Korean Geography*, ed. Timothy R. Tangherlini and Sallie Yea (Honolulu: University of Hawai'i Press, 2008), 40–41.

28. For US readers, Capitol Hall *(Chung'angch'ŏng)* is, for the most part, a misnomer because this structure only briefly doubled as South Korea's legislative complex from 1948 until 1950. Until its spectacular demolition in 1995, it functioned primarily as the country's executive branch.

29. Bae, "The Symbolic Landscape of National Identity," 141–42; and Myungrae Cho [Cho Myŏng-nae], "From Street Corners to Plaza: The Production of Festive Civic Space in Central Seoul," in *Globalization, the City and Civil Society in Pacific Asia: The Social Production of Civic Spaces*, ed. Mike Douglas, K.C. Ho, and Giok Ling Ooi (London: Routledge, 2007), 197. For more on the contexts of the protests in 1960 and 1986, see Kim, "The April 19th Generation and the Start of Postcolonial History in South Korea"; and Namhee Lee, *The Making of Minjung: Democracy and the Politics of Representation in South Korea* (Ithaca, NY: Cornell University Press, 2009).

30. *CI*, July 18, 1949.

31. For more on these events, see Jung Keun-sik [Chŏng Kŭn-sik], "The Memories of August 15 (Day of Liberation) Reflected in Korean Anniversaries and Memorial Halls," *Review of Korean Studies* 8, no. 1 (2005): 11–50.

32. *CI*, Oct. 5, 1953; and *CI*, Dec. 29, 1953. For more on this culture, see Seungsook Moon [Mun Sŭng-suk], *Militarized Modernity and Gendered Citizenship in South Korea* (Durham: Duke University Press, 2005).

33. *CI*, Aug. 14 and 15, 1964.

34. *CI*, Oct. 24, 1958; and *CI*, Nov. 16, 1958.

35. Early South Korean leaders reclaimed other important roads by erasing their Japanese names and replacing them with those of national heroes. These symbolic thoroughfares include Kōganemachi Avenue (Ŭljiro, named after the seventh-century military leader [Ŭlji Mun-dŏk] who defended Koguryŏ [37 BCE–668 CE] against the Sui [581–618] invasions), Honmachi Street (Ch'ungmuro, named after the posthumous title [Ch'ungmugong] of Admiral Yi Sun-sin [1545–98]), and Yamatomachi Avenue (T'oegyero, named after the pen name [T'oegye] of Yi Hwang [1501–70], one of the most prominent Confucian scholars from the Chosŏn period).

36. *CI*, Aug. 17, 1956; *CI*, May 7, 1966; and *CI*, Oct. 3, 1968.

37. For more on Park's projects of anticommunist urbanism, see An Ch'ang-mo, "Pan'gong ideollogi wa tosi kŭrigo kŏnchu'uk," *Kyŏnggi kŏnch'uk taehagwŏn nonmunjip* 9 (2005): 11–27; and An Ch'ang-mo, "Tosi kŏnch'uk tapsa: Pan'gong kwa chŏnt'ong ideollogi ŭi poru: Changch'ungdong," *Kŏnch'uk kwa sahoe* 5 (Sept. 2006): 282–92. On his cultural policy more generally, see O Myŏng-sŏk, "1960–70 nyŏndae ŭi munhwa chŏngch'eak kwa minjok munhwa tamnon," *Pigyo munhwa yŏn'gu* 4 (1998): 121–52; and Chŏn Chae-ho, "Minjokjuŭi yŏksa iyong: Pak Chŏng-hŭi ch'eje ŭi chŏnt'ong munhwa chŏngch'aek," *Sahoe kwahak yŏn'gu* 7 (1998): 83–106.

38. For Rhee's uses of Yi, see Pak Kye-ri, "Ch'ungmugong tongsang kwa kukka ideollogi," *Han'guk kŭndae misul sahak* 12 (2004): 145–59. On shifting perceptions of Yi, see Roh Young-koo [No Yŏng-gu], "Yi Sun-shin, an Admiral Who Became a Myth," *Review of Korean Studies* 7, no. 3 (2004): 15–36. On the memorialization of other national heroes, see Chŏng, "Pak Chŏng-hŭi sidae ŭi 'tongsang kŏllip undong' kwa aegukjuŭi."

39. *CI*, April 28, 1968. For more on Park's uses of Yi, see Pak, "Ch'ungmugong tongsang kwa kukka ideollogi," 159–69; and Sin Ŭn-jae, "Pak Chŏng-hŭi ui kiŏk mandŭlgi wa Yi Sun-sin," in *Hyŏndae ŭi kiŏk sok esŏ minjok ŭl sangsang hada: Han, chung, il ŭi sahoejŏk kiŏk kwa tong asia*, ed. Kim Hak-i (Pusan: Sejong ch'ulp'ansa, 2006).

40. *CI*, Nov. 5 and 9, 1967.

41. *CI*, Dec. 12, 1968.

42. Bae, "The Symbolic Landscape of National Identity," 161; and *CI*, Sept. 6, 1961.

43. For one debate of this sort, see *CI*, March 17, 1982.

44. *CI*, March 17, 1982.

45. Bae, "The Symbolic Landscape of National Identity," 208.

46. *CI*, May 24, 1983. This aesthetic transformation also expanded exhibition space for the 750,000-item collection, only 1 percent of which had been regularly displayed at the old facility. *CI*, March 17, 1982. A similar critique of the Government-General building emerged in postcolonial Taiwan, although that structure still remains in use as the Presidential Office Building. Joseph R. Allen, *Taipei: City of Displacements* (Seattle: University of Washington Press, 2012), 34.

47. By contrast, North Korean officials drew on the ancient traditions of Koguryŏ (37 BCE–668 AD), whose capital was located in P'yŏngyang. For this history, see Suk-Young Kim [Kim Suk-yŏng], *Illusive Utopia: Theater, Film,*

*and Everyday Performance in North Korea* (Ann Arbor: University of Michigan Press, 2010), 60–128.

48. Jin, "Demolishing Colony," 55.

49. For a critique of the Government-General building as an instance of geomantic rape, see Kim Sŏng-nyae, "P'ungsu wa singminjuŭi ŭi kiŏk ŭi erot'ik chusul," *Han'guk chonggyo yŏn'gu* 2 (2000): 123–57. On patriarchal framings of "comfort women," see Hyunah Yang [Yang Hyŏn-a], "Re-membering the Korean Military Comfort Women: Nationalism, Sexuality, and Silencing," in *Dangerous Women: Gender and Korean Nationalism,* ed. Elaine H. Kim and Chungmoo Choi (London: Routledge, 1997), 123–39.

50. *CI*, Dec. 26, 1991.

51. *CI*, April 2, 1993. For scholarship on the contested destruction of this monument, see Bae, "The Symbolic Landscape of National Identity," 220–73; and Jin, "Demolishing Colony."

52. Bae, "The Symbolic Landscape of National Identity," 242. For counter-arguments, see *CI*, June 6 and 8, 1996.

53. *CI*, June 9, 1994. For a full description of these commemorations, see *CI*, Aug. 14, 1995. I borrow the term "folklore of the regime" from Takashi Fujitani, *Splendid Monarchy: Power and Pageantry in Modern Japan* (Berkeley: University of California Press, 1998).

54. Similar problems of authenticity have surrounded the problematic re-creation of the Ch'ŏnggye Stream. On this project, see Kang U-wŏn, ed., *Ch'ŏnggyech'ŏn: Ch'ŏnggye koga rŭl kiok hamyŏ* (Seoul: Mat'i, 2009); Hisup Shin [Sin Hŭi-sŏp], "Uncovering Ch'ŏnggyech'ŏn: The Ruins of Modernization and Everyday Life," *Korean Studies* 29 (2006): 95–113; and Myung-Rae Cho [Cho Myŏng-nae], "The Politics of Urban Nature Restoration: The Case of Cheonggyecheon Restoration in Seoul, Korea," *International Development Planning Review* 32, no. 2 (2010): 145–65.

55. *CI*, Feb. 28, 1995.

56. *CI*, Feb. 16, 2005; and *CI*, April. 21, 2005. Even after its "restoration" in August 2010, the debate over the signboard's linguistic authenticity has continued unabated. When the new signboard cracked after just three months, the Korean Language Society and several other groups favoring *han'gŭl* as the national script lobbied to replace the digitally reproduced Chinese characters with the vernacular letters that, they insist, King Sejong first invented at Kyŏngbok Palace in the fifteenth century. Although some surveys showed nearly 60 percent support, their proposal failed to convince the government of its authenticity. *Yonhap News Agency*, Dec. 5, 2012.

57. *CI*, Aug. 25, 1999.

58. *CI*, Aug. 25, 1999. Although still under constant police patrol and surveillance, the plaza, like other public spaces, has also become an increasingly important site for mass rallies that combine earlier features of political protest (i.e., against US militarism) with new forms of national festivities (i.e., World Cup assemblies). For more, see Cho, "From Street Corners to Plaza," 195–210. On the limitations and potential of this site, see Moon-Hwan Kim [Kim Mun-hwan], "The Plaza as a Public Art: The Case of Gwanghwamun Plaza in Seoul," *Journal of Asian Arts & Aesthetics* 3 (2009): 21–28.

59. For a seminal work positively reevaluating this pivotal period of Korean history, see Yi T'ae-jin, *Kojong sidae ŭi chaejomyŏng* (Seoul: T'aehaksa, 2000).

60. *CI,* Nov. 11 and 15, 2003.

61. *CI,* Nov. 11, 2003. To make room for other historical attractions, officials also plan to move the American Embassy to an alternative, less central location.

62. For an excellent documentary chronicling this predicament, see Katō Kumiko and Kim T'ae-il, *Annyŏng, Sayonara: Chŏnjaeng kwa ch'imnyak sinsa Yasŭkuni rŭl mal handa* (Seoul: Han'guk tongnip yŏnghwa hyŏphoe, 2007). On the historical roots of the contemporary situation, see Takahashi Testuya, "The National Politics of the Yasukuni Shrine," in *Nationalisms in Japan,* ed. Naoko Shimazu (London: Routledge, 2006), 155–80. In Japanese, see Takahashi, *Yasukuni mondai* (Tokyo: Chikuma shobō, 2005), 11–59.

63. *CI,* Aug. 16, 2010. Upon completion of this 540-million-wŏn project, officials will have restored approximately 75 percent of the over five hundred buildings standing during the late nineteenth century.

64. For more on unsanctioned uses of this space, see Jesook Song [Song Chae-suk], "Historicization of Homeless Spaces: The Seoul Train Station Square and the House of Freedom," *Anthropological Quarterly* 79, no. 2 (Spring 2006): 193–223.

65. "Seoul City Hall's Metamorphosis Pleases Book Lovers," *Korea.net,* Oct. 25, 2012, http://www.korea.net/NewsFocus/Society/view?articleId = 103347 (accessed January 9, 2013).

66. *Korea Times,* July 6, 2012. Approximately 70 percent of the population, in fact, favored demolition.

# Selected Bibliography

NEWSPAPERS AND MAGAZINES

*Unless otherwise noted, the place of publication for these sources is Seoul (Keijō). The years given below correspond to known dates of publication for the subject of this book; a question mark indicates doubt about the start or end of circulation.*

*Korean*

Chosŏn ilbo *(CI)* (1920–40, 1945–present)
Hwangsŏng sinmun *(HS)* (1898–1910)
Kungminbo (Honolulu, 1913–68)
Maeil sinbo *(MS)* (1910–45)
Sinmin (1925–32)
Sinsidae (1941–45)
Sinyŏsong (1923–34)
Sŏul sinmun (1945–present)
Taehan maeil sinbo *(TMS)* (1904–10)
Tonga ilbo *(TI)* (1920–40, 1945–present)

*Japanese*

Bunkyō no Chōsen (1925–45)
Chōsen doboku kenchiku kyōkai kaihō (1924–34?)
Chōsen [ihō] (1915–44)
Chōsen kōron *(CK)* (Tokyo, 1913–44)
Chōsen [oyobi manshū] *(COM)* (Tokyo, 1908–41)
Chōsen shimbun *(CSb)* (Tokyo, 1908–21)

*Chōsen shimpō (CSp)* (Tokyo, 1882–1908)
*Chōsen shisō tsūshin* (1926–33)
*Chōsen sōtokufu kanpō* (1910–45)
*Chōsen to kenchiku (CTK)* (1922–42)
*Hantō no hikari* (1940–44)
*Jinja kyōkai zasshi* (Tokyo, 1902–38)
*Jinja shimpō* (1946–present)
*Kaizō* (Tokyo, 1919–55)
*Katei no tomo (Chōsenban)* (1936–41)
*Keijō ihō (KI)* (1921–44)
*Keijō jinja jingi geppō* (1939–41?)
*Keijō nippō (KN)* (1906–45)
*Keijō shimbun (KS)* (1908)
*Keikidō keisatsu buchō* (1941?)
*Kōkoku jihō* (Tokyo, 1930–43?)
*Kokumin sōryoku* (1939–44)
*Naisen ittai* (1940–41?)
*Ōsaka asahi shimbun furoku Chōsen asahi (OASFCA)* (Osaka, 1925–35)
*Rokki* (1936–44)
*Shisō ihō* (1934–43)
*Sōdōin* (1939–40?)
*Torii* (1931–39?)
*Toshi kōron (TK)* (Tokyo, 1918–44)


*English*

*Korea Times* (1950–present)
*Yonhap News Agency* (1980–present)


OTHER SOURCES
*Korean*

An Ch'ang-mo. "Pan'gong ideollogi wa tosi kŭrigo kŏnchu'uk." *Kyŏnggi kŏnch'uk taehagwŏn nonmunjip* 9 (2005): 11–27.
———. *Tŏksugung: Sidae ŭi unmyŏng ŭl anko cheguk ŭi chungsim e sŏda.* Seoul: Tongnyŏk, 2009.
———. "Tosi kŏnch'uk tapsa: Pan'gong kwa chŏnt'ong ideollogi ŭi poru: Changch'ungdong." *Kŏnch'uk kwa sahoe* 5 (Sept. 2006): 282–92.
Chang Kyu-sik. "Ilcheha Chongno ŭi minjok undong konggan." *Han'guk kŭnhyŏndaesa yŏn'gu* 26 (Fall 2003): 71–91.
Chang Sin. "Taejŏng ch'inmokhoe wa naesŏn yunghwa undong." *Taedong munhwa yŏn'gu* 60 (2007): 361–92.
Ch'a Sŭng-gi. *Pankŭndaejŏk sangsangnyŏk ŭi imgyedŭl: Singminji Chosŏn tamnonjang esŏ ŭi chŏnt'ong, segye, chuch'e.* Seoul: P'urŭn yŏksa, 2009.
Cho Chae-ho and Chŏn Pong-hŭi. "Kojongjo kyŏngbokgung chunggŏn e taehan yŏn'gu." *Taehan kŏnch'uk hakhoe nonmunjip* 16, no. 4 (April 2000): 31–40.

Ch'oe Sŏk-yŏng. "Hanmal ilche kangjŏmgi kukka cherye konggan ŭi pyŏnhwa."
*Han'guksa yŏn'gu* 118 (2002): 221–47.

———. *Ilcheha musongnon kwa singminji kwŏllyŏk.* Seoul: Sŏgyŏng
munhwasa, 1999.

Ch'oe Yu-ri. *Ilche malgi singminji chibae chŏngch'aek yŏn'gu.* Seoul: Kukhak
charyowŏn, 1997.

Ch'oe Wan-gi. *Hanyang: Kŭ kot esŏ salgo sipta.* Seoul: Kyohwasa, 1997.

Chŏn Chae-ho. "Minjokjuŭi yŏksa iyong: Pak Chŏng-hŭi ch'eje ŭi chŏnt'ong
munhwa chŏngch'aek." *Sahoe kwahak yŏn'gu* 7 (1998): 83–106.

Chŏng Chae-jŏng. *Sŏul ŭi munhwa yusa t'ambanggi.* Seoul: Sŏulhak yŏn'guso,
1997.

*Ch'ŏnggyech'ŏn: Sigan, changso, saram.* Seoul: Sŏulhak yŏn'guso, 2001.

Chŏng Ho-ki. "Pak Chŏng-hŭi sidae ŭi 'tongsang kŏllip undong' kwa aegukjuŭi:
'Aeguk sŏnyŏl chosang kŏllip ŭiwŏnhoe' ŭi hwaldong ŭl chungsim ŭro."
*Chŏngsin munhwa yŏn'gu* 30, no. 1 (Spring 2007): 335–63.

*Chongnogu-ji.* Vol. 2. Seoul: Chongno-gu, 1994.

Chŏng Sang-u. "1910 nyŏndae ilche ŭi chibae nolli wa chisikinch'ung ŭi insik:
'Ilsŏndongjoron' kwa 'munmyŏnghwa' ŭl chungsim ŭro." *Han'guk saron* 46
(Dec 2001): 183–231.

Chŏn Min-jŏng. "Ilche sigi Chosŏn pangnamhoe (1929 nyŏn) yŏn'gu: Chosŏn'in
ŭi kŭndaejŏk sigak ch'ehŏm chungsim ŭro." Sŏnggyungwan University, PhD
diss., 2003.

Chŏn U-yong. "Chongno wa ponjŏng: Singmin tosi Kyŏngsŏng ŭi tu ŏlgul."
*Yŏksa wa hyŏnsil* 40 (June 2001): 163–93.

———. "Taehan chegukki—ilche ch'ogi Sŏul konggan ŭi pyŏnhwa wa kwŏllyŏk
ŭi chihyang." *Chŏnnong saron* 5 (1999): 39–72.

Cho Ŭn-chŏng. "Yi Sŭng-man tongsang yŏn'gu." *Han'guk kŭndae misul sahak*
14 (2005): 75–113.

Chu Yun-jŏng. "'Chosŏn mulsan kongjinhoe' (1915) e taehan yŏn'gu." MA
thesis, Academy of Korean Studies, 2002.

Hong Sŏng-t'ae. "Singminji kŭndaehwa wa mul saenghwal ŭi pyŏnhwa." In
*Singminji ŭi ilsang, chibae wa kyun'yŏl,* edited by Kong Chae-uk and Chŏng
Kŭn-sik. Seoul: Munhwa kwahaksa, 2006.

Hong Sun-min. "Kojongdae kyŏngbokgung chunggŏn ŭi chŏngch'ijŏk ŭimi."
*Sŏulhak yŏn'gu* 29 (Aug. 2007): 57–82.

Hŏ Pyŏng-sik. "P'yehŏ ŭi kodo wa ch'angjo toen sindo." *Han'guk minhak
yŏn'gu* 36 (June 2009): 79–105.

Hŏ Yŏng-sŏp. *Chosŏn Ch'ongdokbu: Kŭ ch'ŏngsa kŏllip ŭi iyagi.* Seoul:
Han'ul, 1996.

———. *Uri kunggwŏl iyagi.* Seoul: Ch'ŏngnyŏnsa, 2004.

Hwang Min-ho. "Taejonggyo ŭi hang'il minjok undong." In *Ilcheha Kyŏnggido
chiyŏk chonggyogye ŭi minjok munhwa undong.* Seoul: Kyŏnggi munhwa
chaedan, 2001.

Im Tŏk-sun. "Chosŏn ch'ogi Hanyang chŏngdo wa sudo ŭi sangjinghwa." In *Sŏul
ŭi kyŏnggwan pyŏnhwa,* edited by An Tu-sun. Seoul: Sŏulhak yŏn'guso, 1994.

Kang U-wŏn, ed. *Ch'ŏnggyech'ŏn: Ch'ŏnggye koga rŭl kiok hamyŏ.* Seoul:
Mat'i, 2009.

Kang Yŏng-sim, ed. *Ilche sigi kŭndaejŏk ilsang kwa singminji munhwa*. Seoul: Ihwa yŏja taehakkyo ch'ulp'anbu, 2008.

Katō Kumiko and Kim T'ae-il. *Annyŏng, Sayonara: Chŏnjaeng kwa ch'imnyak sinsa Yasŭkuni rŭl mal handa*. Seoul: Han'guk tongnip yŏnghwa hyŏphoe, 2007.

Kim Chin-gyun and Chŏng Kŭn-sik, eds. *Kŭndae chuch'e wa singminji kyuyul kwŏllyŏk*. Seoul: Munhwa kwahaksa, 1997.

Kim Ch'ŏ-lsu. "Chosŏn ch'ongdokbu ŭi chonggyo chŏngch'aek: 'Chosŏn sin'gung chesin nonjaeng e nat'anan hwangminhwa imbo." *Uri sahoe yŏn'gu* 4 (1997): 66–114.

Kim Chŏng-dong. *Kojong hwangje ka sarang han chŏngdong kwa tŏksugung*. Seoul: Pal'ŏn, 2004.

———. *Nama innŭn yŏksa, sarajinŭn kŏnch'ungmul*. Seoul: Taewŏnsa, 2000.

Kim Chong-gŭn. "Singminji Kyŏngsŏng ŭi ijung tosiron e taehan pip'anjŏk koch'al." *Sŏulhak yŏn'gu* 38 (Feb. 2010): 1–68.

———. "Sŏul chungsimbu ŭi ilbon'in sigaji hwaksan: Kaehanggi esŏ ilche kangjŏm chŏnhangi kkaji (1885 nyŏn–1929 nyŏn)." *Sŏulhak yŏn'gu* 20 (March 2003): 181–233.

Kim Ki-ho. "Ilche sidae ch'ogi ŭi tosi kyehoek e taehan yŏn'gu: Kyŏngsŏngbu sigu kaejŏng ŭl chungsim ŭro." *Sŏulhak yŏn'gu* 6 (1995): 41–66.

Kim Kwang-u. "Taehan cheguk sidae ŭi tosi kyehoek: Hansŏngbu tosi kaejo saŏp." *Hyangt'o Sŏul* 50 (1990): 93–122.

Kim Myŏng-sŏn. "1915 nyŏn Kyŏngsŏng kajŏng pangnamhoe chŏnsi chut'aek ŭi p'yosang." *Taehan kŏnch'uk hakhoe nonmunjip* 28, no. 3 (March 2012): 155–64.

Kim Paek-yŏng. *Chibae wa konggan: Singminji tosi Kyŏngsŏng kwa cheguk ilbon*. Seoul: Munhak kwa chisŏngsa, 2009.

Kim Sŏng-nyae. "P'ungsu wa singminjuŭi ŭi kiŏk ŭi erot'ik chusul." *Han'guk chonggyo yŏn'gu* 2 (2000): 123–57.

Kim Sŭng-t'ae, ed. *Han'guk kidokkyo wa sinsa ch'ambae munje*. Seoul: Han'guk kidokkyo yŏksa yŏn'guso, 1991.

———. *Sinsa ch'ambae kŏbu hangjaengjadŭl ŭi chŭng'ŏn: Ŏdum ŭi kwŏnse rŭl igin saramdŭl*. Seoul: Tasan kŭlbang, 1993.

Kim Tae-ho. "1910 nyŏndae—1930 nyŏndae ch'o Kyŏngsŏng sinsa wa chiyŏk sahoe ŭi kwan'gye: Kyŏngsŏng sinsa ŭi unyŏng kwa han'gugin kwa ŭi kwan'gye rŭl chungsim ŭro." In *Ilbon ŭi singminji chibae wa singminjijŏk kŭndae*, edited by Yi Sŭng-il. Seoul: Tongbuk ayŏksa chaedan, 2009.

———. "Ilcheha Chongmyo rŭl tullŏssan seryŏk kaldŭng kwa konggan pyŏnhwa: 1920 nyŏndae singmin kwŏllyŏk kwa kwijok seryŏk ŭi kwan'gye rŭl chungsim ŭro." *Sŏulhak yŏn'gu* 43 (2011): 1–54.

Kim Yŏng-hŭi. "Chosŏn pangnamhoe wa singminji kŭndae." *Tongbang hakji* 140 (2007): 221–67.

Kim Yŏng-mi. "Ilche sigi tosi munje wa chiyŏk undong: Kyŏngsŏng chiyŏk sŏngbuk-dong ŭi sarye rŭl chungsim ŭro." In *Han'guk kŭndae sahoe wa munhwa III: 1920–1930 nyŏndae 'singminjijŏk kŭndae' wa han'gugin ŭi taeŭng*. Seoul: Soul taehakkyo ch'ulp'anbu, 2007.

———. "Ilche sigi tosi ŭi sansudo munje wa konggongsŏng." *Sahoe wa yŏksa* 73 (March 2007): 45–74.

Kim Yŏng-sang. "Hansŏng puminhoe e taehan koch'al." *Hyangt'o sŏul* 31 (1967): 3–47.

Kong Che-uk and Chŏng Kŭn-sik, eds. *Singminji ŭi ilsang, chibae wa kyun'yŏl.* Seoul: Munhwa kwahaksa, 2006.

Ko Tong-hwan. "Chosŏn ch'ogi Hanyang ŭi hyŏngsŏng kwa tosi kujo." *Chibangsa wa chibang munwa* 8, no. 1 (2005): 52–89.

———. *Chosŏn hugi Sŏul sang'ŏp paldalsa.* Seoul: Chisik sanŏpsa, 1998.

———. *Chosŏn sidae Sŏul tosisa.* Seoul: T'aehaksa, 2007.

Kwŏn T'ae-ŏk. "1910 nyŏndae ilche ŭi Chosŏn tonghwaron kwa tonghwa chŏngch'aek." *Han'guk munhwa* 44 (Dec. 2008): 99–125.

———. "1920–1930 nyŏndae ilche ŭi tonghwa chŏngch'aeknon." In *Han'guk kŭndae sahoe wa munhwa III: 1920–1930 nyŏndae 'singminjijŏk kŭndae' wa han'gugin ŭi taeŭng.* Seoul: Sŏul taehakkyo ch'ulp'anbu, 2007.

Mok Su-hyŏn. "Ilcheha pangmulgwan ŭi hyŏngsŏng kwa kŭ ŭimi." MA thesis, Seoul National University, 2000.

No In-hwa. "Taehan cheguk sigi ŭi Hansŏng chŏngi hoesa e taehan yŏn'gu: 'Kwangmu kaehyŏk' kwa migukch'ŭk igwŏn ŭi ilyangt'ae." *Idae sawŏn* 17 (Dec. 1980): 1–27.

O Myŏng-sŏk. "1960–70 nyŏndae ŭi munhwa chŏngch'eak kwa minjok munhwa tamnon." *Pigyo munhwa yŏn'gu* 4 (1998): 121–52.

Ōta Hideharu. "Kŭndae han'il yangguk ŭi sŏnggwak insik kwa ilbon ŭi chosŏn singminji chŏngch'aek." *Han'guk saron* 49 (June 2003): 185–203.

Pak Ch'ang-sŭng. "Sŏul ilbon'in kŏryuji hyŏngsŏng kwajŏng: 1880 nyŏndae–1903 nyŏn ŭl chungsim ŭro." *Sahoe wa yŏksa* 62 (2002): 64–100.

Pak Hŭi-yong. "Chosŏn hwangje ŭi aedalp'ŭn yŏksa rŭl chŭngmyŏng hada: Wŏn'gudan ŭi ch'ŏlgŏ wa Chosŏn hot'el ŭi kŏnch'uk." In *Kunggwŏl ŭi nunmul, paeknyŏn ŭi ch'inmok: Cheguk ŭi somyŏl 100 nyŏn, uri kunggwŏl ŭn ŏdi ro kassŭlkka?*, edited by U Tong-sŏn and Pak Sŏng-jin. Seoul: Hyohyŏng ch'ulp'an, 2009.

Pak Hyo-saeng and Sŏ Chong-min. "Yŏksa ŭi kilmok ŭl jik'in i wa hamkke: Changgong Kim Chae-jun paksa ŭi hoego." *Han'guk kidokkyosa yon'gu* 6 (1986): 4–9.

Pak Kye-ri. "Ch'ungmugong tongsang kwa kukka ideollogi." *Han'guk kŭndae misul sahak* 12 (2004): 145–59.

Pak Se-hun. "1920 nyŏndae Kyŏngsŏng tosi kyehoek ŭi sŏnggyŏk: 'Kyŏngsŏng tosi kyehoek yŏn'guhoe' wa 'tosi kyehoek undong.'" *Sŏulhak yŏn'gu* 15 (Sept. 2000): 187–88.

———. *Singmin kukka wa chiyŏk kongdongch'e: 1930 nyŏndae Kyŏngsŏngbu ŭi tosi sahoe chŏngch'aek yŏn'gu.* Seoul: Han'guk haksul chŏngbo, 2006.

Pak Yun-jae. *Han'guk kŭndae ŭihak ŭi kiwŏn.* Seoul: Hyean, 2005.

———. "Yangsaeng esŏ wisaeng ŭro: Kaehwap'a ŭi ŭihangnon kwa kŭndae kukka kŏnsŏl." *Sahoe wa yŏksa* 63 (May 2003): 30–50.

*Palgul toen kwagŏ, ne bŏnjjae: Kosŭpilmop'ondŭ, palgul yŏngsang moŭm.* Seoul: Korea Film Archive, 2009.

*Se ibang'in ŭi sŏul hoesang: Tik'usya esŏ ch'onggyech'ŏn kkaji.* Seoul: Sŏul yŏksa pangmulgwan yumul kwallikwa, 2009.

Seo Hyŏn-ju [Sŏ Hyŏn-ju]. "Chosŏnmal ilcheha Sŏul ŭi habu haengjŏng chedo yŏn'gu: Chŏngdonghoe wa ch'ongdae rŭl chungsim ŭro." PhD diss., Seoul National University, 2002.

Sin Chu-baek. "Pangnamhoe: Kwasi, sŏnjŏn, kyemong, sobi ŭi ch'ehŏm konggan." *Yŏksa pip'yŏng* 67 (Summer 2004): 357–94.

*Singminji Chosŏn kwa chŏnjaeng misul.* Seoul: Minjok munje yŏn'guso, 2004.

Sin Tong-wŏn. "1910 nyŏndae ilche ŭi pogŏn ŭiryo chŏngch'aek: Han'ŭiyak chŏngch'aek ŭl chungsim ŭro." *Han'guk munhwa* 30 (Dec. 2002): 330–70.

———. *Han'guk kŭndae pogŏn ŭiryosa.* Seoul: Han'ul, 1997.

Sin Ŭn-jae. "Pak Chŏng-hŭi ui kiŏk mandŭlgi wa Yi Sun-sin." In *Hyŏndae ŭi kiŏk sok esŏ minjok ŭl sangsang hada: Han, chung, il ŭi sahoejŏk kiŏk kwa tong asia,* edited by Kim Hak-i. Pusan: Sejong ch'ulp'ansa, 2006.

Son Chŏng-mok. *Han'guk kaehanggi tosi sahoe kyŏngjesa yŏn'gu.* Seoul: Iljisa, 1982.

———. *Ilche kangjŏmgi tosi kwajŏng yŏn'gu.* Seoul: Iljisa, 1996.

———. *Ilche kangjŏmgi tosi kyehoek yŏn'gu.* Seoul: Iljisa, 1990.

———. "Irŭnba 'munhwa chŏngch'i' ha esŏ ŭi tosi chibang chedo yŏn'gu: Kyŏngsŏngbu hyŏbŭihoe rŭl chungsim ŭro." *Hyangt'o sŏul* 50 (1991): 125–94.

Song Sŏk-ki. "Kunggwŏl e tŭlŏsŏn kŭndae kŏnch'ungmul." In *Kunggwŏl ŭi nunmul, paeknyŏn ŭi ch'inmok: Cheguk ŭi somyŏl 100 nyŏn, uri kunggwŏl ŭn ŏdi ro kassŭlkka?,* edited by U Tong-sŏn and Pak Sŏng-jin. Seoul: Hyohyŏng ch'ulp'an, 2009.

*Sŏul 20 segi konggan pyŏnch'ŏnsa.* Seoul: Sŏul sijŏng kaebal yŏn'guwŏn, 2002.

U Tong-sŏn. "Ch'anggyŏngwŏn kwa Ueno kongwŏn kŭrigo Meiji ŭi konggan chibae." In *Kunggwŏl ŭi nunmul, paeknyŏn ŭi ch'inmok: Cheguk ŭi somyŏl 100 nyŏn, uri kunggwŏl ŭn ŏdi ro kassŭlkka?,* edited by U Tong-sŏn and Pak Sŏng-jin. Seoul: Hyohyŏng ch'ulp'an, 2009.

Yamanaka Mai. "Sŏul kŏju ilbon'in chach'i kigang yŏn'gu, 1885–1914." MA thesis, Catholic University (Seoul), 2001.

Yang Sŭng-u. "Namch'on ŭi p'ilji chojik tŭksŏng kwa pyŏnhwa." In *Sŏul namch'on: Sigan, changso, saram.* Seoul: Sŏulhak yŏn'guso, 2003.

Yi Chong-min. "1910 nyŏndae Kyŏngsŏng chumindŭl ŭi 'choe' wa 'bŏl': Kyŏngbŏmjae t'ongje rŭl chungsim ŭro." *Sŏulhak yŏn'gu* 17 (Sept. 2001): 95–128.

———. "Tosi ŭi ilsang ŭl t'ong hae pon chumin saenghwal t'ongje: Kyŏngsŏngbu ŭi aegukban ŭl chungsim ŭro." In *Ilsaeng p'asijŭm chibae chŏngch'aek kwa minjung saenghwal,* edited by Pang Ki-jun. Seoul: Hyean, 2004.

Yi Ch'ung-ho. *Ilche t'ongch'igi han'guk ŭisa kyoyuksa yŏn'gu.* Seoul: Han'guk charyowŏn, 1998.

Yi Kak-kyu. *Han'guk ŭi kŭndae pangnamhoe.* Seoul: K'ŏmyunik'eisyŏn puksŭ, 2010.

Yi KKotme. "Ilban'in han'ŭihak insik kwa ŭiyak iyong." In *Han'ŭihak, singminji rŭl alt'a: Singminji sigi Han'ŭihak ŭi kŭndaehwa yŏn'gu,* edited by Yŏnse taehakkyo ŭihaksa yŏn'guso. Seoul, Ak'anet, 2008.

Yi Kyŏng-min. *Kisaeng ŭn ŏttŏk'e mandŭrŏjŏnŭnga: Kŭndae kisaeng ŭi t'ansaeng kwa p'yosang konggan.* Seoul: Sajin ak'aibŭ yŏn'guso, 2005.

Yi Kyŏng-su. "Ilche sigi kyŏngsŏngbu ŭi karo chŏngbi kyehoek e ŭi han karo pyŏnhwa e kwanhan yŏn'gu." MA thesis, Yonsei University, 1990.

Yi Kyu-mok. "Sŏul ŭi tosi kyŏnggwan kwa kŭ imiji." *Sŏulhak yŏn'gu* 2 (March 1994): 149–96.

Yi Myŏng-gu. "Han'guk kwa ilbon ŭi tosi kyehoek chedo ŭi pigyo punsŏk e kwanhan yŏn'gu: Chosŏn sigaji kyehoengnyŏng kwa ilbon (ku) tosi kyehoekbŏp ŭl chungsim ŭro." PhD diss., Seoul National University, 1994.

Yi Sang-hyŏn. *Chosŏn ŭi nakjo.* Seoul, 2006.

Yi Si-jae. "Ilchemal ŭi chosŏn'in yuŏn ŭi yŏn'gu." *Han'guk sahoehak* 20 (Winter 1987): 211–30.

Yi T'ae-jin, *Kojong sidae ŭi chaejomyŏng.* Seoul: T'aehaksa, 2000.

———. "Meiji Tok'yo wa kwangmu Sŏul: Kŭndae tosi ro ŭi chihyangsŏng kwa kaejo sŏngkwa pigyo." In *Han'guk, ilbon, "sŏyang,"* edited by Watanabe Hiroshi and Park Ch'ung-sŏk. Seoul: Ayŏn ch'ulp'anbu, 2008.

Yi Yun-sang. "Ilcheha 'Chosŏn wangsil' ŭi chiwi wa iwangjik ŭi ki'nŭng." *Han'guk munhwa* 40 (2007): 315–42.

Yŏm Pok-kyu. "1920 nyŏndae huban—30 nyŏndae chŏnban ch'aji, ch'again undong ŭi chojikhwa yangsik kwa chŏngae kwajŏng." *Yoksa wa sahoe* 73 (March 2007): 75–105.

———. "1933–43 nyŏn ilche ŭi 'Kyŏngsŏng sigaji kyehoek.'" *Han'guk saron* 46 (2001): 233–83.

Yŏnse taehakkyo kukhak yŏn'guwŏn, ed. *Ilche ŭi chibae wa ilsang saenghwal.* Seoul: Hyean, 2004.

*Yun Ch'i-ho ilgi.* Seoul: Kuksa p'yŏngch'an wiwŏnhoe, 1968.

Yun Hae-dong. *Chibae wa chach'i.* Seoul: Yŏksa pip'yŏngsa, 2006.

Yun Hyŏng-gi. "Hansŏng puminhoe e kwanhan ilkocha'l." *Tonga yŏn'gu* 17 (1989): 609–32.

Yun Sŏn-ja. "Haebang hu An Chung-gŭn kinyŏm ŭi yŏksajŏk ŭiŭi." *Han'guk tongnip undongsa yŏn'gu* 34 (Dec. 2009): 123–60.


*Japanese*

Abe Yasunari. "Densenbyō yobō no gensetsu: Kindai tenkanki no kokumin kokka, nihon to eisei." *Rekishigaku kenkyū* 686 (1996): 15–31.

———. "'Eisei' to iu chitsujo." In *Shippei, kaihatsu, teikoku iryō: Ajia ni okeru byōki to iryō no rekishigaku,* edited by Miichi Masatoshi, Saitō Osamu, Wakimura Kōhei, and Iijima Wataru. Tokyo: Tōkyō daigaku shuppan, 2001.

Ambo Norio. *Minato Kōbe, korera, pesuto, suramu: Shakaiteki sabetsu keiseishi no kenkyū.* Kyoto: Gakujutsu shuppansha, 1989.

Aoi Akihito. "Chōsen no kyoryūmin hōsai jinja to chōsen sōtokufu no jinja seisaku: 'Shōchi' toshite no jinja keidai no keisei oyobi sono henyō to jizoku." *Chōsen gakuhō* 112 (July 1999): 69–115.

———. *Shokuminchi jinja to teikoku nihon.* Tokyo: Yoshikawa kōbunkan, 2005.

Aono Masaaki. "Chōsen sōtokufu no jinja seisaku: 1930 nendai o chūsin ni." *Chōsen gakuhō* 160 (July 1996): 89–132.

Chen Peifeng. *"Dōka" no dōshō imu: Nihon tōchika Taiwan no kokugo kyōikushi saikō.* Tokyo: Sangensha, 2001.

Chiba Masaji. "Tōa shihai ideorogii toshite no jinja seisaku." In *Nihonhō to Ajia,* edited by Niida Noboru hakushi tsuitō ronbunshū henshū iinkai. Tokyo: Keisō shobō, 1970.

Cho Kyŏng-dal. "Bōryoku to kōron: Shokuminchi Chōsen in okeru minshū no bōryoku." In *Bōryoku no heichi o koete: Rekishigaku kara no chōsen,* edited by Suda Tsutomu, Cho Kyŏng-dal, and Nakajima Hisato. Tokyo: Aoki shoten, 2004.

*Chōsen doboku jigyōshi.* Keijō: Chōsen sōtokufu, 1937.

*Chōsen dōhō ni taisuru naichijin hansei shiryō.* Keijō: Chōsen kenpeitai shireibu, 1933.

*Chōsen hakurankai Keijō kyōsankai hōkokusho.* Keijō: Chōsen hakurankai Keijō kyōsankai hōkokusho, 1930.

*Chōsen hakurankai kinen shashinchō.* Keijō: Chōsen sōtokufu, 1930.

*Dai-Keijō.* Keijō: Chōsen kenkyūkai, 1925.

Fujimori Terunobu. *Meiji no Tōkyō keikaku.* Tokyo: Iwanami shoten, 1990.

Gotō Yasushi. "'Keijō' shiku kaisei (1912–1937) no tokuchō ni kansuru kenkyū." International Symposium on Urban and Architectural Histories under Colonial Rule in Asia, Academica Sinica (Taipei, Taiwan), Sept. 6–7, 2000.

———. "Nihon tōchika 'Keijō' no toshi keikaku ni kansuru rekishiteki kenkyū." PhD diss., Tokyo Institute of Technology, 1995.

———. "Nihon tōchika no taihoku jōnai no gaiku keisei ni kansuru kenkyū." *Dobokushi kenkyū* 18 (1998): 103–16.

Han Sŏk-hŭi. *Nihon no Chōsen shihai to shūkyo seisaku.* Tokyo: Miraisha, 1990.

Hara Takeshi. *Kashika sareta teikokoku: Kindai nihon no gyōkōkei.* Tokyo: Misuzu shobō, 2001.

———. "Senchūki no 'jikan shihai.'" *Misuzu* 521 (2004): 28–44.

Hashiya Hiroshi. *Teikoku Nihon to shokuminchi toshi.* Tokyo: Yoshikawa kōbunkan, 2004.

Hiura Satoko. "Chōsen jingū ōharaishiki e no jidō seitō dōin: 'Sūhai' to 'shinkō' no aida." *Chōsenshi kenkyū ronbunshū* 46 (2008): 215–44.

———. *Jinja, gakkō, shokuminchi: Gyaku kinō suru Chōsen shihai.* Kyoto: Kyōto daigaku gakujustsu shuppankai, 2013.

Ishida Yorifusa. *Nihon kindai toshi keikakushi kenkyū.* Tokyo: Kashiwa shobō, 1987.

———. "Nihon ni okeru tochi kukaku seiri seidoshi gaisetsu, 1870–1980." *Sōgō toshi kenkyū* 28 (1986): 45–87.

Itagaki Ryūta, "'Shokuminchi kindai' o megutte: Chōsenshi kenkyū ni okeru genjō to kadai." *Rekishi hyōron* 654 (2004): 35–45.

*Jissoku shōmitsu saishin Keijō zenzu.* Keijō: Nikkan shobō, 1907.

Kaneko Fumio. "Mochiji Rokusaburō no shōgai to chosaku." *Taiwan kingendaishi kenkyū* 2 (Aug. 1979): 119–28.

Kang Sin-yong. "Kankoku ni okeru kindai toshi kōen no juyō to tenkai." PhD diss., Kyoto University, 2004.

*Kanjō eiseikai jōkyō ippan.* Keijō: Kanjō eiseika, 1914.

*Katei saiji no reikō.* Keijō: Kokuhei shōsha Keijō jinja, n.d.

Kawabata Gentarō. *Keijō to naichijin.* Keijō: Nikkan shobō, 1910.

Kawamura Minato. *Kiisen: "Mono iu hana" no bunkashi.* Tokyo: Sakuhinsha, 2001.

Kawase Takuya. *Shokuminchi Chōsen no shūkyo to gakuchi.* Tokyo: Seikyū sha, 2009.

*Keijō annai.* Keijō: Keijō kyōsankai, 1915.

*Keijōfu-shi.* Vol. 2. Keijō: Keijōfu, 1936.

*Keijōfu-shi.* Vol. 3. Keijō: Keijōfu, 1941.

*Keijōfu toshi keikaku yōran.* Keijō: Keijōfu, 1939.

*Keijō hattatsushi.* Keijō: Keijō kyoryū mindan yakusho, 1912.

*Keijō toshi keikaku chōsasho.* Keijō: Keijōfu, 1928.

*Keijō toshi keikaku kuiki setteisho.* Keijō: Keijōfu, 1926.

Kim Ch'ŏl-su and Nomura Hiroshi. "Chōsen sōtokufu no shūkyo seisaku: 'Chōsen jingū' no setsuritsu o megutte." *Shakai gakubu ronshū* (Bukkyō daigaku) 31 (March 1998): 17–34.

Kim Kŭn-hŭi. "'Kōminka seisakuki' no jinja seisaku ni tsuite." *Nicchō kankeishi ronshū* (2003): 391–438.

Kimura Kenji. *Zaichō nihonjin no shakaishi.* Tokyo: Miraisha, 1989.

*Kokuheisha kankei tsuzuri.* Keijō: n.p., 1933.

*Kokuhei shōsha Keijō jinja saijireki.* Keijō: Kokuhei shōsha Keijō jinja, 1938.

*Kokumin seishin sōdōin kōenroku.* Keijō: Keikidō shakaika, 1939.

Ko Kyo-maeng, ed. *Chōsen Dai-hakurankai no gaikan.* Keijō: Keijō nippōsha, 1939.

Komagome Takeshi. *Shokumichi tekikoku Nihon no bunka tōgō.* Tokyo: Iwanami shoten, 1996.

*Kōrei taidai shidaisho.* Keijō: Keijō jinja, 1929.

Koshizawa Akira. *Dairen no toshi keikakushi, 1898–1945.* Tokyo: Ajia keizai kenkyūjo, 1984.

Kurita Eiji. "Shokuminchika Chōsen ni okeru jinmei jinshi to 'tada no jinshi.'" In *Nihon shokuminchi to bunka henyō: Kankoku, Kyobuntō,* edited by Ch'oe Kil-sŏng. Tokyo: Ochanomizu shobō, 1994.

Matsuda Toshihiko. *Nihon no Chōsen shihai to keisatsu: 1905 nen-1945 nen.* Tokyo: Azekura shobō, 2009.

———. "Nihon tōchika no Chōsen ni okeru 'keisatsu no minshūka' to 'minshū no keisatsuka': Shokuminchi ni okeru minshū tōgōsaku." *Jinbun ronshū* 33, no. 4 (1998): 27–70.

Matsui Shigeru. *Jichi to keisatsu.* Tokyo: Keigansha, 1913.

Matsumoto Takenori. *Chōsen nōson no "shokuminchi kindai" keiken.* Tokyo: Shakai hyōronsha, 2005.

Matsutani Motokazu. "Minami Chōsen ni okeru bei-senryōgun no shintō seisaku: GHQ/SCAP no shintō seisaku to sono hikaku no shiten kara." *Gendai Kankoku Chōsen kenkyū* 3 (Nov. 2003): 64–77.

Miyata Setsuko. *Chōsen minshū to "kōminka" seisaku.* Tokyo: Miraisha, 1991.

Mizuno Naoki, "Kōminka seisaku no kyozō to jitsuzō: 'Kōkoku shinmin no seishi' ni tsuite no ichi kōsatsu." In *Kankoku heigō 100 nen o tō: 2010 nen kokusai shimpōjimu.* Tokyo: Iwanami shoten, 2011.

———, ed. *Seikatsu no naka no shokuminchi shugi.* Kyoto: Jinbun shoin, 2004.

———. "Shokuminchi Chōsen ni okeru Itō Hirobumi no kioku: Keijō no Hakubunji o chūshin ni." In *Itō Hirobumi to kankoku tōchi,* edited by Itō Yukio and Yi Sŏng-hwan. Tokyo: Mineruba shobō, 2009.

Morita Yoshio. *Chōsen shūsen no kiroku.* Tokyo: Gannandō shoten, 1964.

Murayama Chijun. *Burakusai.* Keijō: Chōsen sōtokufu, 1937.

Namiki Naoto. "Shokuminchi kōki Chōsen ni okeru minshū tōgō no ichidan: Souru no jirei o chūshin toshite." In *Chōsen shakai no shiteki tenkai to higashi ajia,* edited by Takeda Yukio. Tokyo: Yamakawa shuppansha, 1997.

Nishizawa Yasuhiko. *Zusetsu Dairen toshi monogatari.* Tokyo: Kawade shobō shinsha, 1999.

Ogasawara Shōzō, ed. *Kaigai jinjashi (jōkan).* Tokyo: Kaigai jinjashi hensankai, 1953.

———. *Kaigai no jinja.* Tokyo: Shintō hyōronsha, 1933.

Oguma Eiji. *"Nihonjin" no kyōkai: Okinanwa, Ainu, Taiwan, Chōsen shokuminchi shihai kara fukki undō made.* Tokyo: Shin'yōsha, 1998.

Oguri Shirō. *Chihō eisei gyōsei no sōsetsu katei.* Tokyo: Iryō tosho shuppansha, 1981.

Ōmura Tomonojō. *Keijō kaikoroku.* Keijō: Chōsen kenkyūkai, 1922.

Sai Kindō. *Nihon teikokushugika Taiwan no shūkyo seisaku.* Tokyo: Dōseisha, 1994.

Sakagami Takashi. "Kōshū eisei no tanjō: 'Dai-nihon shiritsu eisei kyōkai' no seiritsu to tenkai." *Keizai ronsō* 156, no. 4 (Oct. 1995): 1–27.

Sassa Mitsuaki. "Kanmatsu ni okeru Dankunkyō 'jūko' to Dankun nashonarizumu. *Chōsen gakuhō* 180 (July 2001): 29–63.

———. "Shokuminchi Chōsen ni okeru dankunkyō enkaku to katsudō." *Chōsen kenkyūkai ronbunshū* 41 (Oct. 2003): 203–27.

*Shashin hōdō, tatakao Chōsen.* Osaka: Asahi shimbunsha, 1945.

Shirahata Yōzaburō. *Kindai toshi kōen no kenkyū: Ooka no keifu.* Tokyo: Shibunkaku shuppan, 1995.

Shiraishi Yasunari. *Chōsen eisei yōgi.* Keijō: Nikkan insatsusho, 1918.

*Shisei 5 nen kinen Chōsen bussan kyōshinkai hōkokusho.* Vol. 1. Keijō: Chōsen sōtokufu, 1916.

*Shisei 5 nen kinen Chōsen bussan kyōshinkai Keijō kyōsankai hōkoku.* Keijō: Keijō kyōsankai, 1916.

*Shōwa 19 nen 12 gatsu Dai 86 kai teikoku gikai sestsumei shiryō.* Tokyo: Fuji shuppan, 1994.

Suga Kōji. *Nihon tōchika no kaigai jinja: Chōsen jingū, Taiwan jinja to saijin.* Tokyo: Kōbundō, 2004.

*Taima to kamidana: Katei no kamimatsuri kokoroe.* Keijō: Tairiku Shintō renmei, 1939?.

*Tairiku jinja taikan.* Keijō: Tairiku jinja renmei, 1941.

*Taishō 9 nen korerabyō bōekishi.* Keijō: Chōsen sōtokufu, 1921.

Takahashi Testuya. *Yasukuni mondai.* Tokyo: Chikuma shobō, 2005.

Takatani Miho. "Shokuminchi Chōsen ni okeru jinja seisaku no tenkai to jittai." *Nicchō kankeishi ronshū* (2003): 357–90.

*Tōkyō taishō hakurankai jimu hōkoku (gekan)*. Tokyo: Tōkyō fuchō, 1917.

Watanabe Naoki. "Yi Kwang-su to 'Sinsindae.'" *Shokuminchi bunka kenkyū* 10 (July 2011): 46–61.

Watanabe Shun'ichi. *"Toshi keikaku" no tanjō: Kokusai hikaku kara mita nihon kindai toshi keikaku*. Tokyo: Kashiwa shobō, 1994.

Yamaguchi Kōichi. "Shokuminchi Chōsen ni okeru jinja seisaku: 1930 nendai o chūshin ni." *Rekishi hyōron* 635 (March 2003): 53–69.

———. "Shokuminchi Chōsen ni okeru jinja seisaku to Chōsenjin no taiō: 1936–1945." *Jinmin no rekishigaku* 146 (Dec. 2000): 14–32.

———. "Shokuminchiki Chōsen ni okeru jinja seisaku to Chōsen shakai." PhD diss., Hitotsubashi University, 2006.

Yamamoto Tsuneo. *Kindai nihon toshi kyōkashi kenkyū*. Tokyo: Reimei shobō, 1972.

Yamamoto Yūzo. *Nihon shokuminchi keizaishi kenkyū*. Nagoya: Nagoya daigaku shuppankai, 1992.

Yi Chong-min. "Keihanzai no torishimari hōrei ni miru minshū tōsei: Chōsen no baai o chūsin ni." In *Shokuminchi teikoku nihon no hōteki kōzō*, edited by Asano Toyomi and Matsuda Toshihiko. Tokyo: Shinsansha, 2004.

Yoshida Mitsuo. *Kinsei Souru toshi shakai kenkyū: Kanjō no machi to jūmin*. Urayasu: Sōfūkan, 2009.

Yun Chŏng-uk. *Shokuminchi Chōsen ni okeru shakai jigyō*. Osaka: Ōsaka keizai hōka daigaku shuppanbu, 1996.

*English*

Ahn, Changmo [An Ch'ang-mo]. "Colonial Tourism in 1930s Korean Architecture: The Tradition of the Colonized and the Colonial Policy behind the Style of Railroad Station." *Journal of Southeast Asian Architecture* 7 (2004): 13–25.

Allen, Joseph R. *Taipei: City of Displacements*. Seattle: University of Washington Press, 2012.

Ambaras, David. "Social Knowledge, Cultural Capital, and the New Middle Class in Japan, 1895–1912." *Journal of Japanese Studies* 24, no. 1 (1988): 1–33.

Appadurai, Arjun. *Modernity at Large: Cultural Dimensions of Globalization*. Minneapolis: University of Minnesota Press, 1996.

Atkins, A. Taylor. *Primitive Selves: Koreana in the Japanese Colonial Gaze, 1910–1945*. Berkeley: University of California Press, 2010.

Bae, Changmii [Pae Chang-mi]. "The Symbolic Landscape of National Identity: Planning, Politics, and Culture in South Korea." PhD diss., University of Southern California, 2002.

Baldwin, Frank. "Participatory Anti-Imperialism: The 1919 Independence Movement." *Journal of Korean Studies* 1 (1979): 123–62.

Barlow, Tani. "Debates over Colonial Modernity in East Asia and Another Alternative." *Cultural Studies* 26, no. 5 (2012): 617–44.

Betts, Raymond F. *Assimilation and Association in French Colonial Theory, 1890–1914*. New York: Columbia University Press, 1960.

Bishop, Isabella. *Korea and Her Neighbors*. Seoul: Yonsei University Press, 1970.

Bourdieu, Pierre. *The Logic of Practice*. Stanford: Stanford University Press, 1992.

Brazinsky, Gregg. *Nation Building in South Korea: Koreans, Americans, and the Making of a Democracy*. Chapel Hill: University of North Carolina Press, 2007.

Brooks, Barbara. "Reading the Japanese Colonial Archive: Gender and Bourgeois Civility in Korea and Manchuria Before 1932." In *Gendering Modern Japanese History*, edited by Barbara Molony and Kathleen Uno. Cambridge, MA: Harvard University Press, 2005.

Caprio, Mark E. *Japanese Assimilation Policies in Colonial Korea, 1910–1945*. Seattle: University of Washington Press, 2009.

Chakrabarty, Dipesh. *Provincializing Europe: Postcolonial Thought and Historical Difference*. Princeton, NJ: Princeton University Press, 2000.

Chandra, Vipan. *Imperialism, Resistance, and Reform in Late Nineteenth-Century Korea: Enlightenment and the Independence Club*. Berkeley: Institute of East Asian Studies, 1988.

Chatterjee, Partha. *The Nation and Its Fragments: Colonial and Postcolonial Histories*. Princeton, NJ: Princeton University Press, 1993.

Chen, Edward I-te. "The Attempt to Integrate the Empire: Legal Perspectives." In *The Japanese Colonial Empire, 1895–1945*, edited by Ramon H. Myers and Mark R. Peattie. Princeton, NJ: Princeton University Press, 1987.

Ching, Leo T. S. *Becoming "Japanese": Colonial Taiwan and the Politics of Identity Formation*. Berkeley: University of California Press, 2001.

Cho, Myungrae [Cho Myŏng-nae]. "From Street Corners to Plaza: The Production of Festive Civic Space in Central Seoul." In *Globalization, the City and Civil Society in Pacific Asia: The Social Production of Civic Spaces*, edited by Mike Douglas, K. C. Ho, and Giok Ling Ooi. London: Routledge, 2007.

———. "The Politics of Urban Nature Restoration: The Case of Cheonggyecheon Restoration in Seoul, Korea." *International Development Planning Review* 32, no. 2 (2010): 145–65.

Cho, Younghan [Cho Yŏng-han]. "Colonial Modernity Matters?" *Cultural Studies* 26, no. 5 (2012): 645–99.

Choi, Ellie. "Space and the Historical Imagination: Yi Kwangsu's Vision of Korea during the Japanese Empire." PhD diss., Harvard University, 2008.

Choi, Kyeong-Hee [Ch'oe Kyŏng-hŭi]. *Beneath the Vermillion Ink: Japanese Colonial Censorship and the Making of Modern Korean Literature*. Ithaca, NY: Cornell University Press, forthcoming.

Chong Chinsok [Chŏng Chin-sŏk]. "A Study on the *Maeil Sinbo* (Daily News): Public Information Policy of the Japanese Imperialists and Korean Journalism under Japanese Imperialism." *Journal of Social Sciences and Humanities* 52 (1980): 59–114.

Chou, Wan-yao. "The Kōminka Movement in Taiwan and Korea: Comparisons and Interpretations." In *The Japanese Wartime Empire, 1931–1945*, edited by Peter Duus, Ramon Myers, and Mark Peattie. Princeton, NJ: Princeton University Press, 1996.

Clark, Donald. "Protestant Christianity and the State: Religious Organizations as Civil Society." In *Korean Society: Civil Society, Democracy and the State,* edited by Charles K. Armstrong. London: Routledge, 2002.

Cohen, Nicole Leah. "Children of Empire: Growing up Japanese in Colonial Korea, 1876–1945." PhD diss., Columbia University, 2006.

Collins, Sandra. *The Missing Olympics: Japan, the Asian Olympics and the Olympic Movement.* London: Routledge, 2007.

de Bary, Wm. Theodore, Carol Gluck, and Arthur E. Tiedemann, eds. *Sources of Japanese Tradition, Abridged.* Volume 2, *1868 to 2000.* New York: Columbia University Press, 2006.

de Ceuster, Koen. "The World in a Book: Yu Kilchun's *Sŏyu kyŏnmun.*" In *Korea in the Middle: Korean Studies and Area Studies,* edited by Remco E. Breuker. Leiden: CNWS Publications, 2007.

Do Myoun-hoi [To Myŏn-hoe]. "The Implications of Colonial Modernity without Colonialism." *Korea Journal* 44, no. 2 (Summer 2004): 189–209.

Driscoll, Mark. *Absolute Erotic, Absolute Grotesque: The Living, the Dead, and the Undead in Japan's Imperialism, 1895–1945.* Durham: Duke University Press, 2010.

Dudden, Alexis. *Japan's Colonization of Korea: Discourse and Power.* Honolulu: University of Hawai'i Press, 2006.

———. *Troubled Apologies among Japan, Korea, and the United States.* New York: Columbia University Press, 2008.

Duus, Peter. *The Abacus and the Sword: The Japanese Penetration of Korea, 1895–1910.* Berkeley: University of California Press, 1995.

Eckert, Carter J. *Offspring of Empire: The Koch'ang Kims and the Colonial Origins of Korean Capitalism, 1876–1945.* Seattle: University of Washington Press, 1996.

Edwards, Walter. "Forging Tradition for a Holy War: The *Hakkō Ichiu* Tower in Miyazaki and Japanese Wartime Ideology." *Journal of Japanese Studies* 29, no. 2 (Summer 2003): 289–324.

Fiévé, Nicolas, and Paul Waley, eds. *Japanese Capitals in Historical Perspective: Place, Power and Memory in Kyoto, Edo and Tokyo.* London: Routledge, 2003.

Foucault, Michel. "Governmentality." In *The Foucault Effect: Studies in Governmentality,* edited by G. Burchell, C. Gordon, and P. Miller. London: Harvester Wheatsheaf, 1991.

———. "Questions of Method." In *Essential Works of Foucault, 1954–1984.* Volume 3, *Power,* edited by James D. Faubion. New York: New Press, 2000.

———. *Security, Territory, Population: Lectures at the Collège de France, 1977–78.* New York: Palgrave Macmillan, 2007.

———. *"Society Must Be Defended": Lectures at the Collège de France, 1975–76.* New York: Picador, 2003.

———. "Two Lectures." In *Power/Knowledge: Selected Interviews, and Other Writings, 1972–1977,* edited by Colin Gordon. New York: Pantheon, 1980.

Fujitani, Takashi. *Race for Empire: Koreans as Japanese and Japanese as Americans during World War II.* Berkeley: University of California Press, 2011.

———. *Splendid Monarchy: Power and Pageantry in Modern Japan.* Berkeley: University of California Press, 1996.

Gluck, Carol. *Japan's Modern Myths: Ideology in the Late Meiji Period.* Princeton, NJ: Princeton University Press, 1985.

Grayson, James. "The Accomodation of Korean Folk Religion to the Religious Forms of Buddhism: An Example of Reverse Syncretism." *Asian Folklore Studies* 51, no. 2 (1992): 199–217.

Guha, Ranajit. *Dominance without Hegemony: History and Power in Colonial India.* Cambridge, MA: Harvard University Press, 1988.

Guo, Qinghua. *Chinese Architecture and Planning: Ideas, Methods, Techniques.* Stuttgart: Axel Menges, 2005.

Gupta, Akhil, and James Ferguson. "Beyond 'Culture': Space, Identity, and the Politics of Difference." *Cultural Anthropology* 7, no. 1 (Feb. 1992): 6–23.

Han, Do-Hyun [Han To-hyŏn]. "Shamanism, Superstition, and the Colonial Government." *Review of Korean Studies* 3 (2000): 34–54.

Hanscom, Christopher P. "Modernism, Hysteria, and the Colonial Double Bind: Pak T'aewŏn's *One Day in the Life of the Author, Mr. Kubo*." *Positions: Asia Critique* 21, no. 3 (Summer 2013): 607–36.

Hansen, Thomas Blom, and Finn Stepputat, eds. *States of Imagination: Ethnographic Explorations of the Postcolonial State.* Durham: Duke University Press, 2001.

Hardacre, Helen. *Shintō and the State, 1868–1988.* Princeton, NJ: Princeton University Press, 1989.

Havens, Thomas R. H. *Parkscapes: Green Spaces in Modern Japan.* Honolulu: University of Hawai'i Press, 2011.

Hayase, Yukiko. "The Career of Gotō Shimpei: Japan's Statesman of Research, 1857–1929." PhD diss., Florida State University, 1974.

Henry, Todd A. "Assimilation's Racializing Sensibilities: Colonized Koreans as *Yobos* and the "*Yobo*-ization" of Japanese Settlers." *Positions: Asia Critique* 21, no. 1 (Winter 2013): 11–49.

———. "Cheguk ŭl kinyŏm hago, chŏnjaeng ŭl tongnyŏ hagi: Singminji malgi (1940 nyŏn) Chosŏn esŏ ŭi pangnamhoe." *Asea yŏn'gu* 51, no. 4 (Winter 2008): 72–112.

———. "Keijō: Japanese and Korean Constructions of Colonial Seoul and the History of Its Lived Spaces, 1910–37." PhD diss., University of California, Los Angeles, 2006.

———. "Respatializing Chosŏn's Royal Capital: The Politics of Japanese Urban Reforms in Early Colonial Seoul, 1905–19." In *Sitings: Critical Approaches to Korean Geography,* edited by Timothy R. Tangherlini and Sallie Yea. Honolulu: University of Hawai'i Press, 2008.

———. "Sanitizing Empire: Japanese Articulations of Korean Otherness and the Construction of Early Colonial Seoul, 1905–19." *Journal of Asian Studies* 64, no. 3 (Aug. 2005): 643–53.

Hindess, Barry. "The Liberal Government of Unfreedom." *Alternatives: Global, Local, Political* 26, no. 2 (April/June 2001): 93–111.

Hong Chi-mo. "Kim Chae-jun as Seen from the Perspective of Korean Conservative Theology." *Chongshin Review* 2 (October 1997): 5–35.

Hong, Yang-hee [Hong Yang-hŭi]. "Debates about 'A Good Wife and Wise Mother' and Tradition in Colonial Korea." *Review of Korean Studies* 11, no. 4 (Dec. 2008): 41–60.

Hughes, Theodore Q. *Literature and Film in Cold War South Korea: Freedom's Frontier.* New York: Columbia University Press, 2012.

Hur, Nam-lin [Hŏ Nam-lin]. *Prayer and Play in Late Tokugawa Japan: Asakusa Sensōji and Edo Society.* Cambridge, MA: Harvard University Press, 2000.

Hwang, Kyung Moon [Hwang Kyŏng-mun]. *Beyond Birth: Social Status in the Emergence of Modern Korea.* Cambridge, MA: Harvard University Press, 2004.

Hwang Sung Kyu [Hwang Sung-gyu], ed. *The Life and Theology of Changgong, Kim Chai Choon.* Seoul: Hanshin University Press, 2005.

Hyunah Yang [Yang Hyŏn-a], "Re-membering the Korean Military Comfort Women: Nationalism, Sexuality, and Silencing." In *Dangerous Women: Gender and Korean Nationalism,* edited by Elaine H. Kim and Chungmoo Choi. London: Routledge, 1997.

Jin, Jong-Heon [Chin Chong-hŏn]. "Demolishing Colony: The Demolition of the Old Government-General Building of Chosŏn." In *Sitings: Critical Approaches to Korean Geography,* edited by Timothy R. Tangherlini and Sallie Yea. Honolulu: University of Hawai'i Press, 2008.

"Jingū taima." Encyclopedia of Shinto. http://eos.kokugakuin.ac.jp/modules/xwords/entry.php?entryID = 283 (accessed on December 29, 2011).

Josephson, Jason Ānanda. *The Invention of Religion in Japan.* Chicago: University of Chicago Press, 2012.

Jung Keun-sik [Chŏng Kŭn-sik]. "The Memories of August 15 (Day of Liberation) Reflected in Korean Anniversaries and Memorial Halls." *Review of Korean Studies* 8, no. 1 (2005): 11–50.

Jung Tae-hern [Chŏng T'ae-hŏn]. "Two Korea's Perceptions of the 'Colonial Modernity' since 1945." *International Journal of Korean History* 2 (Dec. 2001): 193–219.

Kal, Hong. "Modeling the West, Returning to Asia: Shifting Politics of Representation in Japanese Colonial Expositions in Korea." *Comparative Studies in Society and History* 47, no. 3 (2005): 507–31.

———. "Politics of Visual Comparison: Notes on the Formation of Nationalism in the Colonial Exposition in Korea." *Tong asia munhwa wa yesul* 3 (2006): 217–49.

Kane, Daniel. "Display at Empire's End: Korea's Participation in the 1900 Paris Universal Exposition." *Sungkyun Journal of East Asian Studies* 4, no. 2 (Aug. 2004): 41–66.

———. "Korea in the White City: Korea at the World's Columbian Exhibition (1893)." *Transactions of the Korea Branch Royal Asiatic Society* 77 (2002): 1–58.

Kang, Wi Jo [Kang Wi-jo]. *Christ and Caesar in Modern Korea: A History of Christianity and Politics.* Albany: SUNY Press, 1997.

Kawashima, Ken C. *The Proletarian Gamble: Korean Workers in Interwar Japan.* Durham: Duke University Press, 2009.

Kim Baek Yung [Kim Paek-yŏng]. "Ruptures and Conflicts in the Colonial Power Bloc: The Great Keijo Plan of the 1920s." *Korea Journal* 48, no. 3 (Autumn 2008), 10–40.

Kim, Charles. "The April 19th Generation and the Start of Postcolonial History in South Korea." *Review of Korean Studies* 12, no. 3 (Sept. 2009): 71–99.

Kim, Christine. "The Chosŏn Monarchy in Republican Korea, 1945–1965." In *Northeast Asia's Difficult Past: Essays in Collective Memory,* edited by Barry Schwartz and Mikyoung Kim. London: Palgrave Macmillan, 2010.

———. "The King Is Dead: The Monarchy and National Identity in Modern Korea." PhD diss., Harvard University, 2004.

———. "Politics and Pageantry in Protectorate Korea, 1905–10: The Imperial Progresses of Sunjong." *Journal of Asian Studies* 68, no. 3 (2009): 835–59.

Kim Do-hyung [Kim To-hyŏng]. "Introduction: The Nature of Reform in the Taehan Empire." In *Reform and Modernity in the Taehan Empire,* edited by Kim Dong-no, John B. Duncan, and Kim Do-hyung. Seoul: Jimoondang, 2006.

Kim, Jong-Geun [Kim Chong-gŭn]. "Colonial Modernity and the Colonial City: Seoul during the Japanese Occupation, 1910–1945." PhD diss., University of Cambridge, 2013.

Kim, Jung In [Kim Chung-in]. "Constructing a 'Miracle': Architecture, National Identity and Development of the Han River." PhD diss., University of California, Berkeley, 2008.

Kim, Michael. "The Colonial Public Sphere and the Discursive Mechanism of *Mindo.*" In *Mass Dictatorship and Modernity,* edited by Michael Kim, Michael Schoenhals, and Yong-Woo Kim. London: Routledge, 2013.

Kim, Moon-Hwan [Kim Mun-hwan]. "The Plaza as a Public Art: The Case of Gwanghwamun Plaza in Seoul." *Journal of Asian Arts & Aesthetics* 3 (2009): 21–28.

Kim, Richard E. *Lost Names: Scenes from a Korean Boyhood.* Berkeley: University of California Press, 1998.

Kim, Sonja. "Contesting Bodies: Managing Population, Birthing, and Medicine in Korea, 1876–1945." PhD diss., University of California, Los Angeles, 2008.

———. " 'Limiting Birth': Birth Control in Colonial Korea." *East Asian Science, Technology, and Society: An International Journal* 2, no. 3 (2008): 335–59.

———. "The Search for Health: Translating *Wisaeng* and Medicine during the Taehan Empire." In *Reform and Modernity in the Taehan Empire,* edited by Kim Dong-no, John B. Duncan, and Kim Do-hyung. Seoul: Jimoondang, 2006.

Kim, Suk-Young [Kim Suk-yŏng]. *Illusive Utopia: Theater, Film, and Everyday Performance in North Korea.* Ann Arbor: University of Michigan Press, 2010.

Kim, Sung-Gun [Kim Sŏng-gŏn]. "Korean Christianity and the Shinto Shrine Issue in the War Period, 1931–1945: A Sociological Study of Religion and Politics." PhD diss., University of Hull, 1989.

———. "The Shinto Shrine Issue in Korean Christianity under Japanese Colonialism." *Journal of Church and State* 39, no. 3 (Summer 1997): 503–22.

Kim Tae-woong [Kim Tae-ung]. "Industrial Exhibitions ('Gongjinghoe') and the Political Propaganda of Japanese Imperialism in the 1910s." *International Journal of Korean History* 3 (Dec. 2002): 179–223.

Ko Dong-hwan [Ko Tong-hwan]. "The Characteristics of the Urban Development of Seoul during the Late Chosŏn Dynasty: With a Focus on the Changes in Urban Structure." *Seoul Journal of Korean Studies* 10 (1997): 95–123.

Lee, Helen J. S. "Voices of the 'Colonists,' Voices of the 'Immigrants': 'Korea' in Japan's Early Colonial Travel Narratives and Guides, 1894–1914." *Japanese Language and Literature* 41, no. 1 (April 2007): 1–36.

———. "Writing Colonial Relations of Everyday Life in Senryu." *Positions: East Asia Cultures Critique* 16, no. 3 (Winter 2008): 601–28.

Lee, Namhee [Yi Nam-hŭi]. *The Making of Minjung: Democracy and the Politics of Representation in South Korea.* Ithaca, NY: Cornell University Press, 2009.

Lee Won-deog [Yi Wŏn-dŏk]. "A Normal State without Remorse: The Textbook Controversy and Korea-Japan Relations." *East Asian Review* 13, no. 3 (Autumn 2001): 21–40.

Lefebvre, Henri. *The Production of Space.* Oxford: Blackwell, 1991.

Legg, Stephen. *Spaces of Colonialism: Dehli's Urban Governmentalities.* Oxford: Blackwell, 2007.

Lo, Ming-Cheng. *Doctors within Borders: Profession, Ethnicity, and Modernity in Colonial Taiwan.* Berkeley: University of California Press, 2002.

Lynn, Hyung-gu. "Fashioning Modernity: Changing Meanings of Clothing in Colonial Korea." *Journal of International and Area Studies* 12, no. 1 (Spring 2005): 75–93.

Maliangkay, Roald. "Them Pig Feet: Anti-Japanese Folksongs in Korea." In *Korea in the Middle: Positioning Korea,* edited by Remco Breuker. Leiden: CNWS Publications, 2007.

Manela, Erez. *The Wilsonian Moment: Self-Determination and the International Origins of Anticolonial Nationalism.* Oxford: Oxford University Press, 2007.

Maxey, Trent E. *The "Greatest Problem": Religion and State Formation in Meiji Japan.* Cambridge, MA: Harvard University Asia Center, 2014.

McDonald, Kate L. "The Boundaries of the Interesting: Itineraries, Guidebooks, and Travel in Imperial Japan." PhD diss., University of California, San Diego, 2011.

Mitchell, Timothy. "Society, Economy, and the State Effect." In *State/Culture: State-Formation after the Cultural Turn,* edited by George Steinmetz. Ithaca, NY: Cornell University Press, 1999.

Moon, Seungsook [Mun Sŭng-suk]. *Militarized Modernity and Gendered Citizenship in South Korea.* Durham: Duke University Press, 2005.

Morris-Suzuki, Tessa. "Becoming Japanese: Imperial Expansion and Identity Crises in the Early Twentieth Century." In *Japan's Competing Modernities: Issues in Culture and Democracy, 1900–1930,* edited by Sharon Minichiello. Honolulu: University of Hawai'i Press, 1998.

Munro, Lisa. "Investigating World's Fairs: An Historiography." *Studies in Latin American Popular Culture* 28 (2010): 80–94.

Murray Li, Tania. *The Will to Improve: Governmentality, Development, and the Practice of Politics*. Durham: Duke University Press, 2007.

O'Dwyer, Shaun. "The Yasukuni Shrine and the Competing Patriotic Pasts of East Asia." *History & Memory* 22, no. 2 (Fall/Winter 2010): 147–77.

Oguma Eiji. *A Genealogy of Japanese "Self-Images."* Melbourne: Trans Pacific Press, 2002.

Oh, Se-mi [O Se-mi]. "Consuming the Modern: The Everyday in Colonial Seoul 1915–1937." PhD diss., Columbia University, 2008.

Opitz, Sven. "Government Unlimimted: The Security Dispositif of Illberal Governmentality." In *Governmentality: Current Issues and Future Challenges*, edited by Ulrich Bröckling, Susanne Krausmann, and Thomas Lemke. New York: Routledge, 2010.

Pai, Hyung Il [Pae Hyŏng-il]. "Navigating Modern Seoul: The Typology of Guidebooks and City Landmarks." *Sŏulhak yŏn'gu* 44 (August 2011): 1–40.

Palmer, Brandon. "Imperial Japan's Preparations to Conscript Koreans as Soldiers, 1942–1945." *Korean Studies* 31 (2007): 63–78.

Park, Chan-seung [Pak Ch'an-sŭng]. "Yi Kwang-su and the Endorsement of State Power." *Journal of Korean Studies* 19, no. 1 (Dec. 2006): 161–90.

Park, Eugene Y. "The Phantasm of the Western Capital (Sŏgyŏng): Imperial Korea's Redevelopment of Pyongyang, 1902–1908." Unpublished Manuscript.

Park, Hyun Ok [Pak Hyŏn-ok]. "Korean Manchuria: The Racial Politics of the Territorial Osmosis." *South Atlantic Quarterly* 99, no. 1 (Winter 2000): 193–215.

Park, Se Hoon [Pak Se-hun]. "Care and Control: Colonial Governmentality and Urban Social Policy in Colonial Seoul." In *East Asia: A Critical Geography Perspective*, edited by Wing-Shing Tang and Fujio Mizuoka. Tokyo: Kokon shoin, 2010.

Park, Sunyoung [Pak Sun-yŏng], trans. *On the Eve of the Uprising, and Other Stories from Colonial Korea*. Ithaca, NY: Cornell University Press, 2010.

Park, Yun-jae [Pak Yun-jae]. "Anti-Cholera Measures by the Japanese Colonial Government and the Reaction of Koreans in the Early 1920s." *Review of Korean Studies* 8, no. 4 (2005): 169–86.

Peattie, Mark R. "Japanese Attitudes toward Colonialism, 1895–1945." In *The Japanese Colonial Empire, 1895–1945*, edited by Ramon H. Myers and Mark R. Peattie. Princeton, NJ: Princeton University Press, 1987.

Prakash, Gyan. *Another Reason: Science and the Imagination of Modern India*. Princeton, NJ: Princeton University Press, 1999.

Pratt, Mary Louise. *Imperial Eyes: Travel Writing and Transculturation*. London: Routledge, 1992.

Redfield, Peter. "Foucault in the Tropics: Displacing the Panopticon." In *Anthropologies of Modernity: Foucault, Governmentality, and Life Politics*, edited by Jonathan Xavier Inda. London: Blackwell, 2005.

Reynolds, Jonathan. "Ise Shrine and a Modernist Construction of Japanese Tradition." *Art Bulletin* 83, no. 2 (June 2001): 316–41.

Robinson, Michael. "Broadcasting, Cultural Hegemony, and Colonial Modernity in Korea, 1924–1945." In *Colonial Modernity in Korea*, edited by Shin

Gi-Wook and Michael Robinson. Cambridge, MA: Harvard University Press, 1999.

Rogaski, Ruth. *Hygienic Modernity: Meanings of Health and Disease in Treaty-Port China*. Berkeley: University of California Press, 2004.

Roh Young-koo [No Yŏng-gu]. "Yi Sun-shin, an Admiral who became a Myth." *Review of Korean Studies* 7, no. 3 (2004): 15–36.

Ruoff, Kenneth J. *Imperial Japan at Its Zenith*. Ithaca, NY: Cornell University Press, 2011.

Ryang, Sonia. "Japanese Travelers' Accounts of Korea." *East Asian History* 13/14 (June/Dec. 1997): 133–52.

Rydell, Robert W. *All the World's a Fair*. Chicago: University of Chicago Press, 1984.

Schmid, Andre. "Colonialism and the 'Korea Problem' in the Historiography of Japan: A Review Article." *Journal of Asian Studies* 59, no. 4 (Nov. 2000): 951–76.

———. *Korea between Empires, 1895–1919*. New York: Columbia University Press, 2002.

Scott, David. "Colonial Governmentality." *Social Text* 43 (Autumn 1995): 191–220.

"Seoul City Hall's Metamorphosis Pleases Book Lovers," *Korea.net*, Oct. 25, 2012, www.korea.net/NewsFocus/Society/view?articleId = 103347 (accessed January 9, 2013).

*Seoul through Pictures 1: The Modernization of Seoul and Its Trials, 1876–1910*. Seoul: City History Compilation Committee of Seoul, 2002.

Shin Dongwon [Sin Tong-wŏn]. "Hygiene, Medicine, and Modernity in Korea, 1876–1910." *East Asian Science, Technology and Society: An International Journal* 3 (2009): 5–26.

Shin, Gi-Wook, and Michael Robinson, eds. *Colonial Modernity in Korea*. Cambridge, MA: Harvard University Press, 2001.

Shin, Hisup [Sin Hŭi-sŏp]. "Uncovering Ch'ŏnggyech'ŏn: The Ruins of Modernization and Everyday Life." *Korean Studies* 29 (2006): 95–113.

Song, Jesook [Song Chae-suk]. "Historicization of Homeless Spaces: The Seoul Train Station Square and the House of Freedom." *Anthropological Quarterly* 79, no. 2 (Spring 2006): 193–223.

Son Min Suh [Son Min-sŏ]. "Enlightenment and Electrification: The Introduction of Electric Light, Telegraph and Streetcars in Late Nineteenth Century Korea." In *Reform and Modernity in the Taehan Empire*, edited by Kim Dong-no, John B. Duncan, and Kim Do-hyung. Seoul: Jimoondang, 2006.

Sonoda Minoru. "Festival and Sacred Transgression." In *Matsuri: Festival and Rite in Japanese Life*. Tokyo: Institute for Japanese Culture and Classics, Kokugakuin University, 1988.

Sorensen, André. *The Making of Urban Japan: Cities and Planning from Edo to the Twenty-First Century*. London: Routledge, 2002.

Sørensen, Henrik H. "The Attitude of the Japanese Colonial Government towards Religion in Korea, 1910–1919." *Copenhagen Papers in East and Southeast Asia Studies* 8 (1993): 49–69.

Spiegel, Gabrielle M. *Practicing History: New Directions in Historical Writing after the Linguistic Turn.* New York: Routledge, 2005.

Stoler, Ann L. "Colonial Archives and the Arts of Governance." *Archival Sciences* 2 (2002): 87–109.

Suh, So Young [Sŏ So-yŏng]. "Korean Medicine between the Local and the Universal, 1600–1945." PhD diss., University of California, Los Angeles, 2006.

Sutcliffe, Anthony. *The Rise of Modern Urban Planning, 1800–1914.* New York: St. Martin's Press, 1980.

Takahashi Testuya. "The National Politics of the Yasukuni Shrine." In *Nationalisms in Japan,* edited by Naoko Shimazu. London: Routledge, 2006.

Thomas, Nicholas. *Colonialism's Culture: Anthropology, Travel, and Government.* Princeton, NJ: Princeton University Press, 1994.

Tikhonov, Vladimir. *Social Darwinism and Nationalism in Korea: The Beginnings, 1880s to 1910s.* Leiden: Brill, 2009.

Trouillot, Michel-Rolph. *Silencing the Past: Power and the Production of History.* Boston: Beacon Press, 1997.

Tsurumi, Patricia E. "Colonial Education in Korea and Taiwan." In *The Japanese Colonial Empire, 1895–1945,* edited by Ramon H. Meyers and Mark R. Peattie. Princeton, NJ: Princeton University Press, 1982.

———. *Japanese Colonial Education in Taiwan, 1895–1945.* Cambridge, MA: Harvard University Press, 1977.

Uchida, Jun. *Brokers of Empire: Japanese Settler Colonialism in Korea, 1876–1945.* Cambridge, MA: Harvard University Asia Center, 2011.

Wilder, Gary. *The French Imperial Nation-State: Negritude and Colonial Humanism between the Two World Wars.* Chicago: University of Chicago Press, 2005.

Wright, Gwendolyn. *The Politics of Design in French Colonial Urbanism.* Chicago: University of Chicago Press, 1991.

Vlastos, Stephen, ed. *Mirror of Modernity: Invented Traditions of Modern Japan.* Berkeley: University of California Press, 1998.

Yi Tae-Jin [Yi T'ae-jin]. "The Annexation of Korea Failed to Come into Being: Forced Treaties and Japan's Annexation of the Great Han Empire." *Seoul Journal of Korean Studies* 18 (2005): 1–41.

———. "The Leaders and Objectives of the Seoul Urban Renovation Project of 1896–1904." In *The Dynamics of Confucianism and Modernization in Korean History.* Ithaca, NY: Cornell University Press, 2008.

———. "Seoul's Modern Development during the Eighteenth and Nineteenth Centuries" In *The Dynamics of Confucianism and Modernization in Korean History.* Ithaca, NY: Cornell University Press, 2008.

Yoo, Theodore Jun. *The Politics of Gender in Colonial Korea: Education, Labor, and Health, 1910–45.* Berkeley: University of California Press, 2008.

Yoon, Hong-key [Yun Hong-gi]. *The Culture of Fengshui in Korea: An Exploration of East Asian Geomancy.* Lanham, MD: Lexington Books, 2006.

Yun Hae-dong. "Colonial Publicness as Metaphor." In *Mass Dictatorship and Modernity,* edited by Michael Kim, Michael Schoenhals, and Yong-Woo Kim. London: Routledge, 2013.

# Index